Demons and Spirits in Biblical Theology

Demons and Spirits in Biblical Theology

Reading the Biblical Text in Its Cultural and Literary Context

John H. Walton

J. Harvey Walton

CASCADE *Books* · Eugene, Oregon

DEMONS AND SPIRITS IN BIBLICAL THEOLOGY
Reading the Biblical Text in Its Cultural and Literary Context

Cascade Books
An Imprint of Wipf and Stock Publishers
199 W. 8th Ave., Suite 3
Eugene, OR 97401

www.wipfandstock.com

PAPERBACK ISBN: 978-1-62564-825-9
HARDCOVER ISBN: 978-1-4982-8878-1
EBOOK ISBN: 978-1-7252-4951-6

Cataloguing-in-Publication data:

Names: Walton, John H., 1952–, author. | Walton, Jonathan H., author.

Title: Demons and spirits in biblical theology : reading the biblical text in its cultural and literary context / John H. Walton and J. Harvey Walton.

Description: Eugene, OR: Cascade Books, 2019 | Includes bibliographical references and index.

Identifiers: ISBN 978-1-62564-825-9 (paperback) | ISBN 978-1-4982-8878-1 (hardcover) | ISBN 978-1-7252-4951-6 (ebook)

Subjects: LCSH: Jewish demonology | Demonology in the Bible | Spirits—Religious aspects—Christianity | Biblical cosmology | Good and evil—Religious aspects—Christianity | Demonology—Biblical teaching | Demoniac possession—biblical teaching | Demonology—Judaism | Gods in the Bible

Classification: BS680.G6 W275 2019 (print) | BS680.G6 (ebook)

Manufactured in the U.S.A.   04/05/19

Contents

CONTENTS

Abbreviations

AB   Anchor Bible

AMD   Ancient Magic and Divination

ANF   *The Ante-Nicene Fathers.* Edited by Alexander Roberts and James Donaldson. 10 vols. Christian Literature Publishing, 1885–87. Reprint. Peabody, MA: Hendrickson, 1994.

AoF   *Altorientalische Forschungen*

AOTC   Apollos Old Testament Commentary

Apoc. Abr.   *Apocalypse of Abraham*

Apoc. Zeph. *Apocalypse of Zephaniah*

Apol.   *Apology*

ArBib   Aramaic Bible

2 Bar.   *2 Baruch*

Apoc. Mos. *Apocalypse of Moses*

BECNT   Baker Exegetical Commentary on the New Testament

BibSac   *Bibliotheca Sacra*

CAD   *The Assyrian Dictionary of the Oriental Institute of the University of Chicago.* Chicago: Oriental Institute 1956–.

CBQ   *Catholic Biblical Quarterly*

CC   Continental Commentaries

DDD   *Dictionary of Deities and Demons in the Bible.* Edited by K. van der Toorn, B. Becking, and P. W. van der Horst. 2nd ed. Grand Rapids: Eerdmans, 1999.

De. Pyth. *De Pythiae oraculis*

EJ   *Encyclopaedia Judaica.* 22 vols. Rev. ed. Jerusalem, 2007.

1 En.	*1 Enoch*
2 En.	*2 Enoch*
ESV	English Standard Version
frag.	fragment
Gk. Apoc. Ezra	*Greek Apocalypse of Ezra*
HSM	Harvard Semitic Monographs
ICC	International Critical Commentary
JAAR	*Journal of the American Academy of Religion*
JBL	*Journal of Biblical Literature*
JETS	*Journal of the Evangelical Theological Society*
JSOTS	Journal for the Study of the Old Testament: Supplement Series
JSP	*Journal for the Study of the Pseudepigrapha*
Jub.	*Jubilees*
KJV	King James Version
KTU	*Die keilalphabetischen Texte aus Ugarit.* Edited by M. Dietrich, O. Loretz, and J. Sanmartín. Alter Orient und Altes Testament 24/1. Neukirchen-Vluyn: Neukirchener, 1976. 2nd enlarged ed. of *KTU: The Cuneiform Alphabetic Texts from Ugarit, Ras Ibn Hani, and Other Places.* Edited by M. Dietrich, O. Loretz, and J. Sanmartín. Münster: Ugarit-Verlag, 1995.
LCL	Loeb Classical Library
LSJ	Henry George Liddell, Robert Scott, and Henry Stuart Jones. *A Greek-English Lexicon.* 9th ed. Oxford: Clarendon, 1996.
LXX	The Septuagint
1 Macc	1 Maccabees
2 Macc	2 Maccabees
NAC	New American Commentary
NICNT	New International Commentary on the New Testament
NICOT	New International Commentary on the Old Testament
NIDNTTE	*New International Dictionary of New Testament Theology and Exegesis.* 5 vols. Edited by Moisés Silva. Grand Rapids: Zondervan, 2014.
NIGTC	New International Greek Testament Commentary
NIV	New International Version

NIVAC	NIV Application Commentary
NKJV	New King James Version
NPNF1	*The Nicene and Post-Nicene Fathers,* Series 1. Edited by Philip Schaff. 14 vols. 1886–89. Reprint. Peabody, MA: Hendrickson, 1994.
OTL	Old Testament Library
OTP	*The Old Testament Pseudepigrapha.* 2 vols. Edited by James H. Charlesworth. Peabody, MA: Hendrickson, 1983–85.
PNTC	Pillar New Testament Commentary
Rab.	Rabbah (i.e., Midrash Rabbah)
RevQ	*Revue de Qumran*
RSV	Revised Standard Version
SAA	State Archives of Assyria
SAACT	State Archives of Assyria Cuneiform Texts
SAAS	State Archives of Assyria Studies
SAOC	Studies in Ancient Oriental Civilizations
SBLWAW	Society of Biblical Literature Writings from the Ancient World
Shepherd	*Shepherd of Hermas*
SRHB	Studies in the Reception History of the Bible
STDJ	*Studies on the Texts of the Desert of Judah*
Sym.	*Symposium*
T. Abr.	*Testament of Abraham*
T. Dan	*Testament of Daniel*
T. Iss.	*Testament of Issachar*
T. Job	*Testament of Job*
T. Levi	*Testament of Levi*
T. Naph.	*Testament of Naphtali*
T. Sol.	*Testament of Solomon*
Targ. Neof.	Targum Neofiti
Targ. Onq.	Targum Onqelos
Targ. Ps.-J.	Targum Pseudo-Jonathan
TCBAI	Transactions of the Casco Bay Assyriological Institute

TCS   Texts from Cuneiform Sources

TDOT   *Theological Dictionary of the Old Testament.* 14 vols. Edited by G. Johannes Botterweck and Helmer Ringgren. Translated by Geoffrey W. Bromiley et al. Grand Rapids: Eerdmans, 1974–2004.

UL   *Utukku Lemnutu*

Vit. Ad.   *Vita Adae et Evae (Life of Adam and Eve)*

VT   *Vetus Testamentum*

WBC   Word Biblical Commentary

Wis   Wisdom of Solomon

ZAW   *Zeitschrift für die alttestamentliche Wissenschaft*

ZECNT   Zondervan Exegetical Commentary on the New Testament

ZIBBCOT   Walton, John. H., ed. *Zondervan Illustrated Bible Backgrounds Commentary: Old Testament.* Grand Rapids: Zondervan, 2009.

Introduction

Why a book about demons and spirits?

A BOOK LIKE THIS ONE is needed because it matters—it matters how we understand the world around us; it matters how we think about the Bible's authority and how it informs our understanding of the spirit world; it matters because how we think about the spirit world influences how we think about God, both his person and his role. We cannot afford to be inconsistent in our methodology or careless in our interpretation. Most of all, we cannot afford to diminish our great God and his revelation to us by misrepresenting them. Christianity is in need of a more careful assessment of these issues and we hope to put further information on the table so that we can think together through the complex issues that are involved.

Demythologizing and conflict theology

"There are two equal and opposite errors into which our race can fall about the devils. One is to disbelieve in their existence. The other is to believe, and to feel an excessive and unhealthy interest in them."[1] So writes C. S. Lewis in the preface to *The Screwtape Letters*. When examining modern trends in biblical and systematic theology, we find that the fields are, for the most part, neatly polarized into both of these errors. On the part of unbelief, there is a tendency, often referred to as "demythologizing," to attempt to redefine the Bible's various references to demons in terms of psychology, sociology, or other abstractions that can be fitted within the constraints of a worldview defined by scientific materialism. The part of "excessive and unhealthy interest" is more complicated. It does not refer to what Lewis called "magicians"; that is, those who worship demonic spirits and/or invoke their power. Rather, it takes the form of the practice of constructing a theological system wherein the role and activity of demons takes a prominent, or even central, role, which we refer to heuristically as "conflict theology" due to its emphasis on an ongoing *conflict* between God and Satan and their respective servants or underlings. In recent decades, this position has gained some popularity among evangelical scholars: "One cannot engage in a Biblical study of the power of God without simultaneously exploring the opposing sphere of power—Satan and his

1. Lewis, *Screwtape Letters*, 3.

principalities and powers. The Bible from beginning to end highlights the theme of conflict with the powers of evil. It is integral to the Biblical worldview."[2] Likewise, "believing in [. . .] the devil and demons is not inherently more difficult than believing in a supreme being that is good and may, in fact, be implicit in such a belief."[3] Finally, "the fact that [good and evil spirits warring against each other] constitutes a central component of Scripture's understanding of God and the cosmos should surely inspire us to do so."[4] Statements like these seem to suggest that a major purpose of the Bible is to teach about demons, and that the Christian worldview simply cannot function without them. (For a comparison of priorities, we may note that demons are totally absent from any of the creeds of the church—that is, the documents that establish the fundamental and integral essentials of Christian doctrine—until the Twelfth Ecumenical Council in 1215, where the first canon mentions the devil in passing: "The devil and other demons were created by God naturally good, but they became evil by their own doing. Man, however, sinned at the prompting of the devil."[5]

In our assessment, neither of these approaches is adequate. Through the book we will evaluate them as we consider the methodologies used in approaching the biblical text, and the exegesis of the pertinent texts. Finally, we will engage with them regarding their conclusions concerning theology and the problem of evil. To begin, however, we will briefly examine the approaches and their limitations.

The limits of demythologizing

"Demythologizing" is an attempt to salvage meaning or value from certain biblical texts whose original meaning cannot be reconciled with what is known to be "real" and "true" as those words are defined by a worldview grounded in scientific materialism. As Rudolf Bultmann, the fountainhead of the demythologizing hypothesis, states: "it is impossible to use electric lights and [. . .] to avail ourselves of modern medical and surgical discoveries, and at the same time to believe in the New Testament world of spirits and miracles."[6] Likewise Walter Wink: "it is as impossible for most of us to believe in the real existence of demonic or angelic powers as it is to believe in dragons, or elves, or a flat world."[7] These statements are not admonitions or conclusions; rather, they are observations that serve as an initial premise. Wink continues, "thus a gulf has been fixed between us and the biblical writers. We use the

---

2. Arnold, *Questions*, 30. See also Arnold, *Powers*, 16.

3. Page, *Powers of Evil*, 268.

4. Boyd, *God at War*, 19.

5. This is also referred to as the Doctrinal Decree of the Fourth Lateran Council, The Lateran Creed. The wicked are said to also experience "perpetual punishment with the devil." Translation in Pelikan and Hotchkiss, eds., *Creeds and Confessions of Faith*, 741–42.

6. Bultmann, "New Testament and Mythology," 5.

7. Wink, *Naming the Powers*, 4.

same words but project them into a wholly different world of meanings. What they meant by power and what we mean are incommensurate."[8] The goal of demythologizing is to interpret biblical teachings in forms that are generic or abstract enough to pass over this gulf and thus retain meaning and relevance for a modern audience who are in point of fact incapable of conceiving anything beyond the material. The exact form that these interpretations take varies between theologians and typically follows the broader themes and categories of larger theological movements such as existential theology (e.g., Bultmann) or liberation theology (e.g., Wink). The biblical passages themselves are read as broad insights about the general nature of such things as evil and power, or merely as stories intended to provoke a particular reaction in the reader upon encountering them.

For our purposes, the problem inherent in the demythologizing approach to biblical texts is not the recognition of the gulf, but rather the method used to cross it. It is true enough that modern readers can have no comprehension of the words and meanings of words that were used by the original authors, for the same reasons that modern readers who understand only English can have no comprehension of the original words written in Greek. The gulf in both cases is the same, and in both cases can be bridged by translation. The problem with demythologizing is that the demythologizers are, metaphorically speaking, poor translators. When translating the Bible's language, a linguist must first understand the ideas represented by the Greek, and thereafter choose the English words that most clearly convey the same idea based on what those words mean in English. However, a demythologizer who approached language in the same way that they approach theology would not use this method. Instead, they would look at the Greek letters and observe, correctly, that they have no meaning to modern English speakers. They would then consult their own instinct, experience, reasoning, and circumstances to formulate an idea of what would be appropriate for the text to say. They would then formulate those truths in English words and declare that *this* must be the meaning of the indecipherable Greek, because the Bible is true and therefore its teachings must accord with the truths that they, the demythologizers, have come to know as members and observers of humanity.[9]

This method of interpretation is a problem because it effectively shifts authority away from the text-in-context and onto the reader. Wink writes, "When we 'let the text speak,' therefore, we do not value equally everything it has to say, but fashion

8. Wink, *Naming the Powers*, 4.

9. Wink's own description of his process bears this out. He states that his objective is "to provide a means for developing a Christian social ethic from within the language of the New Testament" (*Naming the Powers*, 5) using a process he describes as "therapy" (ibid., x). What he does not ask, as a proper translator would, is whether or not the language of the New Testament has any interest in providing the means for developing a social ethic. Consequently, the warrant for the conclusions comes mostly from his own peace of mind ("what I found . . . was the thin margin of hope"; ibid., x), and not from an analysis of the logic and structure of the contents of the text itself, although he does try to demonstrate that his overall interpretation is not inconsistent with the semantic domains of some of the words.

an order of ranked priorities in terms of the resonances it establishes with our own unknown but higher potentialities."[10] Note that the valuing, fashioning, ordering, ranking, prioritizing, and resonating are all done by the reader, not by the authors and composers of the documents. Whatever meaning the author wished to convey, or what purpose that conveyance was meant to serve, matters not at all. In this conception, the text does not serve as a medium for the communication of meaning, like a book; it serves rather as a medium for the Holy Spirit to act on the reader, like an icon. The act of reading the text is not a search for comprehension of knowledge, like study; rather it is a rote act of ritual that indirectly initiates contact with the divine, like veneration. The awareness of its content and message is not achieved through the mechanics of semiotics, but by the direct intervention of the Holy Spirit. The words of the text itself are incidental to this process and may as well be written in gibberish. Proponents of this method sometimes claim that it accords with the practice of the church in the apostolic age, but it is worth noting that the Christians in the apostolic age had no Bible (the New Testament had not been written and the Septuagint was not circulated) and therefore needed no Bible. If we are going to imitate them, then, it follows that we should have no need of a Bible either, and therefore we need not bother to use it. (It is also worth noting that they *did* have a source of apostolic authority that could respond—positively or negatively—to particular interpretations of the gospel in real time, which is something Protestants specifically wish to do without.) In contrast, a reader who wishes to treat the text itself as carrying some form of authority must pay attention to the values and priorities evidenced in the text itself and discernible through its composition and presentation, just as a translator who wishes to respect the integrity of the source document must pay attention to the identifiable grammatical and semantic values of the existing words.

The limits of conflict theology

"Conflict theology" is a label we assign for convenience to a trend, most notably within conservative evangelical or fundamentalist theology, of assigning superlative or primary doctrinal priority to the idea of an ongoing war between God and Satan and their respective underlings, either as a dogma in itself (i.e., "something all Christians must believe") or as a necessary element for understanding fundamental points of doctrine such as the power of God, salvation and atonement, or the mission and role of the church. Conflict theology is a trend, not a school, but nonetheless the arguments offered by various interpreters in its defense are relatively consistent. First and foremost, conflict theologians universally insist on the "real existence" of spirit beings as personal entities possessing agency and will, as opposed to personified abstractions. This is because conflict theology sees the powers

---

10. Wink, "Towards a New Paradigm," 26.

as active participants in a war, not as passive obstacles to be demolished. Conflict theology also takes care to emphasize that Satan is a creature, not a god, and that God's ultimate victory in the conflict is certain, thus distinguishing itself from similar yet unorthodox movements such as Manicheanism (where the patrons of good and evil are equal and opposite gods) or process theology (where God's victory is contingent on people choosing to work to bring it about).

Conflict theologians, especially when contrasting themselves with demythologizers, pride themselves on "taking the teaching of the Bible seriously." What this normally consists of is treating the biblical text as a series of propositional statements, each of which, considered independently, is factually true. These propositions, or "proof-texts," are lifted from the text and arranged like a jigsaw puzzle into a coherent system of interconnected logic.[11] Any gaps in the system that are not provided by the text are supplied by appealing to any combination of tradition, philosophy, logical deduction, experience, or common sense; these are verified by the further internal coherence of the system as a whole. If any of these propositions seem to contradict, one or both are adjusted by appealing to literary or historical context, mitigating cultural factors, or semantic elements such as grammar, semantic range, or even copying errors. As a last resort, the conflicting elements can be simply accepted and held in tension as a paradox. The final result is that the "Bible's teaching" is assumed to consist of *the entire system* and everything that can be deduced or derived from it, not merely those statements that can actually be quoted from the biblical text. In this conception, the biblical documents themselves are merely the tip of the iceberg of God's revealed truth.

This method of interpretation is also a problem because it shifts the Bible's authority away from the text-in-context and onto a philosophical construct. It is true that not all of the Bible's statements can be weighted equally; this is the meaning of the conservative evangelical caveat that the Bible's teaching is true "in all it affirms." But while the relative values of statements—that is, what is or is not affirmed—cannot be determined on the basis of their significance to the reader, as demythologizers do, they also cannot be determined by coherence or dissonance with a broader system of logical propositions. The only way the text's statements can be evaluated is by their own context, within the logic and structure of the literary form in which they are presented. Statements cannot be lifted off the page as propositions; they must be considered according to their function within larger units of composition and discourse. Only at the end of a literary analysis can the text's "teaching" be turned over to the systematic theologians for integration with broader concerns of philosophy.

11. For a more detailed discussion of this method and its history, see Vanhoozer, "Lost in Interpretation," 95–96; and also Noll, *Scandal*, 96–98.

The scope of this study

As indicated by these simplistic summaries, this book is not only about demons and spirits; it is also a study in how the Bible is read and interpreted. In particular, it is a study about how we can possibly attain some measure of certainty that our claims about the Bible's teaching can actually trace their warrant to the Bible's text, as opposed to merely deriving from our own speculative philosophy, however sound or persuasive that philosophy may turn out to be. This is the only way by which we might have any basis to claim that the teaching we ascribe to the Bible is actually based on Scripture alone. Consequently, even readers who are not especially interested in the particular topic of demons and spirits might find something of value, in the form of a test case for a method of biblical theology that prioritizes the importance of the text-in-context.

One of the more unfortunate side-effects of the polarization between demythologizing and conflict theology is that rejection of one is automatically assumed to entail adherence to the other. Consequently, many arguments offered in support of either school consist of criticism of the other, with the assumption that their own position will serve as the default alternative. This study is written primarily as a critique of conflict theology, because that is the majority position of our intended audience. However, the criticism that we will offer of conflict theology does not therefore mean that we support the demythologizing process. We consider both of these approaches to be flawed and therefore seek to offer another alternative that falls in between them.

We assume that the various references, direct and indirect, to demons and other spirit-beings, were included in the text by the authors for some particular purpose. What that purpose was, we do not know—at least, not until we read the text they produced. We assume that the text in its final form was written for the purpose of communicating something relatively specific, and despite the gulf of time and culture we believe that comprehension of that message is possible. However, in order for the message to be received it must first be read, and in order to be read it must first be translated. The task of the biblical theologian is to serve as the translator, not primarily of the language and grammar (a task for linguists), but rather of the structure and logic of the discourse that gives semiotic elements their particular meaning. In this way, we can discover what message the text was intended to convey to its original audience—that is, why it was written—and thereby also discover what specific words and ideas are required to communicate that message to us today.

Part 1

How do we go about reading the Bible?

Chapter 1

Reading the Bible for knowledge

WHEN WE ASK ABOUT "what the Bible says," we generally mean that we are turning to the biblical text in order to gain some kind of knowledge. Both approaches to demonology discussed in the introduction, "demythologizing" and "conflict theology," approach the Bible in this way, though the exact nature of the knowledge is variable and includes such things as divine instructions or commands, details about the nature and denizens of the spirit world, insights on the nature of power, or some kind of heightened self-awareness. In all cases, reading the Bible is supposed to result in acquiring some kind of knowledge that the reader did not previously possess, and the knowledge that is gained is supposed to be relatively specific, based somehow on the content that has been read. Normally also this knowledge, whatever it is, is understood to have been intentionally transmitted to the reader by God. This divine intentionality is the most basic understanding of the idea that the Bible's text is *inspired*. The knowledge that is acquired by the act of reading the Bible, whatever it consists of, is what we will call *revelation*—that is, *revelation* is the things that God wants us to know that we did not know before we read the Bible. Debates about biblical interpretation, including the debate between the demythologizers and the conflict theologians, generally consist of disagreements about what this knowledge—the text's revelation—exactly consists of, and what we are supposed to do with it once we have it. Nonetheless the assumption that the text imparts knowledge of some kind is more or less universal.

Conceptions of the kind of knowledge that is gained by reading the Bible are varied and can be somewhat abstract, including such things as moral awareness, aesthetic experience, motivation to act, an attitude of devotion, and so on. For our purposes, however, we will focus on a single kind of knowledge; the transmission of information. Both demythologizers and conflict theologians agree that reading the Bible is supposed to provide *information* about the various things represented by the word "demon" and similar terms, whether those terms refer to abstractions, institutions, psychological forces, or spirit-beings. So, for example, Wink is looking for information about the nature of power dynamics—and the agencies that have been demythologized to describe it—in order "to provide a means for developing a Christian social ethic."[1] Boyd, conversely, is expecting to be presented with information about demons themselves: "Were it not for the revelation given by the angel [in Daniel 10], neither Daniel nor anyone else would have had any knowledge of [the] unseen battle [with the princes of Persia and Greece]."[2] Whatever the information consists of, it is subsequently collated as a collection of data points and employed by theologians in the systematic construction of a world view. The dispute therefore fundamentally concerns what exactly the words mean, which in turn involves a debate about where the Bible's meaning is vested relative to its words.

When we think of a document conveying information, we often think of a book like an encyclopedia, whose content consists essentially of a list of facts. These facts in turn are presented in such a way that they can be easily understood by any reader of the document. This objectivity of information is a goal of those who write encyclopedias. Consequently, when we read the Bible for information, we tend to read it as if it were an encyclopedia; that is, we treat its passages as if they contain clearly and objectively stated *facts*. These facts are then lifted off the page and employed as propositions in theological arguments. The assumed objectivity of the information is defended by invoking the clarity or *perspicuity* of Scripture, which is taken to mean that discerning the meaning of any passage in Scripture will be instinctively intuitive to anyone who reads it.

The Bible, however, was not written to convey information like an encyclopedia. Rather, it conveys information more like a conversation. By this we mean that the meaning it contains is tailored to its particular audience—specifically, the audience to whom the final redacted form of the original literary composition would have been addressed[3]—in such a way that *they will find it meaningful*. The Bible is an act of communication, not a repository of facts. This does not change the veracity of the information it contains, but it does affect the mode in which meaning is conveyed.

The discussion of the relationship of a text's meaning to the text's words is complex and could easily form a book in itself.[4] Rather than bog down the discussion with theory, we will instead examine a test case that involves similar issues as the discussion of demonology but is made clearer by consensus. That test case is the issue of the Bible's presentation of the structure and arrangement of the elements of the physical cosmos, also known as *cosmic geography*.

---

1. Wink, *Naming the Powers*, 5.

2. Boyd, *God at War*, 10.

3. The audience to whom a literary discourse is hypothetically directed is sometimes called the *implied audience*. We will use the terms *original audience*, *ancient audience*, *target audience*, and *intended audience* interchangeably to refer to this same group of people. The historical persons who actually did read, receive, and interpret the literary work are called the *historical audience*.

4. See for example Vanhoozer, *Is There Meaning in this Text?*; Osborne, *The Hermeneutical Spiral*; Wolterstorff, *Divine Discourse*; Brown, *Scripture as Communication*.

A Test Case: Cosmic Geography

Many passages in the biblical text make declarative statements about such structures as the "pillars of the earth" (Job 9:6), the "waters above" held back by a solid sky ("vault" or "firmament"; Gen 1:6–7), and such regions as the netherworld (*šĕʾôl*) or the cosmic ocean (*tĕhôm*). Like the subject of demons and spirits, there are two broad approaches to this material. One approach is the "demythologizing" approach, which in the context of cosmic geography is called *concordism*. This approach tries to redefine the various Hebrew terms in such a way that they correspond—that is, "concord"—with structures that are known to exist in modern cosmology. So, for example, the "firmament" in Genesis 1:6 (Heb. *rāqîaʿ*) is interpreted to refer to the atmosphere. The other approach insists, as conflict theology does for demonology, that the words must mean the same things that they would have meant to the ancient audience, and further that the presence of the ideas in the text of Scripture means that modern readers who wish to be faithful to the teaching of Scripture must adopt a worldview similar to that held by the ancient authors, even in defiance of the observations of modern science. Thus, advocates claim that the earth really is a flat disc floating on the cosmic ocean and supported by pillars, all underneath a solid dome with the stars inscribed underneath. We proposed that both of these approaches were insufficient in regard to demonology, and both are insufficient in regard to cosmic geography as well. We will now briefly examine the reasons why.

Both the Concordist approach and what we might call the "traditional-literal" approach to cosmic geography require that the Bible's declarative statements on the subject be can be read as factual propositions that are universally true. For our purposes it is important to note that, in modern times, proponents of ancient cosmic geography are almost non-existent. Nobody believes that the presence of ideas about cosmic geography in the Bible means that the Bible is trying to teach us information about cosmic geography and therefore that those ideas must be incorporated into the Christian worldview. So how do the interpreters of both schools still manage to "take the Bible seriously" while simultaneously rejecting its explicit cosmology? Once we understand how ancient cosmology can be rejected in modern times without compromising the integrity of the Bible's message, we will be able to examine the subject of demons and spirits as a topic in itself, with conclusions to be accepted or rejected without concern for issues of the integrity of Scripture.

Consistent with the demythologizing method discussed in the introduction, the Concordist solution to the question of cosmic geography is to redefine the Hebrew words as representing ideas that they consider to be meaningful—which, in context, means inserting any definition onto the Hebrew word that will make the resulting statement true according to modern science, regardless of the word's original meaning. So, for a Concordist, Genesis 1:7 roughly translates to "God made the atmosphere," which is a statement that can be comfortably accepted in modern times. Importantly, however, the meaning that any interpreter finds in the text does not simply consist of the translations of the words; it also consists of *the answers to the questions that the interpreter chooses to ask*. When a Concordist approaches the text of Genesis 1:7, they are not seeking an answer to the question, "what does the Bible teach is up in the sky?" Obviously, they have already decided what is up in the sky on the basis of their translation of the word *rāqîa'* as *atmosphere*. They do not read the text as saying, "the thing up in the sky where the water comes from is a layer of gasses [and not a solid dome]." Instead, Concordists are usually also apologists, and so the question they ask is something along the lines of, "where does the Bible teach that the thing up in the sky, whatever it is, came from?" The answer that they find in turn is, "the thing up in the sky came from God's creative action [and not through some kind of purposeless natural process]." Both of these readings translate the words of Genesis 1:7 in the same way—"God made the atmosphere"—but in the first case the meaning of the text and the information gained from it is "the thing up in the sky is a layer of gasses," while in the second case the meaning of the text and the information gained from it is "God made the thing up in the sky." Thus we see that the questions we ask of the text determine the meaning that we will derive from the text and therefore will also determine the information we will receive when we read it.

The question "what does the Bible teach is up in the sky?" is asked by the traditional-literalists. They, in turn, can only derive the answer based on the historical meaning of the word *rāqîa'*, which is not "atmosphere" or indeed anything else that corresponds to modern cosmology.[5] Combined with the need to read all of the Bible's declarative statements as propositions, this approach must affirm that there is indeed a dome in the sky, and if science claims otherwise then science is mistaken. However, for obvious reasons, traditional-literal interpreters of cosmic geography are virtually non-existent. The non-existence of this position means that nobody is actually *asking* the question, "what does the Bible teach is up in the sky?" The reason why nobody is asking this question is because most people understand that it is not an appropriate question to ask. The Bible was not written to teach us about what is up in the sky, so we should not ask it to give us this information, just as we should not ask it which stocks to buy or how to make tiramisu. Thus we see that in order to become effective interpreters, we must learn which questions are appropriate to ask.

Demythologizers, both in demonology and cosmic geography, choose the questions they ask based on questions they want to have answers to. Thus, as we have seen, Wink asks about how to develop a social ethic, and Concordist-apologists look for ammunition to answer whatever philosophical controversies are popular in their time. Traditional-literalists, and also conflict theologians, are more inclined to ask questions

5. The *rāqîa'* is usually thought to refer to the solid sky, but it is possible that the word for the solid sky is actually *šĕḥāqîm*, while *rāqîa'* refers to the space between the solid sky and the earth. See Walton, *Genesis One as Ancient Cosmology*, 155–61.

about what the Bible's authors[6] have believed on whatever subject has captured their interest. However, we should not necessarily assume that the Bible was written in order to place a stamp of divine approval on whatever beliefs of the authors the text makes reference to, and the clearest example of this is the Bible's cosmic geography. Conflict theologians do not believe that we must believe everything the Bible's authors believed on all subjects: as Arnold specifically says, "I am not advocating a complete paradigm shift back to a pre-scientific era."[7] So the question then becomes, "when is it appropriate to ask what the Bible's authors believed, and when is it not?" We need to gain a sense of the questions we should be asking, if we want the answers we receive to contain the information that the text was written to transmit to us.

We know not to ask the Bible about the physical structures of the cosmos because we know that the Bible was not written in order to tell us about the physical structures of the cosmos. But *how* do we know that? It will not do to say that we know this simply because we do not *like* the Bible's answer to the question. If we accept the Bible's information only when it tells us what we wanted to hear, we are not really acquiring information from the Bible and therefore we are not treating the Bible as a source of information. Instead, we are using the Bible as a fallacious appeal to authority to confirm information that we acquired elsewhere. In this case the real veracity or authority of the information would actually come from its original source, not from the Bible at all, thus making a Bible study on the issue irrelevant and redundant. The real presence of information in the text has to come from within the content of the text itself, not from our feelings about that content; in other words, the Bible contains no information about the physical structures of the cosmos because that information *is not there* for us to find. However, by the same token, we cannot assume that the text will necessarily have answers to the questions *we feel like asking*; that information might also not be there for us to find. The text of Genesis 1:7 is not interested in telling us that there is a *rāqîaʿ* up in the sky, but it might *also* not be interested in telling us that, whatever the thing up in the sky might be, God made it. The fact that apologists want to answer the question of where the structures of the sky came from, and even the fact that they like the answer they can wrangle out of Genesis, does not mean that this is the information that the text was written to convey. We cannot assume that a given piece of information is the Bible's inspired affirmation based on the fact that we like it or the fact that it makes sense for the same reasons that we cannot assume that a given piece of information is not the Bible's inspired affirmation based on the fact that we do not like it or the fact that it does not make sense.

The information contained in the text—that is, the inspired affirmation, the message the text was written to convey—must be derived from its contents, not from

---

6. Usually these interpreters are interested in the *historical* authors, but sometimes they also address the beliefs of the *implied* authors. More often they do not distinguish the two unless they are actively engaged in narrative criticism.

7. Arnold, *Powers*, 182.

the feelings or interests of potential interpreters. This in turn means that, in order to figure out which question we should ask of the text, we must ask about what question the text was written to address. In other words, for any given passage in the Bible, we do not ask "what does this tell me about a subject I am interested in?" or "how can I make this meaningful for me/for the intended audience of my theological work?" or "what does this tell us about what the author believed?" or even "is this true?" Instead, the question we must ask is, "what question or concern was this passage written to address?" or simply, "why is this in here?" It is *this* question that will lead us to the information that the text was written to convey.

In the process, of course, we might have to understand what the author would have believed, and we might even receive answers about things we happen to be interested in. On the other hand, however, we might not. The Bible does not tell us about the structures of the physical cosmos, so no matter how curious we are we will have to look for our answers elsewhere. This work will attempt to demonstrate that the same is true for the subject of demons and spirits.

Reading as communication

As we mentioned briefly above, the Bible delivers its meaning less like an encyclopedia—a repository of facts—and more like a conversation. The Bible's information content should therefore not be seen as a list of various facts but rather as a *message* that its author intends to *communicate*. In order for communication to be possible, a kind of "social contract" must exist between the author or speaker and the reader or listener. The author/speaker agrees to use language in a way that the audience would reasonably be expected to understand; this is called "accommodation."[8] The reader/ listener agrees to do his or her best to receive the message as it was intended to be understood. Either party can neglect or ignore their part in the contract, but if they do so, effective communication becomes impossible. "Deferring to the text's authority" means adopting the role of the reader in the contract of communication; that is, it means that we seek for the meaning that the author has placed in the communicative media, rather than create meaning for ourselves.

The reader's role in the contract of communication is to hear what the author[9] has said, but the writer's role is to convey their message in a way that is meaningful to the intended audience of the discourse. So who is the audience? Demythologizers

8. Importantly, a speaker or writer does not accommodate an audience by affirming ideas as true that the speaker believes to be false simply because the audience believes those ideas to be true. Accommodation means that the speaker chooses language and logic that the audience will find intuitive in order to express their ideas. In other words, accommodation takes place in the mode in which ideas are expressed, not in the content of the ideas themselves. Communicating ideas to an audience based on what the audience would prefer to hear is not accommodation; it is simply pandering.

9. Specifically, to hear what the *implied author* has said. The *historical author* does not need to be known or accessible to readers of the documents.

of all kinds assume that the intended audience of the discourse is themselves; that is, modern people who think in modern ways and share the curiosities and concerns of the modern world. Because they assume that the author communicates meaningfully *to them*, they read the text in such a way as to make it meaningful *for them* because they assume that the author is communicating to them personally. This assumption is usually based on the idea that God is the author (the basic meaning of *inspiration*) and God is unconstrained by history, and also on the concept of perspicuity, which they usually understand to mean that the Bible's message will be intuitive to anyone who reads it. Traditional-literal approaches, on the other hand, assume that the author communicated meaningfully to the ancient audience, and therefore the Bible's meaning for us consists of taking those ancient ideas as universal facts. So for example Arnold, "If the realm of spirits and angels is a dominant part of the biblical world view, it should thus be a dominant part of the Christian world view in our age,"[10] and also "we must first strive towards making [the affirmation of the real existence of demons and spirits] as important a part of our world view as it was for Paul."[11]

We propose instead that the Bible was written *for* us, but not *to* us. Its message has relevance for us today, but its audience—the people to whom it was written meaning-fully—are the ancient peoples who spoke the Hebrew and Greek languages in which the documents were written and who were immersed in the culture that provides the context that gives the words of those languages meaning. The author communicated in a way that the ancient audience would have found meaningful.[12] In order to play our role as readers in the contract of communication, then, we have to understand what that meaning would have been. The meaning the text had for the ancient audience is the same meaning it has for us today; the text can *never mean* what it *never meant*. However, by the same token, it is highly reductionistic to assume that the meaning for the original audience would have simply consisted of reiterating things they already knew. The audience of Genesis already knew that there was a *rāqîaʿ* up in the sky, and already believed that God had put it there, and so they did not need to be told that this was the case. Consequently, a statement to the effect of, "there is a thing in the sky called a *rāqîaʿ*, and God put it there" would not have given them new informa-tion. If the text's meaning is the information that the audience is supposed to acquire, and "there is a thing in the sky called a *rāqîaʿ*, and God put it there" is not acquired information, then "there is a thing in the sky called a *rāqîaʿ*, and God put it there" is not what Genesis 1:7 *meant* to them, and therefore not what it *means* to us, either. The *affirmation* of the text is the *new* information that the author intends the ancient audience to acquire, which can consist of completely new ideas but more often consists of clarifying ideas that may have been known but are contested or open to diverse

10. Arnold, *Powers*, 17.

11. Arnold, *Powers*, 182.

12. For a very technical discussion of the contextual nature of literary communication from the standpoint of linguistic theory, see Klutz, *Exorcism Stories*, 15–29.

interpretation. Ideas that the audience already knows, or at least holds with relative certainty, are *referenced* in order to convey this information. The task of the modern interpreter is to sort out the Bible's *affirmations* from its *references* in order to understand the meaning that the text was originally written to convey.

Affirmation and reference

The Bible does not teach that "there is a thing up in the sky called a *rāqîaʿ*" because its declarative statements concerning the *rāqîaʿ* are references, not affirmations. The reason they are references is not because modern science has since taught us otherwise, but because the statements consist of information that the ancient audience of the document already knew. Thus the meaning of the text is not simply to affirm the beliefs of the audience as factual propositions. References, however, are not redundant or superfluous; rather, they are the means by which the text's affirmations are conveyed. In order to know what the author of Genesis wanted to communicate—that is, affirm—to his audience, we have to know what purpose the statement "God made the *rāqîaʿ*" serves in the discourse of Genesis 1. In order to know *that*, in turn, we have to know what the ancient audience would have understood the *rāqîaʿ* to be. This of course means that we cannot begin by reading *rāqîaʿ* as "atmosphere." Thus both the Concordist and traditional-literal approach are misguided and do not serve to discover the meaning of the text.

By itself, read in isolation, the statement "God made the *rāqîaʿ*" does not mean anything at all. Words and phrases need context to mean things, so a word or phrase without a context is effectively meaningless.[13] Of course, Genesis 1:7 does not occur in isolation, but instead occurs in a series of statements that together constitute the cosmogonic hymn or liturgy that is Genesis chapter 1. However, Genesis 1 itself does not occur in isolation either; it is only part of the larger unit of discourse called the *cosmic history* (Gen 1–11), which itself is only part of the larger literary unit called the *book of Genesis*. If we want to know what the author (or, more likely, redactor) of Genesis wanted to communicate when he found a place for the phrase "God made the *rāqîaʿ*" in his composition, we have to understand the literary intent of the entire composition, not merely the meanings of the individual words or phrases. Words need context to mean things, and the context in this case is the literary composition. Consequently, meaning—that is, the message that the text was written to communicate, which is the information that it affirms—is found in *the literary intent of the composition*, not in propositions derived from declarative statements.

---

13. Or, perhaps more accurately, a word or phrase without a context can mean a lot of different things and so its meaning is indeterminate. Neither a word or phrase devoid of meaning nor a word or phrase of indeterminate meaning can serve as effective communication, so the word or phrase communicates nothing.

So, in the case of Genesis 1, the literary intent of the cosmic hymn is to depict the world as having been originally established as a place of *order*, using a metaphor for order that would have had meaning to the ancient audience: a cosmic temple.[14] However, Genesis 1 does not exist in isolation either, and so its affirmations cannot be reduced to "the cosmos is a temple" or "God put the cosmos in order," both of which are ideas that the original audience would have probably understood already.[15] Instead, Genesis 1 is the prologue to the cosmic history, which, as we will discuss in chapters 10 and 12, describes the inability of humans to sustain the order that was originally established. This *is* new information, since the ancient world generally believed that order—at least in the human world—was sustained through human efforts. However, because the cosmic history is part of a larger discourse, we cannot assume that the factual proposition "humans are not good at sustaining order" is the message that the text is communicating to the modern reader. Genesis is written to anticipate the Israelite covenant—of which its original audience is aware—and so tells the story of Israel's ancestors by way of *contrast* to the primordial history that preceded them. In doing so, it *interprets* the covenant in such a way as to depict it as God's (re) establishing the order that humans failed to uphold on their own. However, the final redacted form of Genesis is also written to anticipate the exile. Thus, we also cannot assume that the factual proposition "God establishes order in the human world through human participation in the Israelite covenant" is the meaning that the text is communicating to the modern reader. The exilic audience of the final redacted form of the Pentateuch is trying to make sense of what happened to them. The five books are written primarily to provide insights as to what the covenant *is*, so that the audience in exile can come to understand why it failed. This in turn is also the affirmation for the modern reader: through the juxtaposition with ancient Near Eastern social ideals and the stories of God's provision for Israel's ancestors, we are supposed to gain some kind of knowledge about what the covenant was, and thereby also gain some kind of knowledge of why Israel's actions caused it to fail. This affirmation can then be taken by the systematic theologian and combined with the affirmations of the rest of the Pentateuch, of the rest of the Old Testament, and of the rest of the anthology of texts we call the Christian Bible, all read within the context of their own discourse, in order to produce some kind of coherent theological construct.

Of course, the claim that all of Genesis can be reduced to "the Israelite covenant was supposed to be [X]" is overly simplistic; our purpose is not to exegete Genesis but to demonstrate the relationship between a text's affirmations and its references. For our purposes, two observations are important. The first is that "the Israelite covenant was supposed to be [X]" is *not a proposition that can be derived from any of the text's declarative statements.* This "meaning" of Genesis—the message it was written to affirm—is not found by transcribing words into facts. Instead, the way it is found

14. Walton, *Genesis One as Ancient Cosmology*, 178–83.
15. Walton, *Genesis One as Ancient Cosmology*, 107–10.

is by examining all of the text's *references* and understanding the significance they would have had to the ancient audience who heard them. The second observation is that this affirmation has nothing whatsoever to do with whether or not there is a dome up in the sky, or even how "the thing in the sky, whatever it is" came to be there. Both the Concordist and traditional-literal approach to Genesis 1 have managed to miss the affirmation of the text entirely.

As we will demonstrate throughout this work, all of the Bible's statements about demons or similar creatures are references, just as all of the Bible's statements about the physical structures of the cosmos are references. This means that we need to understand the significance they would have had to the ancient audience, and so cannot read them as referring to psychological abstractions (except insofar as the ancient audience would have done so), but we also cannot arrive at the text's affirmations by transcribing the words of those statements into facts. References are references because they mean things to the audience who heard them, and because they mean things, they are used as a vehicle to convey the author's message, which in turn contains the text's affirmation. What that message is can only be determined by understanding what the references mean. This in turn requires that we be attentive to the meanings of the words as the ancient audience would have understood them, but it also requires that we be attentive to features of composition and discourse which also determine meaning. Arguably the most important of these features is the genre in which the composition was written.

Chapter 2

The genres of Scripture

I MAGINE THAT YOU COME into work and find on your desk a message from your boss. What does it say? It might contain instructions or an assignment. It might be a newsletter describing the state of the company and its plans for the future. It may be an offer of promotion or a threat of dismissal, or a note of praise or censure. It could perhaps be an invitation to the department picnic, or simply a wish to "have a nice day." In order to know what it says, we would first have to read it. Then, and only then, can we begin to ask how we ought to respond to whatever it contains. But to respond to it appropriately we must determine, as we read, what sort of document it is.

The Bible is more complex and sophisticated than an office memo, but it is nonetheless a document, and therefore the initial approach should be the same as for any document. Understanding how a particular genre works is necessary for understanding what an author is trying to say when they use that genre to communicate. Words need context to mean things, and the genre of the text they appear in is one of the most basic elements of the context. This is why quotations cannot be lifted off the page and analyzed in a vacuum as independent propositions. But if we want to understand what the Bible's statements about demons mean in context, we have to understand how the various genres in which those statements appear operate.

The genres of Scripture: historical narratives

Many Bible readers have well-established methodologies for reading the narrative material in the Bible—what they would call "Bible stories." They learned them growing up in the church. They may not have ever thought of trying to describe their methodology, let alone defend its presuppositions, but everyone has a methodology. Since much of the information in the Bible about Satan and demons occurs in narrative, it is important that we evaluate our presuppostions and, if need be, modify our methods and expectations.

Demons and other spirit-beings occasionally appear in the Bible's historical and Gospel narratives, acting alongside and interacting with real people—that is, with characters that the text treats as historical figures. Interpreters who read the

Bible's statements as propositions stake the Bible's integrity on the assumption that these depictions are more or less a transcription of what a video camera observing that time and place would have recorded. Some of the more extreme interpreters try to deconstruct the actions and (especially) dialogue of the spirit-beings in order to gain insight into their nature, motives, and psychology. But this assumption is based on the idea that the genre of "history" as we find it in the Bible is essentially a presentation of objective data that readers are meant to draw on in order to forensically reconstruct events. We will therefore investigate the genre of "historical narrative" to discover whether or not its purpose is really nothing more than the transcription of empirical, forensic data.

Historical narratives are *narratives*

When interpreters of the Bible, both confessional and skeptical, talk about the biblical authors "making up" events, they refer to the practice of presenting persons and events that never existed or never happened as if they had, as is done in the genre we today call *fiction*. Critics of the Bible look for inconsistencies in the details of the text, both compared to itself (i.e., the sequence of events in the different Gospels) and to other "historical" documents (i.e., the date and participants of the battle between the North Kingdom and Moab, as recorded by both 2 Kings 3 and the Moabite Stone) and offer these inconsistencies as evidence that the Bible is unreliable. Consequently, some apologists for the Bible try to preserve its integrity by arguing that, since the teaching of the Bible is true, all of the events it records must have occurred exactly as the text describes them. Both of these approaches take the text's details as if they were a series of objective data points that can be used to forensically reconstruct what a camera present at the event would have recorded.

Both of these approaches are misguided because it is in fact impossible to forensically reconstruct events using the information that the Bible provides. This is because the content is not a spreadsheet of data; it is a narrative. Most critics accuse the Bible of embellishing its record with details that a camera would not have seen; for example, a Red Sea crossing and wilderness wandering that are said to have never occurred but had been invented later as propaganda. Narrative, however, is created, not primarily by *adding* things that a camera *would not* have seen, but by *removing* things that the camera *would* have seen. Narratives create emphasis in order to establish characters and plot, without which the narrative does not exist. In order to create this emphasis, certain details are brought to the reader's attention while others are omitted entirely. We know what Jesus ate for dinner on a particular Thursday, because Jesus is an important character and "the last supper" is an important event in the arc of the plot. But if the text was a camera impartially recording the activities of Jesus, we would know what he ate for breakfast as well. If the text was impartially recording events in the upper room, we would know who was in there on Wednesday and what they ate for dinner as well. For the purposes of forensic reconstruction, however, incomplete data is just as damaging as fabricated data.

The Bible's record of events—or the record provided by any historical narrative, for that matter—is less like footage from a security camera and more like what we see in movies, especially those made before computers. Security cameras impartially record everything that passes in front of the lens. Movie cameras also record what occurs in front of the lens, but they make no attempt to be impartial. A movie camera does not attempt to capture *everything* that is happening on the set while it is recording. Instead, it focuses solely on a small number of people doing a few very specific things—the actors giving their performance. Consequently, when we watch the movie, we pay attention to the way that the things the camera has chosen to record contribute to the overall product of the movie. We do not try to use that footage to forensically reconstruct what was happening on the set on the day that it was shot.

Narratives are unlike real life because in real life there are no such things as "characters" and "plots." Instead there are hordes of essentially indistinguishable people doing a wide variety of things of essentially indistinguishable significance. It requires a director to point the camera at particular persons among the crowd, and to draw attention to which of their actions or which of the events that befall them are of importance, in order to produce a story. A good example of this process is seen in the production of so-called "reality television." These shows are created by filming hundreds of hours of unscripted people interacting with each other, often in humorously contrived or otherwise unique circumstances. This footage is then combed through by the show's producers, and scenes are selected and arranged that depict characters saying or doing things or acting in ways that will appeal to the show's audience. These are taken from their original context and edited together in order to give the illusion of a narrative arc. The characters in a reality show are not (usually) actors giving a performance—their words, actions, and personalities are "real"—but those words and actions are manipulated through editing and presentation so that some characters are the "heroes," some characters are the "villains," and they all take part in a series of actions that increase in conflict leading to a climax and resolution—that is, they take part in a *story*.

The Bible's narratives, like movies and reality television shows, are crafted products. Their content has been selected and presented in a particular way to serve the purposes of the document's author/redactor. Because they are crafted, we cannot think of their contents as empirical data or raw footage. Consequently, the question of whether or not the narratives are "true" has nothing to do with how that data compares to data we collect from other sources. Nonetheless, because the narratives are crafted, they are crafted *for a reason*. Thus, if we want to understand how to read narratives we must examine what the authors expected to accomplish by writing them.

Historical narratives interpret events

Ancient historians were not "journalists." Journalists, at least in theory, attempt to present their audience with impersonal facts that the audience can use to reconstruct the event "accurately"—that is, as a camera would have seen it—and thereby formulate their own interpretations of the event. When a journalist moves beyond the presentation of facts and attempts to persuade the audience to interpret the event a certain way—what we call "spin"—they are, again in theory, acting unethically. This is because journalism as a genre is supposed to be objective, which is why journalists are called "reporters."

Ancient historians, however, did not pretend or aspire to be objective. The documents we call "history" are written for the specific purpose of interpreting the events they describe in a particular way. Their message is not "here is how it happened"; their message is "this is how one ought to understand what happened." The event is significant—and therefore worthy of record—not in itself, but because of what it represents and signifies, which in turn is nothing more than what the author has constructed it to represent and signify. What that is depends on the document itself.

From the ancient Near East, most of the "historical" material that we have comes from monumental commemorative inscriptions. These normally serve to glorify the ruler who created the monument and commissioned the inscription. However, these inscriptions were not widely circulated among the people in order to manipulate popular sentiment, as we imply when we label them "propaganda." Most of the population of the ancient world could not read, and these inscriptions were often carved in inaccessible places, squirreled away in archives, or buried in the foundations of buildings. They did not exist to communicate information; they existed so that it could be said that they had been written. The act of writing itself granted legitimacy to whatever the document was written to convey; that is, the power and the glory of the ruler who was able to cause the inscription to be made.[1] These documents are also infamously prone to exaggerating their details, especially concerning the amount of plunder taken in battle, the size of armies, and the numbers of defeated enemy troops. These particular features have also been widely recognized in the biblical text as well, especially in the books of Numbers and Joshua. But if the accuracy of the details is subject to, let us say, "creative embellishment," then to what extent can we claim that the account is "true?" In other words, we need to examine what it would mean for such an account to be "false."

Commemorative inscriptions normally exist to legitimate the ruler who commissioned them, either as a rightful claimant to the throne, the rightful ruler of a subjugated territory, or as a wise, just, and pious ruler appointed and favored by the gods (or all of these at once). The "truth" of the document is therefore not in its details but in whether or not the ruler was really the legitimate claimant, great military

---

1. Walton and Sandy, *Lost World of Scripture*, 23.

leader, or pious servant of the gods that the document proclaims him to be. Suppose an inscription claims that the king conquered a territory by defeating an army of one million chariots and destroying one hundred cities and leaving behind no enemy that breathed. Suppose also that what "really" happened—i.e., what a camera would have seen—was that he defeated an army of several thousand, conquered two cities, and accepted the surrender of two more. As long as those battles were important victories for the king and important defeats for the enemy that did in fact lead to the subjugation of the territory, the narrative is still "true" in what it intends to convey, even if not in the technical details that it uses to convey that truth; it exists to portray the king as a great and glorious conqueror, which he really was. If, however, the camera would have seen the king knock over a few huts full of peasants, badly frighten some sheep, be repelled by the defenders of a city, and sneak off home with the enemy king still firmly in control of his lands, then the document would be false; not because its details were inaccurate but because it attempts to portray the king as something other than he really was. Historical documents *interpret* events, and so it is the accuracy of the interpretation, not of the selected details, that determines the "truth" of the account. All of the selected details are inherently "inaccurate"—by virtue of being incomplete—due to the selection process that forms an inevitable part of crafting narratives.

At the same time, however, a king would not claim legitimacy based on winning a battle that he had never actually fought. Historians interpret events, but they do not fabricate them. In order for an event to be interpreted, there must have been an event to interpret. This is what sets "history" apart from such genres as parables, fables, and what we call "fiction," which also take the form of stories. By classifying a document as "history," we affirm that an event of some kind took place. What we cannot do is reconstruct the *details* of the event from the details provided in the document. As a result, we cannot appeal to the "authenticity" of the details in order to determine whether or not the genre is history—since the details are always artificial, by definition of *narrative*—and we likewise cannot use the details to render a judgment about whether or not a "real event" actually occurred, since that would be circular.[2] If the genre is indeed "history" then it is based on a real event. If it is a "false" history, that charge would be based on the lack of integrity of the historian (see discussion below) or on the improper interpretation of the event, not on the degree to which the details correspond to what a camera would have recorded.

It is likely that some of the Bible's sources—notably the "annals of the kings" and various battle reports[3]—were documents of this kind; that is, inscriptions and

2. Recent apologetic attempts to "authenticate" the details in (especially) the Gospels serve the purpose of dating the documents to the first century, in contrast to arguments that claim, for example, the Gospels were written in the fourth century to legitimate Constantine's religious reforms in concert with his bid for imperial power. The case that the Gospels are authentic products of the first century (which is sustainable) is different from the claim that every detail they describe is an authentic camera transcript (which is not).

3. Compare also the "book of the law" found in the foundations of the temple by Josiah's

archives. However, documents such as the Pentateuch, Luke-Acts, and the Deuteronomistic History were not monumental inscriptions or documents for the archives; these were circulated and read, or at least read aloud. This form of "history writing" more closely resembles the kind we see in epic poetry and the Greek and Roman histories, which were also circulated and read. Nonetheless, the purpose of these documents is still not to record the details of events. Greek (and later, Roman) historians were also interpreters, although their interpretations had different goals than those represented by ancient Near Eastern monuments.

The story of the past defines the state of the present

Ancient Near Eastern monumental inscriptions were written in order to preserve the king's legacy, either for future kings or for the gods.[4] Therefore, we might say that in these documents, talking about events is a means to an end to talk about the king. This is why their truth and falsity is evaluated based on what they say about the king, not on what they say about the events. The Greek and Roman historical narratives are likewise not "about" the events they describe; those events are likewise a means to an end to talk about something else, though what exactly that thing is varies by author. Broadly, we might say that the purpose of a historical narrative is to describe something about the nature and character of the people and/or community that the story is a history *of*. This is especially true if the account is an origin story, as, for example, the *Aeneid* is the origin story of Augustan Rome and the Pentateuch is the origin story of the Israelite covenant, since describing how a thing came to be is one way of describing what that thing is. This property of *definition* thereby offers the audience a means of understanding the state of affairs as they stand in the world of their present, as opposed to understanding the details of the doings of the past. It is the significance for the present, not the depiction of the past, that gives history its value, and is the reason why anybody took the trouble to write these depictions or to read them. Consequently, the truth or falsity of the narratives has less to do with the accuracy with which they describe the events of the past, and more to do with the accuracy with which they describe the state of the present—although, as discussed previously, the genre of *history* still presumes an event of some kind did actually occur.

We still use this understanding of history today, at least when we re-cast the events of the past into narratives. For example, when I (John) was younger, I was told the story of Christopher Columbus, who defied the ignorant monarchs of his time, who believed the world was flat; who persevered against great hardship; and who was rewarded with discovery, fame, and wealth. This vindication of persistence in the face of adversity and authority was held up as an exemplar of the American spirit, which is why he is honored with a federal holiday and why his story was taught

---

remodelers, which some interpreters think is transcribed in the book of Deuteronomy.

4. Walton and Sandy, *Lost World of Scripture*, 23.

to schoolchildren. Now, several decades later, I still hear the story of Christopher Columbus. Now he is a greedy ignoramus who stubbornly ignored the best science of his time, which argued that the earth was bigger than his own calculations indicated; who lied to his crew and put them through unnecessary hardship and distress through his bungling; and who finally arrived in a peaceful, undespoiled land which he devoured in slavery and genocide. This version is also held up as an exemplar of the American spirit, for which Americans ought to repent. Which of these stories is true and which is false depends on who you ask, but in no case is the truth based on the accuracy (or lack thereof) of the details of the events that the story describes; everyone agrees that an Italian man financed by Spain sailed across the Atlantic in the late fifteenth century. In addition, neither version of the story is told in order to influence people on how to think about Columbus; the story is told in order to influence people how to think about America. The motive for the story is the American holiday celebrated in the present, not the actions and achievements (or lack thereof) of one explorer in the distant past. That is why we tell stories and generate controversies about Columbus, and not about similar figures who have no holidays, such as Amerigo Vespucci (who actually did discover America), or Robert Peary (another celebrated explorer of dubious achievement), or Hérnan Cortés (who was also responsible for the suffering of many natives). The story of the voyage of Christopher Columbus—both versions—in the distant past is a means to an end to talk about the nature and character of the American nation today.

One biblical book at least explicitly states the reason why it was written. In Luke 1:2, the author writes that he "decided to write an orderly account for you, most excellent Theophilus, so that you may know the certainty of the things you have been taught." But what has Theophilus been taught? Certainly not aimless trivia about things that were said and done in various locations around Galilee and Judea. Not doctrine either, since the book of Luke-Acts contains very little in the way of theological argument. What Theophilus has been taught, that Luke is trying to affirm—both for the patron himself and the wider reading audience—concerns the nature and character of Jesus of Nazareth, and of the schismatic Jewish sect that worships him as the Son of God. "Luke-Acts tells the story not simply of the founder of Christianity, but of Christians as a people . . . . [The author] set out their story in an effort to provide them with a definition of who they were."[5] Other books of the Bible do not state their purpose explicitly, but the purpose can nonetheless be inferred. The Deuteronomistic History (Joshua, Judges, Samuel, Kings) is written to the Jewish community in exile in order to explain the exile—that is, to describe their current status. The books of Chronicles are written to the returning exiles in order to reconnect the identity of the returning community with their ancestral heritage. The ancestral narratives of Genesis are the backstory of the nation of Israel as a people, and the narrative segments scattered throughout Exodus-Numbers are the backstory

5. Sterling, *Historiography and Self-Definition*, 19.

of Israel as a nation in the land under the covenant. While the covenant and the exile are "events of the past" for us today, they would have been the present state of affairs for the audience for whom the books were originally written.

Ancient histories derive their veracity from the authority of the historian, not the presentation of evidence

Since historical narratives are interpretations of events, it is important that the historian possesses an authority that entitles him (or her) to interpret properly. Modern historians, following the example of the sciences, try to remove the influence of the observer—that is, themselves—from the results of the study, such that any investigator examining the same evidence would draw the same conclusions. Their authority therefore derives from the relationship between the evidence offered and the conclusions drawn, and the content of their monographs mostly consists of extensive documentation. Ancient historians, however, do not offer "evidence" of this kind; the biblical narratives contain very little documentation of samples from primary and secondary sources.[6] This is because ancient historians vested the authority of their conclusions not in their data, but in themselves: "[the historian] wished to be seen as competent to judge both men and deeds."[7] Historians who record their own experiences, both observing events and interviewing eyewitnesses (as Luke does), do so not to appeal to the authority of the source, but to establish their own credibility as observers. We see similar practice today in such figures as political pundits or sports commentators, who derive their authority from their credentials or personal insightfulness, not from the thoroughness of their arguments and evidence. Perhaps the best example today of this kind of authority comes from professional scientists turned amateur philosophers (i.e., Carl Sagan, Richard Dawkins, Neil DeGrasse Tyson, etc.) who use the personal authority derived from their credentials as scientists, and from the evident intellect required to succeed in their fields and understand very advanced mathematics, as a license to speak with (assumed) authority on a wide variety of non-scientific subjects in generally non-scientific ways.

Some ancient historians did claim to be impartial, but "impartial" in this context does not mean what "objective" means to a scientist today. It does not mean that they have sought to methodologically remove themselves and their cognitive process, along with its biases, from the investigative process. The impartiality of the historian means

---

6. Exceptions can be found in Ezra-Nehemiah where the decrees of the Persian kings are found, and also in the comment at the end of Esther that the events are documented in the "Book of the Annals of the kings of Media and Persia" (Esth 10:2). However, it is worth noting that the "primary sources" in Ezra-Nehemiah are offered to establish the authority by which the temple is being rebuilt, not to establish the authority of the description (and therefore interpretation) of the event of the rebuilding of the temple as depicted by the historian.

7. Marincola, *Authority and Tradition*, 164.

that their insight is unadulterated by the expectation of personal gain.[8] The result is that ancient historians are not even trying to present what we would call an "objective analysis"; that is, they are not compiling and presenting a body of evidence that any observer could examine and draw the same conclusions independently. This in turn means that the details the document provides cannot with confidence be invoked as evidence of *anything*, except for what the author is trying to use it to demonstrate. Truth is vested in the interpretation of the events that the historian describes, not in the meticulousness with which they transcribe details.

Narrators in the Bible construct characterizations of real people to make a point about those people and the events that they are involved in. But it is not the reality of the people or events that is the burden of the narrator—it is the interpretation of the events, particularly with regard to how the plans and purposes of God are being worked out through those events. The narrative construction that is offered is therefore designed to portray the events and people in particularly meaningful ways— meaningful to the audience to whom the narrative is addressed. It is consequently tailored to the cultural context of that audience. Authority resides in that interpretation. This is what makes narrative Scripture.

8. Marincola, *Authority and Tradition*, 160–62.

Chapter 3

The genres of Scripture: prophecy and apocalyptic

MANY OF THE BIBLE's most influential passages about demons and (especially) Satan occur in the Bible's prophetic and apocalyptic literature. These texts are commonly thought to offer a kind of exclusive, behind-the-scenes glimpse of meta-cosmic operations and events of the distant past and future. These events include the purported "fall of Satan" putatively described in Isaiah 14 and Ezekiel 28; eschatological battles described in Daniel and Revelation; the impending destruction of Leviathan in Isaiah 27 and of the "hosts of heaven" in Isaiah 24; or the ongoing activity and opposition of demonic powers in Zechariah 3 and Daniel 10. Therefore, it is necessary to examine what prophecy is and how prophetic literature communicates.

Prophets and prophecy in the ancient world

We often use the word "prophet" today to describe someone who predicts the future. We therefore are inclined to read prophecy in essentially the same way that we read history; as described in chapter 2, we (misguidedly) use history to forensically reconstruct the events of the past, and we (likewise misguidedly) use prophecy to forensically preconstruct the events of the future. This is not, however, what "prophecy" actually means. The role of the prophet is not to predict the future. Rather, a prophet is a messenger from the gods whose role is to communicate what the gods are doing. Prophets do not have special insight into the future; they have special insight into the divine realm and information about the divine plan. This messenger function is expressed in the biblical text by the common refrain of "thus says the LORD."

Unlike historians or philosophers, prophets are told what to say by God, demonstrated by the repeated expression "the word of the LORD came to [the prophet]." This is a necessary part of their "messenger" function. Some interpreters consequently think that the content of these speeches should be treated differently from those genres which are inspired more subliminally. (A similar idea is demonstrated by the practice of many translations of printing the words of Jesus in red, as though we ought to read them differently from the rest of the composition.) However, a prophet is not simply a human dictaphone. Prophetic oracles are communication from the gods, but because they are intended to *communicate*, the message will be presented in a form that both the prophet and the prophet's audience understand (see chapter 1). Further, even the so-called "writing prophets" did not produce the final form of their eponymous documents themselves, although they may have produced some of the source documents. Consequently, the literary compositions that we have should not be thought of as transcriptions of unmitigated divine speech. Literarily they function similarly to other genres of discourse within the inspired canon of Scripture. The difference is that, rather than transmitting insights about the state of the world as histories do (see chapter 2), their purpose is specifically to offer insight on the activity and intentions of God. There is no reason why prophecy should be seen as less embedded in human language and logic, or less literary, than any other discourse. The difference is the subject of the message, not the medium.

Pseudepigraphy

Pseudepigraphy is the word we use to describe a genre of literature that was popular at the time of the Second Temple period, wherein the author assumes the persona of a famous or legendary figure from the past for rhetorical purposes. Although the genre is well-established, some conservatives still balk at the prospect of identifying pseudepigraphic literature in the Bible. Nonetheless, if the message of Scripture is found by reading its text-in-context, then identifying the proper context—including genre—takes primary importance. Therefore, it is important to understand how this genre of document communicates if we want to understand the meaning they were written to convey.

The first objection to recognizing the genre of pseudepigraphy in the Bible comes from the word itself. *Pseudo* means "false"; in the conception of the objectors, nothing in the Bible can be labeled "false" without compromising the Bible's integrity. This is a simple etymological fallacy. We might as well say that no verb in the Bible's text can occur in the imperfect tense because the Bible's text cannot be said to lack perfection. The label is descriptive, not qualitative.

A more reasonable objection comes from the common speculation about the *motives* that underlie the genre. Normally, pseudepigraphy is assumed to be intentionally deceptive, analogous to forgery or fraud. This assumption claims that perfidious authors would illegitimately try to attribute their words to an authority figure in order to usurp that authority for themselves. This conception usually entails further assumptions about the gullibility and credulity of ancient and/or religious people.[1] In actuality, we do not know why pseudepigraphic documents were written this way, but we

---

1. This assumption persists despite clear evidence that the criteria for including a pseudepigraphic work in the canon of Scripture involved more than simple attribution to an author who also wrote biblical literature, as demonstrated by the exclusion of such works as the *Gospel of Peter* or the *Testament of Moses*.

have no reason to assume the motive was fraud. Modern fiction authors, for example, adopt a "false" persona with no intent to deceive; Herman Melville is not trying to trick readers into thinking that his name is Ishmael or that his resume includes a whaling tour on the Pequod. While later readers of pseudepigraphic works often did attribute them to the named author, this is a case of misreading a genre rather than evidence of intended fraud. Literary impersonation can serve a wide variety of purposes and does not automatically amount to deception and fraud.

A final concern involves the familiar misguided practice of reading the Bible's statements as propositions. In this conception, if the text says "In the third year of Cyrus king of Persia, a revelation was given to Daniel" (Dan 10:1), then the authority and integrity of the Bible demands that it is a universally true proposition that the vision was given to *Daniel*, and that it was given in 536 BCE. However, the date stamp, in this case, is one of the conventions of the pseudepigraphic genre. Sometimes the date is vague, as in "the first day of the month [of the 365th year]"[2] in *2 Enoch*, or "the thirtieth year on the twenty-second of the month"[3] in the *Greek Apocalypse of Ezra*. Other times it is quite specific, as in *2 Baruch* ("And it happened in the twenty-fifth year of Jeconiah the king of Judah that the word of the LORD came to Baruch"),[4] and as we also see in Daniel 10. The authority and integrity of the Bible means that whatever the author of Daniel 10 meant to communicate when he wrote his message is true. It does not mean that any statement it employs to convey that meaning can be rephrased as a universal proposition.

Apocalyptic

Apocalyptic is a subgenre of prophetic literature wherein the author narrates a series of visions.[5] Most known apocalypses are pseudepigraphical (that is, attributed to famous figures of the distant past, such as Enoch or Abraham); the two exceptions are the Apocalypse of John, also known as the biblical book of Revelation, and the early Christian *Shepherd of Hermas*.[6] The Bible contains two clear samples of apocalyptic literature—Daniel 10–12 and Revelation—but parts of Ezekiel, Isaiah, and Zechariah contain similar features and may have contributed to the development of the genre. Many of the most well-known passages concerning Satan and demons are found in these books, so a careful understanding of this genre is especially important.

Broadly, apocalyptic literature is commonly misunderstood in two ways. The first of these sees the vision as a more or less literal transcript of events in the author's

---

2. *2 En.* 1.2, trans. Andersen, in *OTP* 1:104.

3. *Gk. Apoc. Ezra* 1.1, trans. Stone, in *OTP* 1:571.

4. *2 Bar.* 1.1, trans. Klijn, in *OTP* 1:621.

5. There are many other characteristic features, but this is the most central. For more detailed discussion on the features of the genre see Aune, *Apocalypticism*, 55–65.

6. Aune, *Apocalypticism*, 3, 61.

future, while the second sees it as a more or less literal transcript of macrocosmic events. In both approaches, the author's vision is essentially equated with camera footage. Within the "newsreel of the future" approach, there are several different approaches to interpreting the specifics of the imagery. One approach sees the vision as *literally* camera footage of future events that the author describes using the limited vocabulary available to him. This approach, for example, might see the fantastic "locusts" of Revelation 9 whose "wings were like the thundering of many horses" as representing military helicopters; John of Patmos has no vocabulary to describe a helicopter, so when he saw them in his newsreel, he groped for whatever imagery he had to convey his impressions of what he saw. A second similar approach sees the newsreel footage as actually containing exactly what the author describes. This approach would see Revelation 9 as claiming that, at some point in the future, we will all see creatures resembling locusts with human faces and scorpion tails; this is the interpretation represented in the popular *Left Behind* series. A third approach sees the vision not so much as a newsreel but as a dramatic re-enactment of future events with the elements represented symbolically in a one-to-one correspondence with their future-historical counterparts—for example, the "ten kingdoms" in Revelation 17 might be thought to represent the United Nations. In this conception, the author does not understand what he sees but faithfully transcribes it so that posterity can correlate the symbols with their referents as they watch the enacted events unfold; this is the interpretation represented by most speculative end-times prediction literature, such as *The Late Great Planet Earth*.

The second misunderstanding sees apocalyptic visions as a kind of "behind-the-scenes" glimpse of metacosmic realities or operations. Once again, in this conception the author is transcribing his impressions of things that he sees but does not understand. We see this interpretation at work when we describe "heaven" in terms borrowed from Revelation 21 (pearly gates and streets of gold). This conception also appears in attempts to identify cosmic beings associated with the various images (such as the dragon in Rev 12), or macrocosmic events occurring behind events in the visible world (the conflict with the woman and the dragon, or the battling princes in Dan 10). This kind of interpretation also lies behind the statement we have noted previously, that Daniel is being told of events of which he would otherwise know nothing.

All of these conceptions are misguided because they misunderstand how both inspiration and prophecy work as a mode of communication. God did not dictate messages to the biblical authors to be transcribed, either in the form of dialog or the form of imagery. Whether the visions reported in the text are a product of a theurgic process or a literary process can be debated—the integrity of the message and its authority as Scripture would not be affected either way—but in either case the images and symbols must have had meaning for both the author and the intended audience. This does not mean that the symbols would necessarily be recognized as having a one-to-one allegorical relationship with their objects, although they might—for example, the kings of the north and south in Daniel 11 stand for the Ptolemaic and Seleucid emperors, and the lamb in Revelation 5 stands for Christ. Most of the time, though, it simply means that the images chosen are not arbitrary and are designed to invoke particular impressions in an intentional manner.

Like all prophecy, apocalyptic literature is supposed to represent a communication from God about what God is doing. It is not a revelation of unknown happenings in the future or in the cosmic realms; it is interpretation of events in the author's present or near-present. In this sense, apocalyptic functions very similarly to historiography, in that it serves *to explain the author's present circumstances*. What historiography conveys through describing and interpreting past events, apocalyptic conveys through symbol and metaphor. In a history, the authority of the interpretation comes from the experience and expertise of the historian who serves as interpreter. In an apocalypse, the authority comes through the cosmic being relaying the vision,[7] not so much from the (typically pseudonymous) author. Additionally, Aune argues that apocalypses are normally produced specifically by communities undergoing oppression or crisis.[8] The purpose of the apocalypse, therefore, is to describe how the particular crisis of the community is connected to God's work, and also what God plans to do to resolve it.

A modern analogue for apocalyptic literature might be found in political cartoons. These pieces of artwork are designed to interpret events in the present by means of metaphorical or symbolic imagery. As is the case in apocalyptic literature, the symbols used by the cartoonist are intended to have meaning for the audience. If we see an elephant or a donkey in a cartoon, we know what that is supposed to represent. Sometimes the symbols represent very specific people or events, but we do not expect them to depict a frame of something a camera would have recorded; compare, perhaps, to the sketches sometimes published of courtroom proceedings where cameras are not allowed. As always, when reading apocalyptic literature, we must ask why those particular images were chosen and what they intend to communicate, and not merely attempt to identify the elements to which they correspond and then arrange those elements into our own interpretation. Therefore, when we read of cosmic events involving spirit beings in this sort of literature, our interpretation should focus on the message that is being given concerning how the cosmic events convey God's work in the audience's crisis. They do not serve to reveal the role of spirit-beings in cosmic events.

7. Aune, *Apocalypticism*, 63, 196.

8. Aune, *Apocalypticism*, 63.

Chapter 4

The genres of Scripture: wisdom and discourse

As discussed in chapter 2, the Bible's historical narratives are stories based on real events, although the specific details of those events as reported in the documents do not necessarily match the details that a camera present at the event would have recorded. This is because the message of the document concerns the interpretation of the event, not the details. The event is a means to an end to talk about something else.

The genre of *wisdom literature* also uses narrative as a means to an end to talk about something else. Unlike those documents in the genre of *historiography*, however, the scenarios described in wisdom narratives are not assumed to be based on events that actually occurred. The most notable examples in this regard are the parables of Jesus. When Jesus says that there was a man who bought a valuable pearl or a field with treasure, nobody would have expected to be able to go into town and find this man. Therefore, as was the case with the genre of historiography, we should not expect to be able to deduce forensic information from the events and actions of characters described in wisdom narratives. However, while historical narratives are limited to interpreting events, wisdom narratives have no events to interpret and therefore can discuss a broader variety of subjects, which in theory could include the topic of the nature and activity of cosmic beings like evil spirits. Several of Jesus's parables—notably the Sower and the Wheat and the Tares—include characters or elements that represent the devil. But beyond this, some biblical narratives that feature demons or creatures commonly identified as demons nonetheless appear to be serving a function other than describing or interpreting the events they depict. These stories would not properly be classified as "history," but they still represent meaningful communication. The most notable of these is the prologue of Job, but the serpent narrative of Genesis 3 and the brief one-sentence story about Michael and Satan in Jude 9 also exemplify this. Additionally, several passages allude to stories or characters that are not themselves presented in the Bible, but are known from the cognitive environment. The most notable of these are the "combat myth" (the perpetual metacosmic struggle between deities and personifications of cosmic chaos, also called *Chaoskampf*), which is referenced especially in Job and Psalms; the myth of the

Watcher Angels, referenced in 2 Peter 2:4; and the cosmic dualism and eschatological conflict found in the Second Temple period and referenced frequently throughout the New Testament. We will discuss the specifics of these narratives later (chapter 9), but for now, if we want to assert that the references to these stories are meaningful, it is important to understand how non-historical narratives convey meaning. Additionally, the same kind of meaning that is conveyed through non-historical narratives can also be conveyed though non-narrative forms. Some examples of this are poetic compositions such as Psalm 82 or Job 41, or extended argument, such as we find in the epistles, notably in 2 Corinthians 10 or James 4. Therefore, we will have to examine the ways in which the details provided in various non-historical genres relate to the broader topic and message of the text.

So-called "myths and legends"

Often the mere presence of a spirit-being in a narrative is enough for critical scholars to classify it as a "myth," by which they mean that it is a literary fabrication that cannot possibly have any significance or value in our contemporary understanding of reality. The "demythologizing" hypothesis agrees that these narratives are literary but tries to salvage meaning from them in terms of, e.g., psychology. Conservatives reject both options and deny that the genre of mythography occurs in the biblical text at all, demanding instead that all of its narratives be classified as "history." Most of the controversy over what counts as "history" versus "myth" occurs between interpreters who use the word "mythical" (or "legendary") as implying that the material is "untrue," and those who believe that the Bible's authority as Scripture means that every statement in the text must correspond to a universally verifiable proposition. Both of these positions are arguably misguided. "Myths" as a genre are not "false"; they are a mode of conveying meaning that is different from the mode we call "history." Classifying a text as "myth" is not an assessment of its veracity; it is an observation about what the text was written to communicate and how it goes about doing so.

Mythographic literature is different from historiographic literature, though not in the commonly assumed sense that the latter is "true" while the former is "false." As discussed in chapter 2, historiographic literature interprets events to describe the state of the historian's present. The authority of the interpretation is contingent on the historian's experience and expertise regarding the event, or regarding its documentation if the historian was not present. Stories classified as "myths" (Gk *mythos*), however, refer to "events" that occur so far outside of the author's expertise or experience, or are so variously or dubiously documented, that no such authority can be legitimately claimed. Consequently, these (often primordial or cosmic) events are not suitable subjects for the genre of historiography.[1] However, they are suitable subjects for another kind of literature that serves a different purpose.

Most modern interpreters of ancient "myths" assume that their purpose is to describe the phenomena of the mechanisms of the cosmos, generally in primitive, unsophisticated, or superstitious ways. Modern interpreters assume, for example, that when the ancients spoke of the sun as a god sailing across the sky in a boat, they were trying to describe the same thing we describe when we speak of the sun as a ball of burning gas with a ball of rock called "earth" orbiting around it. This is a primary motive behind labeling the genre as "untrue." In fact, mythic imagery is intended to describe *function* and *relationship* to other elements of the cosmos, *not* mechanism or phenomena. Classifying the sun as a god does not describe what it is made out of, but rather what it *does*; in this case, that its journey across the sky delineates order for the earth below, since establishing and preserving order is the function of the gods. We continue to affirm this function even today as we use the movements of the sun as the basis for our calendars and clocks. The book of Genesis also affirms this function when it calls the sun a light to mark the days and years (Gen 1:14), but classifying it as a "light" instead of a "god" identifies it as a tool of the high god (Yahweh) rather than a colleague or associate performing its own tasks semi-independently, as for example Šamaš is a colleague of the high god Marduk in Babylon. The affirmation is theological, not phenomenological. In general, mythographic literature is written in order to convey broad truths about the nature and function of the world, and thus is more closely paralleled by what we call "metaphysics" than by what we call "history."

Nonetheless, the Bible actually contains very little of what could be properly called "mythographic literature." With the possible exception of the cosmogony in Genesis 1, the biblical text does not contain narratives featuring divine protagonists interacting with each other or with other cosmic beings in the divine realm.[2] What the Bible does contain is references to stories of this kind that must have been known in order for the reference to be meaningful. While we have no such literature from Israel itself, we have recovered stories of this kind from the cultures of Israel's neighbors, such as the Babylonian *Enuma Elish* or the Ugaritic Baal texts. There is no reason to think that the Bible is referencing these stories specifically, but they do represent the kinds of ideas that were present in the ancient Near Eastern cognitive environment, and therefore most likely reflect the metaphysical conceptions of the world that were also present in Israel.

---

1. Marincola, *Authority and Tradition*, 117–18.

2. Another possible exception is the prologue of Job; however, this passage serves as an integral part of the overall structure of the book of Job. It does not convey general observations about the regular operations of the cosmic realm. See discussion in chapter 13. Likewise passages such as 1 Kgs 22:19–23 and Jude 9 depict singular events that contribute to the broader structure of the discourse, not broader observations about the general operations of the world, even though the original source may have been mythographic in nature and an understanding of those general operations is necessary to understand the significance of the imagery.

When we read these references, then, we should not think of them as propositionally affirming something about cosmic operations or structures. As an example, one of the more prevalent mythographic images found in the Bible is something modern scholars call the "divine council." In comparative literature, this image refers to the pantheon coming together to collectively conduct the business of governing the world; in the Bible the image is invoked in such instances as the gathering of the sons of God in Job 1 and 2, or the "assembly of the gods" in Psalm 82. Conflict theologians especially invest much energy in identifying these beings and arguing that the Bible's integrity demands an affirmation of their real existence. However, the point of these passages is not to affirm that Yahweh has a committee of beings who we—the Bible's reading audience—are intended to identify and classify (as "angels" or otherwise) in a system of cosmic taxonomy.

Mythographic images convey function, not phenomena. The image of the divine assembly, both within Israel and outside of it, serves to identify the *function* of cosmic government, not to identify the functionaries within the cosmic bureaucracy. Divine government is an analogue for human government, which itself is a manifestation of order, as decisions are deliberated and tasks delegated. Since the purpose of the gods is to bring order to the world, it is natural to depict them governing in what would be understood as an orderly fashion. In Israelite (and also Canaanite) literature, where the assembly consists of lesser beings, they emphasize the status and royalty of the high god; a king is not much of a king without a court, after all. Although the court is not an assembly of equals, the courtiers can still offer advice or be delegated tasks, both of which are seen for example in 1 Kings 22:19–22. The point is that the image should be understood in terms of the *function* of the council—establishing order, which they are doing in Job 1 and not doing in Psalm 82—not the *composition* of the council. These references are conveying something about the nature of the world order, not something about the metacosmic activities of beings that are higher than humans but lower than gods.

Another kind of narrative literature found in the Bible is similar in subject and content—if not necessarily in form—to ancient Near Eastern "epics" such as Gilgamesh, Adapa, Atrahasis, and so on. The exact genre of these works is difficult to classify. Many interpreters call them "legends" which, like "myth," is regularly used to mean "a story that is not true." However, like mythography, they simply communicate different things in different ways than what we call "history." We might draw a parallel to the way we use the word "legend" in the context of sports, where it refers, not to a person who is a literary construct, but to a person of great accomplishment and renown. Gilgamesh, the king of Uruk, is a legend in the same sense that Babe Ruth is a legend, not in the same sense that Paul Bunyan is a legend. Ultimately, however, assigning a label to the genre is less important than understanding how it communicates.

Epics are different from historiography in both content and function. They do not interpret events and they do not seek to explain and define the world of the author's present. The Gilgamesh Epic was not commissioned by the king of Uruk to establish his legacy as a doer of great deeds (as compared to ancient Near Eastern inscriptions that describe the deeds of their patrons); neither was it written to describe the nature and identity the city of Uruk or the nation of Babylon through the exploits of their legendary king (as the story of Christopher Columbus is used to describe the nature and identity of America). The lives and deeds of epic heroes instead are supposed to convey more general truths about the human condition. In this sense, the genre functions similarly to what we today call "literature." "Literature" can be essentially historical (Shakespeare's *Henry V* or *Richard II*); can feature fictional characters in more or less historical settings (*War and Peace, Heart of Darkness*); can describe fictional characters in a realistic but nonetheless artificial setting (*Moby Dick, The Great Gatsby*), or can be set in a world that is almost entirely a literary contrivance (*Brave New World, Gulliver's Travels*). Even when the characters or setting are "real," the purpose of the composition is not to create a documentary, but to use them as exemplars in the exploration of broader and more universal themes.

In the Bible at least, the characters in these narratives (Adam, Noah, etc.) seem to be depicted as real people; they are listed in genealogies, and there is no evidence from the ancient Near East that genealogies ever included characters who were purely literary. The ancient Near Eastern epic heroes were probably regarded in the same way.[3] At the same time, the epics include fantastic elements such as battles with monsters or flights to heaven on the backs of eagles. Because the genre is not a documentary, there is no need to try to sort out which parts are "historical" and which are literary; as discussed in chapter 2, *all* narrative by definition has a certain level of artificiality. Episodes in an epic are selected (or constructed) in order to convey the document's themes. When Gilgamesh refuses a proposition by Ištar, the story is not about a failed marriage arrangement to the king of Uruk, either literally from a goddess or from some historical person described in metaphorical terms; the story is about human hubris and its consequences. Hubris, in turn, can be described in either historical or non-historical narratives—our modern story of the sinking of the Titanic is an example of the former; Mary Shelly's novel *Frankenstein* is an example of the latter— and so identifying whether or not the details of the account correspond to anything "historical" is irrelevant to the interpretation of the message. The similar narratives in the Bible—most notably Job and Genesis 1–11—should probably be interpreted in the same way; that is, their truth or falsehood is vested in their themes, not in their details or in depiction of events. Some of the details might correspond to something that a camera would have seen, and some might not, but trying to determine which is which is irrelevant for understanding the message of the text.

---

3. Utanapishtim does not appear in any genealogies, but in the Gilgamesh Epic he is identified as the son of Ubartutu, who is the last king named before the flood in the Sumerian King List.

Discourse

As we have discussed previously, a common misinterpretation of the Bible is to treat its declarative statements as universal propositions. In the context of a narrative, declarative statements tend to describe the actions or speech of characters ("The LORD said to Noah"; "Jacob went to Egypt"; "the sons of Eli were priests"; etc.). The treatment of these statements as universally true propositions is part of what produces a requirement for absolute factual accuracy—that is, a transcript of what a camera would have recorded—onto these documents. However, we have argued that declarative statements should not be treated as propositions; their purpose is not to make universally true statements but *to convey meaning* in the context in which they were written. This remains true even when the context in which the declarative statement is written is not a narrative. We will describe how this works using two genres that are relevant for our purposes: *poetry* and *argument*. Both poetry and argument contain declarative statements, such as "the LORD is good and his love endures forever" (Ps 100:5) or "The reason the Son of God appeared was to destroy the devil's work" (1 John 3:8). However, just as in the case of the histories, these are not to be lifted out of their context and transcribed as propositions. The statements contribute to the communication of a message, and they have to be considered in context in order for that message to be properly received. This is even true if the context is a theological argument, which is worth examining in more detail.

Most of the arguments we will encounter are found in the Epistles, though many of the Psalms are often read as though they were theological arguments as well. Some of these mention demons, or creatures thought to be demons, only in passing (e.g., 2 Cor 4:4; 6:15), while some address them more directly (e.g., Eph 6:12; 1 Cor 10:20; Ps 82). In neither case, however, can we simply lift the statement out of its context and use it as a premise in a systematic theology. We have to consider how the statement functions in the context of its argument, but most importantly, we must understand what the argument itself is attempting to communicate. The author is choosing to present *these* arguments, as opposed to others, for a reason, and is presenting them in a particular *way* for a reason. Therefore, when approaching an argument, we should not ask what this argument tells us about the beliefs of the author, or whether the statement is true. As always, the question we should ask is, "why is this in here?"

Modern readers are inclined to read the Bible's arguments as though they were *proofs*, such as are used by modern philosophers and mathematicians. Our influence comes from René Descartes and the rationalist approach to epistemology he developed in the seventeenth century. In this system, arguments should only consist of premises that are true by necessity—the famous phrase "I think, therefore I am" is one of these—or else have been inevitably derived from previously established propositions. In this way, the conclusions of the arguments will be assured to be necessarily and universally true. Reading the Bible's statements as proofs is normally a reflexive approach to reading the Bible to acquire knowledge, because philosophical proofs are a way in which modern thinkers go about acquiring knowledge. However, none of the arguments in the Bible are designed to work in this way.

Descartes was trying to develop an epistemology—that is, a way of acquiring knowledge. Paul and other biblical writers, on the other hand, are *communicating*; they are conveying knowledge that they have already acquired in a way that the audience will find persuasive. When Descartes started thinking, he did not know what he would end up affirming when he was done. Paul, on the other hand, already knows exactly what he intends to affirm to the audience of his epistle. Descartes traced premises of which he could be certain to reach a conclusion of which he was not certain. Paul demonstrates the truth of a conclusion of which he is certain by means of a train of thought that his audience will find convincing.

The arguments contained in the Epistles are rhetorical, not syllogistic. A *syllogism* is a formula by which the premises guarantee the truth of the conclusion: "if P is true then Q is true; P is true; therefore Q is true." The purpose of a syllogism is to deduce truth. The purpose of rhetoric, on the other hand, is not to deduce, but to persuade. The premises of a rhetorical argument are therefore chosen based on what the audience is inclined to believe. These premises represent the existing knowledge of the author/audience and are part of the means to conveying meaning; they do not represent the affirmation of the communicative act itself. We find meaning in the message the author intended to communicate, not the means by which he chose to communicate it. The premises in a rhetorical argument guide the audience's chain of thought. They do not guarantee the truth of the conclusion (as in a syllogism), and the truth of the conclusion does not demand the affirmation of the premises that were employed to reach it.

The meaning of an argument is therefore not found in the simple transcription of its premises. However, it is not necessarily found in the simple transcription of its *conclusions*, either. If the genre of the text is a work of philosophy, such as Job or Ecclesiastes, the affirmation can perhaps be said to be the conclusion. However, Job and Ecclesiastes are not "arguments"—at least, not entirely—and the "conclusion" is not simply a quotation that occurs near the end, as is commonly thought for Ecclesiastes 12:13, which in fact serves as more of a summary than a conclusion. The conclusion rather derives from the entire thought-picture that has been established over the full course of the document.

The Epistles contain philosophical or theological arguments, but nonetheless they are not abstract works of philosophy or theology. That is not their genre. Paul in Romans is not sharing his thoughts on justification in the same way that the author of Ecclesiastes is sharing his thoughts on the meaning of life. The Epistles are written to more or less specific audiences who are struggling with more or less specific issues and concerns. The answer to the question "why is this in here?" is therefore "to address those issues or concerns," not "to teach the reading audience how justification works."

Addressing that issue or concern might indeed require a particular conception of how justification works, but that would have to be established from context, not simply assumed based on the literary format of "argument" and an appeal to the authority of the author. The arguments expressed in the epistles cannot be read, as they often are, as proofs within a corpus of treatises on systematic theology. They should be read as insight into the problem that the audience is experiencing and consequently as a means to understand the internal logic of the author's proposed resolution in the context of the epistle's cognitive environment. The idea that is affirmed by an argument of this kind is whatever idea prompts the author to propose the stated resolution instead of another. This idea in turn may or may not actually be stated in any of the individual points that are used to advance the argument.

Conclusions from the review of the genres of Scripture

In chapter 1 we used the example of *cosmic geography* to illustrate the difference between the Bible's affirmations—the meaning contained in the message of the text—and its references, which are the actual statements that appear in the documents. Because the Bible's cosmological statements are references, we affirm that the Bible does not actually teach—that is, reveal—details of cosmology. But that conclusion is derived from observations of the structure of communicative acts, not from the fact that we would rather not affirm the details of cosmology that the text provides. Consequently, that same observation applies equally to all of the Bible's communicative acts; not only those that reference cosmology, but also those that reference demons and spirits as well.

Just as the Bible is not a cosmological treatise, so it is not a demonological treatise. The statements of the Bible cannot be lifted out of their context and used as propositions in a study of non-human creatures in the cosmic realm, for the same reasons that they cannot be lifted and used as propositions in a study of the structure and operation of the physical realm; teaching us that information is not the purpose of the text-in-context. Nonetheless, we can still know things about cosmic geography, even though that knowledge is not gained from the Bible. Can we know anything about demons and spirits even though that knowledge is not gained from the Bible? That is what we will discuss in the next section.

Part 2

What are the "demons and spirits" that we want to know about?

Chapter 5

Can we gain knowledge of demons and spirits from outside the Bible?

C ONFLICT THEOLOGIANS OFTEN ARGUE that the Bible's treatment of demons and spirits should be processed differently than its treatment of other subjects—specifically, differently than its treatment of cosmology—because demons are "supernatural." As described in chapter 1, we assume for the sake of argument that the Bible contains revelation of information that cannot be acquired from any other source. Conflict theologians claim that the Bible reveals God's metacosmic war and the spiritual forces that comprise the opposition, which would otherwise remain unknown. To quote Boyd again, "Were it not for the revelation given by the angel [in Daniel 10], neither Daniel nor anyone else would have had any knowledge of this unseen battle."[1] This claim is worth some attention.

Knowledge of demons and spirits

Critical Scholarship has long observed that the Bible is deeply embedded in the literary conventions and discussions common to the ancient Near Eastern and Greco-Roman worlds. This observation, combined with the obligation of the author in the contract of communication (as discussed in chapter 1), means that a large portion of its statements are constructed of ideas that were already known to the audience to whom the original literary composition was addressed. As discussed in chapter 1, this is what we mean when we say that the text's statements are references—they *refer* to known and familiar concepts. If the conflict theologians are correct that God's revelation consists of new information about his cosmic war, they would have to support this claim by demonstrating that the information provided in the text about the war is *actually new*. So, did the original intended audience of Daniel already believe that patron angels did battle to determine the fate of nations, or not?

Most conflict theologians base the warrant for their interpretation on the fact that evil spirits were something that everyone in the cultural context of Scripture— including its authors, audience, and narrative subjects—believed in: "these writers

1. Boyd, *God at War*, 10.

believed in the actual existence of the powers . . . all the writers of sacred Scripture spoke with a common voice on this issue. The tradition of the church also corroborates it."[2] According to Boyd: "the warfare worldview is in one form or another the basic worldview of the Biblical authors, both in the Old Testament and even more so in the New."[3] He goes on to argue that his "warfare worldview"—a specific example of what we have elsewhere called "conflict theology"—is known intuitively to virtually every culture, so as to demonstrate "the myopic nature of the enlightenment Western worldview."[4] Obviously, one cannot have it both ways; information cannot simultaneously be so completely unknown that nobody would have any knowledge of it apart from special revelation delivered in mystic visions, and yet be so intuitive and obvious that everyone everywhere affirms it except for myopic materialists addled by the Enlightenment. We will discuss this problem further in chapter 16. For the moment, however, if we affirm that the ancient world already had knowledge of demons and spirits, how did they come to know what they knew? Not by reading the Bible, since the cosmic battle is asserted to be an operating assumption for the writers of the Bible, and also asserted to be intuitively known by people of many disparate cultures who have never read the Bible. This means that either there are ways of gaining knowledge of the "supernatural" other than the Bible's revelation, or that demons are not, in fact, "supernatural." Either case is theoretically possible, but in neither case can the Bible's special status be appealed to in order to argue that it is the sole source of demonological information that cannot otherwise be known.

Science and the supernatural

In its modern usage, the term "supernatural" refers to anything that cannot be known by means of science; i.e., anything that cannot be explained through recourse to mathematics and natural laws. Therefore, an understanding of the concept of "supernatural" is impossible without an understanding of the concept of "science." When the term "supernatural" was first applied to non-scientific knowledge, "science" referred primarily to a set of epistemological methods designed to study repeatable observable phenomena. By that definition, then, anything that is not repeatable (i.e., history) or not observable or phenomenal (i.e., information and semiotics) cannot be known by means of "science" and is therefore, technically, "supernatural." However, words mean what they are used to mean, and the word "science" as it has come to be used refers to much more than a technical means of gathering particular kinds of knowledge.

When people today use the word "science," they do not normally refer to a process of acquiring knowledge; they refer to a repository of all things that are or can be known. "Science" often now refers to worldview, in many ways indistinguishable

2. Arnold, *Powers*, 178.

3. Boyd, *God at War*, 13.

4. Boyd, *God at War*, 14.

from a religion, that reduces all of existence to purposeless matter moving in accordance with mathematically describable laws. Any perspective on any topic—not limited to observable repeatable phenomena—that fits in accord with this worldview is "according to science"; any other perspective, or any topic that has no such perspective, is "contrary to science." Thus the term "supernatural," which means "not known to science," is normally synonymous with "imaginary" or "fantastical," which carry connotations of untruth.

Conflict theology is a product of its own cognitive environment, and therefore has the same confused relationship to "science" that pervades the entire culture. On the one hand, science is seen as means of gathering knowledge that is suitable for some subjects but not for others. Thus, conflict theologians always take pains to point out that the demonic realm is not a subject that is suitable for scientific study: "If spirits do not have a tangible physical existence, modern science does not have the tools for verifying or denying their real existence. This makes the question of their existence depend not on scientific observation, but upon revelation, worldview, and human experience."[5] Likewise, "the question of the existence of incorporeal beings cannot be proved or disproved by scientific methods. The question is not one that science is capable of answering, as the query is philosophical and theological in nature."[6] On the other hand, the tendency to define what is "true" in terms of science means that the proofs offered by conflict theologians of the "real existence" of evil spirits are fundamentally scientific in nature; that is, based on observation of phenomena and analysis of collected empirical data.

Conflict theologians warrant their claim for the real existence of evil spirits by pointing to observable phenomena such as "radical evil," possession, and the results of "spiritual warfare." These are not scientific in the sense that they could be measured with instruments in a laboratory, but science is a means of knowing, not a means of measuring. So, for example, "the appalling evil that we see around and within us cannot satisfactorily be explained by perversity alone."[7] Likewise, "the potential global annihilation insured [sic] by nuclear war, the untold suffering and killings of an Auschwitz, and the fact that a mother could put her four-year-old child in an oven and burn her to death (Auburn, Maine, 1994), cannot be explained by mere human destructiveness."[8] These arguments are meaningless without a definable standard of "human destructiveness and perversity" that individual events and behaviors can be measured against. The fact that we do not describe "evil" in standardized units is mostly an accident of nomenclature and a consequence of imprecise means of quantification ("natural human perversity cannot exceed 1.6 picohitlers, but burning a child in an oven measures 4.7 picohitlers, which exceeds natural human perversity

5. Arnold, *Powers*, 178.

6. Page, *Powers*, 267–68.

7. Page, *Powers*, 268.

8. Arnold, *Powers*, 179.

and therefore indicates demonic activity"). Nonetheless assertion of a particular magnitude implies that some form of measurement and evaluation is taking place.[9] (For a discussion of evil as a phenomenon and how spirits are thought to explain it using metrics other than magnitude, see chapter 15.)

Some conflict theologians actually call on scientists to measure phenomena scientifically: "psychologists and counselors today are faced with an 'unexplained residue.' Even anthropologists face the same unexplained phenomena in the interpretation of their fieldwork."[10] "Unexplained residue" in context refers to phenomena that cannot be accounted for within existing models of psychology and disease. It does not refer to something that scientific disciplines are unqualified to study, because if it did the assertion that scientists could not describe it with their science would be meaningless.

Similarly, conflict theologians try to demonstrate the reality of spirits by the scientific process of appealing to statistics. "The west . . . is the only contemporary society that denies the reality of evil spirits. The field of anthropology reveals that throughout Asia, Africa, the Pacific Islands . . . the idea of evil spirits is an integral part of the world view of many people groups."[11] Likewise, "Similar warfare stories serving a similar purpose can be found throughout the oral and written traditions of ancient and contemporary primitive peoples,"[12] and "that so many different cultures exhibit some sort of belief in evil spirits demonstrates that the human experience of evil is such as to suggest the involvement of supermundane realities."[13] This argument takes the results of a series of empirical data (drawn from "the field of anthropology") and derives its conclusion based on a statistically significant agreement among the results.[14] A similar appeal to the statistical analysis of experimental data is the "evidence" of the success of various "spiritual warfare" strategies:

> Numerous stories of Christians effectively battling principalities and powers are surfacing from all over the world, including Korea, Argentina, Canada, and elsewhere. A few Christian leaders are now culling insights from these accounts and advocating new and specific strategies for battling higher-ranking spirits that wield influence over neighborhoods, cities, geographical territories, and even whole countries. . . . Even if aspects of the strategy sound strange, different, or even absurd, can we question it in light of its apparent success?[15]

9. See for example Plantinga, *God, Freedom, and Evil*, 55.

10. Arnold, *Powers*, 179. Cited Twelftree, *Christ Triumphant*, 152–56.

11. Arnold, *Powers*, 179.

12. Boyd, *God at War*, 17.

13. Page, *Powers*, 268.

14. This method of assessing information is fundamentally *scientific*, as opposed to rationalist, because it does not appeal to the authority or veracity of the data (i.e., "the beliefs of People X are true; People X believe Y; therefore Y is true") but merely to its quantity.

15. Arnold, *Questions*, 145. In context, Arnold thinks the success is attributable to other factors than the particulars of the strategy (174). He is describing this approach, not advocating it.

In this example, the statistically significant data is the "effective battle" and the "apparent success." Thus, this is another example of a scientific process being used to investigate a topic that is not supposed to be a subject for scientific investigation. The unfortunate result is that the designation "supernatural" is ultimately used as a rationalization for methodological inconsistency. If "science" yields the desired conclusion on the "supernatural" subject, science is willingly employed. However, where the results of scientific investigation are undesirable, they are dismissed out of hand because the subject is "supernatural" and therefore not a legitimate subject for scientific inquiry.

If a thing is "supernatural" it means it cannot be known by the methods of science, period. It does not mean that it can be known by applying the methods of science in a haphazard and imprecise manner. If the scientific methods offered by conflict theologians to defend the existence of spirits are actually evidence of anything, it means that spirits are knowable by scientific methods and therefore are not "supernatural" after all; they are a subject for scientific inquiry that happens to be largely undocumented and poorly understood, like "dark energy" or "antimatter." Nonetheless, if science does not understand them, it is not unreasonable to look to other authorities. As discussed briefly above, this authority is normally the common understanding of non-western cultures, the peoples of the ancient world, and (most importantly) the biblical authors themselves. Therefore, it is worth looking into how the ancients gained their knowledge of the "supernatural."

What the Bible's authors knew

Conflict theologians argue that the Bible's inspired status means that it requires us to take the author's prior knowledge as carrying a stamp of divine authority: "we must strive towards making this as important a part of our worldview as it was for Paul."[16] In this conception, the Bible's affirmations extend beyond declarative statements within the documents themselves to include any statements that the author would have affirmed as being true. The Bible's primary value is thereby seen as providing, not a particular message in a particular context, but insight on what the authors and characters—especially Paul of Tarsus and Jesus of Nazareth—would have thought about a wide variety of topics. Reconstructing the author's thought through either psychoanalysis or extrapolation of their discourse (or both) in this view takes precedent over a literary analysis of the specific contents of the document.

Nonetheless, even within the bounds of this general approach, it is apparent that the Bible's authors would not have thought of demons and spirits as a subject that can only be known through the particular mode of knowledge conveyed in sacred Scripture. They had knowledge of demons and spirits, but they acquired that knowledge in

16. Arnold, *Powers*, 182.

more or less the same way they acquired knowledge of everything else. That way was certainly not "science"—even if it could achieve some of the same results that science can in terms of agriculture, astronomy, metallurgy, etc.—but it was also not by reading Scripture. Paul did not write his letters through some kind of subliminal compulsion and then read what he had written to discover what it said about demons. What exactly the method was we are not likely to discover, since the ancients were not inclined to write treatises detailing their own epistemological theory.[17] But that does not matter, because the point is not that we should acquire knowledge of demons and spirits in the same way the ancients acquired it. The point is that what we decide we can know about demons and spirits should be consistent with the way we decide we can know about anything else. Either an appeal to properly basic human knowledge (as demonstrated by conflict theologians above, which would point to the rationality of belief in the existence of spirits)[18] or an appeal to the demonstrated ability of science to classify the efficient causes of observable phenomena (as advocated by demythologizers, which would point to the rationality of disbelief in the existence of spirits) would serve in this capacity. Even an appeal to a divine stamp of approval on common beliefs in the ancient world as represented in the Bible would suffice, though in that case the entire ancient worldview—including its cosmic geography, as described in chapter 1—would have to be adopted to retain consistency. However, the choice between any of these options, is a matter of internal consistency within our own epistemology. It is not a matter of internal consistency with our doctrine of biblical inspiration. Whether we choose to believe in demons and spirits or not does not affect the way we read and understand the message of the Bible, because the message of the Bible was not given for the purpose of giving us information about demons and spirits.

17. Magical texts of various kinds describe theurgic rituals used to gain knowledge *from* spirits, and also defense of the veracity of knowledge gained in this way, but they do not normally describe how the ritual itself came to be known.

18. Technically, properly basic knowledge is not a warrant for truth. The ability to identify a belief as properly basic places the burden of proof on those who wish to disprove that belief; it does not itself demonstrate that the belief is true. A properly basic belief in spirits combined with the demonstrated *in*ability of science (or other methods) to *dis*prove their existence is a legitimate argument that belief in spirits is rational and reasonable, but it is not a proof of their existence.

Chapter 6

Do evil spirit beings really exist?

F OR MANY PEOPLE, CONSIDERATION of the biblical and theological material about
demons concerns the question of whether demons really exist. Most people have
opinions already based on their cultural location and personal experiences. They
have not necessarily developed those opinions based on the Bible alone. In this book,
it is not our intent to evaluate metaphysical realities. The field of biblical theology as
a discipline is not well suited for discussing the question of existence (or lack thereof)
or for speculating on the efficient causes of observable phenomena. Regardless of
what people may or may not be experiencing in places like Africa or Malaysia, a
study of the text of the Bible will not shed any light on the details of what is happening there. Likewise, no amount of analysis of the phenomena themselves will be of
any use for elucidating the biblical text. This fact is nonetheless unintuitive for many
interpreters, who are used to using the testimonies of missionaries from the developing world as evidence in support of (especially) conflict theology. Therefore, we must
examine these claims further.

If demons are real, the Bible will not tell us anything about them

As a thought experiment, let us consider 1 Kings 20:36, where a man is killed by a
creature called an 'aryēh, which, according to translators across the centuries, is a kind
of animal that we call a "lion." Now, suppose a report comes in from Africa about a
man who was killed by something that, by most evidence, appears to have been some
sort of animal. What information does the teaching of 1 Kings 20:36 give us about
the animal that killed the African man? Most people would realize that the answer is
"nothing at all." We understand intuitively that an anecdote in a narrative account—or
even a direct statement in a discourse, e.g., Proverbs 30:30—concerning an animal is
not a proposition in a universal systematic treatment of "animals." The Bible is not a
bestiary, so when it talks about animals its statements are references that are a means
to an end to talk about something else, just as statements about cosmic geography are
a means to an end to talk about something else (see chapter 1).

Let us then, for example, consider Mark 1:23, where a man is afflicted by something called a *pneuma akatharton*, which is a kind of spirit-creature that we often identify as a "demon." Now, suppose a report comes in from Africa about a man who was afflicted by something that, by at least some evidence, appears to have been some sort of spirit-creature; remember, this thought experiment assumes as a premise that demons are real. What information does the teaching of Mark 1:23 give us about the creature that afflicted the African man? As with the animal, the correct answer is "nothing at all," for the same reasons. Nonetheless, many interpreters prefer to jump to the conclusion that the Bible teaches that the African creature is the *same* kind of creature that Mark describes and, even though the Africans have their own name for it and understanding of what it is, these ideas need to be corrected by the ideas of Second Temple Judaism that are reflected in the language of Mark, as Mark in turn has been interpreted through two millennia of Christian reception. The experience of the African man is therefore invoked by conflict theologians as empirical (read: scientific) proof that their interpretation of Mark, and by extension all other passages that correlate with or support that interpretation, is accurate.

This conclusion, however, is absurd, as we can demonstrate by applying the same logic to a discussion of animals. Imagine that we receive a report of an African man killed by an animal they call a "hippo." Imagine that, in response, we consult our Bibles and discover that, according to God's Inspired Word, the animals that kill people are called *'aryēh*, which means "lions." Admittedly, sometimes a different word, such as "bears" (*dubbîm*; e.g., 2 Kgs 2:24) is used, but similarities in behavior are presumed to indicate that these in fact refer to the same creatures. From the text and from the ancient cultural backgrounds, we determine that, in the perception of the ancient author, "lions" are predatory carnivores. Thus, fortified by God's revealed truth, we conclude that the animal that the Africans call "hippo" and naively believe to be a viciously territorial herbivore is actually revealed by God to be a predatory carnivore called a "lion." Imagine that we then proceed to use our observations[1] of hippos to further our knowledge of lions ("the rivers of Africa are infested with lions and they sometimes attack people who fall out of boats"), and then apply that knowledge to the [hypothetical] systematic profile of animals in the biblical text ("Jonah was attacked by animal after he fell out of a boat, and we know that lions attack people who fall out of boats, so the animal must have been a lion"), and then further use that information to correlate this data with other passages that mention lions ("God sends lions to attack people who disobey his instructions; see Jonah 1:3, 17; 1 Kgs 20:36") and then apply that conclusion to interpret events in real life ("lions attack people who disobey God's instructions"; 1 Kgs 13:23–26; 20:35–36; 2 Kgs 17:26; Isa 15:9; Jer 5:6, see also Jonah 1) and therefore conclude that the hippo victim in Africa must have disobeyed God and been trying to run away. The leaps in logic and unwarranted conflations are no less

---

1. For references to modern phenomena used to supplement biblical material, see for example Boyd, *God at War*, 197.

egregious when the topic under discussion is spirits instead of animals. We should not say that the words *běnê 'ělôhîm* and *daimonion* refer to the same kind of creature that we call *fallen angel* for the same reasons that we should not say that the Hebrew words translated *lion* and *bear* refer to the same kind of creature we call *hippo*.

The reason for this is because the message of the Bible's text is not intended to provide insights about the efficient causes of phenomena. When Jesus makes mud in John 9:6 and heals a blind man, the passage is not intended to be read as a treatise on the pharmacological properties of human saliva mixed with Levantine soil. A scientist should not expect to be able to examine the chemicals and enzymes in a sample of such mud and thereby deduce information about the kind of congenital blindness that those chemicals cured. This is because we understand intuitively that Jesus's healing ministry, even when reagents are involved, is not really about the mechanical process of healing, but about who Jesus is and what his purpose is. When we read about Jesus's exorcism ministry, however, interpreters forget this understanding and focus entirely on the mechanism, as if Jesus's methods of healing could shed insight on the nature of the affliction that was cured. In actuality, the fact that a "possession" can be cured by words of command tells us nothing about the nature of the affliction; after all, lameness can also be healed that way. That a demon can be driven off by words does not tell us anything about a demon, for the same reason that curing paralysis by words (Matt 9:6) does not tell us anything about the human nervous system. Likewise the actual words used tell us nothing more about the malady that is cured than would an analysis of the actual mud from John 9. The details are not meaningless, but they are not the subject of the narrative, either; they are tools used to tell the story. The text talks about demons, but only as a means to an end to talk about something else.

Consequently, once again, it matters very little to the interpretation of the text whether the demons are "real" or not. There really are lions in Africa, and they really do kill people. But no amount of documentation of real attacks by real lions in Africa will help me understand the message of 1 Kings 20:36, and no amount of study of Kings will help me understand real attacks by real lions. In fact, the only reason we know that the ancient Hebrew word *'aryēh* refers to the same creature that English speakers call "lion" is due to the combined efforts of linguists, historians, and zoologists; at no stage in the process are theologians involved. Likewise, theologians have nothing to contribute to the discussion of whether or not demons are responsible for phenomena in Africa. For all of its limitations, the best tool we have for isolating—if not necessarily identifying—the efficient cause of observable phenomena and distinguishing them from observer bias and psychological elements is still some form of scientific method. The scientists would probably not call the agents "spirits"—scientists like to develop their own standardized nomenclature for their subjects—but that would not matter; the relevant comparison would be activity and attributes, not what the thing is called. Lions did not stop being lions (or *'aryēh*) when biologists started calling them *panthera leo*. The case would then have to be made that whatever the data indicates is causing the African phenomena has significant similarities, as best can be determined, to the thing that historians and linguists can identify as being represented by the Greek word *daimonion*. In any case, however, the activity of spirit-creatures recorded in the Bible will not tell us anything about the identity or activity of any spirit-creatures that we might be able to identify in Africa, just as the activity of animals recorded in the Bible does not tell us anything about the identity or activity of animals in Africa. Likewise the presence and activity of real demons in Africa would not inform our understanding of the message of the biblical text, any more so than the presence and activity of real lions in Africa informs our understanding of biblical texts that mention the activities of lions. This is worth further examination.

If demons are real, nothing we observe about them will help us interpret the Bible

There is a different sort of argument that tries to prove the "real existence" of spirits based on the ability of certain activities such as prayer, exorcism, or "spiritual warfare" to bring about certain results. This success is then invoked as a kind of confirmation of the particular interpretation of the Bible that initially inspired the practice. However, the efficacy of these practices (or not), as well as anything that can be proved (or not) on that basis, is also irrelevant to the practice of biblical interpretation.

First, again, the Bible is not concerned with mechanisms. The Catholic rite of exorcism, for example, draws heavily from the biblical text, including such passages as John 1, Luke 10–11, and Mark 16, but the reason for the composition of those passages—i.e., the answer to the question "why is this in here?"—was not "to provide instructions for a ritual of exorcism." Compare this to, say, Leviticus 16, which contains instructions for the Day of Atonement ritual,[2] or to the spells in the Egyptian *Book of the Dead*, which—as far as we know—actually were intended to be used as spells. The purpose of the text of the Gospels in context is not the same thing as the purpose of the text of the *Rituale Romanum* in context. Thus, even if the ritual "works," it does not demonstrate anything about the content of the teaching of the Gospels.

Second, and more importantly, invoking divine assistance through prayer and/or ritual is not a mechanistic process. A contrast can be made to modern medicine, which *is* a fundamentally mechanistic process. If I get sick, I can take an antibiotic. If what is making me sick is a bacterial infection, I will get better; if it is something else, like viruses or prions, I won't. The efficacy of antibiotics in curing certain afflictions is some of the strongest evidence that those afflictions are actually caused by bacteria. But prayer does not work in the same way as antibiotics. If my disease is caused by a

---

2. The message of the final form of the book of Leviticus as a whole is not to instruct its audience in the performance of rituals, but nonetheless the ritual instructions are contained in the text. Neither the Gospels nor any other part of Scripture transcribe instructions for an exorcism ritual. (The elimination ritual of Lev 16 is not properly an exorcism; see discussion of Azazel in chapter 7).

virus, an antibiotic cannot make me better. But if I have a disease caused by a virus, and I pray to God to deliver me from bacteria, God can heal me anyway because God's healing power is not contingent on my ability to correctly identify the nature of my affliction. This is what we mean when we say that prayer or divine action is not a *mechanism*. If a person in the Middle Ages is sick, asks God to "restore the balance of my humors," and gets better, that does not necessarily mean that the affliction was actually caused by an imbalance of humors. Similarly, if a person is sick, asks God to "deliver me from evil spirits," and gets better, it does not necessarily mean that the affliction was actually caused by evil spirits.[3]

Of course, even in medicine it is possible to confuse correlation and causation. I can have a disease caused by a virus, take an antibiotic, and then get better as the viral infection runs its course; this would not be evidence that the disease is caused by bacteria. Once again, the difference between correlation and causation can be (somewhat) reliably established by an analysis of data gathered under controlled experimental conditions; in other words, by "science." All sorts of social, behavioral, or psychological phenomena can be analyzed in this way, even if their material causes cannot be isolated in a laboratory. There is no scientific test for the presence of spirits in the same sense that there is a scientific test for the presence of bacteria (i.e., a microscope), but there is a scientific test for a statistically significant relationship between action and consequence, which in turn, when demonstrated under appropriate experimental conditions, stands as evidence for causation. Without evidence of causation we have evidence of nothing, and belief based on evidence cannot be based on "nothing." Further, since divine action is not a mechanism—that is, there is no mechanical relationship between the nature of the divine act of healing and the nature of the affliction that is healed—such a study would demonstrate only the effectiveness of prayer or ritual; it would not demonstrate anything about the affliction. Further still, since prayer and ritual are not mechanisms either—that is, there is no mechanical relationship between the human act of requesting divine assistance and the divine act of healing—we would not expect their efficacy to be scientifically verifiable, because science as a discipline is limited to the study of mechanisms. That does not mean that prayers and rituals "don't work"; it only means that if they do happen to work, it proves nothing more than "in this particular circumstance, for some reason, God acted and caused it to work." The answer to your prayer proves that your prayer was answered; it does not verify, for example, your "Spiritual Warfare Strategy" or the interpretation of Ephesians upon which it is based. If the strategy is reliable enough to be offered as empirical evidence of something, it is also reliable enough to be scientifically tested as a mechanism. This is simply the way that "evidence" works.

If spirits can be empirically demonstrated to exist, that in itself might be interesting, but it would not be particularly relevant for biblical interpretation. Lions

3. Contra Boyd, *God at War*, 198: "[a] naturalistic explanation fails to account for . . . why Jesus's exorcism worked."

really exist, and zoologists learn a lot of information by studying them, but most of that information is trivial as far as the teaching of the Bible is concerned. Further, the Bible's depiction of demons would probably not be of any value to a (scientific) diabologist, for the same reasons that the Bible's depiction of animals is not normally helpful to a zoologist. Ostriches really exist, but Job 39:16 (notoriously) misrepresents the behavior of ostriches. Diabologists would gain their knowledge of the nature and behavior of their subject matter through their own methodological processes, as zoologists, astronomers, geologists, historians, and others also do. In fact, it is likely that (some) diabologists would use their empirical observations of spirits to try to undermine the teaching of the Bible, exactly as some zoologists use their empirical observations of ostriches (and eagles, i.e., Deut 32:11). The answer to all of these is the same: the Bible is not a bestiary. But because it is not a bestiary, its message is not to give information about the creatures it describes. Consequently, any information that it does happen to offer about the creatures it describes—including "there is such a thing"—is only a reference used to convey the message of the text and should not be confused with the affirmation of the message itself.

Chapter 7

What is a "demon" within the Bible's cognitive environment?

W ORDS IN THE BIBLE mean what the authors use them to mean. That meaning, in turn, reflects ideas and concepts that would have been understood by the original audience. When we read the word *demon* in the biblical text, therefore, we cannot assume that the word would bring to their minds the same idea that it brings to ours (this is the essence of what is called cognitive semantics). We must look to the cognitive environment to discover what the word we translate "demon" would have meant in its original context. Only then can we begin to ask what the author intended to communicate by means of the reference.

Demons in the ancient Near East[1]

One of the ways that comparative studies can contribute to the interpretation of the Hebrew Bible is to provide information from the cognitive environment that fills in gaps where the biblical information is scant. In our interest to fill in such gaps, however, we cannot uncritically adopt ancient Near Eastern views wholesale as if Israel never departs from the mainstream.[2] On the other end of the spectrum, inserting the Hellenistic or the New Testament view into the gaps is methodologically flawed for the same reasons. Both the ancient Near East and the New Testament hold potentially helpful perspectives, but both must be investigated closely in relation to the actual textual data of the Hebrew Bible. One of the areas that has been insufficiently studied, and has often had outside information imposed on it, is the concept and role of demons in the Hebrew Bible. It is especially interesting because demons play such a substantial role in the ancient Near East, in the Hellenistic Period, and in the New Testament, but are largely absent from the Hebrew Bible.

---

1. This section adapted from Walton, "Demons in Mesopotamia and Israel."

2. Note an unfortunately fairly typical comment by Russell, "The minor malicious spirits that appeared from time to time in Hebrew religion resemble those of other cultures and were in large part derived from those of Canaan." See *Devil*, 215.

The first problem we face concerns terminology. No general term for "demons" exists in any of the major cultures of the ancient Near East or in the Hebrew Bible. They are generally considered one of the categories of "spirit beings," along with gods and ghosts. The term *demons* has had a checkered history; in today's theological usage the term denotes beings, often fallen angels, who are intrinsically evil and who do the bidding of their master, Satan. This definition, however, only became commonplace long after the Hebrew Bible was complete. The idea of evil spirits under the control of a chief demon cannot be assumed for the ancient Near East or for the Hebrew Bible, and requires careful assessment even for the New Testament. Some of the general concepts that eventually appear in Judaism and Christianity can be observed to show similarity to Persian Zoroastrianism, though we should hesitate to draw straight lines of influence without further evidence (see chapter 9).

Thus, the English term *demon* is already a prejudicial label that undermines the investigation due to anachronism. Rather than using prejudicial and potentially anachronistic terminology, we need first to establish a taxonomy of spirit beings on a largely descriptive basis. Using empirical data found in the ancient literature, we can discern a taxonomy of spirit beings in three classes: gods (class I), defined as those who receive sacrifices, at one extreme; and at the other extreme, ghosts (class III), defined as those who were formally human.[3] Class II is made up of all that remain and is a large and diverse group. These divisions are more culturally accurate than the common division between good (gods) and evil (demons) because in the ancient world spirits (and gods) were consistently morally ambiguous or neutral.

The role of spirits in general in Mesopotamia[4] must be considered in light of what could be termed the "great symbiosis."[5] Gods were believed to have needs for food,

3. While ghosts were taken seriously and could affect the living in terrifying ways, they were much more limited than class II entities. Scurlock, *Magico-Medical Means*, 5, identifies the obnoxious behavior of ghosts as represented in "emitting ghostly screams, by haunting people in visible form, and by causing a series of physical problems."

4. In this section, we will consider only Mesopotamian civilizations for a number of reasons. The material from Egypt follows many of the same patterns and categories as Mesopotamia with two notable exceptions. The first is that in Egypt the profile is complicated by the involvement of "class II" beings in the passage of the deceased to and through the netherworld. Views of afterlife in Israel have more overlap with Mesopotamia than Egypt, so the comparative study will be more productive using Mesopotamian civilizations. The second is that in Egypt the line between class I and class II is much less distinct because those in class II are sometimes eventually elevated to class I. Mesopotamia does not show the same sort of fluidity, nor does the Hebrew Bible. Ugarit has little to offer to the discussion. The scant information is drawn only from incantations, which offer very little descriptive information about their beliefs (see Spronk, "The Incantations"). Horon, sometimes referred to as "lord of the demons," can be either a threat or a protector (see Rüterswörden, "Horon," 425–26; Choi, "Resheph and Yhwh Ṣeba'ot." For treatment of incantation, see Pardee, *Ritual and Cult*, 172–79, RS 24.244). Horon and Resheph are called "reified horrors" by Wyatt, who considers "demons" to be gods in the making or unmaking (Wyatt, "The Religion of Ugarit," 549). As in Egypt, the line between classes I and II is somewhat blurred, with Resheph being also considered a god. For this reason and others, the data from Ugarit and Egypt merit their own separate investigations.

5. The literature from ancient Mesopotamia evinces diversity of expressions and perceptions of

drink, clothing, and housing. People had been created with the explicit purpose of providing for these needs. At the same time, when the gods were properly provided for, they would in turn provide care and protection for the people. This symbiosis between humans and gods provides the parameters for the Mesopotamian religious system. Religious obligation was defined by the rituals that were performed to meet the needs of the gods. The understanding of the gods was construed in terms of their provision and protection. People were only required to be ethical because ethical behavior brought order to the world, not because the gods were ethical. Gods were not imitated or morally elevated; they were authority figures who demanded attention and offered benefits. Class I spirits (the gods) are here defined as those who are the protagonists in this great symbiosis. They are the focus of the rituals and they provide the benefits. We will discuss the great symbiosis further when we discuss the paradigm-shift that took place between the testaments in chapter 8.

Class II spirits are only tangential to this ritual system. They do not have temples, priests, or sacred space of any kind.[6] They do not receive sacrifices.[7] They are said to need neither food nor drink, so they have no needs to be provided.[8] They can do harm or provide benefits to humans just as the gods can, but the harm they bring is either as the agents of the gods, or as opportunists when the gods have not been properly cared for and are therefore inattentive to human subjects.[9] The incantation texts describe the latter sort of victims as those who "have no personal deity."[10] The benefits these class II spirits bring are also as agents of deity. Thus, their location outside the great symbiosis defines their position in the religious system. The second element that defines class II in Mesopotamia is the nature of the relationship of these beings to the practice of magic and its associations with power.[11] Class II spirit beings exercise

---

spirit beings, so that we must be cautious about making too fine a distinction in each case. Nevertheless, the data are consistent enough across several genres in the ancient literature to make the following taxonomic distinctions. See van der Toorn, "The Theology of Demons."

6. Westenholz, *Dragons*, 15.

7. Blair, *De-Demonising*, 81. P-A. Beaulieu indicates a possible exception in that deified fantastic creatures appear with divine determinatives and are recipients of offering in the Neo-Babylonian period at the temple of Eanna in Uruk, *Pantheon of Uruk*. Ornan, "In the Likeness of Man," 97, however, counters that in this case they "might have been perceived as deified emanations of the god who had defeated them."

8. In Geller, *Utukku Lemnutu* (Hereafter, *UL*) 6:166, it says that "They don't eat food and don't drink water" (needs provided by sacrifices and libations). In 13:27–28, "since no *maṣḥatu*-flour has been scattered for them, nor any divine offering made for them, their behavior is aggressive."

9. Abusch, "Witchcraft," 47–48, identifies three stages of development. (1) The victim is vulnerable to demonic attack because unprotected by a personal god, who is absent or who has fled; (2) the victim is vulnerable because he has sinned and angered personal god, who abandons or calls forth demonic attack; and (3) the victim is innocent but a witch is able to influence the deity to be angry.

10. Cunningham, *Deliver Me from Evil*, 62.

11. Magic is understood here as a subset of religion. I am not suggesting that class I is unaffected by magic, but only noting the particular associations between magic and class II. See Arnold, "Divination and Magic."

power in the human realm by terrorizing or protecting, and are resisted or enlisted by means of power (incantations, exorcism). So as we compare class II spirit beings in Mesopotamia with those in Israel, we must consider them in light of the great symbiosis and the exercise of power in magic.

Akkadian terminology represents class II spirit beings either in corporate groups[12] (for example, *utukku, asakku, rabiṣu, šedu*) or as individual beings (for example, *lamaštu, pazazu, lilitu,* and *ardat-lili*). Descriptions of class II spirits are available throughout the literature. In a piece entitled "The Underworld Vision of an Assyrian Prince," a vision describes a number of such beings who served as attendants to Nergal in the netherworld (for example, "The Evil Spirit had a lion's head, his hands and feet were those of Anzu").[13] All of these are composite beings, as is common for the spirits in class II in Mesopotamia. Combining the features of two or more fierce animals made them more dangerous and also indicated their status as on the periphery of the ordered world; that is, they are liminal creatures.[14] Westenholz observes that "The greater the resemblance to human beings the greater the propensity that the demon would be predisposed toward the benefit of humankind."[15]

People could overcome attacks by class II spirits in a number of ways: (1) regain the favor of their god; (2) call on specialists to exorcise the spirit; or (3) use incantations, figurines, amulets, or other magical means to enlist the help of guardian spirits (for example, Pazazu against Lamashtu). As already mentioned, class II spirits do not receive sacrifices. Westenholz describes them as "a by-product of creation without a fixed place in the universe. . . . Without a place of their own, they roamed the earth and took by force what they did not get by right; mankind was useless to them and therefore they preyed on humanity without restraint."[16] In the *utukku lemnutu* series, the incantations are made of the gods, and presumably whatever sacrifices are offered, are offered to them: "I adjure you by the great gods so that you go away."[17] It should also be noted, however, that the ritual actions, when described, do not generally include sacrifices to the great gods, but ritual acts performed in relation to the patient,[18] and occasionally food and water offerings to the household gods.[19] In tablet 10, the role of Marduk can be observed as he is able to weaken the *utukku*: he notices the

12. Egyptian literature also makes reference to such groups of spirits, generally under the control of the gods. The generic name for them is the seven arrows (*šeseru*). For extensive summary of the information in Egypt, see Meeks, "Demons," 375–78.

13. Livingstone, *Court Poetry*, 71–72, text 32: r.2–9.

14. Cunningham, *Deliver Me from Evil*, 89, indicates their composite nature is symbolic of disorder.

15. Westenholz, *Dragons*, 11. She also distinguishes between those that go on four legs, "monsters," and those that go on two, "demons."

16. Westenholz, *Dragons*, 15.

17. *UL* 6:37.

18. *UL* 7:10–19.

19. *UL* 9:10.

utukku, he gets angry at the *utukku*, he receives the ritual elements arranged around the patient, and orders the *utukku* to depart.

Class II spirits are thought responsible for disease, plague, and all sorts of disasters in the cosmos.[20] They inhabit liminal spaces in sea, earth, and sky.[21] One text about the seven deadly Sebetti describes their nature:

> They are powerful in heaven and earth.
> They are the waves in the sea,
> They are the terrors of the marsh.
> They are the asakku-disease in the canebrake.
> They are the flaming embers in the forest.
> They are the evil web in the mouth of a jar,
> They are the neglected fruit in gardens.[22]

Another text describes them as "agent(s) of harm (and) accessories to evil, maliciously ready to commit murder every day."[23]

In contrast to this negative profile, class II spirits are also seen as having a relationship to the gods (class I). They are "born of Anu's seed,"[24] the evil ones of Ea, throne bearers of gods,[25] and "messengers of Lord Anu."[26] Furthermore, we often find class II spirits as chaos creatures who have been defeated by the gods (class I)[27] and have become their associates. So Wiggermann notes, "For the monsters, outlaws by nature, it is only a small step from the unpredictable servant to rebel, and from rebel to defeated enemy. The role of the god in their relation changes accordingly from master to rightful ruler, and from rightful ruler to victor."[28] Saggs traces this development through three stages determined by tracing ideas through the literature: (1) they arose from ancient numina acting independently of the gods; (2) they became agents of the gods, and in late literature (3) can be seen as hypostases of the gods or gods themselves.[29]

The class II spirits in Mesopotamia can be summarized as powers that can be either malevolent or benevolent. Westenholz suggests that they tended to operate independently, but when their actions were called to the attention of the gods, they could

---

20. Westenholz, *Dragons,* 14.

21. Westenholz, *Dragons,* 12.

22. *UL* 13:6–15.

23. *UL* 16:3–4.

24. *UL* 5:152. *UL* 5:143 says they were "Fashioned in the Netherworld, but spawned in Heaven."

25. *UL* 5:157–58. *UL* 5:158 recalls the demons portrayed on the *nemedu* thrones, e.g., Sennacherib's at Lachish.

26. *UL* 16:12.

27. Wiggermann, *Mesopotamian Protective Spirits,* xii.

28. Wiggermann, *Mesopotamian Protective Spirits,* 153.

29. Saggs, *Encounter,* 105.

be quickly brought into line.[30] Thus, we see that they were subordinate to the gods and largely under their control. "The place of these demonic beings in the universe was as mere agents and executors of the will of the gods."[31] In this sense, they would not be considered as having wisdom and knowledge and being held accountable for their actions, but they are not robots either; they might best be compared to wild animals who act on instinct. The texts specifically say that "They have no understanding"[32] (compare perhaps to Job 39:17). Consequently, Saggs notes that the difference between what we have designated as class II and class I is that divine behavior is purposeful, whereas "demon" behavior is irrational and arbitrary, and even clumsy or ridiculous, but dangerous nonetheless.[33] Given the information developed from the sources, we would also conclude that class II beings, also like animals, have no moral agency; that is, the capacity to know whether something is good or bad, and consequently deciding a course of action based on that knowledge. They could be called morally neutral or ambiguous, but would be best described as *amoral*. In terms of volition and moral agency, class II spirits could be compared to wild animals or meteorological phenomena, as opposed to [sociopathic] humans, as the creatures we call "demons" often are.[34]

Terms for "demons" in the Hebrew Bible

The ancient Near East has no category of creatures called "demons" and therefore no word to describe that category, and biblical Hebrew does not have one, either. However, a number of Hebrew terms have been thought by various interpreters at various times to represent creatures that are essentially similar to Mesopotamian class II spirits. The interpretation of these creatures generally falls into one of three categories.[35] The first is the position of conflict theology, that they are essentially interchangeable with the modern conception of demons; evil spirits allied under a ruler named Satan in a purposeful war of opposition against the will and purposes of God. This position is entirely anachronistic and cannot be supported from the text itself. The second position is commonly held by anthropologists and historians, and argues that the creatures are vestiges from pre-Yahwistic Israelite religion or other ancient Near Eastern mythology that have been artificially or polemically incorporated and repurposed by the Yahwistic biblical authors.[36] This position, while interesting, is merely speculative

30. Westenholz, *Dragons*, 14–15.

31. Westenholz, *Dragons*, 14.

32. *UL* 5:155.

33. Saggs, *Encounter*, 95, citing van der Leeuw, *Religion*.

34. Interestingly, in Hebrew Bible usage there is ambiguity and disagreement among scholars concerning whether the key terms refer to class II creatures or wild animals or destructive forces of nature.

35. See Blair, *De-demonising*, 2–15.

36. For this position also applied to the divine council, see White, *Yahweh's Council*, esp. 173–75.

and in any case is irrelevant for theology; theology is concerned with the use that the various authors have chosen to make of the ideas they have inherited, not where those ideas happened to come from, except insofar as the author's beliefs dictate the meaning of his words and the flow of his logic. As discussed in chapter 1, the Bible's message does not affirm the beliefs of its authors or sources, even though we do need to understand what those beliefs were in order to understand the references that the author uses to convey the message. The third position is held by the demythologizers and argues that the terms have nothing to do with spirit-beings or mythographic characters at all, but instead refer to animals, natural phenomena, or abstractions.[37] This position is likewise anachronistic because it assumes a rigid categorical distinction between spirit-beings and animals or phenomena that does not represent the thinking of the ancient world.

Whether the various terms refer to spirits or not is difficult to determine with certainty and mostly irrelevant, since the categorical distinction between "spirits" and "not spirits" is blurred in the ancient cognitive context, especially regarding liminal creatures. We are primarily interested in whether or not the depiction of the creatures deviates in any significant way from the cognitive environment's general concept of class II spirits, described above, because lack of deviation from commonly held beliefs is one of the strongest indicators that the content in question is a reference, not an affirmation; people do not need a message from God to tell them things they already believed. We are also interested in the various ways that the reception of these terms had led to the classification of the referents of the terms as what we today call *demons*. This we will now briefly examine.

Perhaps the most notable term is *šēdîm*, which occurs in Deuteronomy 32:17 and Psalm 106:37 (NIV "false gods") and which is translated by the LXX as *daimonia*, "demons." This translation is the basis for Paul's argument in 1 Corinthians 10:20 (see chapter 11). What the word *šēdîm* originally referred to we do not know, although context indicates that they would not have been understood as class II spirits (that is, "demons"), since they receive offerings.[38] Broadly, two possible etymologies are suggested. The first is the Akkadian *šedu*, which refers to the winged bull-men who guard entrances to palaces and temples in a manner similar to the Hebrew *kĕrûbîm* (cherubim). *Šedu* are composite creatures who do not receive offerings, which would place them in the realm of class II spirits; however, *because* they do not receive offerings, it is unlikely that the wilderness generation gave sacrifices to them. Thus, a

---

37. The warrant for this position is that none of the terms can be demonstrated *tabula rasa* to refer to spirit-beings without appeals to some combination of etymology or comparative cosmology/mythography; See for example Blair, *De-Demonising*, 14–15. This observation is true enough; however, the embeddedness of the text within its cognitive environment and the necessity of context to determine the meanings of words (see chapter 1) means that we *should* assume that the Bible's cosmology is more or less the same as that of its neighbors unless there is a specific reason to assume otherwise.

38. Blair, *De-Demonising*, 60.

more plausible option is the Aramaic *šdyn*, which are equated with members of the Canaanite pantheon.[39] The LXX's decision to translate the word as "demons" reflects a Hellenistic assessment of intermediate beings that are not gods (Deut 32:17; see further below) which for the translators included any beings other than Yahweh; the Greek word *daimonion* does not reflect the original etymology of the Hebrew term. The fact that the *šēdîm*, whatever they were, were given offerings means that they would not have been thought of as "demons"—that is, class II spirits—in their original context, and instead should be understood as more or less parallel to foreign gods. See further discussion below and in chapter 11.

Another term translated "demons" by the LXX is *śĕ'îrîm* in Isaiah 13:21 (NIV "wild goats"). *Śĕ'îrîm* also occurs in Leviticus 17:7 and 2 Chronicles 11:15 (NIV "goat idols"); as things which receive offerings, translated by the LXX not as *daimonion* but as *mataios* (lit. "empty things"). *Mataios* also translates the Hebrew words *ĕlîl* and *hebel*, which refer to idols (see chapter 11); *ĕlîl* is translated *daimonion* by the LXX in Psalm 96:5. *Śĕ'îrîm*, on the other hand, is a normal Hebrew word for "goats" (e.g., Lev 16:5, 7, 8; Num 7:87; 2 Chr 29:23). In 2 Chronicles 11:15 the "goat idol" is paralleled with Jeroboam's "calf idol," which in turn is not usually interpreted as representing either an animal or a theriomorphic spirit-being in the shape of a bull. Instead, the "calf idol" is normally thought to represent either a deity whose aspect is a bull (e.g., Egyptian Apis) or, more likely, a mount or iconic attribute of a deity who is associated with a bull as a symbol, perhaps Baal or (in Jeroboam's case) Yahweh.[40] Thus, Jeroboam's "goat idols" might likewise be dedicated to a deity with an iconic attribute or symbolic association of a goat. Which deity this may have been is unknown—and may also have been Yahweh—though the use of goats in the Day of Atonement ritual has led many interpreters over the centuries to associate it with Azazel (though see below). However, once again, the fact that the *śĕ'îrîm/mataios* receive offerings means that they are not class II spirits and therefore not conceptually parallel to "demons" in the original context.

The word *śĕ'îrîm* also occurs in a list of liminal creatures who inhabit the ruins of Babylon and Edom (Isa 13:21–22 and 34:13–14). These beings live in liminal regions and do not receive offerings, and thus could be class II spirits. The ancient Near Eastern conception that depicts "demons" as being drawn to liminal areas persists in the Second Temple period; compare Matthew 12:43, "[an impure spirit] goes through arid places seeking rest (*anapausis*), and does not find it (*eurisko*)" with LXX Isaiah 34:14, "Night Creatures" (LXX *onokentaurois*, Heb. *lîlît*) will also lie down and find (*eurisko*) for themselves places of rest (*anapausis*)." This concept of demons being drawn to the wilderness in turn may have informed the translation decisions of the LXX. However,

---

39. Burnett, "Prophecy in Transjordan," 158–59. See also discussion in Hackett, *The Balaam Text*, 85–89; Chavalas and Adamthwaite, "Archaeological Light on the Old Testament," 93–94. See also Stavrakopoulu, *King Manasseh*, 272–74.

40. Blair, *De-Demonising*, 83–84.

the various words used over the years to translate the (sometimes obscure) Hebrew terms for the creatures are nonsystematic, even within the same text, and sometimes rather creative. Sometimes the words are thought to refer to mythographic creatures or class II spirits, i.e., KJV; "dragons" and "satyrs"; other times they are thought to refer to ordinary animals, i.e., NIV, "jackals" and "wild goats." A summary of the relevant Hebrew terms and their various translations is as follows:

Liminal creatures in the judgment oracles of Isaiah

Hebrew	Isaiah 13:21–22				Isaiah 34:13–14			
	LXX	Vulgate	KJV	NIV	LXX	Vulgate	KJV	NIV
śĕʿîrîm	daimonia	pilosis (hairy ones)	satyrs	wild goats	untranslated	pilosis (hairy ones)	satyrs	wild goats
ṣiyyîm	thērion	bestiae	wild beasts	desert creatures	daimonia	daemoniae	wild beasts	desert creatures
iyyîm	onokentauros	ibes (ibises)	wild beasts	hyenas	onokentauros	onocentauri	wild beasts	hyenas
tannîm	exinoi (hedgehogs)	sirenae	dragons	jackals	seirēnes	dracones	dragons	jackals
ōḥîm	ēchon ("sound"; not a creature)	dracones	doleful creatures	jackals	—	—	—	—
bĕnôt yaʿănâ	seirēnes	strutiones (ostriches)	owls	owls	strouthōn (ostriches)	strutiones (ostriches)	owls	owls
lîlît	—	—	—	—	onokentauros	lamia	screech owl	night creatures

As discussed above, Hebrew śĕʿîrîm means "goats." Etymologically it is connected to the word for "hair" (śēʿār, ʿśāʿîr, e.g., Gen 25:25; 27:11), which is the basis of the Latin translation pilosis, "hairy [ones]." LXX daimonia in Isaiah 13:21 might be based on a combination of the use of śĕʿîrîm in other contexts and the Second Temple idea that demons receive offerings on behalf of the gods (as we see with the šēdîm),[41] but if that were the case then the two occurrences of the word in cultic contexts (Lev 17:7 and 2 Chr 11:15) should have been translated daimonia as well, as opposed to mataios. Alternatively, the translation daimonia might come from the idea that both the śĕʿîrîm and the "demons" of the Second Temple period inhabit liminal areas.

41. The Midrash and the Targums render śĕʿîrîm in Lev 17:7; Isa 13:21; 34:14; and 2 Chr 11:15 as šdym, all supposedly meaning "demons." Janowski, "Satyrs," 733.

Whatever the logic of the LXX, the combined concepts of "hairy goat demons" led to the KJV's choice of the word "satyr," which is an English transliteration of a Greek word (*saturos*) that originally referred to the [more or less] human companions of Dionysus, but later became synthesized with the Roman *Faunus*, which refers to composite goat-men. The medieval and modern iconography of the devil as a goat-man is based on the Satyrs/fauns, so the association of demons and goat-creatures was logical enough for the KJV. But the Hebrew word itself contains no indications that the term refers to anything other than goats (so NIV), though we should also recognize that the line between theriomorphic class II spirits and liminal animals is not clearly established in the ancient Near East.

The term *śĕʿîrîm* also occurs in Isaiah 34:14; "the *ṣiyyîm* will meet with the *ʾiyyîm*, and the *śĕʿîrîm* will call to each other." In the LXX, *śĕʿîrîm* is left untranslated, with the subjects of the verb "call" (*boesontai*) being the *ṣiyyîm* and the *ʾiyyîm*, translated "*daimonia*" and "*onokentaurous*," respectively. *Ṣiyyîm* and *ʾiyyîm* also both occur in Isaiah 13:21–22. Both English translations render the words the same way in both passages (KJV "wild beasts of the desert/wild beasts of the island"; NIV "desert creatures/hyenas"), but the LXX and the Vulgate are less systematic. In Isaiah 13:21, the LXX translates *ṣiyyîm* as *theria* ("beasts"), but in Isaiah 34:14 it translates *ṣiyyîm* as *daimonia* ("demons"); the Vulgate follows suit in both passages. In both passages, the LXX translates *ʾiyyîm* as *onokentauros*, which the Latin transliterates in Isaiah 34:14, but renders instead as "ibis" in Isaiah 13:22. LXX also uses *onokentauros* to translate *lîlît* in Isaiah 34:14, which the Vulgate renders as *Lamia* (see below). The Greek *onokentauros* occurs again in the works of the third-century naturalist Aelian, who describes it as a centaur (a composite man-horse) with the equid component being a mule rather than a horse, attributing the description to Pythagoras (d. 495 BCE).[42] The meaning of the Hebrew terms *ṣiyyîm* and *ʾiyyîm* in context is unclear. Psalm 72:9–10 contrasts "desert tribes" (*ṣiyyîm*) with "kings . . . of distant shores" (*melki ʾiyyîm*) as part of a poetic merism that designates "everybody." This usage in psalms is the basis of the KJV translation "[creatures] of the desert/[creatures] of the islands." The NIV "hyenas" follows the RSV and is repeated in most other English translations, though some prefer "wolves" (e.g., ASV, NASB) or "jackals" (e.g., NKJV). All are likely based on a proposed etymology of *ʾiyyîm* as being derived from the root *ʾwh*, "to howl" and serving as an onomonopoeic designation for a "howling creature"; this interpretation is attested as early as 1877.[43] Both terms *ṣiyyîm* and *ʾiyyîm* appear again in Jeremiah 50:39. The LXX translates the phrase as "the *indalmata* [will live] in

42. Aelian, *De Natura Animalium* 17.10. The creature in question is usually inferred to have been an ape of some kind (so LSJ; see also Aelian, *On Animals III books 12–17* trans. A. F. Scholfield (LCL) 333). Aelian calls it a quadruped but notes that it can pick things up as though its forefeet were hands (ibid., 335).

43. Keil and Delitzsch, *Isaiah*, 1:305.

the islands" (*indalmata en tais nēsois*); *Indalmata* means "hallucinations"[44] and *nēsois* is the LXX preferred translation of *'iyyîm* but does not refer to a creature.[45] Both of these are different than either of its choices in Isaiah. The Vulgate translates the terms respectively as *dracones* (dragons) and *fatuis ficariis* (referring to the fauns),[46] both of which are likewise different than either of its choices in Isaiah. KJV and NIV both repeat their consistent translation. Most scholars agree that the terms (in both Isaiah and in Jeremiah) are intended to be impressionistic and not to identify specific creatures, as demons or otherwise.[47]

The third creature that appears in Jeremiah 50:31 beside the *ṣiyyîm* and the *'iyyîm* is the *bĕnôt ya'ănâ* (NIV "owls") which also appears beside *tannîm* (NIV "jackals") in Isaiah 43:20; Job 30:29; and Micah 1:8; in addition to Isaiah 13:21 and 34:13. The translation of these two words is likewise inconsistent:

"Jackals" and "owls" in various passages

	tannîm		*bĕnôt ya'ănâ*	
	LXX	**Vulgate**	**LXX**	**Vulgate**
Isa 13:21–22	*exinoi* (hedgehogs)	*sirenae*	*seirēnes*	*Strutiones* (ostriches)
Isa 34:14	*seirēnes*	*dracones*	*Strouthon* (ostriches)	*Strutiones* (ostriches)
Isa 43:20	*seirēnes*	*dracones*	[daughters of] *Strouthon*	*Strutiones* (ostriches)
Jer 50:39	—	—	[daughters of] *seirēnes*	*Strutiones* (ostriches)
Job 30:29	*seirēnes*	*dracones*	*Strouthon* (ostriches)	*Strutiones* (ostriches)
Mic 1:8	*drakonton*	*dracones*	[daughters of] *seirēnes*	*Strutiones* (ostriches)

The Vulgate consistently translates *bĕnôt ya'ănâ* as "ostrich," which is consistent with its appearance in Leviticus 11:16 and Deuteronomy 14:15 on a list of unclean birds (NIV "horned owl"). The LXX occasionally agrees, but in other places wants to render the term as *Siren*, referring to composite (class II) bird-women from Greek mythology. All of the LXX passages include "Siren" as one of the pair, replacing *tannîm* if

44. LSJ. *indalma* also translates *ṣiyyîm* in LXX Wis 17:3 (NRSV "specters").

45. *nēsos* ("island") is the LXX translation for *'iyyîm* in all occurrences other than Isa 13:22; 34:11 (translated *onokentauros*) and 1 Sam 4:21; Eccl 4:10; 10:16 (translated *ouai*, an exclamation of distress, NIV "woe" or "pity").

46. Holladay, *Jeremiah 2*, 420

47. Holladay, *Jeremiah 2*, 420; Wildberger, *Isaiah 28–39*, 335.

it wants to use "ostrich" for *běnôt yaʿănâ*. The Vulgate also translates *tannîm* as "Siren" in Isaiah 13:22 (though the LXX does not). The more consistent Vulgate translation of *tannîm* as "dragon" might reflect a common confusion between the words *tannîm* ("Jackals," plural of *tan*) and *tannîn*, the word for the chaos monsters (plural *tannînim*; see also Ps 44:19; Vulg. 43:20). This is probably the source of the LXX *drakon* for *tannîm* in Micah 1:8, since *drakon* is the word it uses for *tannîn* in Isaiah 27:1. The Vulgate translates *tannîn* as *draco* in Exodus 7:12; Deuteronomy 32:33; Psalm 74:13 (Vulg 73:13); 91:13 (Vulg 90:13); 148:7; Isaiah 51:9; Jeremiah 51:34; and Ezekiel 29:3; 32:2.[48] The Vulgate also uses *draco* to translate the Hebrew hapax *'ōḥîm* in Isaiah 13:21, which the LXX renders as *echos*. "Echo" is the name of a nymph (a class II spirit) in Greek mythology who was cursed to only be able to repeat the last few words said to her, but here the usage is depersonalized and simply means "sound." Many English translations (including all prior to the KJV) render *'ōḥîm* as "owls";[49] the inspiration for the KJV's "doleful creatures" is uncertain.[50] NIV "jackals" for both *'ōḥîm* and *tannîm* follows Vulgate "dragons." In any case, the Hebrew usage of *tannîm* and *běnôt yaʿănâ* does not indicate that they are anything other than liminal animals; canids and birds of some kind, respectively. The LXX *exinoi* ("hedgehogs") for *tannîm* in Isaiah 13:22 comes from its normal use of the term to translate Hebrew *qippod*, which occurs in lists of liminal creatures in Isaiah 34:11, 15, and Zephaniah 2:14. The conclusion is that the various translators included sirens, ostriches, dragons, mule-centaurs, hedgehogs, and also demons, together in the poetic descriptions of desolation wherever they seemed appropriate, without much consideration for what particular words meant, either in terms of specific animals (hedgehogs versus jackals) or even categories of creatures (animals versus class II monsters or spirits). Nonetheless, the imagery is not inappropriate because, once again, in the ancient Near East—and apparently extending into the Second Temple period as well—the taxonomy of the various inhabitants of the liminal world is somewhat blurred. Wild or predatory animals were not clearly differentiated from theriomorphic demons. But while the lack of distinction is irrelevant for poetic imagery (as here), it does mean that we cannot rely too much on the terms as a guide for theological metaphysics. The conflation of demons with other denizens of liminal regions in the ancient world, reflected in both the Hebrew Bible and the Septuagint, is not a warrant for us to read "evil supernatural spirit-creature" into any Hebrew term or Greek translation thereof that describes liminal creatures. Our word and category "demon" contains baggage that the ancient "creature from the liminal

---

48. *Tannîn* is also translated *ceta* ("whale") in Gen 1:21; Job 7:12; and Isa 27:1; and as *coluber* ("snake") in Exod 7:9–10.

49. Targum Isaiah renders *ōḥîm* with the Aramaic cognate *ōḥîn*, which in Aramaic is thought to refer to the eagle owl (cf. Akkadian *hūa* with metathesis, *CAD* 6:212b). See also Wildberger, *Isaiah 13–27*, 32. The Greek *echos* might in fact be intended as a transliteration of *ōḥîn* based on phonetic similarity.

50. KJV's only other use of "doleful" is in Micah 2:4, where it translates Hebrew *nāhâ něhî*, (NIV "mournful song").

world" designation did not, and therefore serves as a poor translation, even when applied to a Greek semantic equivalent. (It is also worth noting that the recapitulation of Isaiah 13:19–22 in Revelation 18:2 emphasizes the *uncleanness* of the spirits and animals, as opposed to anything evil, although the presence of "demons" and "impure spirits" derives from the terms used in the LXX.)

Regardless of the choices of later translations, most of the Hebrew terms for liminal creatures most naturally refer to animals. One that probably does not, however, is *lîlît* (NIV "owls") in Isaiah 34:14.[51] *Lîlît* is a cognate of the Akkadian *lilitu*, a succubus-demon similar to the Greek *Lamia* and Akkadian *Lamashtu*. She is a seductress of men and a killer of children.[52] Aquila transliterates *lîlît* as *Lilith*, and Symmachus renders the term as *Lamia*, as does the Vulgate. The Vulgate also uses *lamia* for *tannîm* ("jackals") in Lamentations 4:3. However, the LXX for *lîlît* is *onokentauros* (mule-centaur, the same term it uses to translate *'iyyîm*), not *Lamia*. So why would the LXX have used *this* term, instead of the technical term for the same demon (*lamia*) that their language already has? Aelian later used the term *onokentauros* impressionistically to describe a great ape, but that should not lead us to assume that the LXX translators had an apelike creature in mind. An explanation may be found in the *Testament of Solomon*, which appears to represent Second Temple folklore despite being written later.[53] Solomon is introduced to a succubus named Onoskelis, a female Satyr with the legs of a mule.[54] The demon makes her home in caves and identifies her habitat as cliffs, caves, and ravines. A demon named Obyzouth, more closely resembling the conventional Lilith/Lamia in both appearance and activity, is interrogated separately.[55] This in turn might indicate that some diversity regarding succubi existed in the cognitive environment of the Second Temple period. If that is the case, then the LXX decision to depict the succubus in Isaiah 34:14 as the mule-composite archetype might have been a deliberate attempt to invoke the themes of liminal dwelling and unworldly nature (which the *Testament of Solomon* also emphasizes for Onoskelis), as opposed to the themes of torment and infanticide invoked by Lamia (which the *Testament of Solomon* also emphasizes for Obyzouth). This in turn would support the idea that the LXX is choosing words that emphasize desolation as opposed to those that emphasize supernatural evil, although of course any conclusion is speculative. Even if the Hebrew term in context is supposed to

51. Blair's argument that the term must necessarily refer to a night-bird of some kind (derived from the assumption that *lîlît* is a derivative of the Hebrew *lāylâ*, "*night*," which is also the basis for the NIV "night creatures") because every other creature in the list is a natural animal (Blair, *De-Demonising*, 95) is anachronistic because it assumes a rigid categorical distinction between liminal animals and class II spirits, which would not have been present in the original context.

52. Hutter, "Lilith," 520–21.

53. Duling, "Testament of Solomon," 942.

54. *T. Sol.* 4.2.

55. *T. Sol.* 13.1–2; The defining feature of Obyzouth is its hair (*T. Sol.* 13.2), which as described resembles depictions of the *Lilith* in ninth-century incantation bowls (Duling, "Testament of Solomon," 973–74, n13a). Lilith's long hair is emphasized in the Talmud as well (Hutter, "Lilith," 521). See Blair, *De-Demonising*, 28 for comparison between Obyzouth and Lilith.

reference a [kind of] spirit, though, its emphasis is clearly on the liminal habitat of such creatures (and therefore the extent of the desolation that will befall Edom and Babylon by means of their transformation into liminal space), not an authoritative affirmation that such creatures are real and everything the cognitive environment believes about them is true, and is also not intended to saddle the creature with all of the baggage that later interpreters attached to the word "demon."

Several other places in the Hebrew Bible contain allusions to terms or names that correspond to ancient Near Eastern mythic figures. The most notable of these are *rešep* (e.g., Deut 32:24; Hab 3:5); *qeṭeb* (e.g., Deut 32:23; Hos 13:14); and *deber* (e.g., Hos 13:14; Hab 3:5). *Rešep* is the name of a Canaanite plague god; however, since he has a temple and worshippers, he would not be properly classified as a (class II) "demon." In the Bible the difference between metaphysical demonization and literary personification can be difficult to determine. Further, the etymological correspondence of a Hebrew term to an ancient Near Eastern deity does not necessarily mean that the referent is still conceived as a personal entity in Israelite cosmology; for example, the Hebrew term for the sun (*šemeš*) is a cognate of the name of the Akkadian sun god (šamaš), but the sun is neither a god nor a demon in Israel; it is a light (Gen 1:14–16), and it is not normally considered to be demonized when it is personified (i.e., Isa 24:23). Neither does the shared etymology mean that the Israelite reference is a deliberate polemic against the mythology of its neighbors. In all of the occurrences of the name *rešep* (Deut 32:34; Hab 3:5 ["pestilence"]; Ps 78:48 ["bolts of lightning"]) it serves as a weapon or instrument of the warrior God (here, Yahweh), which is a role suitable for either an ancient Near Eastern chthonic deity, an ancient Near Eastern demon, or a depersonalized phenomenon, and in turn indicates that *rešep* has not been conceptually reclassified, no matter which of the three it indicates. Several additional passages are thought to allude to the mythographic image of the plague god, notably Psalm 76:4 (*rišpê qāšet*, NIV "flashing arrows"; *Rešep* in Ugaritic texts is an archer);[56] Job 5:7 (*běnê rešep*, NIV "sparks"); and Psalm 91:5 (*hēṣ yā'ûp*, NIV "arrow that flies.") Reference to a mythographic image does not necessarily indicate a full acceptance of the mythology on which the image is based; for example, the culture of the modern West does not acknowledge Cupid/Eros as a literal deity (or demon), but we can nonetheless speak meaningfully of *love* in terms of being shot through the heart with an arrow, a mythographic image based on the Greco-Roman deity. Likewise, the Israelites could speak meaningfully of *plague* in terms of being shot with arrows, but this does not necessarily mean they would have acknowledged a literal plague god any more than we acknowledge a literal love god. Nonetheless, even if the imagery would have been understood literally, the reference to the plague god in his conventional role is still a reference, not an affirmation.

Psalm 91:5–6 contains a litany of things that the audience/psalmist will not fear: "the terror of night (*paḥad lāylâ*), nor the arrow that flies by day (a mythographic

56. KTU 1.82:3; Wyatt, "Qeteb," 673.

reference to *Rešep*), nor the pestilence (*deber*) that stalks in the darkness, nor the plague (*qeṭeb*) that destroys at midday." All of these are sometimes considered to be references to demonic or chthonic agencies.[57] *Paḥad lāylâ* occurs only here, but *deber* and *qeṭeb* occur elsewhere, often in conjunction with *rešep* as instruments of Yahweh. *Deber* (NIV usually "plague" or "pestilence") is a relatively common word (50+ occurrences) that indicates widespread death alongside famine and war,[58] but it is usually read as being personified in Psalm 91:6, and also in Habakkuk 3:5 (paralleled with *rešep*) and Hosea 13:14 (paralleled with *qeṭeb*). *Qeṭeb* occurs only three other times (Deut 32:24, "deadly plague"; Isa 28:2, "destructive wind"; Hos 13:14, "destruction") and may derive from the name of the Ugaritic deity *qzb*, who is related to the death god Mot. A mythographic allusion to Mot in turn may be intended by the "wasting famine" (*mĕzê rā'āb*) in Deuteronomy 32:24.[59] Alternatively, the *mĕzê rā'āb* may be similar to the Phoenician *lhst lmzh,* mentioned in an incantation against demonized bloodsucking insects. These in turn may be conceptually similar to the *ălûqâ* ("leech"), a hapax in Proverbs 30:15 sometimes thought to reference a vampiric demon or demonized creature of some kind.[60]

The LXX of Psalm 91:6 (along with Aquila and Symmachus) read the "destruction" (*qṭb*) and the "[one who destroys] at midday" (*yāšûd ṣohorayim*) as two separate agencies. The latter was translated as *daimonion mesembrinon,* "midday demon," based on an alteration of *yāšûd* ("destroy," from root *šdd*) to *šēd*, the same word translated 'demon" in Deuteronomy 32:17.[61] This variant is the basis for demonizing all four (or five) evils in Psalm 91:5–6, though in the Hebrew text-in-context they could just as easily be personified abstractions; the *šēdîm*, on the other hand, are always entities and never abstractions. But even if they are understood as entities, *Rešep* and *Qeṭeb* are deities depicted as functioning in the normal capacity of [destructive and chthonic] gods and so it would not be appropriate to classify them as "demons." (Mot has no cult and is essentially a chaos creature, see chapter 9).

The theological innovations of orthodox Israel stripped worship away from all entities other than Yahweh. In that sense (alone) it is permissible to say that the gods of the pantheons have been reclassified as "demons," if demons are simply defined broadly as non-human creatures who do not receive worship. However, the definition of "demon" as "a divine being that does not receive sacrifices" must not be conflated with the later definitions of a demon as "an evil entity opposed to Israel's God." In Israelite perceptions, the gods still retained the same basic functions and same basic position in the divine hierarchy even without their cults; further, they were still

57. For extensive discussion see Blair, *De-Demonising*.

58. del Olmo Lete, "Deber," 231.

59. Wyatt, "Qeteb," 673.

60. Hendel, "Vampire," 887. Fox identifies it as a horse leech found in the Mesopoitamian region that attaches to the inside nostril of horses as they drink from the river, *Proverbs 10–31*, 867–68.

61. Riley, "Midday Demon," 572.

worshipped elsewhere, so the best that could be said is that Israelite orthodoxy *treated the gods the same way they treated demons*, which is not the same thing as saying that Israelite orthodoxy *redefined the gods as having always been the same kinds of things as the things called demons*. On the other hand, denying worship to the gods in the ancient Near East while still conceiving of them as gods (class I spirits) is possible. For example, deliberate neglect of the cults is Enki's proposed solution to the gods' attempts at population control in *Atrahasis*. Neglect of the cults makes the gods angry, and in their anger they might unleash demons or destructive deities (such as *Rešep*) on the negligent humans. The Hebrew Bible's repeated emphasis on the impotence of the gods, especially relative to Yahweh (see chapter 11), is a reassurance to the Israelites that the gods and their anger can be ignored with impunity; this reassurance may be part of the message of Psalm 91.[62] At the same, though, the repeated emphasis not to sacrifice to the gods indicates that they were still conceived of as something that could potentially be sacrificed to, which in turn means that they were not thought of in the same class as demons: Israel does not *need* to be told not to bow down to class II spirits such as the Leviathan or the Cherubim, for example. Thus, even in Israel a strong categorical distinction remains between "demons" and [foreign] gods, even if the latter are destructive and not formally worshipped.

Other terms that could represent either [chthonic] gods, demons, or personified abstractions are the *melek ballāhôt* ("king of terrors") in Job 18:14; *ăbaddôn* ("destruction") in (especially) Job 28:22; and *ăzā'zēl* ("scapegoat") in Leviticus 16. Unlike *Rešeph* and *Qeṭeb*, there is no etymology connecting any of these to ancient Near Eastern deities or demons, so their identification must be made solely on context. The "king of terrors" is sometimes equated with the "firstborn of death" (*běkôr māwet*) in Job 18:13; the assumption that these must be mythographic references has led to the proposal, based on circumstantial evidence, that both titles refer to the Mesopotamian plague god Namtar or a Canaanite near-equivalent.[63] However, like Rešep, Namtar is a deity, not a demon. We have no good reason to assume that Job is *not* invoking a mythographic image of some kind, but in either case the purpose of this passage is not to authoritatively affirm the existence, identity, and activities of Namtar, or to reveal that he is an evil being opposed to Israel's God.

'Ăbaddôn occurs six times, normally in parallel to terms representing the underworld (Prov 5:11; 27:20; Job 26:6; Ps 88:12). In Job 31:12 it indicates a place, which is identified with Gehenna in the Babylonian Talmud.[64] In Job 28:22 neither [personified] *ăbaddôn* nor [personified] death (*māwet*) know where Wisdom comes from. *Māwet* is a cognate of Mot the name of the Canaanite death god, and so on that basis some interpreters assume that both figures here are deities. However, Hebrew *māwet*

---

62. "Israel need not fear demonic forces, though if it does, Yahweh is greater than them." Goldingay, *Psalms 90–150*, 45.

63. Rüterswörden, "King of Terrors," 487.

64. Hutter, "Abaddon," 1.

is often an impersonal abstraction, so it seems more likely that the usage here is literary personification. Second Temple literature develops the idea of an angel who rules over the abyss or the netherworld (Uriel in *1 En.* 20.2; Eremiel in *Apoc. Zeph.* 6.15; compare perhaps Rev 9:2; 20:1), where evil or malicious angels are restrained (*1 En.* 21.9–10; *Apoc. Zeph.* 6.8, 16–17). Either or both of these ideas might inform the portrayal of Abaddon, now a personal name, in Revelation 9:11 as "king" and as "the angel of the abyss"—that is, either the angel who rules the abyss or the king of the angels imprisoned in the abyss. The Greek name *Apollyon* for the same character is derived from the verb *apollumi*, which means "destroy" and is the semantic equivalent of the Hebrew *'bd*, root of *ăbaddôn*, but which is also associated with the destructive aspect of the Greek god Apollo, who acts as both author and averter of evil.[65] However, the character in Revelation represents a trajectory of interpretation and should not inform the understanding of the Hebrew term in its Old Testament context.

Also personified and demonized in the Second Temple reception is *ăzā'zēl* (Azazel), which occurs only in Leviticus 16:8, 10, and 26, all in the context of the Day of Atonement ritual. In the *Apocalypse of Abraham*, Azazel is the name given to the devil, and in *1 Enoch* he is listed as one of the two hundred watchers. The LXX translation *apopompe* (different from the name *Azael* used in Greek renditions of *1 Enoch*) means "cast out" or "be rid of,"[66] and suggests a possible etymology of *'ēz* + *'zl*, "the goat [that] goes away" (which is the basis of the English *scapegoat*),[67] thus identifying the *animal itself* as *ăzā'zēl*. The rite of the Day of Atonement is cosmetically similar to an elimination ritual, which is a kind of exorcism wherein the demon is transferred into an object which is then destroyed. The combined ideas of Azazel being a demon—specifically, a demon that is transferred into the goat and sent away in an elimination ritual—and Azazel being a goat occasionally leads to the association of either or both with the *śĕ'îrîm*, the "goat demons";[68] *śĕ'îrîm* is the term used for the "goats" used in the ritual in Leviticus 16:8.

Alternatively, because one of the two goats in Leviticus 16:8 is "*for* Yahweh" and the other is "*for* Azazel," later interpreters, including some still today, inferred that *ăzā'zēl* should be read as a divine proper name. However, the ritual in Leviticus does not transfer a demon or deity named Azazel *into* the goat, and does not send a goat or goat-demon named Azazel out of the camp, either; the goat is instead sent away *to* Azazel (Lev 16:10, 26). The *Apocalypse of Abraham* implies that the impurity is transferred (via the goat) from the sanctuary and the people onto Azazel: "The corruption which was on [Abraham] has gone over to [Azazel]" (*Apoc. Abr.* 13.14).[69] The place *1 Enoch* specifies as the location of Azazel's imprisonment (*Dadouel, 1 En.*

65. Hutter, "Abaddon," 1; van den Broek, "Apollo," 75.

66. LSJ, 213.

67. Blair, *De-Demonizing*, 17.

68. Janowski, "Azazel," 129; Blair, *De-Demonising*, 60.

69. Translated by Rubinkiewicz, in *OTP* 1:695.

10:4) is the same place where the scapegoat is banished to in *Targ. Onq.* Lev 16:10, 21,[70] implying a tradition wherein the goat is sent to Azazel's location. However, in elimination rituals the object or animal is not given or sacrificed to a demon or chthonic god; it is simply destroyed. Thus, an alternative interpretation sees *'ăzā'zēl* as referring to the *place* where the goat is sent or killed (for instance, *Targ. Ps-J.* Lev 16:22 claims that the goat will be killed by being blown off a cliff). Topographic regions can be personified (as the sea, for example, frequently is) and it may be that a personified wilderness (or region of the wilderness) is "receiving" the goat. Blair suggests that Azazel represents a personified abstraction of chaos, as the sea also does.[71] Whatever *'ăzā'zēl* originally represented, the text of Leviticus in context does not treat it as a demon of any kind, and later interpretation to that effect does not derive from Leviticus and should not be used as insight into the original meaning of the text. Azazel is never mentioned by name in the New Testament.

Another term that becomes interpreted as a proper name in the Second Temple reception is *bĕliya'al,* which normally occurs in collocation with *bĕnê* (lit. "sons of belial," NIV usually "scoundrels"), an idiomatic expression whose etymology cannot be identified with certainty but which is unquestioningly pejorative. One proposed option is that *bĕliya'al* is the name or title of a chthonic deity; this concept is derived from the phrase "torrents of belial" in Psalm 18:4 and 41:9 (NIV "destruction"), where the word is paralleled to "death" and invokes the imagery of the netherworld.[72] Another option is that the term is an abstraction meaning "uselessness" or "nothingness"[73] (so ESV, where "sons of belial" is translated "worthless men"). Whatever its etymology, the word in the Bible is not a proper name; it has a definite article in 1 Samuel 25:25; 2 Samuel 16:7; and 1 Kings 21:13, and Hebrew does not assign definite articles to proper names. Thus, "what we have here is another example of the Hebrew idiom using *ben,* 'son,' with some term in order to indicate an intimate relationship between the person and the character or activity suggested by the term."[74] Those designated as "sons of belial" are always gross and flagrant violators of social propriety or the covenant order or both; those who encourage idolatry (Deut 13:14); murderous gang rapists (Judg 19:22; 20:13); those who reject and despise the king (1 Sam 10:27; 2 Sam 20:1); false witnesses who condemn an innocent man to death (1 Kgs 21:10, 13; 2 Chr 13:7); and corrupt priests who abuse the sacrifices (1 Sam 2:12). In Job 34:18 the designation "*bĕliya'al*" (by itself) is paralleled to "wicked" (*riša'*), and in Nahum 1:11 "[one] who devises *bĕliya'al* plans" is paralleled to "[one] who plots evil (*ra'*) against the LORD." In Proverbs 6:12 a "troublemaker" (*'ādām bĕliya'al*) "goes about with a

---

70. Nickelsburg, *1 Enoch 1*, 222.

71. Blair, *De-Demonizing*, 62.

72. B. Otzen, "בְּלִיַּעַל *bĕliya'al*," 134.

73. B. Otzen, "בְּלִיַּעַל *bĕliya'al*," 133.

74. B. Otzen, "בְּלִיַּעַל *bĕliya'al*," 133–34. He offers as an example *bĕnê 'awlâ*, "sons of injustice" (e.g., 2 Sam 3:34; 2 Sam 7:10; NIV "wicked [people]").

corrupt mouth"; in Proverbs 16:27 a "scoundrel" (*'iš bĕliya'al*) "plots evil"; and in Proverbs 19:28 "a *bĕliya'al* witness mocks at justice." The condition of *bĕliya'al* therefore represents the antithesis of what is considered good, proper, and desirable. This idea led to the adoption of *Belial* as a proper name to designate the prince of darkness, the leader and patron of those who oppose and stand opposite the covenant order, in the documents of Qumran. The term is used in this sense in 2 Corinthians 6:15, but the Greek name *Belial* does not occur in the LXX.

A mythographic allusion to a demon called a *rabiṣu* is sometimes identified in Genesis 4:7 as the basis for the Hebrew hapax *rōbēṣ* (NIV "crouching"). A *rabiṣu* is a Babylonian demon who ambushes its victims in a variety of more-or-less specific places. The usage in Genesis would be metaphorically comparing the "sin" that is "crouching at [Cain's] door" to an ambushing demon. This is theoretically possible (though the grammar is difficult), but it is important to emphasize that the statement does not say that a *rabiṣu* ("croucher-demon") is waiting to influence Cain to commit murder. *Rabiṣu* harm their victims, they do not entice them to sin.[75] A different mythographic allusion may be found in Ezekiel's vision of seven men who slaughter the people and defile the temple in Ezekiel 9:1–8. In appearance and function they resemble a group of Babylonian chthonic deities called the Sebetti (lit. "the seven"), who in the *Poem of Erra* are dispatched to punish the humans for neglecting the worship of Erra and Marduk, just as the executioners in Ezekiel punish the people for neglecting the worship of Yahweh. The Sebetti are also invoked to witness and enforce treaties, which is significant in the context of Israel's broken covenant.[76] In context, they appear in a vision and are intended to be symbolic; the text is not identifying divine agencies behind Nebuchadnezzar's [future] destruction of the city.

Finally, brief mention should be made of the class II spirits that are not in any way considered demonic by theologians: the *Kĕrûbîm* (Cherubim) and *Sĕrāpîm* (Seraphim). *Kĕrûbîm* are composite creatures that guard sacred space; for example the interiors of the temple and the tabernacle (1 Kgs 6:23–28; Exod 37:7–9), and the way to the tree of life (Gen 3:24). They flank God's throne on the lid of the ark of the covenant (Exod 25:18–22), and they provide the motive power for God's chariot (Ezek 10:3–5). In all of these, the *Kĕrûbîm* are similar to Mesopotamian guardian spirits such as the *šedu*. These composite creatures were originally chaotic but were domesticated by the gods[77] and now serve the basic functions of animals; watchdogs (notably the monster Anzu is one of these; see chapter 9), mounts, or draft animals for chariots. The *Sĕrāpîm* appear only in the throne vision of Isaiah 6 and in Numbers 21:6, where the LORD sends "burning serpents" (*nĕḥāšim śĕrāpîm*, NIV "venomous snakes") to torment the people; the serpents are in turn thwarted by the apotropaic image Nehushtan (Num 21:8–9), which itself become an object of idolatrous devotion before being destroyed

75. Barré, "Rabiṣu," 683.

76. Bodi, "Ezekiel," 423–24.

77. Annus, *Ninurta*, 117–19.

by Hezekiah in 2 Kings 18:4. The same creatures may appear as "Fiery serpents" which are the vicious denizens of the desert in Deuteronomy 8:15 (*nāḥāš śārāp*, NIV "venomous snakes"), or as "flying serpents" (*śārāp mĕʿôpēp*, NIV "darting snakes") in Isaiah 30:6. A political leader is metaphorically described as a "flying serpent" in a judgment oracle in Isaiah 14:29. The composite nature of the *śĕrāpîm* (winged serpents), habitat in the desert, and role in afflicting torment are all consistent with ancient Near Eastern class II spirits, as is their function as Yahweh's domesticated heralds in Isaiah 6. In fact, the *śĕrāpîm* may represent the Hebrew Bible's most explicit depiction of ancient Near Eastern "demons." Ironically, however, neither they nor the *Kĕrûbîm* are ever associated with Satan or the Greek *daimonia* in any way.[78] This in turn indicates that the later identification of demons in the Old Testament is more motivated by theological preference than it is by a close examination of descriptions of the creatures within the text-in-context. We will examine this idea further in chapter 16.

In conclusion, we must note that the most conspicuous feature of "demons" in the Hebrew Bible is their absence. Much of what we know about ancient Near Eastern demons comes from ritual literature. A significant portion of the Pentateuch is composed of Israel's ritual literature, yet none of it concerns exorcisms or other apotropaic rites. There is no mention of how to handle someone afflicted by a demon—not even a directive to send them out of the camp—and no mention of what kinds of sacrifices should be offered to Yahweh to expel a demon. Of course, the Bible is not an anthology of ritual texts; the rituals it contains are intended to define the nature of Israel's covenant order by describing the steps that should be taken to maintain it. Presumably the Israelites would have had apotropaic rituals of some kind—it would be odd if they did not—but their exclusion from the biblical corpus means that keeping the camp free of demons was not an especially important concern for the maintenance of the covenant order; note that higher emphasis is placed on skin diseases and molds than on demons. This stands in sharp contrast to the proposed metanarrative of the conflict theologians wherein battling Satan and his minions is the primary purpose of Yahweh and his covenants in both testaments.

Demons in the Second Temple and early Christian period

Christian demonology, both that expressed in the New Testament and developed beyond it, is not exclusively derived from any other extant tradition, but rather merges conceptions taken primarily from Jewish tradition or Greek philosophy in a haphazard and utilitarian manner. This merging does not represent an attempt to puzzle

---

78. Although Satan was later thought to have once been either a cherub or a seraph, this identification is not derived from the demonic nature of the creatures in context. The idea that the devil began as a cherub is based on Ezek 28:14, which was read as describing the fall of Satan (see chapter 13). The idea that the devil began as a Seraph derives from medieval angelology where the seraphim are the most exalted caste of angels (partly because of their station in God's presence in Isaiah 6), and so the devil (being the highest angel) would have been among them.

together a uniquely Christian demonology, because there is little to no systematic coherence between interpreters (though there are occasionally identifiable trends) as each selects different elements to suit their individual purposes. Further, many of these interpretations are borrowed and embellished outside of the Christian community; some of these ideas are later adopted by the Christians themselves, others are rejected along with the original ideas (once advocated by Christians) that inspired them. The final result is that there *is* no "uniquely Christian demonology." We will therefore summarize a selection of conceptions of demons from the first three centuries of the Common Era. Although of course only those of the first century or earlier could be seen as having actual reflection in the text of the New Testament, the later development of those ideas is important for demonstrating the extent to which our modern conception of demons is owed to sources other than the Bible.

Most of the writings of the early Christian era reflect ideas previously expressed in the works of Plato (c. 420–340 BCE) or in the Jewish apocryphal, pseudepigrapic, or apocalyptic literature, such as are preserved in the Dead Sea Scrolls (c. 200–100 BCE). These works represent the cognitive environment of the Second Temple period and therefore influence the New Testament as well. Plato wrote that demons (*daimones*) were bestowed upon individuals as a rational soul,[79] and Socrates famously claimed to be guided by one. Plato also wrote that "demons" were intermediaries between gods and humanity, carrying sacrifices and petitions upward and ordinances downward, and likewise facilitating religious rituals, divinations, and sorcery.[80] These beings were to be worshiped by wise men, though only after offering proper honors to the higher gods,[81] and a human could ascend to demonhood upon death.[82] The Dead Sea Scrolls describe a spirit of deceit placed within humans under the rule of an angel of darkness (see chapter 9), and this angel leads them into sin and grief,[83] while provoking a long list of nefarious traits.[84] The book of *Jubilees* describes a class of angels who were sent down to earth to instruct righteousness but instead produced evil offspring with human women,[85] and the Book of the Watchers (see chapter 9) has the angels descend of their own accord with similar results, including the instruction in astrology, magic, and divination.[86] All these writings contain most of the basic elements that will be elaborated and combined by the writers of the first three centuries CE, including the authors of the New Testament.

79. Gersh, *Middle Platonism*, 1.235. cf. Plato, *Timaeus*.

80. Plato, *Symposium* 202e.

81. Plato, *Laws* 717.

82. Gersh, *Middle Platonism* 1.235, cf. Plato, *Cratylus*. The *Testament of Solomon* also describes a demon who had once been a man (*T. Sol.* 10.2).

83. 1QS 3.18–24, cf. 1QM 13.11–12.

84. 1QS 4.9–13.

85. *Jub.* 4.15; 5.1–2.

86. *1 En.* 6.1–6; 9.10.

The range of opinions on what demons are and where they come from falls into three loose categories. The first is that they were created deliberately. The second is that they were the offspring, transformation, corruption, or ascension of other created beings. The third is that they are a component of the human soul, either living or dead. When external, demons are normally associated with the realm of air, which also associates them with the spirit; the Greek word *pneuma* and the Hebrew word *rûaḥ* can both mean either "air" or "spirit." Philo (20 BCE–50 CE), echoing Plato, argues that "demon" is the general name for a class of creatures that also includes angels, and implies that they, as incorporeal souls, naturally abide in the realm of air.[87] In the next century, the middle Platonist Apuleius (c. 120–180) writes of a class of demons possessing an aerial body.[88] Iamblichus (c. 245–325), also following Plato, writes of demons as a class of supernatural beings, together with angels, archangels, archons, and heroes, all being emanations of the gods.[89] In the Talmud, demons are incorporeal because they were created on the eve of the Sabbath and God did not have time to make bodies for them.[90] The same tractate places demons halfway between man and angels, having some properties of both.[91] Another part of the Talmud indicates that "God . . . combines in himself the powers of the angels and of the invisible demons."[92] In contrast, most of the Christian writers follow Enoch and affirm that demons are either the offspring of the fallen angels[93] or the fallen angels themselves.[94] Some of the rabbinic writers also take this view,[95] though others say that the demons were the descendants of Adam and Lilith,[96] or of the builders of the tower of Babel, along with apes and water-spirits.[97] Aristides and some rabbis associate demons with water instead of air.[98] Josephus (c. 37–100) wrote that demons were the souls of the dead;[99] Justin Martyr (c. 100–165) implied that demoniacs were inspired by dead souls;[100] and Apuleius recognized a

87. Philo, *de Gigantibus* 2.

88. Gersh, *Middle Platonism*, 1:310.

89. Iamblichus, *De Mysteriis* 2.1

90. Ginzberg, *Legends of the Jews*, 1:83. cf. *Tanhuma* 1, 12.

91. Ginzberg, *Legends*, 5:108. cf *Tanhuma* 1, 12.

92. Ginzberg, *Legends*, 3:377. cf. Gittin 68b.

93. See for example Justin Martyr, 2 *Apology* 5.

94. See for example Minucius Felix, *Octavius* 27.

95. Ginzberg, *Legends*, 5:154. cf. *Midrash Bereshit Rabbah* 27.7.

96. Ginzberg, *Legends*, 1.118. cf. *Tanhuma* 1, 20.

97. Ginzberg, *Legends*, 5:204. cf. *Midrash Aggada*.

98. Aristides, *Apologia* 4; Ginzberg, Legends 5:87. cf. *Alphabet of Ben-Sira* 23a–23b; 33a–33b; *Pesahin* 112a.

99. Josephus, *Jewish War* 7.185.

100. Justin Martyr, 1 *Apology* 18.

class of demons as embodied souls and another as departed souls.[101] The *Testament of Solomon* also describes a demon who had once been a man.[102]

Demons are usually considered to be invisible, although in the Talmud they can assume any form they desire.[103] For Apuleius, demons are "visible to nobody," but can "reveal themselves as 'a kind of voice, although not the usual or human kind' or using 'a sign which is the apparition of the demon itself.'"[104] For Iamblichus, they can manifest themselves in visions as frightening forms accompanied by tumult and disorder.[105] The particulars of its manifestation can also determine its nature; whether it is good, or an agent of punishment, or a being of malice.[106] Sometimes demons manifest by possession and indicate their presence by the mania of the demoniac, as Eusebius claims of Montanus.[107] Similarly, demons that compose or indwell a soul manifest their presence by the behaviors they instigate, as is seen in the spirits of light and darkness at Qumran (see chapter 9).

"Demons" are identified not only by what they are made out of (usually air) but also by their activity. One of their most common functions is the facilitation of the Roman cult system. Plato, as mentioned previously, had already affirmed this in 300 BCE, and his position is repeated by Plutarch in the first century CE.[108] Apuleius says that demons "preside over all revelations, various magical phenomena, and all kinds of prophecy";[109] Iamblichus speaks of demons conveying oracles;[110] and even Porphyry (c. 234–305) acknowledges that the theurgists he ridicules are in communication with "fraudulent" demons, as opposed to the gods or "good" demons that they claim contact with.[111] Both Minucius Felix (an early Christian apologist, d. 250) and the Platonic philosopher Plutarch (c. 46–120) engage the question of why the divinations and oracles of Greece and Rome are not functioning as well as they were averred to have done in the past. Minucius claims that the demons "have their lurking places under statues and consecrated images,"[112] while Plutarch agrees that "demons are the guardians of sacred rites of the gods and prompters of the mysteries."[113] Minucius argues that the oracles do not come true because the demons have no knowledge to offer: "they are

---

101. Gersh, *Middle Platonism* 1.233.

102. *T. Sol.* 10.2.

103. Ginzberg, *Legends*, 5:108; cf. note 16. Cf. *Tanhuma* 1, 12.

104. Gersh, *Middle Platonism*, 1:311.

105. Iamblichus, *De Mysteriis* 2.3.

106. Iamblichus, *De Mysteriis* 2.7.

107. Eusebius, *Ecclesiastical History* 5.16.

108. Plutarch, *Isis and Osiris* 361C.

109. Gersh, *Middle Platonism*, 1:310.

110. Iamblichus, *De Mysteriis* 2.10.

111. Porphyry, *Epistle to Anebo*.

112. Minucius Felix, *Octavius* 27.

113. Plutarch, *De Defectu Oracularum* 417A, trans. Babbitt, in LCL 306:389.

both deceived, and they deceive; inasmuch as they are both ignorant of the simple truth, and for their own ruin they confess not that which they know."[114] Plutarch, on the other hand, considers several possibilities but ultimately concludes that the demons had either gone away, diminished in power, or died.[115] Even Minucius' assertion that all the gods worshiped by the Romans are actually demons[116]—a common argument in Christian writings[117]—is echoed by Plutarch when he claims that "the various tales . . . of the gods, their concealments and banishment and servitude, which men rehearse in legend and song, all these are, in fact, not things that were done to the gods or happened to them, but to the demons."[118] The same question is still tossed about a century after Minucius Felix; Porphyry argues that the diviners are deceived by fraudulent demons, and Iamblichus responds by ascribing the problems to errors in theurgical practice because demons are inspired by the gods and cannot deceive,[119] although later he acknowledges a type of corrupt demon that can interfere with the divination process and is recognized by the error that results.[120]

The demotion of the traditional Greco-Roman pantheon from gods to demons (on account of depictions of their behavior in their own mythology) sometimes produced a charge of atheism against the Christians: as Justin Martyr recounts, "we deny that those who did such things as these are gods, but state that they are wicked and impious demons . . . , hence we are called atheists."[121] A similar charge was leveled against Socrates, and so Justin aligns himself with Socrates (and, implicitly, the "demon" whose guidance Socrates claimed) against the demonically-inspired unreason of his accusers: "when Socrates endeavored, by true reason and examination, to bring these things to light, and deliver men from the demons, then the demons themselves, by means of men who rejoiced in iniquity, compassed his death, as an atheist and a profane person, on the charge that he was introducing new divinities; and in our case they display a similar activity."[122] Minucius Felix, on the other hand, condemns Socrates, who was guided by a demon but still did not possess wisdom: "let Socrates the Athenian buffoon see to it, confessing that he knew nothing, although boastful in the testimony of a most deceitful demon."[123] Thus we see that various Christian perspectives on demons sometimes agree with those of non-Christians, and also sometimes disagree with each

---

114. Minucius Felix, *Octavius* 27, trans. A. Cleveland Coxe, in *ANF Fathers of the Third Century* in The Ante-Nicene Fathers, edited by Alexander Roberts and James Donaldson, 190.

115. Plutarch, *De Defectu Oracularum* 420A–C; 438D.

116. Minucius Felix, *Octavius* 27.

117. See for example Justin Martyr, *2 Apology* 5.

118. Plutarch, *De Defectu Oracularum* 417E, trans. Babbitt, in LCL 306:393.

119. Iamblichus, *De Mysteriis* 2.10.

120. Iamblichus, *De Mysteriis* 4.7.

121. Justin Martyr, *1 Apology* 5–6, trans. Coxe, in *ANF* 1:164.

122. Justin Martyr, *1 Apology* 5, trans. Coxe, in *ANF* 1:164.

123. Minucius Felix, *Octavius* 38, trans. Coxe, in *ANF* 4:197.

other. The deceit of demons is also mentioned by Iamblichus, who writes of wicked demons which appear as good demons in order to deceive a just worshiper,[124] and Philo's evil angels "cloak themselves under the name of angels."[125]

The most consistent attribute of demons is their distinctness from the "true" gods, whether that distinction is made in terms of nature, or behavior, or both. Justin Martyr builds the case that demons oppose reason and inhibit virtue, arguing that the demons "demand sacrifices and service from people who live irrationally"[126] and will "divert [the Roman persecutors] from reading and understanding what [Christians] say."[127] Philo describes the "evil angels" as those who pursued sensory pleasures instead of "reason, the sciences, and virtues."[128] Iamblichus writes that demons draw down the soul towards nature[129] and thus impede them from being able to escape the realm of sense perception and fate.[130] Plutarch describes demons who take pleasure in suffering.[131] The gnostic *Apocryphon of John* describes the demons as responsible for, among other things, envy, jealousy, distress, trouble, pain, callousness, anxiety, mourning, empty pride, anger, wrath, bitterness, agony, and shame.[132] Christian writers add idolatry[133] and heresy to this list, including statements that demons inspired Marcion[134] and Montanus.[135] The *Shepherd of Hermas* associates similar activities with an evil angel using language similar to that employed by the Dead Sea Scrolls.[136]

The demons in the Talmud sometimes prefer to slay their victims rather than deceiving or corrupting them. This is similar to the role they play in the ancient Near East, and they are likewise still associated with magic. It is notable that, while demons are the originators of sorcery,[137] they can still be opposed by magic. Justin Martyr scoffed at Jewish mysticism,[138] but some Christians apparently appreciated it, as demonstrated by the *Testament of Solomon*, a Jewish demonology with Christian overtones that describes the magical binding of a host of demons by Solomon to help him build the temple.[139] Solomon's traditional mastery of demons was notorious enough to be also

124. Iamblichus, *De Mysteriis* 4.7.

125. Philo, *De Gigantibus* 4, trans. Colson in LCL 227:455.

126. Justin Martyr, *1 Apology* 12, trans. Coxe, in *ANF* 1:166.

127. Justin Martyr, *1 Apology* 14, trans. Coxe, in *ANF* 1:167.

128. Philo, *De Gigantibus* 4, trans. Colson in LCL 227:455.

129. Iamblichus, *De Mysteriis* 2.4.

130. Iamblichus, *De Mysteriis* 2.6.

131. Plutarch, *Isis and Osiris* 361B.

132. *Apocryphon of John* 18.24–30.

133. See for example *Epistle of Barnabas* 16.7.

134. Justin Martyr, *1 Apology* 58.

135. Eusebius, *Ecclesiastical History* 5.16.

136. *Shepherd* mandate 6; cf. *Epistle of Barnabas* 18.1–2; *Didache* 1.1.

137. Ginsberg, *Legends*, 5:154. cf. *Aggadat Bereshit*.

138. Justin Martyr, *Dialogue with Trypho* 85.

139. Ginsberg, *Legends*, 6.292.

affirmed by Josephus.[140] In the Midrash, demons likewise "assist" in God's purposes by preventing Moses from entering the tabernacle while the cloud is on it.[141] Similarly, after the deluge, the demons continued to harass the descendants of Noah "with pain and all sorts of suffering leading to physical and spiritual death" until the angel Raphael drove away nine-tenths of them, the remainder being left to punish sinners.[142] The role of demons as agents of punishment is found in the Platonists as well. Apuleius describes demons as "an object of terror to evil men"[143] and Plutarch says that some demons "go about as avengers of arrogant and grievous cases of injustice."[144] Christians more commonly depict demons as being on the receiving end of punishment,[145] but this perspective is found in the Platonists as well; Plutarch allows that demons "must pay the penalty for the sins they commit and the duties they neglect," though afterwards they will be restored to their proper station.[146] Similarly, Apuleius tells of demons who "wander erratically" as punishment for their sins, although in his case there is no distinction between this class of demon and a deceased human, since *demon* is the name given to the soul.[147] Some demons are also considered to serve as guardians, much as some modern Christians conceive of guardian angels. Plotinus (c. 204–270) writes an entire essay on the diverse nature of these spirits.[148] Porphyry disdainfully describes a belief wherein demons of various kinds are assigned over the various components of the body, intellect, and soul.[149] Apuleius has demons who are "'guardians assigned to individual men during their lifetime,' coming to our aid when we require 'not council but revelation.'"[150] These demons also serve the role of the psychopomp, escorting the departed soul to its final destination.[151]

The purpose of this survey is not to identify all of the references to demons in early literature. Rather, it is to demonstrate that there is *no unified, monolithic Christian doctrine of demons that either follows a single pre-existent strain or sets itself apart distinctly from all others.* It is also worth noting that the Christian writers do not necessarily appeal to the Bible. In order to argue that the Roman gods are demons, for example, both Minucius Felix and Justin Martyr appeal to the teachings of magicians and philosophers (especially Plato), but neither mentions St. Paul and 1 Corinthians

140. Josephus, *Antiquities* 8.45–46.

141. Ginsberg, *Legends*, 3:210. cf. *Num. Rab.* 14.19.

142. Ginsberg, *Legends*, 1:173. cf. *Sefer Noah.*

143. Gersh, *Middle Platonism* 1.313.

144. Plutarch, *De Defectu Oracularum* 417B, trans. Babbitt, in LCL 306:389.

145. See for example Justin Martyr, *1 Apology* 52.

146. Plutarch, *Isis and Osiris* 361C, trans. Babbitt, in LCL 306:65.

147. Gersh, *Middle Platonism*, 1:313–14.

148. Plotinus, *On Our Guardian Spirit.*

149. Porphyry, *Epistle to Anebo.*

150. Gersh, *Middle Platonism*, 1:312.

151. Gersh, *Middle Platonism*, 1:312.

10:20. Most of the categories described here can also be found in the New Testament, where they are referenced in similar ways; that is, some particular aspect of the general profile is emphasized according to the author's purpose. We will examine these in more detail below and in chapters 11 and 14.

Terms for demons in the Greek New Testament

The Greek word for demon is either *daimon* or *daimonion*; the latter is the preferred term in the New Testament and the Septuagint. Some scholars argue that the distinction is technical and that *daimon* refers to the semidivine intermediate beings of Platonic cosmology while *daimonion* refers to evil spirits allied with Satan.[152] However, this proposal is mostly circular and cannot be demonstrated consistently; Matthew 8:31 uses the term *daimon* where the parallel passage in Luke 8:27 uses *daimonion*, and the LXX of Isaiah 65:11 uses *daimon* to render the name of a deity (Heb. *gad*, NIV "fortune") but states elsewhere that "the gods of the nations are *daimonion*" (LXX Ps 96:5). The term *daimonion* is also used in the neutral Middle-Platonic sense in Acts 17:18 (NIV "foreign gods"). *Daimonion* is Plato's term for the inspiring demon of Socrates,[153] and is also the term he uses for the intermediate divine agencies.[154] It is likely that the Middle-Platonic divine intermediaries (who more or less parallel the functions of the ancient Greek and Near Eastern class I pantheons) would have been seen as somehow distinct from the tormenting and possessing spirits (who more or less parallel the functions of the ancient Near Eastern class II "demons"), but that distinction does not appear to be emphasized by a technical use of *daimon* versus *daimonion*, at least not at the time of the New Testament. The Greek term for a specifically evil or malicious spirit is *kakodaimon*,[155] which does not appear in the Greek Bible.

Other terms used in parallel with *daimonion* are *pneuma akartharton* ("impure spirit") and *pneuma poneron* ("evil spirit"). *Akathartos* is used by the LXX to translate *ṭāmē'*, the same term used to designate unclean animals (also, e.g., Acts 10:14). "Unclean" is a ritual category, not a moral category; the spirit-creature itself is unclean, like a pig, and the person afflicted by one is also unclean, like a person with a skin disease. Uncleanliness is an undesirable state, but most of the elements that cause it (corpses, molds, diseases, menstrual blood) are morally neutral. This designation is consistent with the conception of demons as the cause of disease. *Poneros*, on the other hand, can indicate a moral category. However, like the Hebrew *ra'* (which it translates in the LXX) or the English "bad" (the semantic equivalent), it does not necessarily do so;[156]

---

152. See for example Riley, "Demon," 238.

153. *Apology* 24b, 40a.

154. *Symposium* 202e.

155. LSJ, 861.

156. Kelly, *Satan in the Bible*, 64. For *ra'* attributed to Yahweh, see Walton and Walton, *Lost World*

a *bad man* is immoral, but *bad luck* or a *bad smell* is not. The English translation *evil* is misleading because in modern English the term "evil" designates specifically moral badness. In archaic English (i.e., the KJV), "evil" simply indicates a superlative state of "bad" and has a similar semantic range; *poneros* likewise indicates a superlative state of the badness represented by the Greek *kakos*. Yahweh can bring about *poneros* in LXX Joshua 23:15, and the *pneuma poneron* that afflicts Saul in LXX 1 Samuel 16 is still "from the LORD." Nonetheless, due to the influence of the cognitive environment, especially the ideology represented at Qumran, it is likely that *pneuma poneron* and the related title *ho poneros*, "the evil one" (e.g., Matt 13:19) are indeed intended to reflect a kind of moral character. However, in that same tradition the prince of darkness and his angels are established by God to do what they do, which we also see in the case of the affliction of Saul; they are not enemies that oppose the will of God (see further discussion in chapter 9). The point is that neither "impure spirit" nor "evil spirit" should be read to mean "immoral spirit standing as an enemy of God."

The NIV "devil" is a derivative transliteration of Greek *diabolos*, meaning "slanderer." In the LXX it translates the Hebrew title *śāṭān* (lit. "accuser, adversary") in Job 1:7–12; 2:1–6; Zechariah 3:1–3; and Psalm 109:6; and in the New Testament is used interchangeably with *Satanas,* the Greek transliteration of the same word, which does not occur in the LXX[157] and in the New Testament is used exclusively as a proper name. The LXX also uses the term *diabolos* as a designation for Haman in Esther 8:1 (Heb. *ṣôrēr*, NIV 'enemy"), and the term refers to "slander" or "gossip," or those who engage in it, in LXX Esther 7:4 (NIV "distress"), 1 Timothy 3:11 ("malicious talkers"), and Titus 2:3 ("slanderers"). For further discussion of Satan see chapter 13; for other titles that may or may not also refer to this character see chapter 14.

Finally, Acts 16:16 mentions a *pneuma pythonos* (NIV "spirit by which she predicted the future") which enables the girl it inhabits to practice "fortune telling" (*manteumene*). The classification of the spirit and the divination it facilitates are references to the *Pythia*, the oracular priestess of the shrine of Apollo at Delphi. *Python* was the name of the dragon-serpent who was slain by Apollo when the latter assumed control of the shrine.[158] In Acts, the spirit functions as a herald, proclaiming Paul and his companions to be "servants of the Most High God" (Acts 16:17). After "many days" of this, Paul finally loses patience and exorcises the spirit; the account in context is presented as an explanation of why Paul and Silas were [unjustly] put in jail (Acts 16:19–21, 35–40). However, the spirit's behavior and Paul's response have presented some confusion to interpreters. Clearly Paul is not interested in healing the girl for

---

of the Israelite Conquest, 153–54.

157. The variant *satan* is used in LXX 1 Kgs 11:14, 23 in reference to Hadad and Rezon. Aquila and Symmachus both use it in Num 22:22 in reference to the angel of the Lord (LXX *endiaballein*); 1 Sam 29:4 in reference to David (LXX *epiboulos*); and Zech 3:1 (LXX *diabolos*). LXX *epiboulos* also used for Heb *śāṭān* in 2 Sam 19:22 in reference to Abishai and in 1 Kgs 5:4 (LXX 5:18) in reference to generic enemies.

158. van Henten, "Python," 670.

her own sake or "delivering her from the bondage of Satan" (cf. Luke 13:16); he simply wants her to go away. The spirit itself is not aggressively confronting the apostles (cf. Luke 4:33–34), nor is it harming the girl (cf. Luke 8:29), nor is it responsible for the hostility of the crowds against Paul, nor is it even *lying*. Some scholars suggest that Paul is annoyed to hear the gospel proclaimed by a [supposed] demon, while others assume that the proclamation must have had a tone of sarcasm or mockery. However, if either of these were the case, calling the creature an *evil spirit* would have better communicated this idea. Therefore, we should ask if the reason might not have something to do with what the *python* specifically is.

The oracle at Delphi was a respected source of divination in Greek tradition, but by the first century the shrine had badly declined. In *The Obsolescence of Oracles*, Plutarch and his interlocutors note that "[the Delphic shrine] used to employ two prophetic priestesses . . . and a third was appointed to be held in reserve. But today there is one priestess and we do not complain, for she meets every need."[159] They then proceed to debate the reasons why. In the course of the dialogue they determine that the oracles are overseen not by the gods but by demigods (*daimones*):

> certainly it is foolish . . . to imagine that the god himself after the manner of
> the ventriloquists (who . . . [are now called] "Pythones") enters into the bodies
> of his prophets and prompts their utterances. . . . For if [the god] allows him-
> self to become entangled in men's needs he is prodigal with his majesty and he
> does not observe the dignity and greatness of his preeminence.[160]

They conclude by attributing the decline of the oracles to a waning of the power of the demigods[161] or perhaps to their abandonment of the shrines or even to their death.[162] The "ventriloquist" (*eggastrimithos*) they mention is what the girl in Acts 16 is; these were thought to speak via a spirit (god or demigod) in their stomach, which is what the *pneuma pythonos* is.[163] The spirit is not affecting her mind or manipulating her actions; it is sitting inside her body and speaking through her mouth. Thus, the fortune-teller is not "possessed" in the typical sense, which is why the term "demon-possessed" (*daimonizomai*) is not used to describe her condition. But the debate shows that the idea of mantic divination being facilitated by a *daimon* of some kind is not unique to Paul (the character) or Luke (the author).

Minucius Felix, weighing in on the same issue a century later, writes that "[the] cautious and ambiguous oracle of [Apollo], failed just at the time when men began to be at once more cultivated and less credulous."[164] He correlates this failure with "[the

---

159. Plutarch, *De Defectu Oracularum* 414B, trans. Babbitt, in LCL 306:375.

160. *De Defectu Oracularum* 414E, trans. Babbit, in LCL 306:377.

161. *De Defectu Oracularum* 438d.

162. *De Defectu Oracularum* 418–21.

163. For discussion see Keener, *Acts*, 3:2424–26. The spirit impregnated her with the message.

164. *Octavius* 26, trans. Coxe, in *ANF* 4:189.

time] Apollo had already ceased to make verses," a phenomenon that is also discussed by Plutarch in *The Oracles at Delphi*. The occasion for Plutarch's debate is the observation that "the prophetic priestess [has ceased] to give her oracles in epic verse or in other metres . . . ; this fact above all else militates against confidence in the oracle, since people assume one of two things: either that the prophetic priestess does not [make contact with the god], or else that the spirit has been completely quenched and her powers have forsaken her."[165] The nature of the objection seems to be that the ability of the Pythia to deliver oracles in elevated speech is evidence of the presence of the god;[166] Minucius Felix's ability to make the same accusation a century later indicates that the decline of the oracle was indeed a widely recognized phenomenon. Yet at the same time, the fortune-teller in Philippi is making a substantial amount of money (Acts 16:16). If the "cultivated" are no longer interested in oracles, then the people paying the fortune-teller are the "credulous"; she probably would have had the same kind of reputation that an astrologer or "phone psychic" would have today. However, the people who take her seriously are also the people most likely to respond to her promotion; that is, superstitious rubberneckers interested in a show and maybe a free lunch, the same kinds of people who constituted the "crowds" that Jesus was always trying to avoid. The fortune-teller's promotion is effectively turning Paul's ministry into a farce; we might imagine what would happen if Miss Cleo took it upon herself to loudly promote an event at your church.[167] This in turn is not helping Paul spread the gospel. The issue is not the *python* per se—which explains why he tolerates it for so long—but rather the environment that its promotion is creating due to how it is perceived by the Philippian audience.

All of the references to the various kinds of demons and spirits in both testaments depict them in ways that are entirely consistent with their portrayal in the broader culture. Additionally, the portrayal of demons in the Old Testament has less in common with that of the New Testament than either of them have with the cultures in which they are embedded. Further still, neither of those portrayals has much in common with what we think of when we use the word "demon" today. Importantly, the most notable feature of demons in both the ancient Near East and in the Greco-Roman world is not the quality of *evil*, which is the feature that we are most inclined to associate with them. Rather, their most notable quality is that they are distinct from the gods, and the distinction is emphasized even when they serve as the agents or extensions of the gods. Consequently, in order to fully appreciate what a "demon" is, it

165. *De Pythiae Oraculis* 402B, trans. Babbitt, in LCL 306:303.

166. Plutarch's dialogue consists mostly of demonstrations that it is not unseemly for the gods to speak in prose, and his ultimate conclusion is that the deliverance of the oracles in prose enhances their clarity and thus protects against charlatans who exploit the ambiguity of verse (*De Pythiae Oraculis* 406–7).

167. Miss Cleo was a TV psychic who was spokesperson for a psychic pay-per-call service from 1997–2003.

is also necessary to discuss what a *god* is, and what it means to be different from one. That is what we will examine in the next chapter.

Chapter 8

Demons should be defined relative
to a culture's conception of gods

FROM THE SURVEY IN the previous chapter, we can see that the conception of "demons" is remarkably diverse. Most notably, we observe a significant difference in this conception between the cognitive environments of the two testaments. This observation alone means that proposing a monolithic "biblical presentation of demons" cannot be accomplished without subverting one of the testaments and subordinating its conceptual categories to the other. Most Christian interpreters choose to subvert the Old Testament with the New, but this approach demonstrates a lamentable disregard for the value of the Old Testament's message in its own context and therefore to its status as the inspired word of God with a message to convey. Further, the misinterpretation of Old Testament teachings by the anachronistic imposition of New Testament ideas and concepts has the potential to result in theological conclusions that are inaccurate, theologically problematic, or even outright dangerous, as, for example, when the conquest of Canaan is read as advocating the extermination of non-Christian religions because they are demonically empowered and therefore opposed to God. Consequently, if we want to talk about demons systematically, we have to first identify an overarching category of *what a demon is* that fits in all three contexts (ancient, classical, modern) where we wish to discuss them. As mentioned briefly above, we propose that demons are best conceived of as *"cosmic or spirit beings that are not gods,"* but we now give brief attention to some common alternatives.

The first common definition of demons is that they represent a personification of an abstract conception of evil. According to this theory, a culture's mythology is a projection of its psychology, and this psychology is thought to be universal to all humanity. Thus, in this conception, "demons" can be understood by examining all cultures to see what they think "evil" is and how it is personified in their mythology; using that information to form a composite profile; and then reading that composite profile back into every appearance of "demons" in any of those contexts.[1] This approach is problematic on several grounds. First, it assumes a monolithic human perception of evil that is always defined and always personified in more or less the same

1. See for example Russell, *Devil*, 17–54.

way. So, for example, Russell begins by defining evil as "pain,"[2] which is expected from a twentieth-century humanist but would probably not be affirmed by, for example, a stylite monk. Augustine addresses the issue in *City of God*:

> I see I must now speak of those evils which alone are dreaded by the hea-then—famine, pestilence, war, pillage, captivity, massacre, and the like calami-ties . . . . For evil men account those things alone evil which do not make men evil; neither do they blush to praise good things, and yet to remain evil among the good things they praise. It grieves them more to own a bad house than a bad life, as if it were man's greatest good to have everything good but himself.[3]

Where Russell defines evil as something that people *experience* (pain), Augustine defines it as something that people *do* (vice). Which definition is correct is not the point; the point is that they are different, and both are different from the conception of evil as *disorder* that is found in the ancient Near East. This means that Russell's personi-fied (inflictor of) pain, Augustine's personified (inciter to) vice, and Israel's personified (instigator of) disorder cannot be conflated into a single composite profile without badly distorting all three of them. The result is that both the [hypothetical] composite profile of the demons and the subsequent deconstruction of each culture's [supposed] expression of that profile is essentially arbitrary, consisting (usually) of what the an-thropologist happens to dislike or (at worst) what the anthropologist fancies that the primitive and unsophisticated cultures would have probably disliked. A study of what the various cultures actually dislike in their own terms, on the other hand, does not lead to anything that can be universally applied to all of them.

A second common definition of demons is taxonomic, used today when we de-scribe them as "fallen angels." This approach essentially attempts to identify demons phenomenologically, in the same way we would identify, say, lions or bears. Various cultures might identify a lion in various ways—a heraldic emblem; a totem spirit; a guardian to be revered; an enemy to be feared; an aspect of a god; a manifestation of a demon; a trophy to mount on a wall; a rug *in potentia*—but nonetheless they all refer to the same animal. Some scholars see "demons" the same way, and try to understand them by compiling characteristics of anything that any culture calls a "demon," or anything cosmetically similar to something that some culture calls a "demon," into a single profile. The problem with this approach is that, once again, it is somewhat circular. Without a fixed definition of "demon," it is not possible to know whether any individual creature counts as one; however, without knowing which creatures count as "demons," it is not possible to establish a definition of the category. Most interpreters therefore select the prototypical "demon" somewhat arbitrarily—usually, for our purposes, the possessing spirits in the New Testament designated by the word *daimonion*—and then try to identify other creatures as the same kind of entity either

2. Russell, *Devil*, 17.

3. Augustine, *City of God* 3.1, trans. Dods, in *NPNF* 2.43.

by correlating behavior (the *rûaḥ ra'* in 1 Samuel 16); or by contextual association (the demonized woman "bound by Satan"; Satan as the "prince of demons"); or by the use of the word *daimonion*, both in the LXX (the gods of the nations, the *šēdîm*) and elsewhere (the demon of Socrates). Each of these associations is used to further expand the category; so for example the LXX of Psalm 96:5 is used to argue that the gods of foreign religions are same taxon of entities ("fallen angels") as those who afflict the demoniacs. This composite profile is then employed to project characteristics from any of those creatures onto any of the others, with no regard, and occasionally in direct contradiction to, the way that the creature is portrayed in context. From a metaphysical perspective, however, defining a category requires more than circumstantial association. Claiming that the gods of the nations are the same kinds of beings as the possessing spirits of the Gospels simply because the Greek Bible calls both of them *daimonion* is like claiming that the national animal of Scotland is the rhinoceros because someone at some point used the term *unicorn* to describe both a rhinoceros and a mythical horned equid. In order to define a category meaningfully, all of the members of the category must have some quality common to all of them and distinct from all others.[4] When examined in context, however, there is no universal overlap between all of the creatures who are variously asserted to be "fallen angels" (see full discussion in chapters 11, 12).

Consequently, we propose that demons as a category should not be regarded in terms of their nature (personified evil) or their taxonomy (fallen angels), but rather in terms of the *function* they are given in a particular cosmological system. In a system that contains both gods and demons, the demons are assigned responsibility for anything that cannot be attributed to the gods, for whatever reason. This means that the paradigm shift that occurs between the testaments does not reflect a change in the conception of demons, but rather a change in the conception of gods. Nonetheless, the role of demons as filling the gaps in the cosmology left empty by the conception of gods remains consistent. We will now explore this concept in more detail.

Gods in the ancient Near East and Israel

Gods in the ancient world are the creators and sustainers of the cosmic order. Their role in the great symbiosis (see chapter 7) is directly related to this function. By keeping the gods happy by caring for their needs, the people hoped to retain the gods' favor and thereby enjoy the benefits of the order the gods produced in return. The gods demand morality and justice in the human world because these are conducive to a stable and well-functioning society that will therefore be able to meet

---

4. The technical question of whether that quality exists as a form that the observer recognizes ("that thing possesses the quality of demon-ness") or whether the quality is created by the observer ("'demon' is the word we use for a thing with properties X, Y, and not Z") does not matter for this purpose; in either case the common quality must *be there*.

the needs of the gods effectively, but the gods themselves are neither moral nor just. They are amoral and inscrutable, often petty or arbitrary in the way they take offense. They do not have an essential character that humans are expected to imitate, and humans are not supposed to imitate their functions, either. When the ancients say that the gods are good, they are expressing a hope that the gods will *do* good *for* them. They do not mean that the gods teach humans how to be good or that humans should be good as the gods are good.

Israel's theology differs somewhat from the conventions of the ancient Near East, but those theological innovations do not set up a contrast between a moral God and immoral demons. In the Old Testament, Yahweh is described as a "god" (*'ĕlôhîm*) and therefore would have been likewise understood as inscrutable, inimitable, and operating outside of the limitations and relative nature of human moral systems. Israel's theological innovations come primarily by way of the covenant. Israel's covenant takes the form of a treaty between a vassal and a suzerain.[5] Through the covenant, Yahweh takes on the dual role of an ancient Near Eastern god and an ancient Near Eastern emperor. Serving in the role of the king, he is more directly responsible for Israel's social order and thus is less inscrutable and arbitrary than gods would normally be. However, the role of the king does not entail teaching the subjects how to be good or serving as an example for the subjects to imitate.

The giving of the Torah should not be seen as moral instruction, and the stipulations of the covenant should not be seen as the first principles of a system of applied ethics. Kings would produce documents in the genre of "legal wisdom," which is also the genre of the Torah, in order to establish their legacy as wise and just rulers to the readers of the documents; normally future kings or the gods. The wisdom of the king was also intended to instruct the judges and magistrates to whom authority was delegated so that they could wisely administer justice, somewhat comparable to the way case law is used by lawyers today. However, unlike case law, the statements of legal wisdom do not represent actual sample verdicts. Rather, they represent the kinds of rulings that an ideal judge would make in a variety of circumstances—some practical, some purely hypothetical, and some intentionally absurd. The purpose is to teach judges the underlying principles that they should employ when deciding their own cases.[6] In Israel's case, the most notable magistrate is the human king, who effectively serves as a regent appointed over Yahweh's vassal state. This is what it means that "[the king] is to write for himself on a scroll a copy of this law. . . . It is to be with him, and he is to read it all the days of his life so that he may learn to revere the LORD his God and follow carefully all the words of this law and these decrees" (Deut 17:18–19). The Torah

5. For the most thorough treatment, see the three-volume work of Kitchen and Lawrence, *Treaty, Law and Covenant*.

6. LeFebvre, *Collections*; Jackson, *Wisdom-Laws*; Hayes, *What's Divine?*; Bottéro, "'Code' of Hammurabi"; Van de Mieroop, *Philosophy before the Greeks*, 143–81; Westbrook, *History of Ancient Near Eastern Law*; Walton, *Old Testament*.

teaches the kings (and priests) how to be wise administers of order and justice, and in so doing demonstrates that the fountainhead of this legal wisdom (Yahweh) is a wise and just ruler. It does not teach ordinary citizens how to be moral.

In a similar vein, the statement "be holy because I am holy" in Leviticus 19:2 should not be read as a command to imitate the moral character of Yahweh. First, the verb is a future indicative, not a present imperative; the phrase literally reads, "you will be holy because I am holy." It is a statement of fact, not a command or an admonition. Second, holiness (various forms of the root *qdš*) is a status, not a series of actions, and it is not a moral status; the vast majority of holy things are inanimate objects (the articles of the tabernacle), places (cities, mountains, temples), or periods of time (Jubilee, Sabbath), which are amoral and lack agency of any kind. Third, the holy status is conferred, not earned. Yahweh makes Israel holy (e.g., Lev 21:8); the Israelites do not make themselves holy. Labeling something as *qdš* identifies it as one of the spheres of patronage that collectively define the god's identity.[7] Saying that Israel is holy is not saying that Israel possesses a certain moral character; it is saying that Yahweh is the God of Israel, much like we would say Zeus is the god of thunder or Ares is the god of war. Divine identity determines a god's function and therefore defines how worshippers are supposed to relate to him or her; it does not describe properties of the patronized elements. Saying that Ares is the god of war does not tell us anything about war; it tells us something about Ares. Likewise, saying that Yahweh is the God of Israel does not tell us anything about Israel; it tells us something about Yahweh. "You will be holy because I am holy" means essentially the same thing as "you will be my people and I will be your God" (e.g., Exod 6:7; Lev 26:12), which is a declaration of identity as well as a statement of function.

The point of this is that Yahweh is still seen as an amoral provider of order, and demons are amoral agents of non-order. Theological affirmations that Yahweh is good express a hope that Yahweh will do good for Israel, and also affirm that Yahweh is competently serving his dual function as God and King.[8] However, Yahweh's unique monarchial role does mean that he takes a greater interest in personally maintaining the order of his domain than is normal for deities. While ancient Near Eastern gods were often accorded the title of "king," the concept indicated relationship and power dynamics, in contrast to dictating a specific function. Gods stood over the kings in power and authority much like the kings and officials stood over the people, but the gods did not serve the functions ascribed to the kings (maintaining civil order in the human world). Yahweh, in contrast, actually assumes monarchial *functions* in addition

---

7. *Qādôš* is the semantic equivalent of the Akkadian determinative *dingir*, which is applied to a similar range of objects and abstractions. See Walton and Walton, *Lost World of the Israelite Conquest*, 105–16 for full discussion. For the use of *dingir* as defining divine identity, see Hundley, "Here a God, There a God." For a comprehensive analysis of the Hebrew root, see the second appendix at https://www.ivpress.com/Media/Default/Downloads/Misc/5184-appendix.pdf.

8. For a discussion of the Hebrew word *good* translated as "functioning properly," see Walton, *Lost World of Genesis One*, 50.

to the divine functions ascribed to gods. As a result, Israel's [cultic] service to Yahweh is generally expressed in terms of *service to a sovereign*—especially fidelity to the terms of their vassal treaty, the covenant—rather than the "providing for needs in a symbiotic relationship" that was normal for cultic service to ancient Near Eastern deities. While the form of the service—primarily sacrifices—is the same, in the ancient Near East the sacrifice is seen as food offered to meet the needs of the gods, while in Israel it is seen more as tribute signifying loyalty, respect, and submission (e.g., Mal 1:8–14). Consequently, Yahweh's enforcement of order in his domain also parallels the expected response of a *king*, more so than the expected response of a god. Disorderly conduct on the part of Israel is almost always met with direct divine action in the form of active retribution, not passive divine abandonment leading to the actions of opportunistic demons, which is the normal response of angry ancient Near Eastern deities. When demons do appear in the Hebrew Bible, it is normally as depersonalized weapons or instruments of Yahweh's agency, such as *Deber* and *Qeṭeb* in Deuteronomy 32:24 (NIV "consuming pestilence and deadly plague"; see chapter 7). Israel's theological innovations do not make demons the immoral counterparts of a moral God; they neglect demons as irrelevant, reduced to instruments of a deity who prefers to manage the human world directly. Demons in their typical ancient Near Eastern role—as opportunistic nuisances when the gods have abandoned their people or are not paying attention—are almost completely absent from the Hebrew Bible.

Gods in the classical world

By the time of the writing of the New Testament, the conception of the gods had changed. The amoral steward of order was abstracted and depersonalized and moved to the periphery of the cosmos. In the Dead Sea Scrolls this being is called "the God of knowledge";[9] in Middle Platonism the concept is represented by a transcendent Supreme Mind.[10] The anthropomorphic members of the pantheon (i.e., the gods) were reclassified into a hierarchy of rational beings that also includes humans. By taking their place in this hierarchy, the gods acquired a property that they did not possess in the ancient world: *virtue*. In the classical world, the gods are exemplars of the highest form of being that a rational creature can attain,[11] and the practice of religion is supposed to teach and promote virtue in its practitioners.[12] In the Qumran texts the

9. 1QS 3.15–19, trans. Wise, Abegg, and Cook, *Dead Sea Scrolls*, 129.

10. Ferguson, *Backgrounds*, 388.

11. "Middle Platonists derived from Plato (*Theaet.* 176b) the doctrine that the goal of life as happiness consists in 'likeness to God, so far as is possible.'" Ferguson, *Backgrounds*, 388.

12. This, at least, is the position of the philosophical religions that strongly influenced later Christian theology, especially Neopythagoreanism, Middle Platonism, and Neoplatonism. See Ferguson, *Backgrounds*, 320–21. Popular religion included the worship of personified virtues as gods (ibid., 176), but did not include much in the way of moral obligation or instruction (ibid., 177). The gods of pre-Hellenistic Greek religion, like the gods of the ancient Near East, were amoral (ibid., 153).

paragon of virtue is called the Prince of Light[13] or the Angel of Truth.[14] Other Jewish traditions refer to it as Michael, Melchizedek,[15] or Logos.[16]

Assigning the gods the property of virtue immediately creates two problems. The first is that it is necessary to account for the depiction of the behavior of the gods in ancient traditions, where they act in a manner that is not suitable for virtuous humans to imitate. This is also true of the Israelite conceptions of Yahweh in the Old Testament: "No longer easy in their minds about ascribing rapine and destruction to the will of their God, the Hebrews sought new theodicies; . . . the malignant, destructive aspect of Yahweh was subtracted from him and ascribed to a different spiritual power, the Devil."[17] The misdeeds of the Roman pantheon were likewise ascribed to demons by both the Christians and by the Romans themselves. Justin Martyr, for example, writes "we not only deny that they who did such things as these are gods, but assert that they are wicked and impious demons, whose actions will not bear comparison with those even of men desirous of virtue."[18] He then goes on to add:

> all reckon it an honorable thing to imitate the gods. But far be such a thought concerning the gods from every well-conditioned soul, as to believe that Jupiter himself, the governor and creator of all things, was both a parricide and the son of a parricide, and that being overcome by the love of base and shameful pleasures, he came in to Ganymede and those many women whom he had violated and that his sons did like actions. But, as we said above, wicked devils perpetrated these things.[19]

To this the Greek philosopher Plutarch adds, "As for the various tales of rapine and wanderings of the gods, their concealments and banishment and servitude, which men rehearse in legend and in song, all these are, in fact, not things that were done to the gods or happened to them, but to the demigods [Gk *daimones*, 'demons']."[20]

The second problem is that it becomes necessary to account for manifestations of evil that must necessarily have a cosmic source but could not possibly be perpetuated by virtuous beings. The most notable of these are the suffering of the righteous and the prosperity of the wicked, and also the creation of a world permeated with evil, attributed by Platonists to matter and by some Christians to the fall. The reality of this "cosmic unvirtue" necessitates the acknowledgment of a being with the power of a god (more or less) but without the attribute of virtue. For the Platonic philosophers this

13. 1QS 3.20.

14. 1QS 3.24.

15. Kobelski, *Melchizedek*, 36.

16. Runia, "Logos," 528.

17. Russell, *Devil*, 181–83.

18. Justin Martyr, *1 Apology* 5, trans. Coxe, in *ANF* 1:164.

19. Justin Martyr, *1 Apology* 21, trans. Coxe, in *ANF* 1:170.

20. Plutarch, *De Defectu Oracularum* 15, trans. Babbitt, in LCL 306:416–17.

being is called the *demiurge*, the creator of the material world, and cosmic misman-agement is ascribed to demons on account of the imperfection that arises from their partial material nature. Marcion tried to equate Yahweh the God of Israel with the demiurge, since Yahweh created the material world. Philo, on the other hand, equated Yahweh with the Supreme Mind of Middle Platonism, and found the activity of the demiurge in the plurals in Genesis 1:26:

> God said, "Let us make," an expression which plainly shows the taking with Him of others as fellow workers. It is to this end that, when man orders his course aright, when his thoughts and deeds are blameless, God the universal Ruler may be owned as their Source; while others from the number of his subordinates are held responsible for thoughts and deeds of a contrary sort: for it could not be that the Father should be the cause of an evil thing to his offspring: the vice and vicious activities are an evil thing.[21]

Most Jewish and Christian interpreters followed Philo, casting Yahweh the God of Israel as the abstract Supreme Mind, Christ the logos (or Michael or some equiva-lent in Judaism) as the paragon of virtue, and Satan and demons as the source of cosmic mismanagement. The Manichaeans in the fifth century also tried to ascribe the creation of the material world to the devil, and Origen in the third century argued that materiality was imposed as a punishment for the defection of souls from their original pristine state,[22] but for the most part Christians do not associate corporeality and matter with evil in the manner of the Platonists.[23] Thus, for the classical Chris-tians cosmic mismanagement is generally defined in terms of the persecution of the righteous and the encouragement of unreason and unvirtue.

The price of ascribing virtue to the gods and casting them as exemplars to be imitated is that the role the gods can play in the cosmos is substantially reduced, since much that occurs within the world order does not serve as a guide for human virtue (by both ancient and modern admission). As the role of the gods diminishes, the demons that fill the gaps left by the gods increase in power and prominence. The reason why the demons are more prominent in the New Testament than in the Old is because in the cognitive environment of the Second Temple period God is seen as more abstract and passive, and so the active personalized cosmic beings are his lesser minions, the angels and the demons and their respective commanders. In Manichae-anism, and in similar systems where God remains active while still exemplifying vir-tue (i.e., open theism), he is simultaneously weakened such that the demons occupy the space left by the limits of his power. The point is that in all cases the demons are defined based on the limits of the gods.

21. Philo, *Commentary on Genesis* 24.75, trans. Colson and Whittaker, in LCL 226:58–61.

22. "Let us see then, in the first place, what is the vanity to which the creature is subject. I appre-hend that it is nothing else than the body" Origen, *On First Principles* 1.7.5, trans. Coxe, in *ANF* 4:264.

23. This is largely due to the prevalent desire to defend the doctrine of the incarnation from the Docetists, who held an essentially Platonic conception of matter.

Gods in the modern world

This functional definition of demons can still apply to us today. Our modern cognitive environment is defined by an ideology that historians and philosophers call *humanism*, which is a values system that places the fulfilling of human desires and the promulgation of human happiness (now sometimes called "human flourishing") as its highest values. This is specifically in contrast to a value system that places fulfilling *divine* desires and according proper honors to the *divine* as its highest values, which we might perhaps call *axiological theism*.[24] This was the ideology of the Middle Ages, though modern humanistic Christians will usually conflate them and argue that producing human flourishing *is* the divine will and desire (see further discussion below and in chapter 16). The difference in value is demonstrated as early as Martin Luther's theses; medieval patrons of the arts and of building projects wanted to make fantastic art and spectacular cathedrals to show honor to God (compare Matt 26:8–11), while Martin Luther wanted to give the money to the poor to increase their happiness (compare Matt 25:35–46).[25] The point is that when God exists in a humanistic value system, his purpose is to promulgate human happiness or human flourishing; this in turn is the meaning given to the phrases *God is good* and *God loves us*. The image of Christ the King who demands our service and reverence (the *pantokrator* that dominates every medieval church) is replaced by the image of Christ the Servant (e.g., Matt 20:28; Mark 10:45; Phil 2:7) who meets our every need. Over the course of the sixteenth to the eighteen centuries, European humanists discovered that "science" (and the technology it produced) was far more efficient at meeting some human needs—especially physical needs—than the old religious devotional system had ever been; this observation was one of the chief warrants for the claim that science had replaced God. Religious apologists countered with the idea that religion could meet some human needs—especially emotional and existential needs—that science could not. This debate continues even today, but both sides operate on the premise that God and religion primarily serve to meet human needs and to increase human happiness. In this cognitive environment, the problem of evil—wherein evil is invoked as evidence against rational belief in a good and powerful God, which Boyd correctly observes is absent from the Bible[26] and was mostly ignored in the Middle

---

24. Theism as a value system, where God (or specifically God's will) constitutes the highest value, is not necessarily the same thing as theism as a metaphysical system (our normal meaning of the term *theism*), where an entity with the name or taxon of *God* is thought to exist. There may be some overlap in the sense that definition of the metaphysical *God* (especially according to ontological arguments) might necessarily entail that its will should constitute the highest value, but nonetheless it is theoretically possible to acknowledge a metaphysical God while still measuring values according to some other standard (as is done for example in deism).

25. Critics of both movements postulate spurious political motives to both sides, but for our purposes it is best to be as charitable as possible.

26. "[T]he Biblical authors on the whole seem largely unaware of any antimony between their faith in an all-good and all-powerful God on the one hand the reality of intense suffering in the world on

Ages[27]—takes particular prominence. In a theology where God is the King, God can do as he likes; humans can beg for mercy (the liturgical *kyrie eleison*) or attempt to appease his wrath (formally absent from Catholic doctrine, but often mistakenly associated with penance and propitiation), but cannot question his decisions or call him to account. In a theology where God is a servant, however, God is accountable to the humans and can be called up for scrutiny or review. In this system, if God's provision for human needs and human happiness is found wanting, God can be "fired"; we can abandon our faith and our religion and find another (better) source for our happiness. For those people who find God's provision for human happiness to be lacking but nonetheless for whatever reason wish to retain their faith, demons are called in to account for God's failure to produce human happiness. The whole purpose of conflict theology and its attribution of evil to Satan and demons (which we will further discuss in chapter 15) is to allow its adherents to retain their faith in a God whose purpose is to make them happy by ascribing the suffering (unhappiness) that cannot be attributed to such a God to the demons. Thus, in the modern world demons are still given responsibility for anything that cannot be ascribed to the gods.

The point of this is not that we should affirm any of these conceptions of gods above the others; the Bible's purpose is not to affirm the beliefs of its authors, either for demonology or for theology proper. Rather, the point is that, as systematic theologians, anything we claim about God affects what we can claim about demons, and anything we claim about demons affects what we can claim about God because the concepts are inherently related. Classical theologians from Augustine to Aquinas began their theology with God and when they were finished found little room for the demons. Modern open theists, deists, and atheists often begin their theology with demons (or depersonalized evil, defined in humanistic terms), and when they are finished find very little room for God. Whether any of them were right is not the point; the point is that a systematic theology of demons should not be based on compiling proof-texts about demons or things assumed to be demons; it should be constructed in accordance with the attributes, functions, and limitations of God (if any).

the other." Boyd, *God at War*, 52.

27. "After Augustine the question always gets filed under the category of God's providence." Boyd, *God at War*, 55.

Part 3

Demons and spirits in the Bible and its cognitive environment

Chapter 9

Divine combat and enemies of the gods

ONE OF THE MOST fundamental tenets of the modern conception of demons is their opposition to and perpetual conflict with both God and humanity. This conception is often supported by appealing to various statements lifted directly from the biblical text. However, we have argued that these statements are not intended to be propositions in a systematic treatment of cosmic beings, but rather references that are used to communicate to a particular audience in a particular context (see chapter 1). In order to understand what the references mean, it is necessary to understand what they are a reference *to*. Therefore, we will now discuss the concept of gods in conflict (theomachy) as it was understood in the world of the Bible's cognitive environment.

The struggle against chaos

The motif of the gods doing battle with the monsters or other elements representing chaos—which scholars call *chaoskampf*—is well established in ancient Near Eastern literature, including the Hebrew Bible.[1] Establishing and maintaining order against the persistent threat of chaos is one of the primary functions of gods in the ancient world. Naturally, then, the original establishment of the created order (cosmogony) occasionally involves the *chaoskampf* motif. Chaos, which is the absence of order, is represented by monstrous divine or semidivine creatures or by abstractions such as darkness or the netherworld, and is associated with the [occasionally personified] regions of the earth where humans cannot live, such as mountains, deserts, and especially the sea. The chaos elements either exist before the gods or percolate into being alongside them, but at some point they need to be killed, domesticated, constrained, or otherwise removed so that the ordered world can be established. The most famous instance of *chaoskampf* in cosmogony is the Babylonian *Enuma Elish*, where Marduk fights and defeats Tiamat, the personified ocean, and creates the world from her corpse, in the process becoming king of the gods and receiving

---

1. Major discussions include: Anderson, *Creation Versus Chaos*; Ballentine, *Conflict Myth*; Batto, *Slaying the Dragon*; Day, *God's Conflict*; Kloos, *Yhwh's Combat*; Niditch, *Chaos to Cosmos*; Tsumura, *Creation and Destruction*; Wakeman, *God's Battle*; Watson, *Chaos Uncreated*; Walton, "Creation in Gen 1:1—2:3."

the authority to decree destinies. Chaos creatures are class II spirits (see chapter 7) portrayed typically in iconography as composite creatures or dragons. As class II spirits they were amoral but could also be mischievous or destructive. They caused problems if left unchecked, but they could also be domesticated and become associates of the gods. A sharp delineation between chaos creatures and other liminal beings or class II spirits is not clearly established.

The establishment of the cosmic order does not represent the once-and-for-all defeat of chaos. Maintaining and preserving the created order requires constant vigilance and battle. This ongoing struggle is represented by associating the *chaoskampf* motif with daily or seasonal cycles, such as Ra versus Apophis in Egypt or Baal versus Mot in Ugarit, representing the renewing of creation that accompanies the rising of the sun or the coming of spring. *Chaoskampf* motifs are also extended to the preserving and renewing of order in the human world, most notably in the succession of kings[2] and in the restoration of temples.[3] The chaos monsters or elements can also serve as agents or weapons of the gods when the gods wish to demonstrate displeasure by withdrawing the benefits of order. The most notable occurrence of this is the great flood that wipes out the entire created order, described in the Gilgamesh Epic and the Atrahasis Epic, and also in Genesis 6–9. The gods can also dispatch chaos creatures or lesser agents of non-order (which we call *"demons,"* see discussion in chapter 7) to afflict those who have earned their displeasure in some way or another. Thus, while the chaos creatures are frequently the opponents of the gods and represent obstacles that the gods need to perpetually overcome, they are also not personifications of what we would call "evil" and neither are the gods ubiquitously and unconditionally opposed to them. They are a byproduct of creation and exist outside the ordered world, but there is no systematic program of the gods to exterminate them; the ancients do not foresee a future where the gods finally eliminate all traces of chaos from the world. Chaos is expected to be controlled, not annihilated.

The *chaoskampf* motif is also found throughout the Old Testament, where it serves much the same function as its ancient Near Eastern counterparts with a few minor—though not insignificant—modifications. Like the rest of the ancient Near East, the Hebrew Bible describes its highest values in terms of order, but in Old Testament theology that order is described in terms of the covenant. Consequently, one of the most significant *chaoskampf* images is the parting of the Red Sea (Exod 14:21; Isa 51:10; the sea is a ubiquitous symbol of chaos) which paves the way to Sinai, a theme that continues in the miraculous provision for Israel as they journey through the non-order of the wilderness. The motif is also present in the cosmogony of Genesis 1. The elements of non-order, the darkness and the deep, are "separated" from the light and the land, but unlike Tiamat in the *Enuma Elish*, they are not destroyed.[4] Boundar-

2. Pitard, "Combat Myth."

3. Halpern, "Ritual Background."

4. Some scholars see the separating of the waters in Genesis 1:7 as a conflict image, resulting in

ies are set on the darkness (enforced by the two lights in Gen 1:18) and also on the sea (Job 7:12). Also in contrast to the ancient Near East, Yahweh actually *creates* the chaos monsters (the "great creatures of the sea" in Gen 1:21; Heb. *tannîn*, the same word used of Leviathan in Isa 27:1). Psalm 104:26 says that Yahweh created Leviathan to frolic in the sea, and Job 40:15 classifies the chaos creature Behemoth along with Job as a creature of God. At the same time, however, there is no evidence that the chaos monsters are fallen beings that were originally created as something else, as, for example, is later thought of the devil. They are created, but they are created *as what they are*; they are not "order monsters."[5] Whatever God's plan for creation is, the chaos creatures are a part of it. This is a departure from the ancient Near East, where the chaos creatures are outside of the divine plan and generally serve as obstacles towards it, even as they also occasionally serve as tools.

The basic Hebrew word for the chaos monsters is *tannîn*.[6] The word occurs fifteen times, most notably in Genesis 1:21, where the *tannîn* (NIV "great sea creatures") are created, and Psalm 148:7, where they praise the LORD alongside the rest of creation. The staff of Moses becomes a *tannîn* (NIV "serpent") in Exodus 7:9–10, as do the staffs of the Egyptian magicians in Exodus 7:12. The word is used in parallel to the monster *Rahab* in Isaiah 51:9; to both *liwyātān* (NIV "Leviathan") and *nāḥāš* (NIV "serpent") in Isaiah 27:1; to the sea (*Yām*) in Job 7:12; to both *Yām* and *liwyātān* in Psalm 74:13; to an ordinary cobra in Deuteronomy 32:33; and to cobras and lions in Psalm 91:13. In Ezekiel 29:3 and 32:2 the king of Egypt is metaphorically referred to as *tannîn* (NIV "monster"), and in Jeremiah 51:34 Nebuchadnezzar is said (metaphorically) to have "swallowed [Israel] like a *tannîn*" (NIV "serpent"),

---

the implied "death" of the *tehom*. However, this reading is based on the assumption that Genesis 1 is literarily dependent on the *Enuma Elish*. For a full critique of this hypothesis, see Tsumura, *Creation and Destruction*.

5. Readers of the Masoretic text have noted that the separation of the waters in Genesis 1:6–8 and the creation of the *tannîn* in 1:17 are not concluded with the affirmation that "it was good." However, this should not be read to understand that the waters and the monsters are evil. The word "good" (*ṭôb*) means "properly carrying out its function." However, chaos creatures by definition have no function assigned to them. They have a place in the world (on the periphery) and therefore their presence is part of the divine plan, but they are not part of the created order. See full discussion in Walton, *Lost World of Adam and Eve*, 40, 133.

6. In several passages, there is debate over whether the word in the text is *tannîn*, "monster," or *tannîm*, plural of *tan*, "jackal." In Nehemiah 2:32, the word is used to designate a feature in Jerusalem (NIV "the Jackal Well"), and therefore which animal it is named for is mostly academic. Another instance is Psalm 44:19 (NIV "you . . . made us a haunt for jackals," following MT) which emphasizes the liminal nature of the animals and therefore could be represented by either. Many commentators want to read lit. "crushed us in [a] place of jackals/of a sea monster" as referring to a location (i.e., the sea or the desert, liminal regions; see deClasse-Walford, Jacobson, and Tanner, *Psalms*, 414; Goldingay, *Psalms 42–89*, 46. Day, on the other hand, wants to read "crushed us *instead of* the monster" (Day, *God's Conflict*, 112–13). This interpretation only makes sense if the word is *tannîn*, and would be another example of *chaoskampf* imagery applied metaphorically to political situations. Finally, in Lamentations 4:3 the word is *tannîn*, but should nonetheless be understood as "Jackals" (following NIV; see Day, *God's Conflict*, 112; Niehr, "תנין," 729).

which may be a reference to an image from Canaanite mythology where Mot (a chaos creature personifying death) devours Baal. The "great fish" (*dāg gādôl*) that God sends to swallow Jonah in Jonah 1:17 invokes the same image[7] and may also be a chaos creature of some kind.[8] In many—though, importantly, not all—of these passages, the *tannîn* is depicted in the traditional role of *chaoskampf* antagonist. Sometimes the monster metaphorically represents a political enemy, not a literal mythographic figure or a personified abstraction. We will examine this usage further in the next section ("enemies and divine warriors").

Yām, the (occasionally personified) sea, and *tĕhôm*, the (rarely personified) cosmic ocean, are also occasionally used to invoke the theme of *chaoskampf*. As mentioned above, the (depersonalized) *Yām* and *tĕhôm* are divided in Exodus 14:21 and Genesis 1:7,[9] respectively, as a symbol of the triumph of order over chaos. The Red Sea crossing is referenced in Isaiah 51:9–10, where the [Red] sea (*yām*) is paralleled to both the *tĕhôm* (NIV "great deep"; see also Psalm 77:16 where it is parallel to *mayîm*, "waters") and the monster *Rahab*. *Yām* is paralleled to *tannîn* in Job 7:12 as something that must be guarded; with *Rahab* in Job 26:12 as something churned up (see also Isa 51:15) or cut in pieces, respectively; and with Leviathan as something respectively split or broken in Psalm 74:13. Leviathan is called the "*tannîn* that is in the sea" in Isaiah 27:1, and *Yām* and Leviathan are mentioned together as creations of God in Psalm 104:25. The sea is churned and trampled in Habakkuk 3:15, in parallel to the defeat of the "leader of the land of wickedness" (referring to Babylon)[10] who is crushed and pierced through the head with a spear. Additionally, many passages speak of God creating the sea (e.g., Exod 20:11; Ps 95:5), ruling over the sea (e.g., Ps 89:9), or containing or restraining the sea (e.g., Job 38:8; Prov 8:29). The (personified) *Yām* and *tĕhôm* do not know where wisdom is found in Job 28:14, and the *tĕhôm* is released to bring the flood in Genesis 7:11. The association of chaos creatures and the sea undergirds the idea that both are reflections of either potential disruptors of order or indicative of where non-order resides.

Several chaos monsters are also indicated with proper names. *Rahab* is named six times as a chaos monster. It is parallel to *tannîn* in Isaiah 51:9; to *Yām* in Job 26:12; to Babylon in Psalm 87:4; and to generic enemies in Psalm 89:10. It cowers before God in Job 9:13 and is metaphorically compared to Egypt in Isaiah 30:7. Leviathan (*liwyātān*) is created by God in Psalm 104:26; killed by God in Psalm 74:14 (where it is paralleled with *Yām*) and Isaiah 27:1 (where it is associated with both *Yām* and *nāḥāš*);

7. Day, *God's Conflict*, 110–11.

8. Walton, "Jonah," 104–5, 117; Sasson, *Jonah*, 150.

9. The word used in Genesis 1:7 (Hiph of *bdl*, NIV "separated") is not the same word used in Exodus (Hiph of *hlk*, "divided"); however, Proverbs 3:20 does refer to the "dividing" (*hlk*) of the *tĕhôm* in reference to the cosmogony.

10. "The conflict with the powers of chaos here enacted clearly involves their identification with a hostile political power that has invaded Judah (cf. [Hab 3:12–14, 16]), which . . . is presumably the Babylonians." Day, *God's Conflict*, 105.

and invoked as part of an anti-cosmos incantation in Job 3:8, which begins "let there be darkness" (Job 3:4, NIV "may [the day] turn to darkness") in an inversion of the creation formula in Genesis 1.[11] Leviathan, together with the chaos creature *Behemoth*, is also the subject of an extended discourse in Job 40–41. Despite the subject of the chaos creatures, Job 40–41 is not an instance of the *chaoskampf* motif; neither Behemoth or Leviathan are depicted as consuming or devouring, or being crushed, trampled, or broken (although there is a passing mention of Job's inability to spear the Leviathan in Job 41:1, 7–9, which might invoke the theme). Likewise, these chapters are not a bestiary that provides authoritative teaching on the [biological] characteristics of the beasts, as is assumed by some interpreters when they try to identify the creatures as, e.g., a hippopotamus, a crocodile, or a dinosaur. (Note also that the discourse in Job 38 describes cosmic geography and Job 39 describes the characteristics and behavior of familiar animals, most of which are [infamously] inaccurate according to science.) Rather, the discussion serves a particular literary purpose in the context of the broader argument of Job. In Job 7:12, Job has complained that God is treating him like a chaos monster ("Am I the sea, or the monster of the deep, that you put me under guard?") and in Job 30:20–33 Job accuses God of essentially acting like a chaos creature: "In Job's perception, God has joined [personified] Terrors and Night in behaving towards Job as a chaos creature, as author of disorder and death."[12] In Job 40–41 Yahweh picks up both of these accusations and twists them around.[13] Job is indeed like the chaos creature Behemoth (Job 40:15),[14] but not in the sense that he needs to be put down or monitored. Rather, Behemoth is a creature of God, strong, steadfast, indifferent to turmoil, and invulnerable, as Job was (or ought to be). Likewise, Yahweh is like the chaos creature Leviathan (Job 41:10), but not in the sense that he is senselessly and indiscriminately destructive. Rather, he is mighty, untamable, unassailable, unequaled, and lord of his domain.[15] The creatures are not in any way presented as evil (or even antagonistic, although Leviathan is dangerous), and the passage is not simply God reminding Job that he is not up to the task of running the cosmos (as in Job 38; running the cosmos includes the duty to subdue the chaos monsters), although that is also perhaps implied.[16] The discourses of Yahweh are intended to readjust Job's—and the reader's—assumptions about the nature of the governance of the cosmos, and recasting the chaos creatures in an unconventional light is part of that process.[17]

The chaos imagery is also picked up in the New Testament, although by then it has been filtered through the interpretive lens of the Second Temple period. Consequently

---

11. Walton, *Job*, 119.

12. Walton, *Job*, 317.

13. Walton, *Job*, 407.

14. Walton, *Job*, 408; esp. n28.

15. For full discussion see Walton, *Job*, 408–9.

16. Walton, *Job*, 402.

17. Walton, *Job*, 406.

we cannot blend Old and New Testament usage to descry a systemic biblical profile of chaos, and we certainly should not read the New Testament's conceptions backwards into the Old Testament context. In the Second Temple period the chaos creatures and the liminal realm in general are reclassified from disruptively nonfunctional to actively evil (see discussion in chapter 10). No longer simply threats to the world order that can be subdued or employed at need, they are now active opponents and obstacles of the divine plan and must be eliminated before creation can be perfected. This is most clearly demonstrated in the Dead Sea Scrolls, where the *tannîn* are associated together with Beliar.[18] In contrast, a tradition preserved in *4 Ezra, The Apocalypse of Baruch* (*2 Baruch*), and *1 Enoch* describes the Leviathan as a monstrous *animal* who is preserved to be food for God's elect,[19] and the *Apocalypse of Abraham* depicts Leviathan in its conventional Old Testament role of threatening the cosmic order.[20] However, the New Testament does not refer to the Leviathan by name, instead invoking literary references to combat from (especially) Psalms and Isaiah. Jesus's calming of the storm (Matt 8:23–27; Mark 4:35–41; Luke 8:22–25) is a reference to the restraining of the sea in Job 38:8–11 and Psalm 89:9,[21] and his walking on the water (Matt 14:22–23; Mark 6:45–52; John 6:16–21) is a reference to Job 9:8, "[God] treads on the waves of the sea."[22] In context, these passages are intended to describe the divine nature of Jesus by casting him in the role assigned to God in the source material; they are not intended to describe the nature of the sea or to depict the sea as an evil force opposed to God. Likewise, the dragon character in Revelation (e.g., Rev 12:3) can be understood as a reference to the Leviathan in Isaiah 27:1, but this allusion derives from a history of eschatological interpretation and apocalyptic imagery and is not intended to clarify the identity of the character in Isaiah (see full discussion in chapter 10). Finally, the vision of the New Jerusalem in Revelation 21 specifically mentions the absence of darkness (Rev 21:25) and sea (Rev 21:1), both of which are images of chaos (e.g., Gen 1:2). However, these images are not intended to affirm a metanarrative about God's desire to purge the world of chaos that we are supposed to read back into the Old Testament. The purpose of the image is to invoke the perfection of the created order, using the symbols of chaos as they were understood in John's time. We might contrast the idyllic image of Revelation 21 to that of Psalm 104:25–26, where the praise of God through celebration of the created order *includes* both the sea and the Leviathan.

While chaos in the Hebrew Bible is not opposed to God, it is still the absence of order and order is still portrayed as the highest good, at least in the human world. Consequently, chaos is disruptive to humanity at best, and destructive at worst, and

---

18. 11QApPsa 5.1. Niehr, "תנין," 731. Cited Puech, "*11QPsApa*," 377–408; Puech, "Dead Sea Scrolls: Forty Years of Research," 64–89.

19. *4 Ezra* 6.49–52; *2 Bar.* 29.4; *1 En.* 60.7–10, 24. See Whitney, *Two Strange Beasts*, 31–58.

20. Whitney, *Two Strange Beasts*, 77.

21. Hays, *Echoes of Scripture in the Gospels*, 67.

22. Hays, *Echoes of Scripture in the Gospels*, 71.

chaotic states are almost always adversarial and unpleasant—in other words, when the narrator depicts an event or circumstance using the imagery of chaos, that event or circumstance is almost always negative. This does not make them inherently evil in any moral sense. The most notable instances of this are when the *chaoskampf* motif is used to describe conflict with human enemies, which are sometimes metaphorically presented as chaos monsters, as for example is sometimes thought to be the case in Psalm 74:14 and Isaiah 27:1.[23] But divine combat with human enemies involves more than the use of the *chaoskampf* motif to describe them, which we will now examine further.

Enemies and divine warriors

Warfare ideology in the ancient Near East included the idea that the gods fought alongside the human armies, and indeed were ultimately responsible for victory. However, the ancients did not conceive of themselves as carrying out the will of the gods in the form of moral or ideological purges in the way that many think of *holy war* today. In the ancient world, the city or nation represented the cosmic order in microcosm, and indeed served as the foundation of that order: "The Mesopotamian visualized his or her city as being located at the center of a world that could not exist without it."[24] War in the ancient Near East was not the opposite of peace; it was a response to encroaching disorder, which usually manifested as either rebellion or invasion. The gods fought alongside the armies because preserving the order was the primary function of the gods. The rituals used to invoke the gods to war and the presence of the gods with the army (usually represented by an image or standard; compare the ark of the covenant in Joshua 6:4, 13) were observed to ensure that the wars were conducted in a proper and orderly manner so they would not produce a greater disorder than they intend to correct; we might compare this to our modern practice of devising rules (i.e., the Geneva Convention) that we follow when waging war in order to make sure that the war does not produce more "evil" than the evils it is intended to correct. Both the disorder of rebellion and the disorder of invasion are represented in the Hebrew Bible, and both invoke the imagery of Yahweh as the divine warrior fighting alongside human armies.

The presence of the divine warriors alongside the army—which modern scholars call the "divine vanguard"—was commonly represented in the ancient Near East by symbols or images of the gods carried into battle alongside the army. Egyptian armies carried divine effigies as battle standards, as well as an image of the king's patron god.[25] In Assyria, "the presence of the gods in battle was symbolized visually

23. For Psalm 74, Watson, *Chaos Uncreated*, 156–68; and for Isaiah, Day, *God's Conflict*, 112–13.

24. Van de Mieroop, *Ancient Mesopotamian City*, 42. See also Pongratz-Leisten, "The Other and the Enemy," 202.

25. Kang, *Divine War*, 101.

by the standards and flags carried by the armies, and also by the presence of priests and diviners who represented the gods physically."[26] In Israel the presence of the divine warrior is normally symbolized by the Ark of the Covenant (Josh 6:6; 1 Sam 4:3). Divine warriors were thought to wield the elements of the cosmos as weapons against enemy armies, which is also reflected in certain biblical passages (e.g., Ps 18:8–14; Exod 14:19–26; Judg 5:20–22; Josh 10:11; 1 Sam 7:10). Images such as thunder, earthquake, and panic; combat by stars, water, fire, and cloud; hail and lightning wielded as weapons; and divine warriors soaring on clouds or cherubim are all well-attested throughout the ancient Near East.[27]

Rebellion occurs when a vassal kingdom violates a treaty. In the ancient Near East, treaties were witnessed by the gods, and the gods were called upon to enforce the penalties of the treaty if it was broken. In ancient Israelite theology, the nation of Israel was a vassal kingdom of Yahweh, and their treaty was the covenant (see discussion in chapter 8). In Deuteronomy 30:19 the heavens and the earth are called to witness the terms of the covenant (see also Deut 32:1); in Isaiah 1:2 they are called on again to observe Israel's infidelity. The elements of the cosmos are not gods, but elsewhere in the ancient world it would be the gods performing this role. Thus, the actions of Yahweh the divine warrior against rebels are almost always directed against Israel. Israel's covenant infidelity is called "rebellion" (e.g., Ezek 2:3, "I am sending you to the Israelites, to a rebellious nation that has rebelled against me") and accordingly Yahweh as the divine warrior marches against them: "This is Jerusalem, which I have set in the center of the nations, with countries all around her. Yet in her wickedness she has rebelled against my laws and decrees. . . . I myself am against you, Jerusalem, and I will inflict punishment on you in the sight of the nations" (Ezek 5:5–8). "In the center of the nations" means that Jerusalem—a synecdoche for the nation of Israel—is the center of the world order. The nation's rebellion threatens that order, and so the deity steps in to deal with the problem. In most of the ancient Near East the gods were concerned with order in the human world because a stable and well-ordered society allowed the humans to meet the needs of the gods efficiently. In Israel, however, Yahweh preserves order not for the sake of allowing people to meet his needs, but for the sake of his reputation as a competent ruler; this is what it means that he will "inflict punishment *in the sight of the nations*" (Ezek 5:8). This is the same motive that ancient Near Eastern kings would have for preserving order in their domains (see discussion in chapter 8). Yahweh also fights alongside the Israelite kings against rebels in 2 Kings 3:7–26, and refuses to fight with Rehoboam against rebels in 1 Kings 12:19–24.

Enemies are different from rebels because enemies have no treaties to violate and therefore cannot violate treaties. Ancient Near Eastern literature frequently portrays enemies as subhuman or demi-human monsters of the liminal world who appear at the design of the gods and wreak havoc until the gods destroy them. The archetypal

26. Craigie, *War*, 119.

27. Weinfeld, "Divine Intervention." See also Kang, *Divine War*, 24–42.

portrayal of these "invincible barbarians" is found in the Babylonian *Cuthean Legend of Naram-Suen*, where they are designated by the epithets "Umman-manda," and "brood of destruction." Their creation is commissioned by the great gods, though they are raised by the chaos monster Tiamat, and they are sent to ransack Babylonia for no specified reason.[28] Naram-Suen, king of Babylon, consults oracles to seek the favor of the gods in repelling the invaders, but does not receive permission.[29] Trusting in his own strength, he decides to engage the enemy anyway and is soundly defeated on three occasions. In the process, he discovers that the enemies are monstrous bird-like demi-humans, and he has to test and see if they can bleed before he is certain that they are not spirits.[30] After capturing several of the enemy, he again consults the oracles about whether he should execute them, and is told that they should be spared because "one day Enlil will summon them for evil" (that is, to have evil done to them by the gods).[31] The story is written to portray pacifism as piety and emphasize the value of trusting in the will of the gods.

The literature of the Neo-Assyrian and Neo-Babylonian empires sometimes depict their historical enemies according to the archetype of Naram-Suen's enemies in the *Cuthean Legend*. Ashurbanipal refers to the king of his enemies the Cimmerians as "offspring of Tiamat" and "king of the Umman-manda"; Nabonidus of Babylon also refers to his enemies the Medes as "Umman-manda." Because the invincible barbarians are chaotic (by virtue of their liminal habitat, monstrous appearance, and association with Tiamat), and because their defeat and destruction is engineered by the gods without Mesopotamian interference, the confrontations with the Umman-manda can be seen as an allusion to the *chaoskampf* theme. The application of the label to historical enemies would therefore represent a historicization of the *chaoskampf*, much as is also demonstrated in the Bible through the portrayal of human enemies as monsters or the sea.

The imagery of the Cuthean legend is used in the Bible in Ezekiel 38–39 to describe the armies of Gog.[32] Hordes of enemies from the surrounding regions pour into Israel, where they are destroyed by God with no Israelite interference. Ezekiel's imagery is heavily influential in the development of the image of the eschatological combat in later literature (see below), which in turn is reflected in Revelation 20. The imagery of the invincible barbarians may also be invoked in the Pentateuch in the general depiction of the peoples of Canaan and the surrounding regions, especially by the designation *rĕpā'îm* (e.g., Deut 2:10–12),[33] which normally refers to the shades of the dead (8x, e.g., Isa 14:9; 26:14, 19) but in the Pentateuch is historicized to refer to human enemies.

28. Westenholz, *Legends*, 309–11.
29. Westenholz, *Legends*, 317.
30. Westenholz, *Legends*, 315.
31. Westenholz, *Legends*, 323.
32. Bodi, "Ezekiel," 484–85.
33. See Walton and Walton, *Lost World of the Israelite Conquest*, 148–50.

However, most of the historicized *chaoskampf* images in the Bible do not invoke the tropes of the Cuthean legend specifically, but instead use the more generic images of chaos, such as the *tannîn* for the Babylonians in Jeremiah 51:34[34] and for Egypt in Ezekiel 29:3 and 32:2,[35] and the sea for Assyria in Isaiah 17:12–14 and 8:5–8[36] and for Babylon in Habakkuk 3:15.[37] The waters refer to the nations in general in Psalm 46:3–4.[38] More indirectly, Psalm 74 invokes the power of Yahweh demonstrated by the defeat of the chaos monster at creation to plead for aid against enemies, although those enemies are not explicitly depicted as monsters themselves.

It is worth noting that this depiction of enemies in the ancient literature, including the Bible, is not like what we now call *demonization*; that is, an excuse to exterminate the enemy on moral, proprietary, or otherwise ideological grounds—whether sincerely held or merely expedient—without regret or remorse. Ashurbanipal made a treaty with the Cimmerian king, and Nabonidus fought alongside the Medes against Nineveh. The purpose of the rhetoric is for the creators of the documents to depict themselves and their nation as the ideal center and manifestation of the world order. Chaos in the ancient world is not an evil to be exterminated, but it does need to be kept in its place (that is, *outside*) so that the world order can function smoothly on both the cosmic and civic level. We should note that, in the NIV of Isaiah 27:1, Yahweh is said to "punish" Leviathan, which in context may refer metaphorically to a human enemy, i.e., whoever is causing Israel to "[perish] in Assyria and [be exiled] in Egypt" in Isaiah 27:13. However, the word translated "punish" (*pqd*) does not necessarily mean "punish for crimes." What it more accurately means is "put in its proper place."[39] If the referent is a criminal it can indeed mean punish, but the use of the word does not imply criminality in the referent. The "proper place" for a chaos creature (or anything that embodies chaos) is outside the world order.

In Israel this basic idea of preserving the order is tied specifically to the covenant; "covenant fidelity in the land" represents to Israel what "order in the city and the realm" represents to the rest of the ancient Near East. Enemies are depicted as chaos elements when they are disturbing the covenant order, either at the command of God (comparable to the barbarians in the Cuthean legend) or as a threat that God must overcome as in conventional *chaoskampf*. It is also clear, then, that when the Old Testament talks about the enemies of Yahweh in mythographic terms (i.e., as chaos elements), it is not talking about demonic powers operating through or behind the enemy armies or nations. The rhetoric assigns the enemy a place in the world order (that is, outside of it); it does not speculate on their metaphysical or moral characteristics.

34. See Day, *God's Conflict*, 109.

35. See Day, *God's Conflict*, 93–94.

36. See Day, *God's Conflict*, 101–4.

37. See Day, *God's Conflict*, 104–9.

38. See Day, *God's Conflict*, 120.

39. Creason, "PQD Revisited," 30.

However, instances of conflict against divine enemies that are not chaos creatures or otherwise associated with the liminal world is also present in both the ancient Near East and the Bible. This we will now examine.

Rebellion in heaven

In the polytheistic world of the ancient Near East, the various hierarchies of gods do not always get along, and so occasionally the gods fight wars among themselves. One of the most common reasons for divine conflict is the function of the gods in marching beside their human armies and fighting on their behalf (see above). When armies battled, the gods of the armies fought with each other as well. However, there is evidence that the gods of the losing side were not necessarily killed, punished, or even vilified in any way. A Hittite text reports the subduing and subsequent destruction of a rebel city in a manner reminiscent of the actions of Joshua at Jericho.[40] After the battle is over and the city destroyed, however, the enemy gods are not smashed and destroyed; rather, the victorious king offers them appeasement and petitions them to approve and enforce the ban he has set on the site.[41] In the Bible, Jephthah in Judges 11:23–32 engages the Ammonites in a kind of "trial by ordeal" with the understanding that the gods of the armies (Yahweh and Chemosh) will approve the outcome and settle the dispute.[42] Chemosh and the Ammonites lose this battle, but Chemosh is still around afterwards. Other times, however, the enemy gods are humiliated, with their images smashed or carried away in captivity and their temples destroyed.[43] Even so, there is no evidence that the losing gods were thought to be punished for crimes against the victors. They are simply defeated and their humiliation or destruction is a testimony to the relative power of the victor. This image occurs frequently in the Bible, especially in the prophetic literature, where the "idols" (referring both to the images themselves and the gods that the images represent) are smashed, broken, or carried into exile. However, the emphasis of these passages should be read as an affirmation of Yahweh's superior power. It does not contain or imply any kind of indictment against the losers; like the chaos creatures, they are enemies to be defeated, not criminals to be disciplined. For further discussion, see chapter 11.

In other instances, disputes arise among the pantheon as to who will have the right to rule over the gods. Normally these narratives serve as the origin story of the current structure of the pantheon and describe how whichever god is exalted as ruler earned that position. In this sense, they function very similarly to royal legitimation documents created by human kings to defend their right to rule. Gods in the ancient Near East did not rule the world by virtue of having made it; the gods in fact did not

40. Del Monte, "Hittite Herem," 22.
41. Del Monte, "Hittite Herem," 44.
42. Kang, *Divine War*, 195.
43. Holloway, *Aššur is King!* 193–97.

make the world but merely set the habitable parts of it in order. In Mesopotamian literature, the right to rule is tied to the possession of something called the *tablet of destiny*, which allows the bearer to assign functions (i.e., to decree destinies) for everything in the world. In the *Enuma Elish*, Marduk demands the tablet of destiny in exchange for fighting the chaos monster Tiamat; in *Anzu and Ninurta* the warrior god Ninurta has to recover the tablet after it is stolen by the chaos creature Anzu. Anzu wants to gain the ability to order the gods around out of spite for making him their doorkeeper;[44] Tiamat wants to kill the gods because they make too much noise and they disturb her sleep. These relatively low ambitions are part of the impulsive nature of chaos creatures. In the Baal texts from Ugarit, Baal counters an unspecified threat (the text is broken) from Yamm, the personified sea, in exchange for a palace, which carries similar connotations of kingship and authority.

The installation of a new king in the ancient Near East is seen as a triumph over chaos, and so regnal succession can be represented literarily by *chaoskampf* both in the human world and the divine world, since divine government is analogous to human government. In the Bible, this imagery may inform the symbolism in Daniel 7, in which beasts rise out of the sea and are supplanted by the Ancient of Days and the rider on the clouds (Dan 7:13).[45] However, the beasts in Daniel 7:3–8, 17–18, 23–25 (as also 8:3–8, 20–25) are normally interpreted as metaphorically representing human nations and rulers[46] as opposed to literally describing divine beings; the king of Greece (*melek yāwān*) in Daniel 8:21 is not the same character as the prince of Greece (*šr yāwān*) in Daniel 10:20. The rider on the clouds may be a divine figure since the description invokes divine warrior archetypes, but some interpreters read the image as a metaphor for a human messiah.[47] In either case, the biblical text is employing mythographic imagery—which may

44. "In Anzu, there is no general revolt against the gods, only the greedy desire for power by an individual. Anzu's theft of the Tablet is more an act of treachery than rebellion, though he does desire to control the responsibilities of the gods." Walton, "Anzu Myth," 77.

45. For full discussion of parallel imagery, see Walton, "Anzu Myth," 73–83.

46. See Porter, *Metaphors and Monsters* for a discussion of the metaphorical significance of the imagery. Whatever its influences, Daniel 7 is not a corruption or transmission of an existing mythographic text, so there is no reason why it cannot be composed to invoke both mythographic themes and metaphorically significant images at the same time.

47. There is some uncertainty as to whether the "one like a son of man" in Daniel 7:13 is supposed to represent a divine being or not. While the image of riding on the clouds is unquestionably theophanic, it is less clear whether the character is literally a divine being or a metaphorical presentation of a king or a kingdom, as the beasts are. Both interpretations are attested even into the early Christian period. In favor of the metaphorical reading, the beasts are all divine/cosmic creatures that represent kings and nations, and so it would be odd for them to be juxtaposed with a literal divine figure. In this reading, the "one like a son of man" metaphorically represents Israel and/or its king, the messiah, just as the beasts represent kings/kingdoms. In favor of the literal reading, the "one like a son of man" is separated from the beasts by a description of the Ancient of Days, who literally represents God. The statement that "all nations will worship him" would also be odd if "he" is supposed to represent a corporate political entity or a human ruler. Aram. *pᵉlaḥ* in the Bible always takes a divine object. When Jesus claims the title "son of man" for himself in Mark 14:62, the High Priest calls it blasphemy, which it would not be if the figure was human, but that does not tell us what the author of Daniel

derive from the Anzu myth[48]—in order to deliver its message, which specifically concerns the restoration of Israel's covenant order from the chaos of exile; it is not providing a behind-the-scenes description of cosmic entities and operations, as is consistent with the genre of prophecy (see chapter 3).

In other ancient Near Eastern texts, however, the antagonists are not chaos monsters trying to achieve something relatively petty; instead they are rebels and usurpers—normally lesser members of the pantheon—trying to wrest the rule of the cosmos from the established deities. This element is found in *Enuma Elish* (where the rebels recruit Tiamat to aid their cause) and in *Atrahasis*. In both of these texts, the lesser gods are angry with the greater gods because the lesser gods have to do all of the work. The rebellion is eventually put down and the gods create humanity to bear the burden of the labor of the gods. As familiar as the theme of a lesser divine being trying to steal the throne of heaven sounds to us due to a reception history spanning from pre-Christianity to Milton, this divine rebellion imagery is not actually presented anywhere in the Old Testament. The closest possible reference is the allusion to the mysterious character *hêlēl ben šaḥar* (NIV: "morning star, son of the dawn"; KJV "Lucifer, son of the morning") in Isaiah 14:12. While the name is clearly a reference to something, no consensus has developed as to exactly what. The LXX translates *hêlēl* as *ʾeosphoros*, the name of the planet Venus, which is the basis of both English translations (*lucifer* is the name of the planet Venus in Latin, lit. "bringer of light," *lux* + *ferre*). Forsyth argues that this translation, along with other similarities, should lead the reader to equate *Hêlēl* with the Greek character Phaethon, who unsuccessfully attempts to drive the chariot of the sun before being killed by Zeus.[49] Forsyth also draws parallels between Phaethon and Anzu[50] and ultimately argues that all three characters—Anzu, Phaethon, and *Hêlēl*—are essentially interchangeable. However, there is little direct support for this from the text itself. The boast in Isaiah 14:13 ("I will ascend to the heavens; I will raise my throne above the stars of God") is ascribed to the king of Babylon, and we should not necessarily assume that he is reenacting the aspirations of the mythic character *Hêlēl*, whoever that is. For example, if someone today refers to (say) a disgraced politician metaphorically as *Icarus*, it does not mean that he was injured or killed while failing to operate an experimental flying device. The reference refers to a plummet—literal or figurative—facilitated by hubris. Similarly,

---

meant in context. If the "one like the son of man" is indeed supposed to be a divine being then the ancient Near Eastern divine enthronement motif becomes even more apparent, but the passage becomes more problematic for orthodox Judaism since it would feature two divine beings interacting. This has led to the interpretation of the figure as angelic rather than divine, sometimes specifically identified as Michael (though of course angels are not [supposed to be] worshipped any more than kingdoms are), or a member of the divine council (White, *Yahweh's Council*, 130–34). See Collins, *Daniel*, 304–10 for a summary of the various positions.

48. Walton, "Anzu Myth," 69–89.

49. Forsyth, *Enemy*, 135.

50. Forsyth, *Enemy*, 132.

the metaphorical reference to the king of Babylon as *hêlēl ben šaḥar* may refer to the themes of the myth rather than its circumstances, in which case the specifics of the king's boast may not have been paralleled in the original myth.

An alternative interpretation tries to identify *Hêlēl* with the Canaanite minor deity Athtar, based on the claim that he "will sit . . . on the heights of Mount Zaphon" in Isaiah 14:13. This rather specific reference to the seat of Baal in Canaanite religion would be an odd statement for a Babylonian king, which suggests that the words of the mythological character *Hêlēl* are being placed in the king's mouth as part of the metaphorical comparison. In the literature of Ugarit, Athtar is chosen to rule in place of Baal after Baal is (temporarily) devoured by Mot. After discovering that the throne is too big for him to sit on, he declares that he "cannot be king in *Ṣaphon*" and leaves to become the king of the earth or perhaps the Netherworld.[51] Athtar is not a rebel or a usurper[52] and is not sent down to the earth (or netherworld) as punishment. If *Hêlēl* is intended to be a reference to Athtar, then it would mean that the Babylonian king is not equal to his aspirations. However, if this is the case then the reference to *Hêlēl* /Athtar is not a reference to the theme of conflict and rebellion in the divine realm. For a further discussion of Isaiah 14 and the Bible's references to heavenly rebellion in general, see chapter 13.

It should not be surprising that the idea of victory over a revolt or conflict leading to a power shift within the pantheon would be absent from ancient Israel, where Yahweh is alone in the pantheon and has held his office since the beginning.[53] Nonetheless, the concepts remain in the cognitive environment and some of the themes begin to emerge in the reception of the material. We might especially note that the theme of the enthronement of a divine being who is given power and authority after overcoming a hostile adversary is very similar to some of the language used to describe the exaltation of Christ (e.g., 1 Cor 15:24–27; Rev 11:15; to a lesser extent Eph 1:22).[54] This imagery

51. Watson, "*Hêlēl*," 393–94.

52. Contra Forsyth, *Enemy*, 130. The epithet of Athtar, *ʿrz*, which Forsyth renders as "rebel," is better translated "Tyrant" (e.g., Watson, "*Hêlēl*," 393). Some interpreters argue instead that *ʿrz* should be translated "luminous" and offer the title as a further parallel between Athtar and Hêlēl (Craigie, "Helel, Athtar and Phaethon," 223; see also Wyatt, *Religious Texts from Ugarit*, 132).

53. Some scholars, trying to anthropologically reconstruct the history of Israelite religion, argue that at some point the Hebrews had [at least] two gods; El/*ʾĕlôhîm*, more or less the counterpart to Canaanite El, and Yahweh, more or less the counterpart to Canaanite Baal. The theory states that at some point Yahweh succeeded El as the head of the pantheon, but later writers in an attempt to promote monotheism merged the two characters together. This hypothetical redaction process is supposed to account for some of the variance in the titles and images used to describe Israel's God in various parts of the Hebrew Bible. While interesting, this hypothesis is speculative and has little bearing on the imagery and theology of the biblical text-in-context; we are interested in the literary intent of the final redacted form, not the beliefs that might be extrapolated from its [hypothetical] sources.

54. 1 Cor 15:27 quotes Ps 8:6, but the messianic application of the psalm comes through the influence of Dan 7; see Ciampa and Rosner, *First Letter to the Corinthians*, 775. For the allusion to Dan 7:13–14 in Rev 11:15 see Koester, *Revelation*, 515; Osborne, *Revelation*, 441–42; Beale, *Revelation*, 611. For the allusion in Ephesians 1:21 see Hoehner, *Ephesians*, 77.

derives from Daniel 7 (which, as discussed above, may derive from the imagery of *Anzu and Ninurta* and thereby carry the rebellion theme implicitly), although Daniel's cloud rider does not actually fight and defeat any of the beasts. Nonetheless, the reception of the tradition and the strong emphasis on the divinity of the redeemer, as is the case in Christianity, makes the semblance to the ancient Near Eastern material even stronger (see also the Christian reception of Psalm 110). This would have been even more obvious in ante-Nicene Christological systems, such as those of Arius or Origen, wherein the Father and the Son are two different beings. However, the most notable reception of the rebellion theme occurs in the interpretation of Genesis 6 and the fall of the watcher angels, which we will now examine.

The fall of the watchers

The narrative of the watchers (Aramaic *'îrîn*) is a Second Temple tradition based partially on the Hebrew Bible (or possibly a parallel tradition), especially Genesis 6.[55] The title "watchers" for the eponymous beings is derived from Daniel 4:10, 14, 20 (NIV 4:13, 17, 23), which the tradition interprets interchangeably with the *bĕnê 'ĕlôhîm* (NIV "sons of God") of Genesis 6:2, 4. The character Azazel (taken from Leviticus 16; see chapter 7) also makes an appearance in the narrative,[56] as do the angels Michael (Dan 10:13, 21; 12:1) and Gabriel (Dan 8:16; 9:21). The narrative of the fall of the watchers is primarily found in the pseudepigraphical book of *1 Enoch*, especially chapters 1–36 called the Book of the Watchers.[57] The narrative is also referenced in many later works, including notably the book of *Jubilees*[58] and the New Testament (especially 2 Peter 2:4 and Jude 6).

The Book of the Watchers presents two distinct narratives, the first featuring an extrabiblical character named Shemihazah and the second featuring Azazel, who has been cast as one of the watchers. The second narrative functions as a commentary on some of the features of the first.[59] Shemihazah and two hundred of the watchers (called "angels" in some manuscripts),[60] including Azazel (*1 En.* 6.7), observe the beauty of human women and desire to take them as wives. After swearing an oath that they will not abandon their resolve to carry out this "great sin" (*1 En.* 6.3),[61] they descend to earth, marry the women, and begin to teach them "sorcery and charms

---

55. See discussion in Harkins, *Watchers*; Stuckenbruck, *Myth of Rebellious Angels*; Wright, *Origin of Evil Spirits*.

56. For equation of Heb. *ʿăzāʾzēl* (LXX αποπομπήν) with Ἀζαήλ in *1 En.* 1.8, see Janowski, "Azazel," 130–31.

57. Nickelsburg, *1 Enoch 1*, 72–76.

58. *Jub.* 4.15; 5.1–2.

59. Fröhlich, "Mesopotamian Elements," 13.

60. Nickelsburg, *1 Enoch 1*, 174.

61. Nickelsburg, *1 Enoch 1*, 174.

and the cutting of roots and plants" (*1 En.* 7.1),[62] later elaborated to include spells, mysteries, and the signs of the earth, sun, moon, stars, and lightning (*1 En.* 8.3). Azazel meanwhile teaches the forging of weapons and the craft of jewelry and cosmetics (*1 En.* 8.1).[63] The children of the union of the watchers and the women are the *gibbōrîm* ("Giants," a reference to Genesis 6:4, NIV "heroes"), and the children of the giants are the Nephilim (also from Genesis 6:4).[64] The giants and their offspring eat all of the humans' food; then they eat the humans; and finally they eat each other (*1 En.* 7:3). Observing this, the angels Michael, Sariel (or *Uriel*), Raphael, and Gabriel bring accusation of the watchers and the giants before God (*1 En.* 9.1–11). In response, Sariel is sent to warn Noah of the impending deluge (*1 En.* 10.1–3); Raphael is sent to bind Azazel in darkness in the wilderness (*1 En.* 10.4–8); Gabriel is sent to destroy the children of the watchers by sending them to war against each other (*1 En.* 10.9–10); and Michael is sent to "bind [the watchers] for seventy generations in the valleys of the earth . . . until the eternal judgment is consummated" (*1 En.* 10.12).[65] Michael is further instructed to "destroy all perversity from the face of the earth" (*1 En.* 10.16) and "cleanse the earth from all impurity and from all wrong" (*1 En.* 10:20), presumably in reference to the flood.[66] The narrative of the watchers is mentioned again in a different section of *1 Enoch* called the Animal Apocalypse (*1 En.* 85–90) where Azazel (represented by a single star, *1 En.* 86.1) descends first and teaches his knowledge to humanity prior to the arrival of Shemihazah's band (represented by many stars, *1 En.* 86.3). The variation may be an attempt to clarify the narrative sequence of the book of the watchers and also to associate Azazel's instruction with the appearance of metalworking among the line of Cain in Genesis 4:22.[67] Placing Azazel's transgression first may support a possible interpretation of the Book of the Watchers wherein the cosmetic arts taught by Azazel allowed the human women to seduce the watchers, thus making Azazel ultimately responsible for the entire affair.[68] However, in the Animal Apocalypse (where Azazel descends first) there is no indication that the watchers were seduced.[69] The idea of a seduction of the watchers by the women is sometimes proposed to be the basis for Paul's odd assertion that women should keep their heads covered "because of the angels" in 1 Corinthians 11:10.[70]

62. Nickelsburg, *1 Enoch 1*, 182.

63. Nickelsburg, *1 Enoch 1*, 188.

64. Nickelsburg, *1 Enoch 1*, 184–85.

65. Nickelsburg, *1 Enoch 1*, 215.

66. "The devastation of the flood following these events signifies the purification of the earth." Fröhlich, "Mesopotamian Elements" 13.

67. Hogan, "The Watchers Traditions," 115.

68. Hogan, "The Watchers Traditions," 110.

69. Hogan, "The Watchers Traditions," 116.

70. See for example Lewis, "'Because of the Angels,'" 88. Alternatively, Paul's emphasis on the presence of the angels may simply be emphasizing a need for extreme purity and propriety; the Qumran War Scroll states that "any man who is not ritually clean in respect to his genitals [compare Lev

The binding of the watchers is mentioned again in the Animal Apocalypse (*1 En.* 88.3), as is the binding of Azazel (*1 En.* 88.1). In the book of *Jubilees*, the binding of the watchers is mentioned (*Jub.* 5.6, 10) but Azazel is not. However, *Jubilees* reports that after the flood, the "polluted demons began to lead astray the children of Noah's sons."[71] These demons are specified as the children of the watchers in *Jubilees* 10.5. In response, God orders all of the demons to be bound (*Jub.* 10.7). However, Mastema (Satan) requests that one tenth of the spirits remain free:

> Leave some of them before me, and let them obey my voice. And let them do everything which I tell them, because if some of them are not left for me, I shall not be able to exercise the authority of my will among the children of men; because they are (intended) to corrupt and lead astray before my judgment, because the evil of the sons of men is great. . . . And [the angels] acted in accord with all his words: all the evil ones, who were cruel, [they] bound in the place of judgment, but a tenth of them [they] let remain so that they might be subject to Satan upon the earth.[72]

However, the binding of the [watchers/angels/sons of God] is not recorded in Genesis, and the second binding and allocation of the children of the watchers to the control of Satan is not found in either Genesis or *1 Enoch*. Nonetheless, the binding of the angels is mentioned in 2 Peter 2:4 and Jude 6, and probably also informs the imagery used in Revelation 20, where the dragon is bound in the abyss "to keep him from deceiving the nations" (Rev 20:1–3) and subsequently released to deceive them again (Rev 20:7–8). The devil's binding is comparable to the fate of Azazel in *1 Enoch*, especially *1 Enoch* 88:1, "[the angel] seized the first star that had fallen from heaven, and he bound it by his hands and feet and threw it into an abyss";[73] and also to the fate of the "polluted demons" in *Jubilees* 10.1, 6–7. The devil's release is comparable to the tenth of the [demons] in *Jubilees* 10.9 who are left free.[74] Finally, depending on the date of its composition, the *'îrîn* in Daniel 4 may be a reference to the Enochic tradition, rather than the other way round. If this is the case then the word in Daniel invokes the title "watchers" as applied to good angels (e.g., *1 En.* 39.12–13; 71.7),[75] not to the malefactors of the Book of the Watchers.

In the Book of the Watchers, the angels teach various skills to humans, a detail not recorded in Genesis. This has led some scholars to speculate that the profile of the

---

15:16] on the day of battle shall not go down with them into battle, for holy angels are present with their army" (1QM 7.6; trans. Wise, Abegg, and Cook, *Dead Sea Scrolls,* 157). This imagery in turn derives from Exodus 19 and Joshua 3, not Genesis 6.

71. *Jub.* 10.1, trans. Wintermute, in *OTP* 2:75.

72. *Jub.* 10.8, 11, trans. Wintermute, in *OTP* 2:76.

73. Nickelsburg, *1 Enoch 1,* 364.

74. Aune, *Revelation 6–16,* 669; Aune, *Revelation 17–22,* 1078–80, 1082; Koester, *Revelation,* 770; Osborne, *Revelation,* 699–701.

75. See Collins, *Daniel,* 224–25. Collins dates Daniel 1–6 contemporarily with *1 Enoch.*

watchers is derived from the *apkallu*, the antediluvian sages who taught humans the arts of civilization in the mythology of Mesopotamia.[76] Annus offers a further series of parallels between the *apkallu* and the watchers as follows:

- The seven antediluvian *apkallu* were fully divine, but the four that appear after the flood are "of human descent," which indicates that the *apkallu* were divine beings that could procreate with humans as the Enochian watchers also do.

- The *apkallu* are composite beings (fish-men) that arise out of the cosmic ocean. As such they are associated with the liminal and chaotic realms, even though their function (teaching the arts) contributes to the establishment of order.[77] Nonetheless, they are sometimes depicted as malicious beings associated with demonology and witchcraft.[78] In Enoch, the watchers bring disorder (the conventional activity of chaotic beings) and teach sorcery.[79] In Genesis, however, the *běnê 'ĕlôhîm* are not chaotic beings (even though they do contribute to disorder, see chapter 12); they do not teach the arts to humanity; and there is no mention of magic.

- In the *Poem of Erra*, in the aftermath of the flood, Marduk banishes the *apkallu* back into the ocean (*apsu*) and commands them not to come out again. This is superficially similar to the binding of the watchers in *1 Enoch*,[80] which as stated above is not mentioned in Genesis.

- Figurines of the *apkallu* were buried in the foundations of houses to ward off evil spirits. The word for these figures in Akkadian ritual texts (*maṣṣarē*) is the semantic equivalent to the Aramaic *'îrîn*, "watchers."[81]

Kilmer also observes that Adapa, the most famous of the *apkallu*, is called "son of Ea,"[82] which is similar enough to the title "son[s] of God" (*běnê 'ĕlôhîm*) in Genesis 6 that it may have inspired the Enochian tradition to equate them. Nonetheless, none of the specific parallels to the *apkallu*—chaotic origin and malicious nature; teachers of crafts; confined to the liminal realm after the flood; called *watchers*—apply to

76. The authors of the book of *1 Enoch* would have been aware of the *apkallu* tradition through Berossus, a fourth-/third-century priest in Babylon who refers to Oannes (= Adapa), a monster from the sea who taught the arts of civilization to humanity.

77. *Jubilees* depicts the watchers as having been originally tasked with instructing humans in proper ritual or ethical conduct (*Jub.* 4:15), although this aspect of the watchers is not emphasized in Enoch. Several other documents depict them positively as well, sometimes with Mesopotamian parallels. See Annus, "Origin of the Watchers," 297–303.

78. See further Annus, "Origin of the Watchers," 291–94.

79. The various "signs" and skills that the watchers teach in *1 Enoch* 8:3 all have counterparts in Mesopotamian ritual and omen literature. Sages were not supposed to teach this information to wives or children even in Mesopotamia, though this is what the watchers are depicted as doing. Annus, "Origin of the Watchers" 290–91.

80. See further Annus, "Origin of the Watchers," 309.

81. Annus, "Origin of the Watchers," 281–83.

82. Kilmer, "The Mesopotamian Counterparts," 39.

the characters in Genesis 6. Consequently, while we can infer that the Mesopotamian traditions of the *apkallu* informed the interpretation of Genesis found in *1 Enoch* and afterward, we cannot assume that Genesis 6 in context is also referring to the *apkallu*. See chapter 17 for a discussion of Genesis 6 in context.

If the watchers in the Enochian tradition are derived from Mesopotamian concepts, then it would make sense that the Enochian conceptions of their children, the Nephilim and the *gibbōrîm*, are as well. As mentioned above, the *apkallu* give rise to a series of creatures called the *ummianu*, which survive the flood.[83] The Jewish *Book of the Giants* (a derivative of Enoch found at Qumran)[84] includes the names of Gilgamesh and Utnapishtim (the Mesopotamian flood hero) among the children of the watchers.[85] The Babylonian Talmud identifies the postdiluvian Amorite kings Sihon and Og (Num 21:21–35) as descendants of Shemihazah;[86] Og is called "last of the *rĕpā'îm*" in Deuteronomy 3:11. The terms *rĕpā'îm* and *Nephilim* are used to describe the inhabitants of Canaan, in particular the Anakites (Num 33:13; Deut 2:11). Other traditions identify Nimrod (the "mighty hunter before the LORD" in Genesis 10:8–9) with the *gibbōrîm*, and by extension with Nephilim.[87] This tradition also implies that Noah himself was one of the "giants," since Nimrod was descended from him through Ham and there would have been no other way for the bloodline to survive the deluge;[88] compare to the presence of Utnapishtim (the Mesopotamian equivalent of Noah) among the children of the watchers in the *Book of the Giants*. All of these traditions assume that "Nephilim" is fundamentally a *biological* taxon signifying a line of divine-human hybrids that gradually diminishes over time. In contrast, the book of *1 Enoch* itself claims that the Nephilim were deprived of their bodies in the flood and became demonic spirits: "The spirits that have gone forth from the body of their flesh are evil spirits, for from humans they came into being, and from the holy watchers was the origin of their creation. Evil spirits they will be on the earth, and evil spirits they will be called" (*1 En.* 14.9).[89] Yet another tradition identifies the "sons of god" not as divine beings but as righteous human beings (sometimes the children of Seth) who intermarry with wicked human beings (sometimes the children of Cain)[90] and produce offspring who are biologically human but morally degenerate. Evidence suggests that this was the interpretation preferred in the synagogue.[91] Against all of these

---

83. Kilmer, "The Mesopotamian Counterparts," 39.

84. See Nickelsburg, *1 Enoch 1*, 76.

85. Annus, "Origin of the Watchers," 282.

86. *Niddah* 61. See Annus, "Origin of the Watchers," 285.

87. LXX uses the word *gigas* for all three; See Wright, *Evil Spirits*, 7.

88. See Stuckenbruck, *Myth of Rebellious Angels*, 5–7.

89. Nickelsburg, *1 Enoch 1*, 267; Wright, *Evil Spirits*, 22.

90. See for example Doedens, *Sons of God*, 6–7.

91. Doedens, *Sons of God*, 6–7.

hypotheses, the text of Genesis 6 itself does not even clearly state that the Nephilim are actually the offspring of the *běnê 'ělôhîm* (see discussion in chapter 12).

Some scholars have further speculated that the character of Azazel, and by extension the rest of the watchers, shows some similarities to the Prometheus character from Greek mythology—or perhaps an unidentified ancient Near Eastern near-equivalent— as described in Hesiod's *Theogony* (507–616) and *Works and Days* (42–105) but especially in *Prometheus Bound* by Aeschylus.[92] Prometheus is depicted in Aeschylus as a benefactor of mankind who teaches them the arts of civilization, especially metalworking, as the *apkallu* also do in Mesopotamia and as Azazel does in *1 Enoch*. Prometheus also angers Zeus by stealing fire and giving it to humanity, for which he is bound and tormented as Azazel also is.[93] The means by which evil comes to be present in the world in *1 Enoch* also shares thematic similarities with Hesiod. Angry at Prometheus and not wishing humanity to be able to enjoy the gifts that Prometheus stole, Zeus creates a beautiful woman, Pandora, and sends her to inflict evil onto men who will marry her or the women who originate from her (described in a misogynistic rant in *Theogony* II 590–612). This is similar to the Enochian tradition in the sense that evil originates through lusting after women.[94] In *Works and Days*, Pandora brings evil, not by marriage, but by being given a jar that contains all evil, which she promptly opens. This has some similarity to the birth of demons in *1 Enoch* who come from women indirectly, being children of the watchers. Interestingly, Hesiod in *Works and Days* identifies the *daimones* (intermediate demigods) as being the spirits of those who lived in the primordial golden age and who now administer human affairs,[95] though in this perception the "demons" are not evil (see chapter 7).

Finally, we should note that, despite the similarities of its details, the *genre* and *themes* of *1 Enoch* differ from any of its purported sources, including Genesis. *1 Enoch* in general is an apocalypse, and its purpose therefore is a kind of social commentary that situates a crisis being faced by the audience in a broader context (see chapter 3).[96] In the process it doubles as a theodicy, describing how evil came into the world. Its most notable feature in this regard is that the advent of evil is laid entirely on the angels: "the author makes the human race . . . victims to be vindicated rather than the perpetrators of violence."[97] The specific actions of the watchers—"they began to defile themselves" (*1 En.* 7.1)—is connected with [contemporary] Jewish ideas about purity

92. Nickelsburg, *1 Enoch 1*, 192–93; Wright, *Evil Spirits*, 34.

93. Nickelsburg, *1 Enoch 1*, 193.

94. Nickelsburg, *1 Enoch 1*, 193.

95. Riley, "Demon," 235.

96. "[Enoch's] purpose is to expound sacred tradition so that it speaks to contemporary times and issues; . . . a story about the origins of evil in primordial times is, in reality, an explanation of the author's time, which is situated at the threshold of the end time, its judgment, and the new age." Nickelsburg, *1 Enoch 1*, 29.

97. Nickelsburg, *1 Enoch 1*, 167. Similarly, "The narrative does not mention human responsibility. The authors and agents of the deeds are the watchers." Fröhlich, "Mesopotamian Elements," 19.

and the nature of sin: "the first stage of the birth of evil is dysfunction in the cosmic order, a result of the mixing of heavenly and earthly beings, a deed considered as a sin related to sexual relations . . . and a case of ethical impurity (sin resulting in the impurity of the sinner and the land)."[98] These specific offenses in turn are derived from Leviticus, not Genesis.[99] In contrast, the description of evil on the earth in Genesis 6:5–7 mentions humans repeatedly, but does not mention the sons of God or the Nephilim at all. Further, the story of the origin of evil on earth in Genesis is usually thought to be found in chapter 3, not chapter 6. Additionally, Genesis is not an apocalypse and does not address the contemporary situation of its audience, except insofar as Genesis contributes to the description of the covenant that its audience is under, and also insofar as the genre of *literature* addresses themes and issues common to all humanity (see chapter 4).

Also in contrast to Enoch, the Greek and Mesopotamian sources are not theodicies at all; rather, like Genesis, they deal with the dynamics of divine-human relations. In Hesiod, Zeus hates humanity and wishes to inflict misery on them, which includes preventing them from benefitting from the gifts of Prometheus. There is no flood in Greek mythology, but Zeus sends evil on humanity in the form of Pandora and her jar. The moral of the story is that the will of Zeus is incontrovertible, and even the clever titan Prometheus could not succeed in subverting it: "So it is not possible to deceive or go beyond the will of Zeus; for not even the son of Iapetus, kindly Prometheus, escaped his heavy anger, but of necessity strong bands confined him, although he knew many a wile."[100] Likewise, in the ancient near Eastern flood story *Atrahasis* the gods hate humanity because the humans are too noisy. After several failed attempts to reduce the population, the gods finally send the flood to wipe out the humans entirely, though Atrahasis is saved when the god Enki subverts the pantheon and warns him. Too late, the gods realize that, with humanity gone, they have nobody to feed them and nobody to do their work for them. Atrahasis offers a sacrifice, and the gods, grateful that their mistake has been corrected, allow him and his descendants to live. The moral of the story is that gods and humans are dependent on each other. In Genesis, and also in *Jubilees* 5.1–2, God is angry with humanity because of their unrighteousness (violence, not cultic offenses or transgression of divine will or command) and wipes out most of the humans as a corrective. In *1 Enoch*, as we have seen, God is not angry with the humans at all.

Thus, we see that the Enochian tradition, which interprets Genesis 6 as representing a rebellion (or at least a determined defiance) of lesser divine beings against the ruling deity, actually represents a complex amalgamation of a variety of elements from

98. Frölich, "Mesopotamian Elements," 19.

99. See Frölich, "Mesopotamian Elements," 15–16.

100. Hesiod, *Theogony* 2.613–16, trans. Evelyn-White, in LCL 57:122–25. *Works and Days* ends the account similarly: "So is there no way to escape the will of Zeus" (105, trans. Evelyn-White, in LCL 57:8–9).

a variety of sources which it appropriates for its own purposes. It is not derived solely from Genesis 6 and should not be assumed to authentically reproduce the contextual meaning of Genesis 6. Consequently, later New Testament references to Enochian themes should be read as references to *1 Enoch*, not to Genesis, and should not inform our interpretation of the meaning of Genesis. We will discuss the New Testament use of Enochian traditions in chapter 14 and Genesis 6 in context in chapter 12.

The eschatological battle

The eschatological battle tradition develops in the Second Temple period as an extrapolation of prophecies concerning the postexilic restoration of Israel, as depicted especially in Ezekiel 38–39. This restoration would include a reconstruction of the temple (as described in Ezekiel 40–48) and reinstatement of the Davidic dynasty, both important aspects of Jewish identity. The concept of a future Davidic ruler, an idea established as early as the eighth-century prophets, became the basis for the various messianic traditions, including those referenced and propagated by the New Testament. Understanding the development of these traditions is important for understanding the meaning that is intended to be conveyed by the references. Although the various permutations of both battle and messiah traditions are highly non-systematic, there are nonetheless some general trends which we will briefly examine.

The Jewish diaspora generally viewed their captivity in Babylon as a recapitulation of the captivity of their ancestors in Egypt, and the release of the exiles by Cyrus was seen as a parallel to the exodus. This imagery is present even in the Bible itself, for example Hosea 11:1 calling the diaspora out of Egypt, and Ezra's reading of the law (Neh 8:2–18) as a recapitulation of Moses. The parallelism is so deeply ingrained that some scholars even propose that the entire Old Testament was *composed* in the exilic period (by revisionists) in order to establish the theme. This theory is extreme and generally unsustainable, though postexilic *interpretations* of the Hebrew Bible (such as the Targum and the Septuagint) occasionally manipulate the text to emphasize parallels between exodus and exile.[101] However, the release of the exiles and even the building of the Second Temple did not fit the Jewish expectation of what their restored nation would look like. Israel in the exodus had the tabernacle, but nonetheless they had no land; they wandered in the wilderness as penance for their sin and the sins of their predecessors. This seems to be how (some of) the diaspora came to see themselves; they have a temple of some sort, but not the grand edifice of Ezekiel's vision, and they have land to live in but no political autonomy. Accordingly, they conceived of the restoration as a recapitulation of the conquest, an idea also found in Ezekiel 48 by the depiction of the division of the land. The talionic oracles of destruction against Babylon in, e.g., Ezekiel 39 ("magog") and Habakkuk 3 ("the land

---

101. See for example, *Tg. Ps.-J.* and *Tg. Neof.* Gen 15:12.

of wickedness") are recast as a glorious *Reconquista* wherein the sinners and idolators are purged from the holy land just as Israel itself was purged at the exile, and as (in their reinterpretation) the Canaanites had been purged before that (see for example Wisdom 12:3–27)[102] and the Nephilim even before that (compare their fate in *1 Enoch*, described above).[103] Sometimes the restoration was thought to be achieved through literal military conquest, just as Joshua's original occupation was; this is the conception behind the Maccabean revolts, behind the zealots of Jesus's time, and behind the Jewish revolts against the Romans that culminated in the destruction of Herod's Temple. This military image led to the conception of the restoration according to the terms and categories of warfare, including the idea that wars were fought on both the human and divine level (see above). However, the divine warrior who fought for Israel could not be Yahweh himself; the return of Yahweh to the side of Israel would signal the final consummation of the restoration (see Ezek 43:7), so Yahweh could not be beside Israel during the war that *brings about* the restoration. Further, the affliction of the diaspora was thought to come from the hand of Yahweh (e.g., 2 Macc 7:18) just as the affliction of the wilderness generation had also come from Yahweh, and Yahweh could not fight against himself on both sides. A solution was found in the character of the commander of the army of the LORD in Joshua 5:14, who was also identified with the angel that the LORD promised to send to drive out the people of Canaan (in his absence) in Exodus 33:2–3.[104] This character was also associated with Michael (e.g., *T. Abr.* 1.4),[105] who appears as one of four archangels in the Book of the Watchers and is entrusted to "destroy all perversity from the face of the earth" (*1 En.* 10.16) in order to bring about idyllic conditions, invoking the same imagery used for the restoration of Israel in Isaiah 65–66 (*1 En.* 10.16—11.2).[106] Michael is also associated with the commander of the army of the LORD in Daniel 10:21 by virtue of being given the same title (Heb. śr; see chapter 12). Additionally, just as the divine commander of

102. For a better understanding of the fate of the Canaanites in context, see Walton and Walton, *Lost World of the Israelite Conquest*.

103. "Just as God redeemed humanity in the person of Noah, God again will cleanse the cosmos; . . . the eschaton will bring about the restoration of the law of the cosmos and, the cleansing of heaven and earth, and the redemption of Israel." Wright, *Evil Spirits*, 49.

104. *Bereshit Rabbah* 97.3.

105. The title given to Michael here (*archistrategos*) is the same word the LXX uses to render "commander of the army [of the Lord]" in Josh 5:14; see Sanders, "Testament of Abraham," 882. The *Testament of Abraham* cannot be dated with certainty, but it may be as early as the second century BCE (ibid., 874). Later Jewish writings would eventually come to associate this character with Metatron; God says of the same angel in Exod 23:21, "my Name is in him," which correlates to descriptions of Metatron as "lesser YHWH." See Orlov, *The Enoch-Metatron Tradition*, 95. However, this particular strain of the Metatron traditions may in fact be based on Michael: "Metatron and Michael were one and the same angel bearing an esoteric and a common name: Michael was the common name and Metatron was the esoteric, magical name. However, at some point the connection between Metatron and Michael was obscured, and a new independent archangel with many of Michael's powers came into being." Ibid., 85. Cited Philip Alexander, "3 (Hebrew Apocalypse of) Enoch," 243–44.

106. Nickelsburg, *1 Enoch 1*, 227–28.

the army of the LORD has a human counterpart in Joshua, Michael was also expected to have one—or sometimes more—human counterparts, which are usually given the title *messiah* (Gk *christos*, lit. "anointed one"). The Old Testament was mined for prophetic hints about the appearance and identity of this individual, and about signs that would signal that the time of the restoration was at hand. The New Testament makes extensive use of these references in order to establish the events it describes as the arrival of the messianic age, even though the anticipated political and military uprising never occurs; it is not a coincidence that the name the angel assigns to the messiah is *Joshua* (Matt 1:21; Heb. *yĕšûaʿ*, Gk. *Iesus*, "Jesus"). A similar hermeneutic to that which produced those expectations is also employed (using different OT passages) to rationalize and interpret the crucifixion and resurrection that *did* occur. The point of the references in the New Testament is to establish the identity of Jesus of Nazareth as the expected and prophesied messiah, and thereby establish the new covenant and the church he inaugurates as the expected and prophesied restoration of Israel through which the divine plan is now being enacted (see chapter 14).

It is important to recognize that the expectation of a messiah—especially a specifically *military* messiah—is neither universal in Judaism nor systematic when it appears. While the imagery of the recapitulated exodus is ubiquitous, some Jewish writers chose to emphasize the exodus, not as a precursor to a conquest, but rather as a demonstration of God's faithfulness that in turn invokes a particular response. "The exodus created both a requirement to follow divine laws and a basis of the promise for Israel's future redemption . . . [despite the loss of God's presence in the temple], prayer is possible, [and] through prayer a person can relate to the divine and experience God's presence [and], in turn, the divine is accessible. Likewise . . . everyday experiences become opportunities to be reminded of the divine and to relate to the divine's manifestation in the world."[107] Where the "military" conception of the exodus emphasized what the wilderness generation did *not* have (land, temple, "rest on every side") and therefore envisioned a future where those things would be gained through divine intervention, the "devotional" conception of the exodus emphasized what the wilderness generation *did* have (a special status before God, God's provision for them) and envisioned those things in their own experience in exile. Thus, the benefits of the messianic age—restored experience of the presence of God—were moved from the realm of the social and political to the internal and spiritual: "[the rabbis] sought to transmute messianic hopes into personal experiences."[108] In the military conception, the kingdom of God—that is, God's manifested presence—appears when the enemies of God are destroyed. In the devotional conception, the kingdom of God appears when the people of God do God's will. Both of these conceptions are depicted side by side (variously and non-systematically) in both the New Testament and elsewhere. However, our purpose is not to trace the development of these trends literarily, but

107. Bokser, "Messianism," 243–45.
108. Bokser, "Messianism," 237.

instead to speculate as to how the various interpretations of the exodus paradigm led to the development of the "enemy" character, known in various documents as Belial, Satan, the devil, or the prince of darkness.

Conflict theologians usually assume that the military imagery of the eschatological battle develops around a preconceived understanding of the "enemy" character, and that the battle emerges as one potential method among several to resolve the problems created by this character. The argument usually derives from the assumption that a more or less monolithic and more or less personalized principle of evil is a dominant feature in all cognitive environments and all cultures, even if it is only tangentially or subliminally alluded to in their literature. This assumption is supported by a sweeping (cosmetic) comparison of a large cross-section of mythology from widely diverse settings and sources, occasionally supplemented by anthropological and psychological speculation.[109] The specific permutation of this supposedly universal intuition in ancient Israel is most commonly asserted to be the *chaoskampf*, which we discussed above. This assumption in turn is invoked to argue for a single more or less linear and more or less systematic combat theme running unbroken through both testaments,[110] with the differences between the presentations amounting mostly to literary emphasis (prominent in the NT; understated but identifiable in the OT) and a preference for certain names over others (NT *devil* and *Satan* preferred over OT *Leviathan* and *sea*). Alternatively, a separate strain of interpretation sees the combat image as wholly innovative and unprecedented, introduced into later Judaism either as a polemic against their more distasteful early traditions[111] or as a product of syncretism with Zoroastrianism (see further below). What we are proposing is an alternative to both of these options. As suggested above, the combat imagery does not originate with the conception of an enemy; rather, it develops naturally as an extension of the ubiquitous exodus paradigm and the expected recapitulation of the conquest that the paradigm entails. The "enemy," when it does eventually appear, is not derived from anything in the Old Testament text-in-context; however, it can be traced back to Old Testament roots by an identifiable sequence of logic. Thus, the identity of the "enemy" is neither an original feature of the Israelite cognitive environment nor an entirely novel imposition. Rather, it represents a *trajectory of interpretation* embellished and integrated with ideas from a variety of (extrabiblical) sources, just as the Enochian material represents a trajectory of interpretation embellished by a variety of sources. We will now examine this possibility further.

As proposed above, the protagonist of the battle motif, Michael, emerges as a recapitulation of the commander of the army of the LORD from Joshua 5:14 and of the angel who goes before the army in Exodus 33:2. Notably, the earliest depictions of

109. See especially Boyd, *God at War*, 11–18; Russell, *Devil*, 36–121.

110. See especially Forsyth, *Old Enemy*, 6–18; Longman and Reid, *God is a Warrior*, 16–19; Boyd, *God at War*, 13–14.

111. Russell, *Devil*, 197–220.

the Michael character (*1 Enoch* and Daniel) do not depict him in conjunction with an equal and opposite antagonist. Similarly, the original conquest account that informs the exodus paradigm does not feature a Canaanite counterpart to either the angel or to Joshua; the enemy armies simply appear one after the other and are each defeated in turn. Likewise, in Daniel 10:20, the princes of Persia and Greece appear one after the other and are fought in turn. In *1 Enoch* 10, Michael is sent to bind the two hundred watchers (except, notably, for Azazel), destroy their children the giants, and to bring renewal on the earth afterward. Azazel, the watcher given the highest prominence—and later identified with the devil in, e.g., the *Apocalypse of Abraham*—is opposed by Raphael, not by Michael. This is consistent with Raphael's opposition to the demon Asmodeus (also sometimes identified with the devil) in the book of Tobit, but Raphael is not ordinarily given any eschatological or military role. Raphael appears again opposite Asmodeus in the *Testament of Solomon*, which lists a series of demons each with an opposing angel whose name can be invoked to counter their influence. Once again, however, this opposition is ongoing and perpetual, and is unrelated to either the final destruction of the demons or the eschatological restoration of Israel. Finally, the *devotional* conception of the exodus paradigm conceives of the "enemy" to be overcome as trends and inclinations, not personal agents, although personal agents are sometimes seen as responsible for inducing those inclinations, whether social-historical (e.g., the "Hellenizers" from the Second Temple period or the Moabites and Midianites from the original exodus in Numbers 25) or spiritual-allegorical (e.g., the serpent in Philo [see chapter 10] or some of the demons in the *Testament of Solomon*). However, these inclinations—regardless of their source—are seen as a persistent feature of human existence, not a temporary affliction that God will eventually intervene to destroy. These three distinct elements—equal and opposite angelic opposition; external prompting of the inclination to disobedience and vice; and the divinely-facilitated destruction of Israel's enemies at the eschaton—are neither systematic nor mutually exclusive, and many sources employ any combination of them in order to serve their particular purpose. At least one tradition, however, managed to combine the three elements into a more or less unified eschatological theme. One of the most sweeping and coherent expressions of this synthesis is found in the community at Qumran, specifically in two documents called the *Two Spirits* and the *War Scroll*. We will now briefly examine these in order to speculate how the synthesis develops as an extension of the Old Testament under the influence of the exodus paradigm.

The *Two Spirits* (1QS 3.15—4.26) is a lengthy aside in a larger document, which appears to be a charter describing the rules for membership in the Qumran sect. The text describes two spirits appointed to each person, one of truth and light and one of falsehood and darkness (1QS 3.17–19). The former engenders righteousness and virtue; the latter engenders evil and sin (1QS 4.2–14). Importantly, both spirits have been established specifically for their purpose by God: "[God] created the spirits of light and darkness, making them the cornerstone of every deed" (1QS 3.25); "God has appointed these spirits as equals" (1QS 4.16, 25). At the same time, however, "The God of Israel [assists] all of the sons of light. . . . God's love for one spirit lasts forever. He will be pleased with its actions for always. The counsel of the other, however, he abhors, hating its every impulse for all time."[112] The two competing inclinations are present within the hearts and minds of all humans (1QS 4.24), which is conceptually similar to the devotion theme discussed above. However, the document further divides corporate humanity into two opposing camps; those who obey the inclination to darkness (elsewhere called "children of darkness," e.g., 1QS 1.10; or "men of the pit," e.g., 1QS 10.16) and those who obey the inclination to light (called "sons of light," 1QS 3.24–25, or later "sons of righteousness," e.g., 1QS 9.14) and implied to consist of the members of the sect (the *Yahad*) and those who might wish to join it. The followers of darkness in turn are cast in the role of the enemies of the people of God, who are destroyed at the eschaton (1QS 3.23; 4.18–26; also 10.19–20). In this way, the perpetual internal struggle between virtue and vice (the devotion theme), as well as the equal and opposite spirits who incite it, are all cast as part of the temporary afflictions of the people of God that will be rectified in the last days by divine intervention.

Many commentators suggest that the specific mythographic image of equal and opposite spirits is derived from the influence of Iranian religion on Judaism. This is theoretically possible, since the *Two Spirits* does exhibit cosmetic similarity to Zoroastrian theology, and Persian cultural influence on Jewish literature can be clearly demonstrated;[113] for example, *Asmodeus* (the demon opposite Raphael in Tobit) is a Persian name sometimes thought to be derived from *Aeshma Daeva*, the Zoroastrian devil. At the same time, however, the *Two Spirits* is not a copy of the Iranian Avesta, nor dependent on it: "the dualism of the Two Spirits at Qumran, with the accompanying paraphernalia of light and darkness, truth and iniquity, could have evolved from inner-Jewish developments."[114] The same tension between Yahweh's establishment of and simultaneous opposition to Israel's oppressors is part of the exodus paradigm and is also presented in Ezekiel and (especially) Habakkuk, and can be seen in the original exodus as well in, e.g., Judges 2:10–22 (in the context of the incomplete conquest). Further, the name of the angel of darkness is *Belial* (1QS 1.18, 24; 2.5; 10.21), not *Aeshma Daeva*, *Angra Maiynu*, *Asmodeus*, or any permutation thereof. The name Belial, in turn, is derived from the Old Testament in accordance with the devotion theme, which is well in keeping with the content and themes of the *Two Spirits*. As discussed in chapter 7, the name *Belial* comes from the Hebrew collocation *běnê běliya'al* (lit. "sons of belial"), which designates gross violations of the covenant order. 1 Samuel 2:12 describes the corrupt sons of Eli as "sons of belial (NIV "scoundrels") [who] did not know the LORD," thus setting up an antithetical juxtaposition between those associated with *běliya'al*

---

112. 1QS 3.24–4.1, trans. Wise, Abegg, and Cook, *Dead Sea Scrolls*, 130.

113. de Jong, "Iranian Connections."

114. Yamauchi, "Did Persian Zoroastrianism Influence Judaism?" 296, citing Barr, "Question of Religious Influence," 226.

(whatever that specifically means) and those who "know the LORD"; that is, those who keep God's covenant and stand as God's people. In the Qumran texts, the abstraction *běliya'al* is converted into the personal name of the angel of darkness, but the essential significance of *covenant antithesis* is nonetheless retained. The Angel of [God's] Truth (1QS 3.24) is not named, and is involved in the final destruction of the darkness only implicitly (1QS 4.19–20, "then shall truth come forth in victory upon the earth . . . by his truth God shall then purify all human deeds").[115]

The military imagery of the exodus paradigm is understated in the *Two Spirits*, but explicit in the *War Scroll* (1QM), which narrates the events of the Battle of Armageddon. While Michael and Belial both eventually participate (1QM 16.11; 17.4–6), the primary emphasis is on the human armies, consisting of the "sons of light" (implicitly the members of the *Yahad*) against a roster of Israel's archetypal enemies, including Edom, Moab, Ammon, the Amalekites, the Philistines, and the "Kittim of Assur" (which is probably a euphemism for Rome),[116] in addition to "those who have violated the covenant" (1QM 1.1–2). The "exiles of the sons of light" "return from the wilderness of the peoples" (1QM 1.3, an explicit correlation of exodus and exile) and begin a war that lasts for thirty-five years (1QM 2.9). Most of the document describes the manufacture of the weapons and heraldry of the army (1QM 2.16—5:2; compare perhaps Exod 25–30); the ordering of the camp and deployment of the troops (1QM 5.3—9:18; compare Num 2:1–34); and instructions for engaging the enemy (1QM 15.4—18.2; compare Josh 6:2–16). Present but understated is the messianic figure leading the army of the sons of light, called the "prince of the congregation" (1QM 3.15),[117] though a prayer of the high priest does invoke the [messianic] star of Jacob (1QM 11.6–7) in reference to Numbers 24:17–19. In general, the *War Scroll* emphasizes the role of the priests and Levites in a recapitulation of Israel's military history (compare Josh 3:3–17; 6:4–5)[118] more than a cosmic confrontation between angels, although angels are present on both sides (1QM 1.15; 7.6); the high priest's prayer specifically invokes God's past military assistance, with reference to Exodus, Numbers, Isaiah, and Ezekiel (1QM 11.5–17). This in turn supports the idea that the eschatological battle is primarily focused on the restoration of Israel[119] and only tangentially concerned with the destruction of a specific cosmic being.

While Belial and the prince of the congregation are minor characters in the *War Scroll*—at least in the parts of it that survive—the appearance of the messiah and the concurrent destruction of Belial are nonetheless consistent features of the restoration of Israel in the Qumran documents. Sometimes the messiah is a military commander recapitulating Joshua, as the prince of the congregation does; in a fragment called the

---

115. Trans. Wise, Abegg, and Cook, *Dead Sea Scrolls*, 131.
116. Wise, Abegg, and Cook, *Dead Sea Scrolls*, 150.
117. Evans, "Messiah in the Dead Sea Scrolls," 96.
118. Evans, "Messiah in the Dead Sea Scrolls," 96.
119. Evans, "Messiah in the Dead Sea Scrolls," 90.

Rule of War, the same character is depicted as ending the war by sentencing the human leaders of the enemy army to death (4Q285 frag. 4–5). Additionally, a text called the *Damascus Document* mentions two messiahs, a kingly type of David and a priestly type of Aaron.[120] The same text also introduces an anti-messiah figure called the "man of mockery" (compare 2 Thess 2). Despite a lack of systematic continuity, messianic themes are present throughout the Qumran texts.[121] The point is that even in a messianic tradition, even where the military eschatology and "devil" figure are clearly established—more clearly than they are in the New Testament—the *fact of* the devil's destruction is not the aspect that the texts choose to emphasize. Rather, the appearance of the messiah and the destruction of the devil are both asides that occur in the course of the all-important restoration of Israel, and the status of fighting alongside the messiah and participating in the destruction of the devil (and his human agents) identifies the true people of Israel; that is, those who are restored to God's favor and who will receive the blessings of the promised new covenant. As we will discuss in chapter 14, this is the theme that the New Testament prefers to emphasize as well; the restoration of Israel is at hand, and the followers of Jesus of Nazareth are the true people of Israel who inherit the promised restoration. The various references to battles against the devil are asides that serve to emphasize this point in the context of the cognitive environment, the influence of which is also evidenced at Qumran.

Having now discussed the larger questions about cosmic battle, we are ready to proceed with consideration of the major passages of Scripture. We will consider how they have been interpreted and we will propose our own conclusions as we re-evaluate the evidence of the biblical text.

120. Evans, "Messiah in the Dead Sea Scrolls," 94–95.
121. Evans, "Messiah in the Dead Sea Scrolls," 100–101.

Chapter 10

The serpent

MANY PEOPLE BEGIN TO build their understanding of demons, and their pur-ported chief, the devil, with Genesis 3. One of the most familiar images from all the biblical narratives is the temptation of Adam and Eve by the serpent, who is traditionally assumed to be the devil. The account in Genesis 3 is normally read as the opening act of a grand metanarrative that sweeps across the story of the cov-enant and reaches its climax in the Gospels and its finale in the book of Revelation. It is interesting, then, to note that the Old Testament *never* equates the serpent with Satan. Indeed, the episode is never mentioned or alluded to again at any point the Old Testament. Romans 16:20 perhaps identifies the serpent with Satan by alluding to Genesis 3:15, and Revelation 12:9 and 20:2 refer to Satan as "the ancient serpent," also perhaps in reference to Genesis. However, a reference by the New Testament authors does not tell us what the original text meant in context. We cannot therefore assume that Paul and John are offering a positive identification of the character in Genesis, and on that basis assume that we can examine the serpent as portrayed in Genesis to learn something about the devil. We must deal with the text-*in-context*; Genesis in the context of the ancient Near East, and Romans and Revelation in the context of the Second Temple period, which includes not only the text of Genesis but also a long history of interpretation.

In Genesis 3

When examining a text-in-context it is important to determine its genre as best as we can. Unfortunately, there is no direct parallel to the narrative of Genesis 3 anywhere in ancient Near Eastern literature that we have discovered. Nevertheless, several of the elements found in the Genesis narrative are also present in ancient Near Eastern epics. The element of a plant that gives life and is lost due to the activity of a serpent is found in the Gilgamesh epic, and the element of food that grants eternal life and is lost due to trickery and deception is found in the tale of Adapa. The elements are used in different ways, so we cannot say that Genesis is an adaptation or corruption of these stories specifically; however, the similarity of the elements indicates that the stories are written to communicate similar things in similar ways, and that the issues are a matter of curiosity in the culture.

In the Gilgamesh epic, Gilgamesh, the king of the city of Uruk, is on a quest to achieve immortality for himself, having become painfully aware of his own mortality after witnessing the death of his friend Enkidu. He journeys to the paradisiac island of Dilmun to meet his ancestor Utnapishtim, who was granted immortality after surviving a worldwide flood. There he learns of a plant that will restore youth to one who eats it, which can be found at the bottom of the *apsu* (the cosmic ocean). He retrieves the plant, but before he can eat it, it is stolen and eaten by a serpent, which consequently "renews its youth" by shedding its skin.

In the tale of Adapa, the sage Adapa is summoned to heaven to give account for breaking the wings of the south wind. He is warned by the god Enki not to eat any food while in heaven or it will kill him. When the high god Anu offers him food, he refuses, and only learns afterwards that the food would have granted him immortality. Neither of these stories are presented as explanations for why humans are mortal (or even as an account of how humans became mortal) and the Gilgamesh story is not an etiology of why snakes shed their skins. Both Gilgamesh and Adapa are presented as paragons of humanity; Gilgamesh is a mighty king of legend, "two parts god and one part man," while Adapa is the first of the *apkallu*, the semidivine sages who taught the arts of civilization to humanity (see chapter 9). If anyone, then, should be able to escape the human destiny of mortality, it should have been them. The point of these stories is that even the greatest heroes cannot escape mortality. The human destiny of death is inevitable.

The portrayal of Adam as a paragon of humanity comes later in Jewish tradition (e.g., Sir 49:19), but nonetheless in Genesis he is still depicted as exceptional. Serving as a priest in the garden of God at the source of the rivers—an iconic image associated with the divine realm—with the tree of life near at hand, if anyone should have been able to escape the human destiny it should have been him. Furthermore, in all three stories, the *means* by which the chance at immortality is lost is somewhat ironic given the portrayal of the paragon. Gilgamesh the mighty king has the plant stolen while he is taking a bath; Adapa the wise sage is tricked. In Genesis, Adam is given an ally to help him rule over the creatures of the earth. Instead, his ally helps him submit to one of those same creatures. The point of the irony is that the inability of humans to escape their destiny is inherent within them; even the mightiest of humans bring their own weakness with them.

The Old Testament in general does not see death and mortality as an obstacle to be overcome. Death is still an undesirable state, especially when one receives it prematurely,[1] but mortality is generally seen as a reality to be accepted; this point is

---

1. The idea of being "redeemed from sheol" or of the victory over the grave in Hosea 13:14 refer in context to being saved from the threat of an early death, not to a reversal of the condition of mortality.

emphasized in Job and especially in Ecclesiastes. While we normally refer to Genesis 3 as *the fall*, this terminology is never used in either testament. Genesis 3, like the ancient Near Eastern stories, is not offered as the story of why humans are mortal, or even as a story of how humans became mortal. Humans in fact are *created mortal*, as indicated by their being associated with dust (Gen 2:7); compare Psalm 90:3 ("You turn people back to dust, saying, 'Return to dust, you mortals'") and Genesis 3:19 ("until you return to the ground, since from it you were taken; for dust you are and to dust you will return"); and also Psalm 103:14–16 ("he remembers that we are dust . . . the wind blows over it and it is gone, and its place remembers it no more").[2] Note also that immortal people would have no need of a tree of life. Consequently, the Old Testament offers no means to restore the original pristine state of humanity (since no such state is ever presented), and also offers no means to escape the destiny of death, since this destiny is portrayed as inevitable. The old covenant promises hope and prosperity for the living while they live, but does not offer anything beyond death. (The new covenant, of course, promises the opposite; suffering and death followed by resurrection.) The point is that nothing in the genre of Genesis 3, as best can be determined from ancient Near Eastern parallels, or in later use of the material within the Old Testament, indicates that Genesis 3 was intended to be read as an etiology of the human condition. Instead, Adam's inability to gain eternal life is *an assertion of the fact* of the inevitability of human mortality, as it also is in Gilgamesh and Adapa. In context, this emphasizes a theme of human weakness and failure that is recapitulated throughout the rest of the cosmic history (see below and in chapter 12).

The second indicator that Genesis 3 is not a component of a larger metanarrative is the literary structure of Genesis itself. The book of Genesis is divided into a series of sub-narratives, each demarcated by the Hebrew word *tôlēdôt* (NIV "this is the *account* of"). The *tôlēdôt* indicates a shift in narrative focus and a transition from one section to another. Because Genesis is mostly a record of ancestry, the shift in narrative focus often—though not always[3]—indicates a shift forward in time. Consequently, conditions established in an earlier narrative often continue in subsequent narratives, because events in the past affect conditions in the future. Nonetheless, although conditions from one *tôlēdôt* can continue into later narratives, the *tôlēdôt* narratives are always more or less self-contained. *In no case* does a narrative arc stop halfway through a *tôlēdôt* section only to be picked up and continued in a later *tôlēdôt*. This indicates that the common interpretation that reads the conflict with the serpent (Gen 3:15, sometimes called the *protoevangelium*) as beginning a narrative arc that is

---

2. "Adam was created outside the Garden of Eden (Gen 2:7) and only afterwards put in Eden on the condition that he could avoid death; . . . if this is so, then the real focus of Genesis 2–3 is that Adam received a possibility to gain eternal life, which is well-known in ancient Mesopotamian myths like Gilgamesh and Adapa." Laato and Valve, "Understanding the Story of Adam and Eve," 5.

3. Examples of *tôlēdôt* sections that do not move forward in time (at least not initially) are the account of Shem in Gen 11:10 and the account of Ishmael in Gen 25:12.

later picked up by the blessing of all people through Abraham (Gen 12:3) cannot be sustained within the composition of Genesis itself.

Most readers of Genesis read chapters 2, 3, and 4 as if they were all separate and more or less isolated; the creation of Adam and Eve, the fall, and Cain and Abel. However, Genesis 2, 3, and 4 are all part of the *same tôlēdôt* that begins in Genesis 2:4 ("this is the account of the heavens and the earth") and continues up until Genesis 5:1 ("this is the account of Adam's family line"). Consequently, instead of reading the fall, the covenant with Abraham, and the covenant at Sinai—not to mention the New Testament—as a single connected narrative, as is often done, we should instead read the creation of Adam, the fall, and the story of Cain and Abel (Gen 2:4—4:26) as a single continuous narrative.[4] Further, we should expect this narrative to be more or less self-contained, as all the individual *tôlēdôt* sections are. What happens in Genesis 3 should therefore tie in very closely with what happens in Genesis 4, and should not tie in specifically with anything else unless it is referred back to elsewhere (which, for example, Noah is in Isaiah 54:9, and Abraham, Isaac, and Jacob also frequently are, but Adam and the serpent are not).

This observation allows us to reexamine the proclamations in Genesis 3:14–19, especially those made to Eve and her offspring. Because chapters 2–4 are self-contained, we propose that the reference to Eve's offspring in Genesis 3:15 does not refer to all of humanity, but rather to her literal offspring—that is, her family, Cain and Abel. The statement "I will make your pains in childbearing [lit. 'conceiving'] very severe; with painful labor you will give birth to children" means that the whole process of conceiving and bearing children will be fraught with anxiety; the word for "pain" refers to *mental* distress, not physical anguish.[5] Most interpretations of this passage insert a hard break between Genesis 3:15 and 3:16, as if God has finished speaking to the serpent and now addresses Eve, similar to the break in Genesis 3:17 when God finishes speaking to Eve and now addresses Adam. However, the language of the passage indicates that this is not the case. Both Genesis 3:14 and 3:17 begin with the formula "because you [did] . . . cursed," but verse 16 does not begin this way. Genesis 3:16, like 3:15, begins with God saying, "I will [do]." The repeated formula indicates that these passages are parallel. Thus, we propose the following arrangement: Genesis 3:14 addresses the serpent directly; Genesis 3:15–16 addresses the woman and the serpent together, one after the other; Genesis 3:17 addresses Adam directly. There is no "because you [did] . . . cursed" statement directed towards the woman. This indicates that Genesis 3:16 should continue the thought of 3:15, not introduce a non-sequitur about the woman's future condition. Thus, the reason for the anxiety ("pain") in Genesis 3:16 is the impending strife promised in Genesis 3:15. Therefore, Genesis 3 arguably does not describe the conditions that will prevail for all of humanity going forward; it describes the conditions that will prevail as the narrative continues in Genesis 4.

4. German, *Fall Reconsidered*, 80; 105.

5. Walton, *Genesis*, 227.

The final redacted form of Genesis is the backstory of the nation of Israel, not an anthology of literature. The stories are literature in the way they communicate—that is the genre—but if Genesis 3 is about the inevitability of the human destiny, then that message contributes in some way to the story of Israel because it is included in the book of Genesis. For our purposes, understanding the genre is important for understanding the characters and the role they play. This in turn allows us to examine in more detail what the serpent is and how it fits into the narrative of Genesis 2–4.

The serpent is not identified as the devil in Genesis or anywhere else in the Old Testament. The word *nāḥaš* is the ordinary word for snake, and it is identified as a "beast of the field" (Gen 3:1, NIV "wild [animal]"). However, as discussed in chapter 7, the line between animals—especially dangerous, predatory animals like snakes—and demons is somewhat blurred in the Old Testament and the ancient Near East. The spirit-creatures we call "demons"—though as discussed in chapter 7, the label is anachronistic—are classified interchangeably with liminal animals, the spirits of the dead, and even living people, normally outcasts from society[6] or the hordes of "invincible barbarians." The category of "liminal creatures" also includes the chaos monsters (i.e., Hebrew Leviathan; Ugaritic Litan), described in chapter 9. In Isaiah 27:1, the word *nāḥaš* is used to designate the Leviathan. Thus, the description in Genesis does not necessarily mean that the serpent would have been understood as what we think of as a mere ordinary animal.

Many interpreters make much out of the fact that the serpent can talk.[7] However, we must remember that the genre is literature, not documentary. The serpent speaks because the role it has been assigned in the narrative requires it to speak. Its portrayal is intended to convey its character, not its taxonomy or its anatomical capacities. At the same time, though, we should not reduce the character to a merely symbolic image. Genesis 3 is not an etiology, but it also is not an allegory, parable, or extended metaphor. Much scholarly debate has been devoted to analyzing serpent symbolism in the ancient world, with suggestions ranging from protection (as in the Egyptian Uraeus) to enmity (as in the chaos creatures, especially Apophis) to wisdom and magic to sexuality.[8] However, the encounter with the serpent should not be reduced to Adam and Eve—or, metaphorically, humanity—dealing with a [personified] abstraction. The serpent is a character in a narrative, not a symbol in a thought experiment. The fact that the character *is a serpent* is significant—Genesis is not a documentary, so the portrayal of the characters is a deliberate decision by the author—but the image of the serpent informs the character, it does not over-write the character with an abstract idea.

Based on the imagery of the crushing of heads in Genesis 3:15, Averbeck argues that the encounter with the serpent should be read as variation of the *chaoskampf*

6. Malul, *Knowledge, Control, and Sex*, 274.

7. See for example Page, *Powers*, 13.

8. Joines, *Serpent Symbolism*; Charlesworth, *Good and Evil Serpent*.

theme, specifically the version in the Baal texts of Ugarit where Baal is said to have crushed the heads of Leviathan (using language virtually identical to that of Isaiah 27:1, where the creature is called *nāḥāš*) in a context that does not involve cosmogony, as Genesis 3 also does not.[9] He therefore argues that the serpent should probably be understood to be a chaos creature of some kind. The theme of Genesis 2–4 that carries over into the broader composition is therefore a variant on the *chaoskampf* and depicts the triumph of chaos over order in the human world, a theme that is repeated in the other vignettes of the cosmic history (Gen 1–11) that sets the stage for the introduction of the covenant with Abraham. Once again this departs from the normal literature of the ancient Near East, wherein the primordial history commonly describes the successful establishment of order. By echoing known images, plots, and motifs from contemporary literature while also distorting them to emphasize disorder, the author is saying that true order is not established either in the creation of the cosmos or in the founding of civilization. True order is established in the Israelite covenant, which the book of Genesis is written to anticipate. However, the repetition of common themes is not the same thing as the establishment of a narrative arc. The *themes* of Genesis 3 (the inevitability of the human destiny and the inability of humans to countermand disorder) are picked up in later literature; the *plot* of Genesis 3 (traditionally, temptation and rebellion followed by toil and death) is not.

The serpent is not classified as evil. If the serpent is indeed a chaos creature, we might infer that it is *in a sense* evil, insofar as chaos is the absence of order, order is the highest good in the ancient world, and evil is the absence of good, but the label *evil* is misleading. That the serpent is chaotic does not mean that we can ascribe any property to it that *we* associate with evil; it is not, as Boyd puts it, "that which God is unequivocally against."[10] The only description given of the serpent is that it is wise ('*ārûm*, NIV "crafty"). '*Ārûm* is a neutral trait that can be either used positively (Prov 1:4; 8:5) or negatively (Exod 21:14; Josh 9:4). It indicates that the possessor is skilled in the use of words.[11] This trait, however, is not an indicator of the serpent's essential nature. It is mentioned because this property allows the character to perform its function in the narrative; that is, it is able to persuade. Although the serpent's action is commonly referred to as "temptation," the text does not say that the serpent tempts Eve. In fact, the text ascribes no motive to the serpent at all; the serpent merely speaks ("he said to the woman"; Gen 3:1). Eve in Genesis 3:13 says that the serpent deceived her, but Eve is not exactly an objective observer of the situation; the evaluation conveys more about Eve's mindset than the serpent's, and the text gives no indication that the narrator endorses Eve's assessment.[12] There is no indication that the serpent

9. Averbeck, "Ancient Near Eastern Mythography."

10. Boyd, *God at War*, 57.

11. Walton, *Lost World of Adam and Eve*, 132.

12. "The narrative does not emphasize that the snake told lies to Eve." Laato and Valve, "Understanding," 7.

formulated a scheme or that it desired the outcome that occurred. If the serpent is indeed a chaos creature, we would expect its actions to be opportunistic rather than premeditated, and arbitrary rather than calculated (see discussion in chapter 9). Like the serpent in the Gilgamesh epic who ate the restorative plant, the serpent in Genesis simply does what its disruptive nature drives it to do at an opportune moment.

The serpent is also interpreted to be evil because of the assumption that the curse in Genesis 3:14 is a punishment, and therefore the punishment must have been earned. However, if the serpent is a chaos creature, it is disruptive by nature and therefore *anything* it does is potentially subject to divine reaction or rebuke. As discussed previously, the proclamation in Genesis 3:14 is not an explanation of why snakes crawl or why people dislike snakes. The formula in Genesis 3:14 resembles incantations found in the Egyptian pyramid texts that are intended to ward off or pacify aggressive serpents (or demons in serpent form) by rendering them innocuous.[13] If Genesis 3 is indeed an iteration of the *chaoskampf* motif, then this proclamation represents God neutralizing the threat of the chaos creature, which Adam could not do since he was the loser. God is not the opponent of the serpent, however; here he serves as an arbiter.[14] In the *chaoskampf* of Psalm 74:14, Yahweh crushes the heads of the Leviathan; in Genesis, however, the crushing of heads is left to the humans (Gen 3:15, though using a different Hebrew word). It is also worth mentioning that Adam's "loss" of his "battle" leads to a condition of non-order imposed upon the land ("thorns and thistles," 3:18); likewise, Baal's defeat by Mot in Ugaritic texts leads to a condition of non-order imposed on the land (drought). The Baal text is one of the few instances where the *chaoskampf* resolves—albeit temporarily—in favor of the monster, and the world order suffers as a result, as we also see in Genesis. Adam was not killed as Baal was, but in choosing to take the fruit of wisdom, Adam and Eve have set themselves up as administrators of the world order. The task of administering the world order is now delegated to them, including the task of subduing chaos.[15] This is what it means that enmity will now exist between the offspring of the serpent, who promulgate chaos (see below) and the offspring of Eve, who (in theory) preserve order. Genesis 4 immediately goes on to record that the offspring of Eve are not especially adept at the role of preserving order. Indeed, the exchange of potentially mortal injuries—crushing the head and striking the heel—indicates a perpetual stalemate, where neither side will succeed in completely subduing the other.

But who are the offspring of the serpent? The (collective) offspring of Eve include Cain, Abel, and Seth, and all their descendants recorded in Genesis 4 until the *tôlēdôt* section ends in Genesis 4:26. There is therefore no reason to think that the enmity represents the inauguration of conflict between countless future generations of humans and future generations of snakes. Further, if what is meant is that Eve's offspring

13. Walton, *Lost World of Adam and Eve*, 129–31.

14. Contra Averbeck, "Ancient Near Eastern Mythography," 354.

15. A similar delegation of administrating order is given in Genesis 9:3–6.

will struggle against abstract chaos, that chaos is represented and personified by the serpent itself (as when its head is struck); Genesis 3:15 should read, "I will put enmity between *you* and the offspring of the woman." Some later interpreters identified the offspring of the serpent as Cain and the "enmity" as therefore referring to the fratricide of Genesis 4,[16] though Genesis itself gives no indication of this. If the serpent is a chaos creature, however, we can guess from the literature of the ancient Near East what its offspring would be. The Babylonian *Cuthean Legend of Naram-Suen* (introduced in chapter 9) describes the invasion of Babylon by hordes of monstrous barbarians who descend out of the mountains and ravage the kingdom. The typology of these enemies is invoked throughout the literature of the ancient Near East, occasionally under the label "offspring of Tiamat."[17] Tiamat is a chaos creature, the personified cosmic ocean. The label "offspring of Tiamat" consistently refers to foreign invaders who appear from liminal regions (usually mountains) outside the bounds of the nation's sphere of order.[18] There are no references to the *offspring of nāḥaš*, but in Genesis the cosmic ocean is depersonalized and therefore it would be odd to ascribe offspring to it. *Nāḥaš* is a personified chaos creature (as Akkadian Tiamat also is) and is conceptually close enough to carry the same meaning.

The offspring of the chaos creature, then, are foreign peoples or outsiders, especially those who live in liminal regions, which in ancient Near Eastern literature includes those who live outside of cities.[19] Cain is afraid of somebody in Genesis 4:14, and Cain also builds the first city (Gen 4:17). The people whom Cain fears therefore live outside the city, which itself represents the sphere of order that Eve's offspring are delegated to establish, since cities in the ancient Near East were embodiments of order. Cain's enemies are therefore the kinds of people that later literature would describe as *offspring of Tiamat*. Therefore, there is enmity between the offspring of Eve and the offspring of the chaos creature, just as Genesis 3:15 states there would be.

The main point of Genesis 2–4, like the rest of the cosmic history, is to juxtapose the conception of order found in Israelite theology with that found in the rest of the ancient Near East. Where most of the ancient Near East located order in cities and civilization, Israel locates it in the *covenant*. Genesis 3 records the delegation of the task of administering order to humans, and Genesis 4 records those humans trying to carry out this role by establishing cities and civilization. However, the city does not succeed in establishing order; Lamech in Genesis 4:19–24 glorifies Cain the murderer and revels in violence. Genesis does not, in fact, establish any kind of resolution to disorder

16. German, *Fall Reconsidered*, 96. Cain is the offspring of the devil in *Tg. Ps.-J.* Gen 4:1, though Cain is still the offspring of *Eve* even in traditions where his *father* is the devil/serpent.

17. Adalı, *Scourge of God*, 60.

18. Adalı, *Scourge of God*, 85–90. "[T]he reference to Tiamat in Ashurbanipal's text comes from her role in creating the forces of chaos in Enuma Elish. . . . [The enemy who are called offspring of Tiamat] is associated with the forces of chaos the goddess created, similar to the myth" (86).

19. See for example Liverani, *Assyria*, 60–61. See also Pongratz-Leisten, "The Other and the Enemy," 205–8.

or the establishment of true order, although the book itself is written to anticipate the covenant. Some insight in what is to come, however, is provided in Genesis 4:26, when, in contrast to the disorder of Cain's city, people "begin to call on the name of the LORD." This idiom indicates a proclamation of loyalty and service to God (see Ps 116:2, 13, 17)[20] and is an action repeated routinely by Abraham (Gen 12:8; 13:4; 21:33) and Isaac (Gen 26:25). The act of people "calling on the name of the LORD" sets the stage for the favor of God towards the descendants of Seth (Enoch and Noah, described in the next *tôlēdôt* section, Gen 5:1—6:8). Building a city and establishing civilization does not produce order in the human world; faithfulness and service to God ("calling on the name of LORD") is the proper way to go about it. However, true order is not established until the covenant is given in Exodus (for a discussion of disorder in the antediluvian period see chapter 12). Disorder is abolished, at least in theory, when God's presence comes and dwells among his people—the imagery of Solomon's temple invokes the ordered world of the Garden of Eden—and the enmity with the offspring of the chaos creature is resolved when God grants Israel "rest from their enemies on every side" (1 Kgs 5:4). But Genesis is not written to be read as part of this larger metanarrative, to which it contributes only incidentally and only in hindsight; its function in context is to contrast the building of cities with the faithful service of God as the (generic) means to produce order in the human world in anticipation of the covenant. In light of this interpretation, we propose that nothing in the contextual understanding of Genesis 2–4 suggests that the serpent should be identified as the devil or in any way providing a foundation for understanding Satan or demons.

In the Second Temple period

By the time of the New Testament, the text of Genesis 3 is no longer being read in its original context. Instead, a long history of interpretation has adopted a meaning of the text that has a specific relevance for their present time. They are not aspiring to what we today call "exegesis." Consequently, their interpretations tell us more about the mindset of the times than they do about the Old Testament text-in-context, and this includes the use of the material by the New Testament authors as well. Two documents in particular offer insight into some of the ways in which Genesis 3— specifically, the character of the serpent—was received by the Second Temple audience: the *Life of Adam and Eve*, and the *Allegorical Interpretation of Genesis 2 and 3* by Philo of Alexandria. The *Life of Adam and Eve* is a text known from a variety of manuscript traditions, the earliest of which is a first-century Greek document called the *Apocalypse of Moses*.[21] Despite the title, the narrative is not an apocalypse in the

20. It can also refer to invoking God's power (1 Kgs 18:24; 2 Kgs 5:11; Ps 116:4) but this meaning does not make sense in any of the contexts where it is used in Genesis.

21. The text also appears in Latin, Georgian, and Armenian versions, each of which offers a slightly different presentation of the material. However, these do not necessarily reflect later anachronistic

conventional sense (though it does contain visions), and its social setting, or even original form, cannot be determined with certainty. It describes the activities of Adam and Eve after their expulsion from the garden and offers their interpretation of their fall. Philo's commentary is a work of philosophy that attempts to present the Jewish tradition as "a rational religion and the source of the wisdom of the Greeks."[22] Philo's thought was deeply influential for later Christian theologians and his influence can be seen in the New Testament as well.[23] These documents will offer some insight into how the story of Adam—specifically, his relationship with the serpent—was understood in the cognitive environment of the Second Temple period. It is *this understanding*, not the original meaning of the narratives in the context of the ancient Near East, that arguably informs the New Testament's references to Adam and the serpent.[24] Consequently, in order to understand the meaning of the references in the New Testament, we must first understand the Second Temple context in which those references were written. This we will now briefly examine.

The *Life of Adam and Eve* opens just after the couple has been expelled from the garden. Their first action is to mourn and do penance before God, first for seven days and then for a further forty days.[25] The account in Genesis, however, records no penance of any kind. Why would the author depict them doing this? We can guess what was on the author's mind from a second piece of evidence, also not found in Genesis: the specific form that the penance takes. Adam stands in the Jordan River, which is in the promised land of Israel, while Eve stands in the Tigris, the river of Babylon.[26] In a later section of the *Life*, Adam states that his condition has come about "since you have forsaken [God's] covenant,"[27] likewise using language not found in Genesis.[28] The

---

innovations: "The archetype of the present Greek version has the best papers to represent the earliest stage in the literary development of the Life of Adam and Eve. . . . [T]he fact that [other material that found a place in one or more versions of the *Life*] was only incorporated later does not tell against its age or importance." de Jonge, "Literary Development," 249. For our purposes, we are more interested in the extent to which the texts represent the cognitive environment of their time than the literary development of any particular document. If all of the versions reflect an authentic Adam tradition—regardless of how late that tradition was actually written down—then even the text of the later versions may be of relevance. For the first-century date of the Greek version, see Johnson, "Life of Adam and Eve," 252.

22. Ferguson, *Backgrounds*, 479–80.

23. Ferguson, *Backgrounds*, 482–83.

24. "There is . . . a history of interpretation of Adam from Genesis to the first century AD, a history revealing a bold and astonishing diversity in which one might say accurately that authors made of Adam what they needed of Adam. . . . Jesus's and Paul's views do not stand over against but instead are instances of this diversity of interpretations." Venema and McKnight, *Adam and the Genome*, 149.

25. Anderson, "Penitence Narrative," 5.

26. The Tigris is also one of the rivers that flows from Eden (Gen 2:14), but the Jordan is not; the mention of the Tigris is therefore more likely intended to juxtapose Babylon with Israel rather than invoking the original location of the garden.

27. *Apoc. Mos.* 8.2, trans. Johnson, in *OTP* 2:273.

28. The language of "covenant" does not occur in Genesis 2–4. God's "command" to Adam in Genesis 2:16; 3:11; 3:17 (Heb *ṣāwâ*) is the same word as the "commands" given to Moses (e.g., Deut

Life depicts Eve as going off to Babylon to do penance for transgressing against the covenant of God. Therefore, it seems that the Second Temple author is interpreting the events that befell Adam and Eve as essentially a repetition of the events that befell the nation of Israel in the exile. "The Jews of the Second Temple period would have no difficulty in decoding the story of Adam as an earlier version of their own story: placed in the garden; given a commission to look after it; being the place where God wanted to be at rest, to exercise his sovereign rule; warned about keeping the commandment; warned in particular that breaking it would mean death; breaking it and being exiled. It all sounds very, very familiar."[29] Nonetheless, prefiguring the exile was not the meaning of the original text-in-context. That is why the *Life of Adam and Eve* has to embellish the text with non-biblical material in order to complete the paradigm. However, the prefiguring of the exile was how the Adam story was read in the Second Temple period, and evidence suggests it is *this* appropriation of the story, not the original text-in-context, that the New Testament authors are thinking of when they reference Adam, or Eve, or—importantly for our purposes—the serpent.

A very different understanding of the events of Genesis 3 is offered by Philo. Philo is trying to present the Jewish tradition as the original and superior philosophy, which (he claims) was later adopted and diluted to varying degrees by the Greeks. Where *The Life of Adam and Eve* applies an interpretation of Genesis to the conditions of the Jewish people specifically, Philo's philosophical reading tries to universalize the teaching of Genesis into a cosmological and ethical application for both Jews and Greeks.[30] While other Jewish works extrapolate Adam's general circumstances to all of humanity, for example Sirach,[31] and others portray the actions of the serpent in the past as having repercussions for all of future humanity, as in the Wisdom of Solomon[32] or *Jubilees*,[33] the portrayal of the *actual encounter with the serpent* being recapitulated in the experience of all people is much rarer. Philo portrays all people as having encounters with their own personal serpents. This understanding will be useful in regard to the New Testament, where the actions of the serpent-characters are depicted as occurring in the authors' present, as opposed to referring back to one event long ago.

6:24), but this term and its noun form (*miṣwôt*) refers to "charges or mandates coming from those with recognized status"; they are not laws that delineate punishable offenses (as demonstrated by Gen 27:8). See Walton and Walton, *Lost World of Torah*, 40.

29. N. T. Wright, in Walton, *Lost World of Adam and Eve*, 177. See also Venema and McKnight, *Adam and the Genome*, 149: "Adam's sin is characterized as disobedience to God's commandments and functions as the prototype of the historical transgressions of Israel."

30. See Ferguson, *Backgrounds*, 478–81.

31. "God gave to each person in the world the choice, and each can do with it whatever one wishes. . . . Sirach has broadened [this notion] from Adam to Israel and to everyone." Venema and McKnight, *Adam and the Genome*, 151. The reference under discussion is Sirach 15:11–15.

32. "[T]hrough the devil's envy sin entered the world, and all who belong to his company experience it" (Wis 2:23–24).

33. *Jub.* 3.28–30.

For Philo, the narrative of Genesis 3 is a historically-enacted allegory that illustrates the way temptation and sin work in the abstract. What Philo is most interested in is the symbolism of the characters, their portrayal, and their actions, both in regard to the origin of human mortality[34] and as an allegory of the mechanisms of temptation and vice. In Philo's allegory, Adam and Eve represent components of the human consciousness. Adam represents the intellect; Eve represents the senses.[35] The way in which they were tempted, and succumbed to temptation, and punished, reflects the way that temptation works on the mind and the way that sin affects the mind, body, and soul. The serpent, therefore, represents both a historical animal and also the human inclination to vice:

> the serpent is truly more cunning than all the beasts. To me, however, it seems that this was said because of the serpent's inclination toward passion, of which it is the symbol. And by passion is meant sensual pleasure, for lovers of pleasure are very clever . . . in finding devices, both those which produce pleasure and those which lead to enjoyment of some kind.[36]

Desire for pleasure (here, the serpent) presents the object that is desired (presumably here the forbidden fruit, although Philo refers to objects more abstractly[37]) to the outward senses (here, Eve), which in turn presents it to the intellect (here, Adam). Desire is inherently neutral, able to direct the intellect towards either good or evil. The serpent in Genesis brought evil, but immediately after identifying the serpent as the symbol of pleasure Philo ties the narrative of Genesis to the narrative of the bronze serpent in Numbers 21:4–9, thus identifying and contrasting two serpents:

> [The body] encounters pleasures which bring death, not the death which severs soul from body, but the death which ruins soul by vice. For we read, "[Then the LORD sent venomous snakes among them; they bit the people and many Israelites died"; Num 21:6]. For verily nothing so surely brings death upon a soul as immoderate indulgence in pleasures. [. . .] How, then, is a healing of their suffering brought about? By the making of another serpent, opposite of that kind of Eve, namely, the principle of self-mastery, . . . a virtue that defends itself against pleasure, its foe [. . .]; if the mind, when bitten by pleasure, the

---

34. "In order that they may be potentially mortal he deceives by trickery and artfulness." Philo, *Questions and Answers on Genesis* 33, trans. Marcus, in LCL 380:20.

35. "[W]oman is the symbol of sense, and man, of mind." Philo, *Questions and Answers on Genesis* 37, trans. Marcus, in LCL 380:22.

36. Philo, *Questions and Answers on Genesis* 31, trans. Marcus, in LCL 380:18–19. See also Philo, *Allegorical Interpretation of Genesis* 74, trans. Colson and Whitaker, in LCL 226:271: "The reason pleasure is likened to a serpent is this. The movement of pleasure is like that of the serpent is tortuous and variable."

37. "[I]t was necessary that both [the mind and the senses] should come together for the apprehension of objects around them." Philo, *Allegorical Interpretation of Genesis* 71, trans. Colson and Whitaker, in LCL 226:269.

serpent of Eve, shall have succeeded in beholding in soul the beauty of self-mastery, the serpent of Moses, . . . he shall live.[38]

The extended metaphor of the serpent representing [the desire for] pleasure is continued to include the rod of Moses (Exod 4:3)[39] and Jacob's blessing on Dan in Genesis 49:17.[40] The consequence of Philo's allegory is that the serpent and its encounter with Adam and Eve is removed from the context of the Israelite covenant; as such, it no longer pertains only to the history and/or status of the Jewish people but now speaks to the universal condition of all of humanity. But this universal application is also far removed from the text of Genesis in context; likewise, it lacks the element of affliction for breaking God's covenant that is found in the *Life*. Thus, we can identify the components of the Adam narrative as it develops into the New Testament, in contrast with its original meaning:

- Adam *archetypally represents* the condition (mortality, inability to establish true order) of all humanity (original context).

- Adam was *afflicted* (with mortality and labor) specifically for violation of divine stipulations, just as Israel was afflicted at the exile (e.g., the *Life of Adam and Eve*).

- All humanity duplicates Adam's specific experiences (e.g., Philo).

- All humanity is afflicted (with mortality) specifically for transgression against God (e.g., Rom 5).

The New Testament authors do not refer directly either to Philo or to *the Life of Adam and Eve*. However, these texts represent the kinds of ideas about the narrative of Genesis 3 and its characters that would have been found in the cognitive environment at the time of the writing of the New Testament. The New Testament's use of the material of Genesis cannot be derived from the original context of Genesis alone without the influence of the ideas of the Second Temple period, which themselves are not derived from Genesis, or even necessarily from the Bible at all. What this means is that the New Testament is not interpreting the Old Testament—that is, telling us what it did or should mean—rather, it is using an *existing interpretation* of the Old Testament as a resource to talk about its own issues in its own way. Both of the themes that we have explored—the story of Genesis 3 as a covenant paradigm and the application of its elements to all of humanity—are made use of by the New Testament authors as they pursue their own literary and theological purposes. That is what we will now examine.

38. Philo, *Allegorical Interpretation of Genesis* 77–81, trans. Colson and Whitaker, in LCL 226:273–75. Interestingly enough, this connection is also affirmed recently by Joseph Ratzinger (later Pope Benedict XVI), who writes that "Christ is the antitype of the serpent, as is indicated in John 3:14" (*"In the beginning . . . ,"* 76). John 3:14 portrays Christ as the bronze serpent that Moses raised in the wilderness.

39. Philo, *Allegorical Interpretation of Genesis* 88–93.

40. Philo, *Allegorical Interpretation of Genesis* 94–108.

In Romans

Romans 16:20 ("The God of peace will soon crush Satan under your feet") is normally thought to be a reference back to Genesis 3:15 ("he will crush your head, and you will strike his heel"). This is possible, although the word Paul uses for "crush" (*sintripsei*) is notably different than the word used in the LXX of Genesis (*teresei*). Further, enemies being put under the feet is a standard motif throughout the entire Old Testament (e.g., Ps 110) and is not unique to Genesis 3:15. Consequently, the reference in Romans may have less to do with Genesis or the serpent than usually thought. At the time of the New Testament it was not normal to actually *equate* the serpent character of Genesis with the Satan character of intertestamental literature; the serpent is more commonly depicted as a tool or instrument of the devil, rather than a manifestation of the devil itself.[41] In the *Life of Adam and Eve*, the devil tricks the serpent into speaking to Eve on his behalf, although he later appears to Eve in the Tigris with no mention of the serpent, and later in the text a beast (specified in the Latin version as a serpent) attacks Seth—that is, strikes Eve's offspring—with no influence from the devil. In *Jubilees*, the serpent is mentioned (e.g., *Jub* 3.17), but the devil is not, and in the Wisdom of Solomon (Wis 2:23–24) the devil is mentioned, but the serpent is not. Thus, Paul's audience would not have necessarily recognized a transparent allusion to Genesis based on the mention of Satan. If no reference to Genesis is intended, the passage may simply be invoking the defeat of Satan as a reference to the eschatological conflict of the messianic age[42] (see discussion in chapter 9). If it would have been understood as a reference to Genesis, however, it is worth asking what meaning would have been conveyed to the audience who would have heard it as such.

First and foremost, the reference is too vague to be able to claim that the passage serves to identify the characters in Genesis 3. The only way it could even be recognized as a reference is if the audience already understands the recipient of the head-crushing in Genesis 3:15 to be Satan. Therefore, we have to ask what significance the audience may have attached to the image of the combat being translated into their own time, with the serpent/devil being crushed under *their* feet.

One option, mentioned above, is that the person being crushed is literally Satan, the character identified in other literature as the "prince of darkness." In this case, the hope for his defeat is a purely eschatological image and carries a similar meaning to the statement "Come, Lord Jesus" in Revelation 22:20; that is, an expression of hope for the consummation of the messianic age. This reading is possible, but has very little to do with Genesis. Another option, however, is that the reference to "Satan" is a metaphor or synecdoche for those who serve or do the work of Satan; that is, those

41. Though it is not unknown; in the *Apocalypse of Abraham* (first/second century CE) Azazel is variously equated with an allegorical personification of corruption, with the serpent, and with the devil (*Apoc. Abr.* 23.1–14; 31.5–6).

42. See for example Dunn, *Romans 16–20*, 905: "the hope of Satan being 'crushed under foot' is part of a larger eschatological hope for the final binding or defeat of the angelic power hostile to God."

identified in other literature as the "sons of darkness." Some commentators think that this refers back to the false teachers in Romans 16:17, sometimes specifically as an exhortation to religious violence.[43] If this is indeed the intent, the description of the false teachers as "deceiving" by "smooth talk and flattery" might be intended to invoke the activity of the serpent in Genesis 3:1. Most commentators, however, think that the interpretation of "Satan" as "community outsiders or deviants" is unlikely,[44] or at least incomplete.[45] The destruction of the sons of darkness is also an eschatological image, but if that was what is intended the emphasis is still informed mostly by eschatological speculation and not the imagery of Genesis:

> Similar sentiments about the influence of Satan and the fate of his adherents are expressed in the Testament of the Twelve Patriarchs. "And Beliar shall be bound by him. And he shall grant to his children the authority to trample on wicked spirits" (T. Levi 18:20). "Then all the spirits of error shall be given over to being trampled underfoot" (T. Sim. 6:6). . . . [W]hen Satan is deposed, [the agitators from Rom 16:17] will suffer humiliation along with him. The call to wisdom [in Rom 16:19], then, should be understood in the light of the promise of eschatological victory.[46]

Alternatively, the reference could be allegorical rather than literal, as in Philo, where the designation "Satan" does not represent an entity (human or demonic) but a [personified] abstraction, which may or may not be specific: "may the God of peace give you victory over anything that is thought to originate from Satan." Once again, this emphasis could be either immanent or eschatological, but would likely carry connotations of both. However, none of these interpretations draw much on the specific imagery and themes of Genesis 3.

We might ask, therefore, what the allusion to Genesis might add to the significance of the statement if it were recognized as such. We may recall that the combat in Genesis 3:15 is reciprocal; the one who crushes the head is the one whose heel is struck. Consequently, Paul's audience may feel that they are being attacked and suffering mortal injury, and Paul is assuring them that the other shoe will drop soon. Their "attackers" might be the false teachers, in which case the church's posture towards them is defensive (i.e., they feel like they are under threat) rather than aggressive (i.e., they

43. See for example Jewett, *Romans*, 994–95. He laments that "the choice of the word συντρίβω ("shatter, crush") leaves no doubt about the violent means required to subdue the church's enemies. The word is used in connection with mistreating people, beating them severely, bruising them, or annihilating them; . . . the reference to Satan implies that the church's enemies are perceived to be his evil minions." He goes onto argue that this endorsement of violence is evidence that the passage is not Pauline: "Paul's vision of the impartial righteousness of God and of the inclusive holy kiss have repeatedly been crushed under the church's feet, as if the very idea of agapaic coexistence were Satan's offspring." Ibid., 996.

44. See for example Cranfield, *Romans 9–16*, 803.

45. See for example. Moo, *Romans*, 933.

46. Schreiner, *Romans*, 804–5.

do not see themselves as righteous avengers). However, we also recall that the imagery of Adam and Eve for a Second Temple audience also invokes the exile and the plight of the Jewish people. The church throughout the New Testament also identifies itself with Israel, so it seems probable that they would apply the condition of both Adam and the Jewish people to themselves. If the Second Temple audience, following the exilic paradigm read back into Genesis 3, read the conflict of Eve's offspring and the serpent as recapitulating their own conflict with foreign oppressors, then a reference to that conflict in a Christian context might invoke conflict between the church (as the new Israel) and its various persecutors—represented metaphorically by Satan, who in the Second Temple period is thought to motivate the oppression of God's people—and include a promise that God will deliver them. This reading does not substantially change the meaning of the passage—which is still an evocation of future hope—but it does add a bit of depth, since relief from oppression is more significant than abstract eschatology. But in no case does the passage offer an authoritative declaration that the serpent character in Genesis 3 ought to be interpreted as having been Satan.

In Revelation

Revelation 12:9 and 20:2 both refer to a character described as "that ancient serpent called the devil, or Satan." The same character is referred to simply as "the serpent" in Revelation 12:14–15, and Revelation 12:9 specifies that it "leads the whole world astray." For our purposes, we must examine whether the combined designation of "serpent" and "devil" is intended to communicate that the character in Genesis was in fact the same entity as the Satan character of the Second Temple tradition.

Our first observation is that the reference to "the dragon, the ancient serpent" is more of a direct reference to Isaiah 27:1 than it is to Genesis 3. The LXX translates the Hebrew word *liwyātān* (NIV "Leviathan"), and also the word *tannîn* (NIV "monster") both as *drakōn*, the same word translated "dragon" in Revelation. Genesis, however, uses only the word "serpent" (Gk *ophis*), with no mention of a dragon. Thus, "the dragon, the ancient serpent" is much more clearly a reference to "[the dragon], the gliding serpent, [the dragon], the coiling serpent, the [dragon] in the sea" from Isaiah 27:1 than it is to "the serpent . . . the [beast of the field]" in Genesis 3:1.[47] Nonetheless, that itself does not mean that the imagery of Genesis is completely absent from the picture. We argued previously that the *tannîn* in Genesis 1:21 (LXX *kētē ta megala*), the *nāḥaš* in Genesis 3, and the Leviathan in Isaiah 27:1 (also called both *tannîn* and *nāḥaš*) all reference the same mythographic image of the chaos monsters, despite none of them being direct literary allusions to each other. That same mythographic image, albeit filtered through a Second Temple history of interpretation, also serves as the

47. See also Beale and McDonough, "Revelation," 1145: "the LXX of [Isaiah] 27:1 has 'the dragon, the serpent' which is almost identical to Rev 20:2: 'the dragon, the ancient serpent.'"

basis of the imagery in Revelation.[48] We can therefore see the imagery of Genesis as part of the "melting pot" of ideas that shape the imagery of Revelation 12 and 20, even if the text is not a direct literary allusion. The multiple heads of the dragon (Rev 12:3) is another invocation of the chaos monster image and obliquely references Psalm 74.[49] The point is that the imagery of Revelation is complex and cannot be reduced to an exposition of the character in Genesis—or any of the characters that inform the image, for that matter. The image in Revelation does not say that the *nāḥaš* in Genesis is the same thing as Satan, and it does not say that the Leviathan is the same thing as Satan, either. (For a discussion of what the Leviathan is, see chapter 9.)

The imagery of Genesis 3 is more clearly invoked in Revelation 12:14–15, where the dragon attacks the [offspring] (see also Rev 12:3 and especially 12:17) of the woman [clothed with the sun] (Rev 12:1, 4, 13, 17), in what is clearly a reference to Genesis 3:15.[50] Here the character is called *the serpent*, with no reference to Satan or the devil, though it is called *the dragon* again in Revelation 12:3, 4, 16, and 17. What is important to realize is that this passage is not interested in identifying qualities of the Second Temple character called *Satan*, including identifying cameos of him in previous literary works. Rather, the passage is identifying *the apocalyptic character called "the dragon" by means of inserting him into various established literary motifs.* The image in Revelation is not identifying various things that *Satan* did, but rather is identifying various things that "the dragon" (whoever that represents) did or will do, with the purpose of the identification being not documentary, but rather a statement concerning the *significance* of the actions.

So, for example, most interpreters of Revelation 12:7–12 read the passage to be authoritatively affirming that an entity called *Satan* lost (or will lose) a war with an entity called *Michael*, and therefore both of these entities "really exist" more or less exactly as they are depicted—a depiction that is read to confirm Second Temple speculation about the characters—and further that the literary allusions authoritatively identify this same being (who lost or will lose a war) as the serpent of Genesis and the Leviathan from Psalms and Isaiah, and also as the character mentioned by name throughout the New Testament. This interpretation is used to freely interpose any traits or qualities of any of those characters onto all of the others. However, we recall that, for the Second Temple audience of Revelation, the war between Satan and Michael is not only something that they already "know" about—and therefore do not need a vision to reveal it—but it also has a particular significance; the war inaugurates the messianic age (see chapter 9). A similar theme is found in the imagery of the "binding" of the dragon in Revelation 20:2, where he is also identified as Satan.[51] The

48. See Forsyth, *Old Enemy*, 253–54.

49. Forsyth, *Old Enemy*, 252.

50. See Aune, *Revelation 6–16*, 708; Beale, *Revelation*, 679–80; Osborne, *Revelation*, 485.

51. See Beale and McDonough, "Revelation," 1145 for a discussion of the messianic/eschatological significance of the binding of Satan, with reference to *1 En.* 54, *T. Levi 18.12*, and *Jub.* 48.15–17.

dragon character is identified as Satan in these instances not to present trivia about Satan but to emphasize that the overthrow of the dragon (whoever that represents) will represent the same thing—that is, the inauguration of the messianic age—that the overthrow of Satan is known to represent in their existing conception.

In the same way, the identification of the dragon character (again, whoever that represents) in Revelation 12:17 with the serpent character of Genesis 3:15, as filtered through the lens of Second Temple interpretation, is designed to comment on the actions of the dragon character, *not* the actions of the Genesis serpent. In this case, the significance would be very similar to what we postulated for Romans 16:20. The dragon character (whoever that represents) is the heel-striker; the offspring of the woman, identified as "those who keep God's commands and hold fast their testimony about Jesus" (Rev 12:17), are suffering aggression and the invocation of reciprocal combat assures them that their fortunes will eventually change. We recall that apocalyptic literature as a genre is a response to a crisis affecting the community and a hope for its resolution (see chapter 3); thus, the allusion to Genesis might be intended to stand as a reminder to the community that the head of their antagonist will eventually be crushed, thus resolving the crisis. Further, the specific identification of the implied head-crushers as "those who keep God's commands" may be a reference to a messianic interpretation of Genesis 3:15 from Jewish literature,[52] thus continuing the idea that the downfall of the dragon will usher in the coming of the messianic age from Revelation 12:7–12.

Identifying with any kind of certainty who (or what) the dragon character represents is virtually impossible, although presumably it would have been more transparent to the original audience. As discussed in chapter 3, we might imagine the plight of someone two thousand years in the future who knows very little about American popular politics but has discovered an American cartoon with an elephant in it. We today (the original audience of the cartoon) would have a fairly clear idea of what it is supposed to refer to, but the hypothetical future interpreter likely would not. This is the situation we find ourselves in when trying to interpret apocalyptic imagery. Nonetheless, while we cannot be certain who or what the dragon represents, we can make a few educated guesses.

Apocalypses are written to address a community in crisis, so it is possible that the dragon represents one of the figures behind whatever crisis the community is

52. "Rev. 12:17 is also a partial fulfillment of the promise in Gen. 3:15, where God prophecies that the individual (messianic) and corporate seed of the woman will bruise fatally the head of the serpent. *Targ. Neof.* Gen. 3:15 interprets the 'seed' corporately: 'when the sons of the woman keep the commandments of the law . . . they will smite you on the head; when they abandon the commandments you will wound them in the heel . . . in the days of King Messiah.' Likewise *Targ. Pal.* and *Targ. Jer. Frag.*" Beale, *Revelation*, 679–80. See also *T. Levi* 18.12: "Beliar shall be bound by him [the messiah] and he shall give power to his children to tread upon the evil spirits." See Beale and McDonough, "Revelation," 1145. It is worth noting, however, that in the Targum the combat is more abstract and allegorized, much as we also saw in Philo: the combat is carried out *by means of* obeying commands (or not); it does not represent actual combat against agents who try to deter others from keeping commands.

experiencing. In the *Psalms of Solomon*, a "dragon" represents the Roman consul Pompey, who before his death—which the text celebrates—had generated crisis by planting an Aquila in the temple.[53] The beasts in Daniel 7, from which the imagery of Revelation borrows heavily, are identified more or less explicitly as representing human rulers, and Rome is represented transparently as being the source of the crisis that Revelation addresses, especially in Revelation 17–19, where it is referred to as "Babylon"; note especially Revelation 18:23 where Babylon/Rome "[leads] all the nations astray" as compared to the dragon doing the same in Revelation 12:9. Thus, it may be possible that the dragon character is supposed to represent a person, as the beast and false prophet in Revelation 19:20 (who suffer the same fate as the dragon in Revelation 20:10) are also normally thought to do. If this is the case then the author of Revelation is communicating that the end of this person would signal the beginning of the messianic age and thereby end the crisis that the community is experiencing. (For the significance of co-identifying a person with Satan, as the dragon character is, see chapter 14).

A second similar option is that the dragon is literally supposed to represent the devil, who in the Second Temple mindset is just as real as any human oppressor would be. To see the devil as the motivating force behind adversity would be natural enough for the time—it was done by the Qumran community, for example (see chapter 9)—but we must remember that Scripture does not exist to provide a stamp of approval on things the audience already believed (see chapter 1). Scripture communicates new information into their world—revelation—and the identity, activity, and destiny of the devil as portrayed in Revelation is something they already knew. Consequently, if the dragon is indeed the devil, then the devil is being presented in his traditional role not to affirm the details of that role but to talk about *something else*. Further, that something else is *not* the identification of other characters in biblical literature, such as the serpent or the Leviathan. Apocalypses address a community in crisis. Whatever the audience is being told about what the devil is doing, it is something that is happening in their present, not trivia about something the devil did in the past.

Although apocalypses address a community in crisis, simply reiterating what they already believed—that the devil is the ultimate source of their trouble and would eventually be defeated by the messiah—seems like a rather *laissez-faire* approach to crisis resolution. Therefore, if the dragon is supposed to represent the devil in his traditional role, the emphasis of the book is probably not on the devil but rather on someone else *interacting with* the devil—someone about whose role and place in the established eschatological narrative they might be less certain. The most likely candidates for this are Christ, cast in the traditional role of the Prince of Light, or the community of the church—that is, the audience itself—cast in the traditional role of the sons of light. The emphasis in this case is not that the devil will be defeated—they already knew that—but that it will be *Christ specifically* who

53. *Pss. Sol.* 2.25; for identification of Pompey see Wright, "Psalms of Solomon" in *OTP* 2.640–41.

accomplishes his defeat, and *themselves specifically* who will receive the blessings of the messianic age as the remnant of Israel. The point of the book of Revelation in this case is to identify Christ and to identify the church, not to identify the devil; consequently, anything it happens to say about the devil is incidental and serves only to communicate the message in a way that will be meaningful within the cognitive context of the audience. The book is not offering a new and unknown narrative about the end times; we recall that apocalypses do not predict the future and do not identify metacosmic operations of which the audience is unaware (see chapter 3). Rather the book—at least in those parts where it references the dragon as Satan—is *situating* the audience within the established eschatological narrative. This option is perhaps the most likely. However, in no case does the profile of the dragon given in Revelation tell us anything about how we should interpret characters from earlier biblical literature, including the serpent in Genesis.

In conclusion, there appears to be no biblical basis for associating the serpent character in Genesis 3 with the Satan character from later literature. In the context of Genesis itself, the serpent is a chaos creature, a morally neutral agent of nonorder behaving according to the nature it was given when it was created. It is not evil and it is not acting in opposition to God. Nothing in the New Testament provides any information to alter this profile. Second Temple literature embellished the character in a variety of ways, including associating it with the Satan character, and the New Testament authors sometimes reference these embellishments to make their own points, but references to Hellenistic speculation by the New Testament do not affirm that those speculations (which are not accorded the status of Scripture) were accurate interpretations of the Old Testament text (which *is* accorded the status of Scripture). Consequently, because the serpent and the devil are unrelated, the serpent should not be used to extrapolate any information about the activities of Satan or the demons, and the activities of the demons should not be used to extrapolate information about the serpent. But what exactly are the activities of the demons? This we will now examine.

Chapter 11

Demons and idolatry

ONE OF THE MOST persistent ideas about demons in the Bible is the assumption that the text teaches—or more accurately, *reveals*—that the gods of the non-Israelite nations, and by extension the gods of non-Christian religions, are in fact evil demons. As Page puts it, "Pagans were not worshipping what they thought they were worshipping."[1] Arnold elaborates: "The Old Testament makes it clear that all of these idols . . . are in reality rebellious angels, or demons, masquerading as 'gods.' They are pridefully diverting to themselves the worship that properly belongs only to the one true God."[2] The classic passage that supports this interpretation is 1 Corinthians 10:20, where Paul states that "the sacrifices of pagans are offered to demons, not to God," in reference to the LXX of Deuteronomy 32, which conflict theologians systematically combine with details taken from Psalm 82 and Daniel 10, and occasionally also from Genesis 6 and Isaiah 14. The results of these amalgamations are then used to launch broad speculations about the reasons for the prohibitions of idolatry in Israel and the true motives behind the various acts of judgment and/or violence against the nations, so for example: "The Old Testament connects idolatry with the demonic—that is with the cosmic enemies of God who rebelled against him. . . . God's commands to Israel to wipe out Canaan's idols and false, immoral worship illustrate the cosmic warfare between Yahweh and the dark powers opposed to his rule."[3] Therefore, we will examine what exactly the pagans thought they were worshipping and what 1 Corinthians and the Old Testament say about them in context.

Demons in 1 Corinthians 10:20

As discussed in chapter 7, the rhetoric of 1 Corinthians 10:14–22 invokes the concepts and categories of a contemporary dispute within Greek culture between the advocates of philosophical religion and the advocates of popular religion. The gods of popular religion were derived from the ancient traditional heritage of Greece and

1. Page, *Powers*, 225.

2. Arnold, *Questions*, 153.

3. Copan, *Is God a Moral Monster?* 167.

Rome, most notably from Homer; they were amoral and required little from their worshippers except sacrifices and the observance of festivals. The philosophers, on the other hand, especially the Middle Platonists who heavily influenced Christianity, had a conception of deity wherein the gods, now exemplars of virtue (see chapter 8), were associated with reason and nature and both *exemplified* the good and, through some combination of reason and nature, *directed* their followers in the pursuit of the good. Even so, the philosophers valued their cultural heritage and did not wish to discard the traditions. Their solution was to depict the traditional Homeric gods as actually representing intermediate beings called "demons" (*daimones*) who were not flawless and who could partake in sub-ideal behavior on account of their essentially material (albeit incorporeal) nature. One of the functions of these intermediate beings, according to both Plato[4] and Plutarch,[5] was to serve as mediators between the cults on earth and the gods in heaven, bringing sacrifices and petitions upward and blessings and commands downward. Thus, it is not in fact true that "the pagans were not worshipping what they thought they were worshipping"; everyone understood that the offerings at the pagan shrines were presented to the "demons." What is of interest to us is *how* Paul is making use of this common knowledge in order to advance his particular argument.

Sometimes in the apologetic debates of the philosophers the gods are called "demons" in order to deride the gods, their cults, and their worshippers, and to juxtapose them unfavorably with whatever the philosopher is advocating. This, for example, is what Justin Martyr is doing when he calls Zeus a "parricide and the son of a parricide."[6] However, Paul does not appear to be making an argument of this kind; he does not say, "the sacrifices of pagans are offered to demons, not to God, and we know this because those who receive the sacrifices are affirmed by their own followers to do things that those followers themselves admit are unseemly for true gods to do." Instead, he says "I do not want you to be participants with demons. You cannot drink the cup of the Lord and the cup of demons too; you cannot have a part in both the Lord's table and the table of demons" (1 Cor 10:20–21). This indicates that his audience already understands that the sacrifices are offered to demons, but they have failed to properly appreciate why this is bad.

4. Plato speaks of demons "interpreting and transporting human things to the gods and divine things to men; entreaties and sacrifices from below, and ordinances and requitals from above. . . . [T]hrough [demons] (*to daimonion*) are conveyed all divination and priestcraft concerning sacrifice and ritual and incantations, and all soothsaying and sorcery." *Symposium* 202e, trans. Lamb, in LCL 166:179.

5. "Let us not imagine that the god . . . is present at these ceremonies and helps in conducting them; but let us commit these matters to those ministers of the gods to whom it is right to commit them, as to servants and clerks, and let us believe that demigods [*daimonas*, "demons"] are guardians of sacred rites of the gods and prompters in the Mysteries." *Obsolescence of Oracles* 417, trans. Babbitt, in LCL 306:389.

6. *1 Apology* 21, trans. Coxe, in *ANF* 1.170.

Most interpreters assume that the Corinthians thought that the sacrifices were of-fered to "nothing" (inferred from 1 Cor 10:19), but that Paul wishes to inform them that what they thought was "nothing" was really "a demon."[7] For these interpreters, the badness of the sacrifice comes from the natural consequences of contact with demons, in contrast to the assumed contact with "nothing." However, we have proposed that the Corinthians already knew that their offerings were made to demons. Interestingly, then, Paul's explanation for why the sacrifice is bad does not include any natural con-sequences of contact with demons: he does not say that they should not be participants with demons because "worship of false gods exposes the worshipper to the influence of evil forces, whether or not the worshipper is conscious of the exposure"[8] or anything of that kind. Instead, he references Deuteronomy 32:16–17: "They made him jealous with their foreign gods and angered him with their detestable idols. They sacrificed to false gods (LXX *daimoniois*, 'demons'), which are not God." Therefore, we must examine this passage to understand how it contributes to Paul's argument.

As discussed in chapter 7, the Hebrew word translated "false gods" in the NIV and "demons" in the LXX is *šēdîm*. There is no consensus as to what the word specifically refers to, but for the purposes of this argument it does not matter much. Paul's point is not to affirm that the things the Israelites sacrificed to in the wilderness are the same things that stand behind the pagan altars, which are the same things that carry all of the baggage assigned to the word *demon*. The use of the word *daimonion* in the LXX allows Paul to conceptually connect the activity of the Israelites with the activity of the Corinthians and thereby also connect the consequences. Notably, in Deuteronomy 32:21–42 the consequences are all things that *God* does, not things that the "demons" do, and he does them because Israel "made him jealous." It is *this* consequence that Paul wishes to invoke in 1 Corinthians 10:22: "Are we trying to arouse the Lord's jealousy? Are we stronger than he?" The "demons" are not going to do anything to the Corinthi-ans—after all, Paul affirms that an idol is nothing—but *the Lord* might.

The properties of the *šēdîm* that provoke jealousy and anger from Yahweh are twofold: they are not-God, and they are *tôʿēbâ* (NIV "detestable"). Despite the con-notations of the English translation—and occasionally the choices of the LXX as well[9]—the Hebrew word *tôʿēbâ* is morally neutral and means "contrary to order."[10] What is or is not contrary to order depends on the order in question. In Genesis 46:34, for example, we read that "all shepherds are *tôʿēbâ* to the Egyptians," as are Jewish

7. See Heiser, *Unseen Realm*, 35–36; Page, *Powers*, 68; Conzelmann, *1 Corinthians*, 173; Garland, *1 Corinthians*, 480; Ciampa and Rosner, *1 Corinthians*, 478; Fee, *1 Corinthians*, 471; Thiselton, *1 Cor-inthians*, 773–76.

8. So Page, *Powers*, 69.

9. *Tôʿēbâ* in Deut 32:16 is translated *bdelygma* ("abomination") in the LXX; *bdelygma* also notably translates *šiqqûṣ* (see next section below) in e.g., Deut 29:17; Ezek 20:7–8; Dan 11:31; 12:11, as well as several other words elsewhere. *Tôʿēbâ* is also translated using various Greek words in other places, including the amoral *akathartos* ("unclean") in Prov 3:32; 16:5; 17:15; and 20:10.

10. Walton and Walton, *Lost World of the Israelite Conquest*, 151–53.

sacrifices in Exodus 8:22. Things classified as *tôʿēbâ* —sometimes specifically "*tôʿēbâ* to Yahweh"—are things that are contrary to Israel's covenant order. Worshipping gods other than Yahweh is *tôʿēbâ*, as are Canaanite worship practices (e.g., Deut 12:31; see also Deut 20:18; 2 Chr 28:3; 33:2). However, we should not assume that describing something as *tôʿēbâ* means that it is universally immoral or inherently opposed to the will of God. The covenant order of Israel does not represent God's ideal state of the world, as Christians under the new covenant know perfectly well. Consequently, there is no indication that the worship of idols is inherently wrong anywhere that it is practiced; it is only wrong when *Israel* does it. The concept can perhaps be illustrated by reference to the common metaphor of the covenant as marriage. In principle, there is nothing inherently wrong with dating or courting another person. However, if I happen to be married, then *for me* dating or courting become very wrong, even though they are still perfectly acceptable for others. Another related metaphor for Israel's covenant infidelity is adultery. If I sleep with my neighbor's wife, it counts as adultery and it is wrong. But if my neighbor sleeps with his own wife it is not adultery and is not wrong, even though it is the same action with the same woman. Likewise, worship of foreign gods *by Israelites* counts as covenant infidelity and is *tôʿēbâ*, but worship of foreign gods by foreigners is never condemned in the Old Testament, although the inability of their gods to defend them is occasionally mentioned with scorn. See below for further discussion on the oracles against the nations.

The consequence for *tôʿēbâ*, as recorded in Deuteronomy 7:26 and 13:14–15, is *ḥerem* (NIV "set apart for destruction"; "destroy completely"). *Ḥerem* is what the Israelites are supposed to do to the people of Canaan (e.g., Deut 7:2). Despite the English translation, *ḥerem* does not mean "destroy"; it means to prohibit, proscribe, or remove [from use].[11] It is conceptually similar to the idea of being "cut off from the community," which is the penalty for such offenses as making anointing oil for non-cultic use (Exod 30:33) or failing to be circumcised (Gen 17:14); in other words, *non-moral* offenses. Neither *ḥerem* nor *kārat* ("cut off") is a punishment; both are done for the sake of the rest of the community that the referent is removed or cut off from, as opposed to being done for the purpose of doing something *to* the offender. Something that is *ḥerem* is removed from the community of the covenant people and/or removed from the land, not to inflict injury on *it* but so that proper order within the community or the land may be restored. It is the removal from the land that is described in Deuteronomy 32 as a consequence of worshiping *tôʿēbâ* idols that are not-God.[12]

The consequence of the LORD's jealousy in Deuteronomy 32:16 is that the Israelites are cut off from the covenant order by the covenant curses. However, Paul in Corinthians probably does not imagine that such things as plagues, famines, or armies

11. Walton and Walton, *Lost World of the Israelite Conquest*, 169–94; cf. Milgrom, *Leviticus 17–22*, 2418.

12. For a more detailed discussion of *ḥerem*, *tôʿēbâ*, and the Israelite covenant order, see Walton and Walton, *Lost World of the Israelite Conquest*, 151–56; Walton, *Old Testament Theology*, 134–35.

will fall upon his audience as a result of their sacrifices; the order of the new covenant does not usually work that way (though see, e.g., 1 Cor 11:30). He is concerned, however, that they will be nonetheless cut off from the community of the people of the new covenant; this is what he means when he says "You cannot drink the cup of the Lord and the cup of demons too; you cannot have a part in both the Lord's table and the table of demons." The cup and table of the Lord are symbols for the Christian community; compare to the decision to eat with gentile believers (or not) in Galatians 2:12, and the injunction to "not even eat" with immoral Christians in 1 Corinthians 5:11. The argument of 1 Corinthians 5 ends with an appeal to "expel the wicked person from among you" (1 Cor 5:13), which is a reference to Deuteronomy 13, which in turn describes the process that should be used to preserve the integrity of the covenant order, including use of the *ḥerem*. The word used in the LXX to translate *ḥerem* is *anathema*, which Paul uses in parallel to the phrase "cut off from Christ" in Romans 9:5. Thus, the concepts of *tôʿēbâ*, *ḥerem*, expulsion from the community, cut off from Christ, and [not] eating together are all conceptually linked, which in turn explains Paul's use of Deuteronomy 32 in 1 Corinthians 10:22. Because one cannot partake in the cup of Christ and the cup of demons, those who choose to partake in the cup of demons will cut themselves off from the new covenant, just as the ancient Israelites by worshipping the *šēdîm* (whatever they were) cut themselves off from the old covenant. However, the severance does not happen because the objects of worship are demons specifically; it happens because they are *not-God*. Nonetheless, it is not the action of sacrificing to not-God that inherently brings the consequence; sacrificing to not-God happens to be *tôʿēbâ* to the order of both the old and new covenant. But that does not mean that only sacrifices and only demons are *tôʿēbâ*; many things were prohibited in Israel that had nothing to do with idolatry, or even with anything like what we would call *morality* (i.e., what we like to say is universally opposed to the will of God). Why idol meat in particular is inimical to the covenant order is never explained, just as the Old Testament never explains why Yahweh adopts certain ancient Near Eastern religious practices for his own cult (blood sacrifice, circumcision, a temple, etc.) while rejecting others (sacrificing under trees, eating meat with the blood in it, sacrificing pigs). Any speculation as to the motive, including that the rejected practices are somehow inherently harmful or immoral, is arbitrary and unwarranted. Sacrificing children (Deut 12:31) might be harmful or immoral (though see below); sacrificing outside a central sanctuary is not (Deut 12:5–7), though both are demarcated by the injunction "You must not worship the LORD your God in their way." We can assume that there was some logic behind it that would have made sense within the original cognitive environment, but there is no clear consensus as to what that logic may have been and we should not assume that it was something that would necessarily make sense in the context of our own culture.

1 Corinthians 10 actually does go on to provide a logic for the prohibition of idol meat: "if someone says to you, 'This has been offered in sacrifice,' then do not

eat it, both for the sake of the one who told you and for the sake of conscience. I am referring to the other person's conscience, not yours. . . . Do not cause anyone to stumble, whether Jews, Greeks, or the church of God" (1 Cor 10:28–32). This reason has nothing to do with anything related to the meat itself or to the idol itself, or to any demon that may or may not be associated with it. The offense that cuts off from the community is "causing another to stumble" or "seeking one's own good rather than the good of others" (1 Cor 10:24, 33). There are many ways in which one could seek one's own good or cause others to stumble that have nothing to do with demons or idols; consequently, there may well be other things that cannot be partaken with at the same time as the table of Christ that have nothing to do with demons or idols at all.[13] (Note that the reiteration of the same argument in Rom 14:13–23 says nothing about idols or demons whatsoever.)

In conclusion, Paul is not revealing to his audience (or to the modern reader) anything about the metaphysics of how idols work; neither is he commenting on the taxonomy of anything that was worshipped either in ancient Israel or in contemporary Rome. The consequence of eating idol meat has nothing to do with idols or demons inherently and everything to do with what is allowed within the community of the people of the new covenant. An idol *is* nothing, and a demon is nothing too. It is not the demon behind the altar that delivers the consequence; rather, it is *the Lord's jealousy* and desire to protect and preserve the functioning order of his covenant people against those who selfishly focus on their own good or those who provoke other members of the community to do things that they believe to be wrong.

Thus, we see that 1 Corinthians 10:20 is not giving us any information that we can read into other parts of the Bible to discover details about the metaphysical or moral nature of gods. Nonetheless, several passages in the Old Testament are occasionally thought to present evidence that the gods of the nations are evil beings opposed to the will and purposes of God. These we will now examine to see what they are intending to communicate in context.

Idols and idolatry in the Old Testament

If, as we have proposed, idols and idolatry are not inherently, metaphysically, ontologically evil, then it is worth examining the condemnation of idols and the worship of idols in the prophetic literature. Idolatry is one of the most frequent accusations against Israel, as for example Jeremiah 22:8–9: "People from many nations will pass by this city and will ask one another, 'Why has the LORD done such a thing to this great city?' And the answer will be: 'Because they have forsaken the covenant of the LORD their God and have worshiped and served other gods.'" In contrast, "because they worshipped and served gods other than Yahweh" is never indicated as a reason

13. For further discussion see Walton and Walton, *Lost World of the Israelite Conquest*, 85–86, 239–52.

for the devastation of Israel's neighbors. We have proposed that this is because the prohibition of idolatry in Israel has less to do with the nature of idols per se and more to do with the nature of the relationship between Israel and Yahweh. This is worth further examination.

The covenant between Yahweh and Israel is commonly recognized to take the form of an ancient Near Eastern suzerain-vassal treaty.[14] This means that the Israelites would have thought of Yahweh as their national patron deity, as for example a Babylonian would have thought of Marduk, but they would have also thought of him as their emperor, as a Babylonian would have thought of Nebuchadnezzar. Most interpreters assume that idolatry is a fundamentally cultic offense because it involves worship, and therefore assume that it is offensive to Yahweh in his function as a deity. Combined with modern theological monotheism,[15] the offense against deity is extended universally to all humanity and combined with speculative rationalizations, so for example: "Idolatry [is] within the realm of that which incurs the wrath of God. . . . It issues in a catalog of vice and viciousness, polluting every aspect of human life."[16] However, the language of exclusivity in lordship is common in vassal treaties, and therefore we propose that idolatry is in fact a *political* offense and is offensive to Yahweh *in his role as Israel's emperor*. A Hittite treaty between Mursili II and his vassal Kupanta-Kurunta includes the injunction that "you shall not desire any other power over you,"[17] and the succession treaty of Esarhaddon stipulates "[do not] set any other king or any other lord over yourselves, nor swear an oath to any other king or any other lord."[18] Ezekiel 2:3 accuses Israel of rebellion (*mārad*, a normal word for political revolt, e.g., Jeremiah 52:3), citing the offense in Ezekiel 5:9–11 as idolatry ("Because of all your *tôʿēbâ* idols; . . . because you have defiled my sanctuary with all your vile [*šiqqûṣ*, see below] images and *tôʿēbâ* practices"). Idolatry is therefore *a treaty violation*, but treaty violations can only be committed by those who are actually under a treaty. Yahweh did not make a treaty—that is, a covenant—with any nation other than Israel, and so accordingly the nations are never said to "rebel" against Yahweh by setting up another lord over themselves (i.e., by serving their own gods).

The gods of the nations do make the occasional appearance in the judgment oracles against the nations, however. Thus, it is necessary to understand how these oracles operate as a genre. With the exception of Jonah (and to a lesser extent Daniel),[19] no

---

14. For the most thorough treatment, see the three-volume work of Kitchen and Lawrence, *Treaty, Law and Covenant*.

15. What we now call *monotheism* is anachronistic to the ancient world and is not represented in the biblical text-in-context. For a discussion on monotheism in the context of ancient Israelite religion versus modern understandings of the word, see Smith, *The Origins of Biblical Monotheism*, 10–14; Lemaire, *Birth of Monotheism*, 43–47.

16. Wright, *Mission of God*, 179.

17. Beckman, *Hittite Diplomatic Texts*, 72.

18. Parpola and Watanabe, *Neo-Assyrian Treaties*, 71–72; *COS* 4.157, 158, 160.

19. The book of Jonah is a narrative, not a compilation of oracular prophecy, and therefore is not

Old Testament prophet delivers an oracle of doom from Yahweh to any nation other than Israel. Even when the oracle begins, for instance, "say to the ruler of Tyre" (Ezek 28:2), we should not imagine that the prophet actually sends the message off to be read to the king in Tyre. The message is delivered to Israelites, in Israel. So, for example, when Jeremiah says that "In Moab I will put an end to those who make offerings on the high places and burn incense to their gods" (Jer 48:35), he is not telling the Moabites (or even the Israelites) that Yahweh is punishing the Moabites because the Moabites burned incense to Chemosh. The offense for which Moab is being destroyed is "because she defied the LORD" (Jer 48:42), not by burning incense to Chemosh, but by mocking Israel (Jer 48:27–30). However, the oracle is not really about Moab per se; Moab is being used vicariously to describe Israel (explicitly in Jeremiah 48:13; Moab will be ashamed of Chemosh as [the northern kingdom of] Israel was ashamed of [Jeroboam's altar at] Bethel) and therefore the fate of Moab is implied to be the same fate that awaits Israel. Chemosh will go into exile (Jer 48:7; this is a common fate of gods whose nations are conquered, see chapter 9) and the people of Chemosh will be destroyed (Jer 48:6), but eventually their fortunes will be restored (Jer 48:7). The point is that Moab burned incense to Chemosh, yet Chemosh could not save them. Israel likewise burns incense to Chemosh, and Chemosh will not be able to save Israel either.

The impotence of the gods is a common theme in the Bible's prophetic literature.[20] One of the most notable examples is Isaiah 44:6–22, where the prophet scornfully describes the process of manufacturing idols: "Half of the wood he burns in the fire; over it he prepares his meal. . . . From the rest he makes a god, his idol; he bows down to it and worships. He prays to it and says, 'Save me! You are my god!'" (Isa 44:16–17; see also 40:19–20; 41:7). It should be easy to see that a thing cannot both be impotent, such that those who revere it are comically foolish, while simultaneously being a cosmically powerful force of darkness that successfully promotes all manner of evil and opposes the will of Yahweh. The word here for "idol" (*pesel*) refers to the

---

comparable to the judgment oracles found in books like Obadiah or Amos. The message he delivers to Nineveh contains no indictment, for idolatry or anything else; Yahweh simply declares that the city will be destroyed. The penance of the Ninevites likewise does not include putting away their idols (Jonah 3:7–10); they cease only their evil ways and violence (Jonah 3:8). Their response is probably a negative foil for Israel, who receives similar oracles and does nothing (compare to the similar idea expressed in Luke 10:13). Daniel, on the other hand, delivers no oracles, but is twice called on to interpret an omen of doom in Dan 4:4–27 and 5:7–29 (compare Joseph in Gen 41). In neither case is the offense that prompts the omen the worship of Marduk or any Babylonian gods. In Dan 5, Belshazzar does "[praise] the gods of silver and gold, of bronze, iron, wood and stone, which cannot see or hear or understand" (Dan 5:23), but his actual offense is his disrespect for Yahweh by abusing the articles from his temple (Dan 5:23), which he should have known not to do because of the experiences of his predecessor (Dan 5:20–21), and therefore the accusation against him is that he has "not humbled himself" (Dan 5:22). The demonstrated power of Yahweh (with reference to Dan 4:31–33) is contrasted with the impotence of the gods of stone (and with the ignorance of the wise men; Dan 5:10–12); the point is not that Belshazzar has violated Yahweh's decrees by worshipping idols.

20. See for example Isa 16:11–12; 18:13; 21:9; Jer 50:38; 51:17–18, 52; Ezek 30:13; Hab 2:18–20; Nah 1:14.

object; some interpreters therefore anachronistically invoke the supposed contrast in 1 Corinthians 10:19–20 between the idol (which is nothing) and demon *behind* the idol (which is powerful) and use this to differentiate between the statue itself and the entity that the statue represents.[21] The supposed dichotomy is further supported by appealing to Daniel 10 and Psalm 82, which we will discuss in chapter 12. For now, though, we will note that the concept of impotence extends beyond the image (*pesel*) and onto the deity itself. The word translated as "worthless idols" in, for example, Deuteronomy 32:21—"They made me jealous by what is no god and angered me with their worthless idols"; compare to Deuteronomy 32:16, the passage Paul references in 1 Corinthians 10:22—is *hebel* (lit. "meaningless" or "worthless").[22] The word for the *idol* that is nothing in 1 Corinthians 10:19 (*eidolon*) is also used by the LXX to translate *hebel* in Deuteronomy 32:21, which refers to the beings behind the idols. However, the word *pesel* in Isaiah 44:15, 17, which refers to the object, is translated *gluptos* ("carved [thing]"; also 42:17), and in Isaiah 40:19–20 it is translated *eikon* ("image").[23] *Eikon* and *gluptos* never translate *hebel*. Thus, it is in fact the beings who are worshipped through the idols that are "worthless" or "meaningless" (*hebel*) in the Old Testament, and who are identified by the word *eidolon* and likewise affirmed to be nothing in 1 Corinthians 10:19 (see above).

Hebel is occasionally paralleled with the designation "[not] god" (*lo' 'ēl*, Deut 32:21; *lo' 'ĕlôhîm*, Jer 16:19–20[24]); with inanimate things (the [depersonalized] sky in Jer 14:22, *pesel* in Jer 8:19; 10:14–15; 51:17–18); or with other things that are worthless (the worshippers themselves in 2 Kgs 17:15; Jer 2:5; practices that are worthless, senseless, and foolish in Jer 8:3–10). Following *hebel* is scornfully contrasted with serving Yahweh in 1 Kings 16:13, 26 and Jonah 2:8. So, while the *hebel* are the recipients of idol worship, they are only called *gods* in Jeremiah 16:20, which is immediately negated. However, the recipients of idol worship are also frequently called gods (*ĕlôhîm* or some variation thereof); see for example 1 Kings 18:24: "Then you call on the name of your *ĕlôhîm* [Baal], and I will call on the name of the LORD. The *ĕlôhîm* who answers by fire—he is *ĕlôhîm*." Thus, we should not see the classification "god" or "not-god" as metaphysical in nature—i.e., a question of whether or not an entity bearing the taxonomy of *god* is present—but rather an indicator of whether or not the entity is able to carry out the *functions* of a god. Statements that affirm that the gods are not gods are neither oxymoronic nor affirmations of what we call *metaphysical monotheism*.

21. See for example Heiser, *Unseen Realm*, 35–36.

22. Compare Ecclesiastes 1:1, where "everything is *hebel*."

23. *Pesel* is translated by *eidolon* in Exod 20:4 and Deut 5:8 (the second commandment); in 2 Chr 33:22 and 34:7 (the idols made by Manassah and destroyed by Josiah, respectively), and Isa 30:22 (in a rude metaphor describing the Israelites forsaking their idolatry in frustration and disgust); all of these imply the function of worship of the image and never only the manufacture of the image itself; thus *eidolon* never refers exclusively to the image.

24. NIV's translation of *šqr* as "false gods" and *hebel* as idols in reference to the idols from Jeremiah 16:20 appears to be correct: Holladay, *Jeremiah 1*, 481; Lundbom, *Jeremiah 1–20*, 772.

Rather, they simply mean that "the things you worship cannot carry out the functions you expect from a god." Whether this impotence is because they do not exist (modern monotheism), because they are evil and disinclined to carry out divine functions (conflict theology), or are simply weak and ineffectual, especially relative to Yahweh (the persistent affirmation throughout the Old Testament) is not especially relevant; the text is interested in affirming that gods other than Yahweh cannot carry out divine functions as well as Yahweh can and it does not especially matter why.

One word that is explicitly paralleled to *gods* is *ĕlîl* ("worthless [things]"; see Zech 11:17), most notably in 1 Chronicles 16:26 and Psalm 96:5: "For all the *ĕlôhîm* of the nations are *ĕlîl*, but the LORD made the heavens." The LXX translates *ĕlîl* in 1 Chronicles 16:26 as *eidolon*, but in Psalm 96:5 the same word is mistranslated *daimonia*, "demons." This translation choice reflects the conflation of the demigods who receive worship at the altars with the pantheons of traditional religion that was present in the cognitive environment at the time of the translation of the LXX; it should not be read as an authoritative classification of the taxonomy of the entities, as is evidenced by translating the same word *in the same phrase* in two different ways. It should certainly not be read to infer that everything the text calls *eidolon* (or any Hebrew word translated as such) can or should be assigned all of the properties that we associate with the word "demon." In fact, there is little to no overlap with the concept of "demons" as they were understood in the ancient Near East (though as we have already shown, the label "demon" is anachronistic; see chapter 7) and the imagery used by the Old Testament to describe the gods of the nations. "Demons" are associated with the liminal and chaotic, but none of the gods are ever described with chaotic or liminal imagery, or compared to the chaos monsters in any way (although the nations sometimes are; see chapter 9). Likewise, the chaos monsters are never called *ĕlîl* or *hebel* and are rarely portrayed as impotent and undeserving of attention or respect (only sarcastically, as a metaphor for Egypt in Isa 30:7). The power and potency of the Leviathan is emphasized specifically in Job 41, and indeed is inherent in chaos imagery even when the particular element is depersonalized. Thus, there is no conceptual overlap whatsoever between the gods of the nations and the kinds of beings that most closely resemble what would later be called *demons*.

The word *ĕlîl* is paralleled to *ĕlôhîm* (Lev 19:4); to *pesel* (Lev 26:1; Ps 97:7; Hab 2:18); to *gillûlîm* ("idols") (Ezek 30:13) and *massēkâ* ("image") (Hab 2:18, see below); to "the work of their hands" (Isa 2:8); and to "his own creation" (Hab 2:18). They are contrasted with Yahweh (Isa 2:18; 10:10–11; Jer 14:14) and will be thrown out (Isa 2:20; 31:7). In Isaiah 19:1, the *ĕlîlîm* cower along with their people as Yahweh sweeps down on Egypt, but no offense is ever specified for the Egyptians, except perhaps that they have become impotent fools (Isa 19:11–16). Once again, this judgment oracle is not specifying that Egypt is being punished for violating Yahweh's decrees, let alone that these violations consisted of worshipping the *ĕlîlîm*. The purpose of the oracle is to demonstrate to Israel the helplessness of Egypt, Judah's erstwhile ally, as is commonly seen throughout the prophets (e.g., Isa 20:1–6; 30:1–11; 31:1–3; 36:4–6; Ezek 17:15–18; 29:1–16).

Other Hebrew words that refer to idols are *gillûlîm* (NIV "idols," occurring thirty-nine times in Ezekiel and only nine times elsewhere); *aṣab* (NIV normally "idol" or "image"); *massēkâ* (NIV normally "image"); and *těrāpîm* (NIV normally "household gods"). None of these are ever depicted as cosmic demonic powers and all of them are portrayed as ineffective or impotent. The "idols" that Manasseh makes and Josiah destroys, called *pesel* in 2 Chronicles 33:22 and 34:7, are called *gillûlîm* in the parallel accounts in 2 Kings 21:11 and 23:24. The word *gillûlîm* contains connotations of impurity and thus represents an increased amount of contempt and disgust, as compared over the more neutral *ĕlîlîm* (Ezek 30:13) or *pesel*.[25] The emphasis on impurity is especially clear when dead bodies are heaped on top of the *gillûlîm* in Leviticus 26:30. However, we should not infer that the emphasis on impurity is somehow an indication of the level of evil that the activity entails; many actions that incur impurity in Israel are not evil in any way (e.g., menstruation, burying the dead). The emphasis is similar to that of Isaiah 30:22 when the idols (*pesel*) are tossed away like a menstrual rag. Consequently, we should not read Ezekiel 30:13, where the "*gillûlîm* of Egypt" are destroyed, as if God is thereby purging the world of something especially evil or unclean. *Gillûlîm* in Ezekiel 30:13 is paralleled to *massēkâ* ("images") and in context represents the familiar theme of the inability of the gods to defend themselves or their people. *Massēkâ* (lit. "cast image") is similar to *pesel* (lit. "carved image") and refers to the process by which the object was manufactured; the two are used together in Deuteronomy 27:15. In Habakkuk 2:18, *pesel* ("idol"), *massēkâ* ("image"), and *ĕlîlîm* ("idols") are all asserted to be valueless and lifeless. *Aṣab* is paralleled to *gillûlîm* ("idols") in Jeremiah 50:2 and to *ĕlîlîm* ("idols") in Isaiah 10:11, and they are derided as being made with human hands in Psalms 115:4; 135:15; and Hosea 8:4. Finally, the *těrāpîm* are thought to refer to a specific kind of idol that represents family gods and ancestors, as opposed to cult images for established deities in temples.[26] These are the "household gods" that Rachel steals from Laban in Genesis 31;[27] the "idol" that Michal uses to impersonate David in 1 Samuel 19; and the "idol" that Micah makes in Judges 17–18. Micah's *těrāpîm* (an image for his personal family shrine) is listed together with a *pesel* and a *massēkâ* in Judges 18:14. The references in Genesis 31 and 1 Samuel 19 might include subtle derision at the ignominious treatment of the objects; Rachel

25. H. D. Preuss, "גלולים," 2–3.

26. *ZIBBCOT*, Walton, "Genesis," 1:112; Heltzer, "New Light from Emar on Genesis 31"; Van der Toorn, "Nature of the Biblical *Těrāpîm*."

27. Some interpreters claim that the "foreign gods" (*'ĕlôhîm*) that Jacob confiscates and buries in Gen 35:2–4 might be these same gods; see for example Hamilton, *Genesis 18–50*, 375. However, the use of a different word and the parallel context in Josh 24:23—there is no specific indication that the Israelites of the conquest generation possessed *těrāpîm*—indicate that the *ĕlôhîm* might refer to cult images plundered in battle; from Egypt or the cities of Canaan in Joshua, or from Shechem in Gen 34:29 (*ZIBBCOT*, Walton, "Genesis," 1:118).

hides the *tĕrāpîm* from Laban by sitting on them and claiming to be menstruating (compare Isa 30:22), and Michal treats the *tĕrāpîm* as a common everyday object, used to create a man-shaped bed stuffing. Other passages indicate that the *tĕrāpîm* had a specific divinatory function; Nebuchadnezzar is directed (by Yahweh) to attack Jerusalem by means of consulting the *tĕrāpîm*—among other oracular sources—in Ezekiel 21:21 (NIV "idols"), and Zechariah 10:2 parallels "*tĕrāpîm* [that] speak deceitfully" with "visions that lie." Hosea 3:4 lists the *tĕrāpîm* among cultic accoutrements that the Israelites will have to do without in their exile; there *tĕrāpîm* is paired specifically with *ephod*, which normally refers to the garments of the priests (Exod 28:6-8; 1 Sam 2:28), though the term is used inconsistently to indicate other things as well (Judg 8:27). An *ephod* is present with the *tĕrāpîm* in Micah's shrine (Judg 17:5; 8:18, 20) and somehow serves a divinatory function in 1 Samuel 23:9-12 and 30:7-8. Finally, in 1 Samuel 15:23 Samuel tells Saul that "rebellion is like the sin of divination, and arrogance like the evil ('*āwōn*) of *tĕrāpîm*" (NIV "idolatry"). '*Āwōn* can be used for cultic or covenant violations of all kinds (i.e., improperly offered sacrifices in Exod 28:38, 43) and so does not inherently refer to something intrinsically immoral,[28] and *tĕrāpîm* is again paralleled to divination. What is most interesting in this context is the juxtaposition of the *tĕrāpîm* with rebellion (*mĕrî*, conceptually similar to *mārad*; the two are paralleled in Neh 9:26),[29] thus further indicating the connection between Israelite idolatry and (political) rebellion. Saul is not an idolater, but he is a rebel. In context, Saul is treating Yahweh like a typical ancient Near Eastern warrior god; he is taking a portion of the spoils to sacrifice as a gift of gratitude for his victory (1 Sam 15:15), as any pious and diligent ancient Near Eastern king would do. However, in doing so he has fundamentally misunderstood the nature of Israelite kingship, wherein he is supposed to be a regent of a vassal state. By erecting a monument to himself (1 Sam 15:12—probably crediting Yahweh with the victory as his divine patron),[30] he has effectively declared independence from his sovereign. The sovereign's response accordingly follows standard ancient Near Eastern procedure; the rebellious regent is dethroned and replaced (1 Sam 15:26-28).

---

28. '*Āwōn* is commonly translated "sin" in the NIV, but the real emphasis of the word is not moral culpability but rather the fact of consequence; the term usually means either "something you did [that has caused/will cause something bad to happen to you]," or "something that has happened/will happen to you [because of something you did]." The offence that produces consequence can be either moral, legal, or cultic in nature. Occasionally the term refers more specifically to calamity (i.e., "something that happens to you") without specifically emphasizing any cause. This is especially seen in Ps 40:12, where '*āwōn* (NIV "sin") is paralleled to the "trouble" (*ra*') experienced by the [righteous] psalmist, and also in Gen 19:15 where the '*āwōn* of Sodom, referring to its destruction (NIV "when the city is punished"; lit. "in the '*āwōn* of the city"), can potentially engulf the [righteous] Lot. See Walton and Walton, *Lost World of the Israelite Conquest*, 54–57.

29. "But they were disobedient (*mrh*) and rebelled (*mārad*) against you." *Mrh* is the verbal root behind the noun *mĕrî*. See Schwienhorst, "מָרַד," 1–5, and Schwienhorst, "מָרָה," 5–10.

30. Tsumura, *1 Samuel*, 397.

Finally, an additional word used to describe the gods is *šiqqûṣ*, translated "vile" or "abomination." The word always refers to gods or cultic objects, with the exception of Zechariah 9:7, where it is paralleled to "blood" and refers to unclean food, and Nahum 3:6, where it implicitly refers to excrement.[31] This context indicates that it refers to the impure or unclean, and therefore might carry connotations similar to *gillûlîm* (see above). The term is parallel to *gillûlîm* in 2 Kings 23:24 and Ezekiel 37:23. In Ezekiel 7:20 and 11:18 *šiqqûṣ* (NIV "vile images") is paralleled to *tôʿēbâ* (NIV "detestable idols"), which as described above refers to something that is outside the bounds of the covenant order and therefore unacceptable for the covenant community. Neither impurity (*niddâ*, e.g., Ezra 9:11) nor uncleanliness (*ṭāmēʾ*)[32] nor "off-limits" (*tôʿēbâ*) are moral categories, and so there is no reason to assume that *šiqqûṣ*, which seems to combine the concepts, would be any different; blood and excrement, as natural elements and by-products of living beings, are not evil and revolting to God in and of themselves either. In Isaiah 66:3, choosing one's own way (implicitly, instead of the covenant order) is compared with delighting in *šiqqûṣ*; disregarding the covenant order is conceptually comparable to *tôʿēbâ* (see discussion on Gen 6 in chapter 12). The *šiqqûṣ* (NIV "vile images") are called "lifeless" in Jeremiah 16:18, thus emphasizing their impotence. Thus, there is no indication in the word that the named gods of the nations made themselves morally reprehensible to Yahweh by exercising power; *šiqqûṣ* is not a moral standing and the "vile images" are powerless. *Šiqqûṣ* is applied to Molech, Chemosh, and Ashtoreth by name (1 Kgs 11:5, 7; 2 Kgs 23:13), and is the term for the "abomination that causes desolation" in Daniel 9:27; 11:31; 12:11, which in context refers to the altar to Zeus erected in the temple by Antiochus Epiphanes.

In conclusion, all of the Hebrew words that refer to the gods of non-Israelite nations or their images (or both at once) are conceptually similar, although there are subtle distinctions in technicality and connotation. *None* of them are ever portrayed as demonically powerful, morally offensive, or opposed to the will of Yahweh. Instead they are helpless and impotent and unworthy of attention or consideration. Worshiping or serving them is a violation of Israel's covenant and confers cultic impurity (as eating unclean food or touching a corpse also does; deliberately incurring cultic impurity is a severe covenant offense that carries the death penalty, e.g., Lev 7:27; 20:18), but *not because they are evil or demonic*; rather, serving a lord other than Yahweh is against the terms of the vassal treaty that Yahweh has made with Israel. The violation comes from the nature of the covenant relationship, not from the nature of the gods. Further, the passages should not be taken as either an affirmation or a denial of the "existence" of such gods. The cognitive environment of the ancient Near East believed in a wide

31. Christensen, *Nahum*, 344.

32. *Niddâ* can refer to (amoral) menstruation (Lev 15:19–33); *ṭāmēʾ* can refer to amoral things such as unclean food (Lev 11) and mold (Lev 14:40–45). For a detailed discussion of these terms and their usage as applied to foreign peoples and their practices, see Walton and Walton, *Lost World of the Israelite Conquest*, 128–29.

variety of gods, and therefore we would expect the Bible's language to reflect (but not necessarily affirm) that belief. Further, that such beings possess relative amounts of power is also part of the cognitive environment. In 2 Kings 18:33–35, Sennacherib mocks the gods of the enemies of Assyria (including the God of Israel) using language very similar to that used by Israel's prophets: "Has the god of any nation ever delivered his land from the hand of the king of Assyria? Where are the gods of Hamath and Arpad? Where are the gods of Sepharvaim, Hena, and Ivvah? Have they rescued Samaria from my hand? Who of all the gods of these countries has been able to save his land from me? How then can the LORD deliver Jerusalem from my hand?" The point of the taunt is for the audience (in this case, the besieged citizens of Jerusalem) to submit to the rule of Assyria, not for them to deny that their god really exists or to take the herald's word as empirical evidence that Hamath, Arpad, et al. must have really had gods after all. This objective is similar to the taunts against the gods addressed to Israel and recorded in the Bible; they are to submit to Yahweh. Other gods are not evil, they are merely weak and unworthy of service, trust, or attention.

The gods and human sacrifice

Another common argument that the gods of the nations are evil involves the practice of human sacrifice—especially child sacrifice—rendered in the NIV as, e.g., "sacrifice children [in the fire] to Molek" (Lev 18:21; 20:2–4; 2 Kgs 23:10; Jer 32:35); and especially "in worshiping their gods, they do all kinds of detestable (*tôʿēbâ*) things the LORD hates (*śnʾ*). They even burn their sons and daughters in the fire as sacrifices to their gods" (Deut 12:31). The argument mostly relies on the assumption of emotional and moral connotations to the words "detestable" and "vile" (*tôʿēbâ* and *šiqqûṣ*) all read through the lens of a modern humanistic aversion to human sacrifice, which our culture regards as particularly heinous and barbaric and so we naturally assume that God must regard it the same way. Thus, the common interpretation holds that the gods are depraved demons who demanded and encouraged human sacrifice among their worshippers, and this practice was so revolting and abhorrent to God that he put the gods to death (inferred from Ps 82 and Isa 24; see chapter 12) and further dispatched the Israelites to annihilate their depraved and perverse cultures (inferred from Leviticus, especially Lev 18:24), and later dispatched the Babylonians to annihilate the practice in Israel for the same reasons (inferred from Jeremiah, especially 32:35).[33] This argument is worth further examination.

First, the phrase translated "sacrifice [children]" (in Lev 18:21; Deut 18:10; 2 Kgs 17:17; 21:6; 23:10; 2 Chr 33:6; and Jer 32:35) is not the normal word for "sacrifice"; the Hebrew reads literally "pass seed" (*ʿābar zeraʿ*) either "to Molek" (Lev 18:21), or "through the fire" (all others), or both (2 Kgs 23:10; Jer 32:35). Children are "passed"

---

33. See for example Milgrom, *Lev 17–22*, 1559.

to idols (*gillûlîm*) in Ezekiel 16:20 and 23:37, but this may or may not refer literally to the same practice indicated elsewhere since these passages are extended metaphors. A similar phrase "give seed" (*nātan zeraʿ*) [to Molek] is used in Leviticus 20:20–4. Similarly, the word translated "burn [as sacrifices] to [their gods]" (*śrp*) in these texts (Deut 12:31; 2 Kgs 17:31; Jer 7:31; 19:5) is not the normal word for a burnt offering (*qṭr*), and indeed refers to the burning of that which is unsuitable for sacrifice; in Leviticus 4:19–21 the fat is burned (*qṭr*) on the altar, while the rest of the carcass is taken and burned (*śrp*) outside the camp. In 1 Kings 13:2, an altar is defiled by burning (*śrp*) human bones on it. Consequently, a longstanding tradition interprets the language of "passing seed" to refer, not to human sacrifice, but rather to exogamy; "Molek" is read as a metaphor for "worshippers of foreign gods," and "pass seed" refers either literally to impregnating a [foreign] woman (*zeraʿ* can mean either "children" or "sperm") or to giving a child in marriage (a common meaning for *nātan*) to a foreign family. The warrant for this derives from the context of Leviticus 18:21, since every other offense in Leviticus 18:6–23 is sexual rather than cultic in nature.[34] However, it is difficult to understand what this would mean when seed is "passed through fire." Consequently, these passages are occasionally interpreted together with those using the word *śrp* to refer to some kind of ritual branding or perhaps a consecration or purification rite.[35] In Numbers 31:23 metals are purified by being "passed (*ʿābar*) [through] fire," but the word *śrp* never clearly means anything other than *destroy by fire* (e.g., Judg 14:15; the word commonly refers to the immolation of cities or the consumption of fuel).[36] *Nātan* and *ʿābar* are paralleled to normal words for sacrifice in Ezekiel 16:20–21: "you took your sons and daughters . . . and [sacrificed] (*zbḥ*) them. . . . You [slaughtered] (*šḥṭ*) my children and [gave them (*nātan*) to be passed (*ʿābar*); NIV "sacrificed"] to the idols." However, the children in Ezekiel 16:20 were born to (personified) Israel by Yahweh, which is very clearly a metaphor—Yahweh did not literally sire the children who were burned in other passages, even though this was something that ancient Near Eastern gods could theoretically do—and so we cannot necessarily take the rest of the passage literally. Further, the firstborn children are *nātan* to Yahweh in Exodus 22:29, which is not normally interpreted to mean "sacrifice" no matter what Ezekiel 16 says,[37] even though the firstborn are paralleled with sacrificial victims (cattle and sheep). Further, again, *śrp* never refers to cultic offerings and we would expect a more

34. See discussion in Milgrom, *Lev 17–22*, 1152–53; Heider, *Molek*, 68–69; Stavrakopoulu, *King Manasseh*.

35. In scholarly literature, the term "februation" is often used. See discussion in Milgrom, *Leviticus 17–22*, 1553–54; Heider, *Molek*, 69–81.

36. The word for nonlethal fire damage (e.g., searing or scorching) is *kawa* (Prov 6:28, 43:2).

37. Studies of the history of Israelite religion occasionally propose evidence of orthodox human or child sacrifice to Yahweh prior to the deuteronomistic reforms; see for example Heider, *Molek*, 402–9. Regardless of the merits of this hypothesis, it is irrelevant for a discussion of the meaning of the text in its final redacted form (since the final form does not confirm the beliefs of its sources) and is not acknowledged by advocates of conflict theology.

appropriate word—*qṭr* ("burnt offering"), *'olâ* ("sacrifice"), *zbḥ* ("slaughter," usually with cultic connotations), or *yqd* ("kindle/burn")—to be used if a meaning of "sacrifice" was intended. Thus, all interpretations have their own problems, but ultimately identifying what the practice specifically represents—or even whether it always represents the same thing—is not especially important; the text is clear that the Israelites were not supposed to do it (whatever it was) and yet they did it anyway, and that is sufficient to convey the message. The point is that the absence of the normal vocabulary for sacrifices in these passages means that they cannot be asserted to definitively describe the practice of killing a human as an offering to the gods.

Second, "Molek" might not even be the name of a deity. The NIV uses "Molek" to translate the various words *Milkom, Malkam,* and *Molek/Molech.* Milkom is the patron deity of Ammon, called "*šiqqûṣ* of the Ammonites" in 1 Kings 11:5, 33 and 2 Kings 23:13. Malkam is implicitly indicated as the god of Ammon in Jeremiah 49:1–3, and as a deity of unspecified patronage in Zephaniah 1:5. Neither of these are ever mentioned in conjunction with the alleged sacrifices. The remaining term, *Molek/Molech,* is problematic, because the varying contexts do not make clear whether it is a title (perhaps a corruption of *melek,* "king"),[38] an adjective, or a proper name, and if so, whose. 1 Kings 11:7 calls Molech "*šiqqûṣ* of Ammon," which is the basis of the conflation with Milkom, but Beal observes that the shrine in 1 Kings 11 is built "on a hill east of Jerusalem," while the topheth to Molech in Jeremiah is in the Hinnom valley in the southwest;[39] thus they are probably not the same deity. Cogan suggests that both references in 1 Kings 11 are to Milkom, with the differing name in 1 Kings 11:7 being a (perhaps deliberate) misidentification;[40] thus Molech has nothing to do with the patron of Ammon.[41] Other supposed referents are a Mesopotamian chthonic deity or class of deities called *Malik(u),*[42] or even perhaps the Phoenician national patron Melqart, though the latter is unlikely.[43] Another alternative interpretation suggests that *molk* is not a name at all but indicates a technical ritual procedure, i.e., "pass through fire [as a *molk*-offering]."[44] The primary problem with this suggestion is that the four occurrences of *Molech* in Leviticus 20:2–5 contain a definite article (lit "[sacrifice] to *the mlk*"), which negates the linguistic basis on which the "type of offering" interpretation is based. Further, the phrase "play the harlot with" (NIV "prostitute yourselves by chasing after") in Leviticus 20:5 usually has a deity, or at least the central object of a cult (e.g., Judg 8:27), as its object.[45] However, on the other hand, in Hebrew

38. See Milgrom, *Leviticus 17–22,* 1556–57; George Heider, "Molech," 581.

39. Beal, *1 & 2 Kings,* 171.

40. Cogan, *1 Kings,* 328; see also Heider, "Molech," 583.

41. See also Day, *Yahweh and the Gods,* 213.

42. Heider, "Molech," 582–83; Milgrom, *Leviticus 17–22,* 1558.

43. Heider, "Molech," 583.

44. See Heider, "Molech," 582; Milgrom, *Leviticus 17–22,* 1556; Heider, *Molek,* 174–79.

45. Heider, "Molech," 583; Day, *Yahweh and the Gods,* 209–10.

a definite article never precedes a proper name, either, which would indicate that *mlk* is a title. Still another argument contends that *mlk* is a *verb*, derived from the root *hlk* and referring to an act of offering,[46] though verbs do not take definite articles either and, once again, interpreting the action as an offering of any kind is problematic due to the semantic range of *śrp*.[47] The point is that there is no basis to definitively conclude that Molek is the name of a deity whose demand for child sacrifice can be extrapolated to all other non-Israelite deities as evidence that all of those deities are evil, since both of the terms "sacrifice" and "Molek" (and in some cases even the word "children") are unclear as to what exactly they refer to.

Third, as described above, *tô'ēbâ* and *šiqqûṣ* do not carry connotations of either moral degeneration or emotional aversion, though *šiqqûṣ* does convey contempt and disgust. *Śn'* ("hate") refers to aversion on all levels, but in the context of ancient Near Eastern treaties "hatred" (Akkadian *zeru*) specifically refers to a violated or broken covenant.[48] Thus, "detestable things that Yahweh hates" (Deut 12:31) does not express emotional or moral revulsion; it means "forbidden things that will break Yahweh's covenant." "Burning children" (whatever that means) will do that, but sacrificing outside the sanctuary will also do that; compare Deuteronomy 12:4–7, where the imperative "you must not serve the LORD your God in their way" is repeated. From the choice of emphasis in Deuteronomy 12:31 we might infer that "burning children" (whatever that means) was generally considered distasteful, but the practice under the kings is never elsewhere described as, for example, "an outrageous thing in Israel" (see Gen 34:7; Josh 7:15; Judg 20:6–10; Jer 29:23), i.e., something that everyone generally agrees should never be done. Yahweh does say in Jeremiah that the practice is something "I did not command, nor did it enter my mind" (Jer 7:31; 19:5; 32:35), but the phrase is not clear enough to definitively state that something that "does not enter Yahweh's mind" is something beyond the pale of the moral order.[49] Some of God's commands leave room for ambiguity or embellishment. For example, Joshua builds an altar of "uncut stones" (Josh 8:31), in deference to Exodus 20:25. The word for "uncut" (*šalēm*) originally referred to field stones without engraving. However, the word *šalēm* eventually came to also refer to ashlar masonry, which is what the temple is built out of. That kind of stonework is not technically what God commanded, but it is still considered acceptable. Likewise, institutions such as the monarchy and charismatic prophecy are not established—that is, commanded—by Yahweh in the Pentateuch,

46. Reynolds, "Molek: Dead or Alive?"

47. Reynolds suggests that the "burning" takes place separately from the sacrifice proper: "the victims were first killed and drained of blood before being burned." Reynolds, "Molek: Dead or Alive?" 149.

48. Riley, "Zeru," 176–78.

49. The collocation *'ālh 'al lēb* ("enter [my] mind") is usually paralleled with "remember" (*zkr*, e.g., Isa 65:17; Jer 3:16; 44:21). Other things that "do not enter the mind" [of the people] are the ark of the covenant (Jer 3:16) and "the former things" (Isa 65:17). In Jeremiah 44:21 something *does* enter Yahweh's mind, which is the memory of past idolatry.

although they are mentioned in passing and both are eventually formally sanctioned as they appear. David's syncretistic sacrificial ritual in 2 Samuel 6:13–19 was not commanded, but is nonetheless accepted, or at least portrayed in a positive light by the narrator. Holladay suggests that the phrase in Jeremiah might be commenting on an archaic or syncretistic understanding held by Jeremiah's contemporaries about what was meant by the "sacrifice (*natan*) of the firstborn" [to Yahweh] in Exodus 22:29[50] (gloss: "that is not at all what I was talking about").

Finally, there is very little evidence that any of the ancient Near Eastern cults actually employed human sacrifice as a regular practice.[51] None of the ritual literature contains instructions for sacrificing humans, and no archeology has unearthed victims who were inarguably sacrificed. This implies that human sacrifice was not institutionalized or practiced on a wide scale, in contrast with what we see, for example, in the Aztecs. What archeology has uncovered are the remains of children or infants, occasionally mixed with the remains of small animals and occasionally exhibiting damage by fire, interred in a manner inconsistent with what are considered to be ordinary burial practices, sometimes in locations that indicate ritual significance, such as in front of altars or in the foundations of buildings.[52] A small number of inscriptions referring to what might be human sacrifice also exist. For example, an Assyrian contract compels the violator to "burn (*šarapu*, cognate of Hebrew *śrp*) his first-born son before Sin, and . . . burn his eldest daughter . . . before Belet-ṣeri."[53] Šarapu can refer to ritual burning, especially reagents in the context of magic,[54] but it is not the normal word for "[burnt] offering" (*niqû*).[55] In addition, the burning of the children in this text is a penalty, not a voluntary act of ritual devotion; besides burning their children, the violator is also forced to "eat one mina of oxhide

---

50. Holladay, *Jeremiah 1*, 268. This reading is harder to apply to Jeremiah 32:35, which specifies "to Molek." In Jeremiah 19:5 the Hebrew is unclear whether the children burned in the fire and the offerings to Baal are to be equated (as NIV) or are different practices.

51. The most thorough treatment of the archaeological and textual material is still Green, *Role of Human Sacrifice*. For child sacrifice, see Dewrell, *Child Sacrifice in Ancient Israel*.

52. See overview in Heider, *Molek*, 204–22.

53. Kwasman and Parpola, *Legal Transactions*, #102:r.5–9. See also Weinfeld and Sperling, "Moloch" 429.

54. *CAD* 17.51.

55. *CAD* 10.252. A text from Ashurnasirpal claims that he "burned (*gibíl*, Sumerian for *šarapu*) adolescent boys *as an offering*" (*maqlutu*; Grayson, *Assyrian Rulers of the Early First Millennium BC I (1114–859 BC)*, 2.260), but these are prisoners of war, not his own children, and the "offering" is listed in parallel with acts of intimidation and oppression such as impaling on stakes, razing cities, and piling heads; therefore the context is different from the circumstances in Israel (and, of course, the semantic range of the word is different; *maqlutu* can mean "offering," *śrp* cannot). Additionally, Ashurnasirpal does not name any gods to whom the boys were offered, and *maqlutu* can also refer to non-cultic destruction by fire ("conflagration"); the context of general rapine and destruction in Ashurnasirpal's text might indicate that the non-cultic meaning is intended (compare Hebrew *zbḥ*, which usually refers to cultic slaughter, but in certain contexts—notably warfare—does not).

and drink a full *agganu* vessel of tanner's paste,"[56] and so the circumstances are not comparable to ordinary cultic "sacrifice," or to the ritual of the topheth described in the Bible (which appears to be voluntary). A small number of reliefs and cylinder seals also depict what may be rituals presenting humans as offerings.[57] This general absence makes sense because within the logic of the ancient Near Eastern cult system the sacrifices are usually intended to feed the gods, and the gods are thought to eat the same kinds of things that human eat; humans prefer not to eat people, so the gods do not want to eat people either. The Greek myth of Tantalus recalls the consequences of the protagonist trying to feed a human to the gods. However, we do have several examples of *ritual killing* of humans that nonetheless are not technically *sacrifice*; that is, the victim is not offered as a gift/food to the gods. The most notable of these is the Assyrian "substitute king ritual," wherein a human standing in place of the king is killed in order to avert an omen of disaster.[58] A Hittite expiation ritual also involves passing between the bisected corpses of various animals, including a human.[59] Pongratz-Leisten suggests that these instances of "sacred killing" served primarily to eliminate disorder affecting the community.[60] However, the details of the ritual of the Topheth are unclear, so any assertions that it represents an elimination ritual are necessarily circular, except for the observation that it occurs outside the normal cultic precincts (in the Hinnom Valley).[61]

By far the most notable archeological findings are a series of sites from Carthage, often called "topheths" by scholars after the word used in the Bible on the assumption that it represents a similar structure; however, the association is purely circumstantial. The Punic sites consist of walled structures in which are buried urns containing the burned remains of animals and human children. Some of the later burials are marked with stele, sometimes containing the inscription *lmlk*.[62] The sites are located in the vicinity of Phoenician colonies and date from the sixth/seventh centuries BCE, roughly contemporary with the Babylonian exile. Thus, some scholars propose that the evidence points to a widespread practice of a child sacrifice cult originating in Phoenicia that spread to its colonies in Carthage and also to its neighbors in Israel. Cultural integration between Israel and Phoenicia is attested; the Baal worship under

56. Kwasman and Parpola, *Legal Transactions*, #102:r.5

57. Heider, *Molek*, 188–92; Day, *Yahweh and the Gods*, 211–12; Green, *The Role of Human*, 27–43, 192–93.

58. Bottéro, "Substitute King," 138–55; Parpola, *Letters*, ##350–52.

59. Collins, "Hittite Ritual" 221–26.

60. Pongratz-Leisten, "Sacrifice in the Ancient Near East." This might be what the burning of victims in the Assyrian contract is supposed to achieve, and may even be what Mesha's sacrifice (2 Kgs 3:27) was for as well; an Ugaritic text describes the offering of a bull and a "firstborn" in order to "drive the strong foe from your gate"; however the text is broken and the words "offer" (*qdš*) and "firstborn" (*bkr*) are unclear (Pardee, *Ritual and Cult*, 150, RS 24.266).

61. See Garroway, *Children*, 178–79.

62. Heider, *Molek*, 185–86.

Jezebel is Phoenician in nature, as is the altar of Ahaz in 2 Kings 16:10–16. The design of the Jerusalem temple likewise indicates Phoenician cultural influence. However, evidence to support this wholesale association between the Punic archeology and the biblical Molek ritual is lacking. Heider notes that most of the Punic "topheths" do not occur in conjunction with temples or shrines, arguing against a cultic function; this includes the oldest evidence of the *mlk* inscription, which is in Malta. Further, the practice of inscribing stele does not begin until two centuries after the earliest burials. Thus, it is unlikely that the Carthaginians brought the practice of cultic sacrifice to *mlk* with them from Phoenicia.[63] Additionally, the ratio of human remains to animal remains at the sites *increases* over time, which indicates that the practice (whatever it was) might not have begun as especially emphasizing *human* subjects, which reached its height in the fourth century BCE, long after Manasseh and Jeremiah.[64] Third, the inscription *lmlk* at Carthage, which refers to a kind of sacrifice, is linguistically unrelated to the biblical *Molek*, which as discussed above probably refers to a title.[65] Finally, no counterpart to the Punic "topheths" has ever been discovered in Phoenicia itself or anywhere else in Syrio-Palestine, including the Hinnom valley.[66] This does not indicate that the Phoenicians (or the Canaanites, or the Israelites for that matter) did *not* practice human sacrifice, but it does mean that the burials in Carthage, whatever they represent, should not be assumed to stand as evidence of a ubiquitous and ongoing practice throughout the entire West Semitic world.

Finally, the practice of *cremation* is well-attested in Phoenicia, Transjordan, and Palestine,[67] including notably at a temple in Amman once thought to be a site of cultic human sacrifice.[68] Cremation of the dead was not the common practice in Israel, however, and may have been viewed unfavorably as a result. The Gilgamesh epic indicates that the soul of one who dies by fire does not enter the netherworld, but goes up in smoke with the body and ceases to exist.[69] Maintaining cohesion within the family among the dead was very important in Israel; compare the common phrases "gathered to his people" (e.g., Gen 25:8) and "[he] slept with his fathers, and was buried with his fathers" (e.g., 1 Kgs 14:13; 15:24).[70] If the Mesopotamian understanding of cremation was common in Israel, the practice would thus be particularly abhorrent for reasons unrelated to idolatry or sacrifice. Cremation was commonly practiced by the Phoenicians and Hittites, who introduced the practice into the Levant,[71] but without the connotations of

---

63. Heider, *Molek*, 198–99.

64. Heider, *Molek*, 199–200.

65. Day, *Yahweh and the Gods*, 209; Heider, *Molek*, 185–87.

66. Heider, *Molek*, 210.

67. Bloch-Smith, *Judahite Burial Practices*, 52–55.

68. Heider, *Molek*, 213–22.

69. Katz, *The Image of the Netherworld*, 215.

70. See for example Hays, *Covenant*, 159–61.

71. Bloch-Smith, *Burial Practices*, 52.

annihilation.[72] Given the use of *śrp* to refer to non-cultic immolation, it may be possible that the ritual at the topheth was funerary rather than sacrificial, perhaps involving the dedication of the deceased to a chthonic deity with the designation or title *mlk*.[73] Note that dedication, rather than sacrifice, is also the fate of the [firstborn] children who are *nātan* to Yahweh in Exodus 22:29. Israelite imitation of Canaanite funerary rites is forbidden in Leviticus 19:21 and Deuteronomy 14:1 ("Do not cut your bodies for the dead"). The practice as a funeral rite would add an additional level of irony to God's pronouncement in Jeremiah 7:32 that "they will bury the dead in Topheth until there is no more room." A funerary interpretation of the topheth can be supported by Isaiah 30:33, where an oracle of destruction against Assyria (Isa 30:31) declares "Topheth has long been prepared; it has been made ready for the [Assyrian] king. Its fire pit has been made deep and wide, with an abundance of fire and wood."[74] However, evidence for any conclusion remains purely circumstantial.

Regardless of what the Punic burial sites or the ritual of the topheth represent, we do know that human sacrifice was performed intermittently because it is depicted in the Bible. In 2 Kings 3:27, the king of Moab, presumably in an attempt to turn the tide of a losing battle, "took his firstborn son, who was to succeed him as king, and offered him as a sacrifice on the city wall." The word used here is a normal word for a sacrifice (*ʿōlâ*, "burnt offering"), usually performed in connection with a petition to deity. Whatever the sacrifice was intended to accomplish, it apparently succeeded: "The fury against Israel was great; they withdrew and returned to their own land." Boyd in particular makes much of this passage, offering the vignette as empirical proof that, not only do spiritual entities really exist and really empower human armies, but they are also potentially strong enough to defeat Yahweh and thwart his plans.[75] This interpretation is well-suited to Boyd's open theism, which requires God to be relatively weak and therefore largely unable to look after the wellbeing of his chosen people despite a presumed desire to do so,[76] but such a reading is highly out of place in the general context of the Deuteronomistic History. Thus, the passage is worthy of further consideration.

2 Kings 3 is the account of Joram king of Israel attempting to pacify Mesha of Moab, a rebellious vassal, who implicitly was allowed to rebel because Joram did evil in the eyes of the LORD (2 Kgs 3:2–6). Joram forms an alliance with Jehoshaphat of Judah and with the king of Edom—presumably another vassal—and all three promptly get lost in the desert (2 Kgs 3:9). After the water is gone, the kings visit the prophet

72. Hays, *Covenant*, 96–97; 130–31.

73. Day argues that *mlk* may refer to the underworld god Nergal or a Semitic near-equivalent. Day, *Yahweh and the Gods*, 214.

74. Oswalt, *Isaiah*, 568–69.

75. Boyd, *God at War*, 118, 133, 163.

76. "[T]he warfare worldview must accept that at least sometimes God is *unable* to prevent [evil]." Boyd, *Satan and the Problem of Evil*, 16 (emphasis original).

Elisha to ask Yahweh for help (2 Kgs 3:11–12). Elisha snubs Joram but agrees to invoke Yahweh for Jehoshaphat's sake (2 Kgs 3:13–15). Yahweh the divine warrior uses the elements of the cosmos to defeat the Moabites, which is "an easy thing in the eyes of the Lord" (2 Kgs 3:16–24), and also promises that they will "overthrow every fortified city" (2 Kgs 3:19). Eventually every city is indeed overthrown except one (2 Kgs 3:25); there the king of Moab sacrifices his son and drives Israel away (2 Kgs 3:27). Thus, Boyd argues that what should have been "an easy thing in the eyes of the Lord" was in fact prevented by the sacrifice, and his promise through Elisha goes unfulfilled. But is that really the best reading of the passage?

Most commentators on 2 Kings 3:27 address the question, "whose fury goes out against Israel?" Boyd assumes that the fury is that of Chemosh (the god of Moab), but the text does not say—nor does it specify to whom the sacrifice was offered—and other interpretations have been proposed. One possible option is that the fury is that of the Moabite army, who failed to "break through" in 2 Kings 3:27 but who are now sufficiently motivated by the death of the crown prince that they try again and succeed. The word translated "fury" is indeed used of human anger in 2 Kings 5:11 and 13:19,[77] but the collocation "great fury" used here always refers to the wrath of the Lord (Deut 29:28; Jer 21:5; 32:37; Zech 1:15; 7:12).[78] This leads some commentators to propose that the fury is that of Yahweh. This interpretation states that Yahweh continues to rage against Omri's dynasty and therefore intervenes at the end to deny Ahab's son a victory; the sacrifice in this reading becomes more or less a coincidence.[79] However, if this was the intended message, we would expect the sacrifice not to be mentioned at all, and instead see something to the effect of "But the Lord remembered the sins of the house of Ahab" (compare perhaps 2 Kgs 23:26). The context indicates that the sacrifice is the more or less direct cause of the fury. A third option is that the wrath is Israel's against itself; disgusted with themselves by the extreme measures to which they have pushed their enemies, they give up and go home.[80] However, this kind of empathetic emotional reaction towards enemies is unlikely in a culture where besieging armies frequently force their victims to *eat* their children (Lev 26:29; Deut 28:53–55; 2 Kgs 6:28–29). Further, the use of the collocation "great wrath" to indicate a divine subject and the nature of the inciting action as a *sacrifice* (a cultic act), combined with the understanding of divine warfare that exists in the cognitive environment of the time (see chapter 9), indicates that we should indeed understand the fury to be that of Chemosh or some other Moabite warrior god. Nonetheless, that in itself is not sufficient to conclude that the message the passage wishes to convey is that Chemosh is real and sometimes he is stronger than Yahweh.

77. See Beal, *1 & 2 Kings*, 315–16.
78. Patterson and Austel, "1, 2 Kings," 819.
79. Beal, *1 & 2 Kings*, 316.
80. Patterson and Austel, "1, 2 Kings," 819; Fritz, *1 & 2 Kings*, 245.

Our next consideration should be to recall that historical narratives in the Bible are not transcriptions of phenomena (see chapter 2). The historian is not sitting there with a tablet recording that first he saw "fury" (whatever that was) and then saw Israel run away. The details are chosen in order to convey a particular message, and even the choice *to include the vignette at all* in the final redacted compilation is part of the choice to convey the message. But should we really suppose that the message was to tell readers that there really are gods other than Yahweh and that Yahweh can really lose fights with them? Normally when the Deuteronomist presents battle reports, they serve one of two purposes. If Israel wins, the point is that Yahweh is mighty in battle and able to triumph over Israel's enemies (e.g., Jos 6:2–24; 1 Sam 17:32–53; 1 Kgs 20:13–30; 2 Kgs 18:20–37). If Israel loses, the point is that Yahweh has allowed them to lose because they have violated the covenant in some way or another (e.g., Jos 7:1–12; 1 Sam 4:1–11; 1 Kgs 22:29–38; 2 Kgs 24:1–20). However, neither of these points are being made in 2 Kings 3:27. Therefore, we must turn again to the fundamental question of interpretation: why is this in here?

The key to interpreting this passage is to recognize that it occurs as part of a series of vignettes about Elisha that runs from 2 Kings 2:19—9:13. Thus 2 Kings 3 should not be read as a battle report highlighting the prowess of the divine warrior; rather, it is an Elisha story. Specifically, the purpose of all of the Elisha vignettes is to legitimate Elisha as the true successor of Elijah; to confirm that he has indeed received a "double portion" of Elijah's spirit (2 Kgs 2:9). In terms of inheritance, this does not mean that Elisha has twice the spirit that Elijah had; the "double portion" means "twice what any other beneficiaries get" and goes normally to the firstborn. The double portion designates the true heir and successor. Elisha's status is critical for the Deuteronomistic History because it is his proclamation that legitimates Jehu as Yahweh's approved successor to Omri's dynasty (2 Kgs 9:3). If Elisha is not a true prophet, Jehu is not a true king; not an instrument of divine vengeance but a usurper and a regicide of the LORD's anointed (see 2 Sam 1:14–16; cf. 1 Sam 24:6, 10; 26:9, 11). All the Elisha narratives in 2 Kings 2–8 are therefore intended to establish Elisha's status as Yahweh's chosen prophet. With this in mind, we should examine the details of 2 Kings 3 to see how the vignette serves the purpose of legitimating Elisha.

Historical documents do not record phenomena; they interpret events (see chapter 2). On a level of pure phenomena, this episode does not look very good for Elisha. In Israel and in the surrounding cultures, a prophet is legitimized—or not—by the truth of his (or, less often, her) predictions; that is, by whether or not the gods do what the prophet says they will do (see chapter 3). History remembers that Israel never succeeded in repatriating Moab; Mesha himself reports his successful campaigns against Omri's successor in an inscription called the Moabite stone. The Israelites at the time of the Deuteronomist would likewise remember this, and they would also remember that Elisha said they *would* succeed. Further, the success that Elisha promised was to go to Joram of the house of Ahab, which Elijah had condemned. Thus, from this episode Elisha resembles Elijah much less than he resembles the false prophets of Ahab who send him to his death at Ramoth-Gilead in 1 Kings 22; note that Jehoshaphat's presence and virtually identical inquiry (in 2 Kgs 3:11 and 1 Kgs 22:7) indicate that the Deuteronomist does indeed have this earlier episode in mind. Does Elisha truly have a double portion of Elijah's spirit, or does he have a "lying spirit" sent from the LORD to destroy those foolish enough to listen to him (2 Kgs 22:19–23; Ezek 14:9–10)? The details supplied by the Deuteronomist are intended to interpret the event in such a way as to set the record straight and establish that Elisha is indeed the true successor of Elijah.

Elisha is first introduced as a former servant of Elijah (2 Kgs 3:11), which serves to establish his pedigree as a suitable "prophet of the LORD" of whom the kings may inquire. The Deuteronomist immediately clarifies that Elisha does not promise victory to Joram; if not for Jehoshaphat, Joram would indeed be abandoned to die (2 Kgs 3:14), as he himself claims in 2 Kings 3:10, 13. Thus, it is Jehoshaphat, not Joram, who is promised victory over Moab. Elisha's contempt for Joram and his family (2 Kgs 3:13) is fully in keeping with the attitude of Elijah before him (e.g., 1 Kgs 18:19). Elisha prophesies water (2 Kgs 3:16), which duly appears (2 Kgs 3:20), and also the devastation of Moab (2 Kgs 3:19), which is carried out in 2 Kings 3:25. Only one city remains, and it is besieged; so far, all that Elisha has claimed has come to pass.

But the final city is never taken, and tradition remembers it. Since the purpose of the narrative is to legitimate Elisha, the details supplied by the Deuteronomist in 2 Kings 3:26–27 should be read as an explanation of *why* the siege failed, construed in such a way that Elisha does not turn out as a false prophet. Consequently, the explanation cannot be that Yahweh has decided that he will not grant final victory to Ahab's house; this reading would make Elisha a false prophet by definition, since he has failed to accurately convey the intent of the gods. Further, it is unlikely that the explanation is that Yahweh tried to do what he planned but failed. Due to the conception of divine warfare in the minds of the original audience of Kings—and also in the minds of the besieging army the narrative describes—it would theoretically be possible for their God to lose in battle. However, the purpose of the passage is not to explain the phenomena of a military defeat but to vindicate Elisha, and the biblical authors never rationalize a failure on the part of a human (an inaccurate prophecy) by appealing to failure on the part of God (defeat in battle). Apart from theological considerations, such an explanation would be unlikely to persuade and thus would not suit the document's purpose.[81] The test of a true prophet is true prophecy and the nature of the test is strictly empirical: "If what a prophet proclaims in the name of the LORD does not take place or come true, that is a message the LORD has not spoken" (Deut 18:22; com-

---

81. Or, said another way, proving that the god is weak would not serve to exonerate the prophet. When Baal is shown to be the weaker of two gods in the contest on Mt. Carmel in 1 Kgs 18:27–29 his prophets are not excused for their failure; instead they are put to death (1 Kgs 18:40) in accordance with the fate of false prophets (Deut 13:5; 18:20).

pare also 1 Kgs 22:28). The most likely explanation, then, is this: God has promised to "deliver Moab into [their] hands" (2 Kgs 3:18), but he has not promised *to strike down Moab on their behalf* (contrast 2 Kgs 18:24). *If* Israel fights *then* they will win, but they still have to go and fight (see 2 Kgs 3:24). However, when faced with the (manifested or impending) power of the enemy deity in response to the king's sacrifice—that is, the "great fury against Israel"—they do not fight, but instead they give up and go home: "they withdrew and returned to their own land" (2 Kgs 3:27).[82] If they had stayed to fight then they would have won, but it is neither the fault of Yahweh nor the fault of Elisha that they chose not to claim the victory that had been promised.

Therefore, 2 Kings 3:26–27 does not depict Yahweh being thwarted by the power of an enemy deity and does not offer biblical proof that there are such things as deities who can successfully oppose the will of Yahweh. However, the passage does depict a deity, presumably Chemosh, accepting a human sacrifice. An additional reference to human sacrifice might occur in Psalm 106:37–38:[83] "They sacrificed their sons and their daughters to false gods (*šēdîm*). They shed innocent blood, the blood of their sons and daughters, whom they sacrificed to the idols (*'ăṣabîm*) of Canaan." These verses are a reference back to Deuteronomy 32:17, "They sacrificed to *šēdîm*, which are not God." The LXX translates *šēdîm* in both passages as "demons," but as discussed above, that does not give any guidance to interpreting their taxonomy in context. The word "sacrificed" in both passages is *zbḥ*, which is a normal word for a cultic offering. We should note, though, that in Psalm 106:37 the word is paralleled with "the shedding of innocent blood," which more commonly refers to (non-cultic) murder.[84] The specific consequence in Psalm 106:38—"the land was desecrated (*ḥānap*) by their blood" is a reference to Numbers 35:33 ("bloodshed pollutes [*ḥānap*] the land"),[85] which again refers specifically to murder, not to cultic rituals. The root *zbḥ* refers to generic slaying in 1 Kings 13:2, where a prophet promises that Josiah will "sacrifice (*zbḥ*) the priests of the high places [i.e., humans] who make offerings here." In 2 Kings 23:20 Josiah does exactly that, though he presumably does not do so as a cultic offering. The choice of the word is meant to be an ironic juxtaposition with the "offerings" that the priests had made there; in the parallel account in 2 Chronicles 34:5 Josiah burns (*śrp*) the bones of the priests on the altar, not as an offering, but to desecrate it. The word "sacrifice" (the noun form of the same root, *zbḥ*) is used metaphorically in both Isaiah 34:6 and Ezekiel 39:17–19 to refer to the wholesale slaughter of armies. The context in Psalm

82. "Done in view of the allies, [the sacrifice] horrified them with the prospect of the vengeance of the local god thus drastically entreated, so that they hastily decamped." Gray, *1 & 2 Kings*, 490.

83. Hosea 13:2 may record something similar (so NIV; see also Andersen and Freedman, *Hosea*, 632). The phrase *zbḥ 'ādām* does use a normal word for sacrifice, but the Masoretic text is difficult and several alternate translations have been proposed that do not indicate human sacrifice (Stuart, *Hosea-Jonah*, 202; Carroll R. (Rodas), "Hosea" 296).

84. Goldingay, *Psalms 90–150*, 236.

85. Hossfeld and Zenger, *Psalms 3*, 92. Adultery defiles the land in Jer 3:1–2, which is subsequently metaphorically compared to idolatry in Jer 3:9. Jeremiah 3 makes no mention of human sacrifice.

106 (paired with innocent blood) and the potential ironic or metaphorical usage of the word *zbḥ* means that the action described might not be a literal cultic sacrifice.[86] The point of Psalm 106 is to recall the past offenses of Israel that God forgave and compare them with the sins of Israel that led to the exile, in order to invoke the hope that God will forgive these sins as well (Ps 106:47);[87] the psalmist may be combining the idols and bloodbaths of Manasseh (2 Kgs 21:2–16; 24:4), and also perhaps the rituals of the topheth (if relevant), with the ancient apostasy of Israel into a single lurid image.[88] In any case, we should not assume that Psalm 106 is a historical document, filling in details that the Pentateuch glossed over. Deuteronomy 32 makes no mention of human sacrifice to the *šēdîm*, and we should not use Psalm 106 to infer that human sacrifice was indeed occurring at the time of the wilderness generation. Psalm 106 emphasizes Israel's historical offenses, punishment, and especially subsequent restoration; its message is to invoke Yahweh's historical acts of mercy and forgiveness, not to clarify the details of what exactly the offenses consisted of.

At the same time, though, it is conceivably possible that humans were literally sacrificed to the *šēdîm* (whatever they were) since we know the practice did occasionally occur, just as at least one human was sacrificed to Chemosh. Does this particular detail in itself prove that Chemosh or the *šēdîm* are evil? Or, to put the question another way, can a god who is *not* evil nonetheless accept a human sacrifice?

The difficulty with claiming that only an evil god opposed to the will of Yahweh can accept or demand human sacrifice is that Yahweh himself is shown to do both. The first instance is Genesis 22:2, where God tells Abraham "Take your son . . . [and] sacrifice [him] as a burnt offering." The phrase here does mean "sacrifice" and is the same phrase used in 2 Kings 3:27. This passage is one of the most extensively interpreted in the Hebrew Bible and it is beyond the scope of this study to cover it. Nonetheless, we make several observations. Most importantly, from a theological standpoint, the test of Abraham (Gen 22:1) is not normally considered to consist of seeing whether or not he is morally complacent enough to commit atrocities simply because God has asked him to. God does sometimes command people to do what they consider to be outrageous things (e.g., Ezek 4:12–15; Hos 1:2), but these are not described as *tests*. That in turn indicates that human sacrifice is *not* something that Abraham, and by extension his cognitive environment, would consider abhorrent or outrageous. If human sacrifice does not carry connotations of unspeakable atrocity for the ancient culture to whom it was written, we cannot read those connotations into the text, regardless of our own sensibilities (though of course we recall that the purpose of the text is not to *shape* our sensibilities; *we* can still regard human sacrifice

86. Goldingay, for example, suggests that the choice of words is rhetorical, contrasting cultic piety with vicious violence. Goldingay, *Psalms 3*, 236.

87. Goldingay, *Psalms 3*, 222–23; Hossfeld and Zenger, *Psalms 3*, 94–95.

88. "[T]he psalmist deliberately paints the Judges period in colors borrowed from the fateful last pre-exilic centuries." Allen, *Psalms 101–150*, 55.

as inherently barbaric and immoral even while acknowledging that Abraham or Israel might not have). Further, even though Yahweh stops Abraham from going through with the sacrifice, Yahweh never commands people to *sin*—that is, to do things that *Yahweh* considers to be wrong—simply to see whether or not they are willing to do it. There is certainly something oxymoronic about confirming a person's willingness to obey God's commands by making them demonstrate a willingness to break another of God's commands. Thus, if Yahweh is not commanding Abraham to [attempt to] do something reprehensible to Yahweh (since that would not make sense), we must conclude that what Yahweh is commanding Abraham to do (human sacrifice) is not, in fact, something the text wishes to portray as reprehensible to Yahweh. The test of Abraham in fact consists of seeing whether he is willing to serve God if serving God means giving up his blessings. Isaac does happen to be a human, but in this passage, he serves more as the embodiment of the covenant promises. The test of Abraham, like the test of Job, is whether Abraham's obedience is pragmatic and benefit-driven, or whether he will "serve God for nothing." To demonstrate Abraham's proper fear of God, he is commanded to sacrifice his son. Nevertheless, this action is not a barbaric atrocity in Abraham's world—it is something the gods can, and sometimes do, ask for—and does not prove that Yahweh is evil. Therefore, Chemosh accepting a (similar) human sacrifice does not prove that Chemosh is evil, either.

The second instance of Yahweh requesting—and this time accepting—human sacrifice is found in Judges 11:30–34. Similar to the king of Moab in 2 Kings 3:27, Jephthah the judge offers Yahweh a sacrifice in exchange for military victory: "whatever comes out of the door of my house . . . I will sacrifice it as a burnt offering." The word for "sacrifice" is the same as that used in Genesis 22:2 and 2 Kings 3:27. The nature of the vow is divinatory and allows the deity to choose its own offering, which the deity will make known by the specified indication; here, the first thing to come from his house to greet him, which turns out to be his daughter. Some interpreters suggest that Yahweh ignores the syncretistic divination and the appearance of the daughter is pure chance, but this would not have been plausible to the original audience—for whom there is no such thing as pure chance, especially in oracular contexts—and other syncretistic divination practices by the judges nonetheless work as intended (i.e., Judg 6:36–40). Other interpreters argue that the fate of the daughter is other than sacrifice, perhaps dedication to the temple as a kind of vestal virgin. However, the word for what Jephthah vows to do most naturally means "sacrifice," and Judges 11:39 says specifically that "he did to her as he had vowed." Thus, the most natural reading of this passage is that Yahweh both chose and accepted a human sacrifice. The overall behavior of the judges, including Jephthah, is consistently portrayed negatively; however, it is portrayed negatively from the perspective of the covenant order (compare perhaps Samson's corpse contact; Judg 14:8–9) and also in terms of personal consequences,[89] not from the perspective of absolute divine ideals. Humans are not ac-

---

89. See also to the fate of Samson in Judg 16:21–30. In Jephthah's case, the repeated emphasis that

ceptable sacrifices within the Israelite cult system (any more than unclean animals), so human sacrifice to Yahweh is *tôēbâ*, as is sacrifice of any kind to any other god within Israel. But the covenant order is not the measure of absolute divine morality, and *tôēbâ* practice does not automatically make someone evil and opposed to Yahweh. Yahweh himself makes use of *tôēbâ* practices on a number of occasions: his last message to Saul is delivered through a forbidden medium (1 Sam 28); he causes Balaam to bless Israel through a forbidden oracle (Num 23–24); and he directs Nebuchadnezzar to attack Jerusalem through forbidden divination (Ezek 21:21). Thus, we cannot conclude from the practice of human sacrifice that the gods who accept it are therefore evil and opposed to Yahweh.

Finally, some interpreters infer that the word *herem* (NIV usually "devoted" or "utterly destroyed") constitutes a form of human sacrifice.[90] The Moabite Stone reports a city being "*hrm* for Ashtar-Chemosh" and in Joshua 6:21 Jericho is *hrm* ("devoted") to Yahweh; in both reports everything in the city, including humans, is "destroyed with the sword." *Hrm* of Edom in Isaiah 34:2 is described metaphorically as "sacrifice" (*zbh*) in Isaiah 34:6, and Deuteronomy 13:15–6 commands that a city and its people be *hrm* and then "burned (*śrp*) . . . as a whole burnt offering." As discussed above, however, *hrm* most accurately means "removed from use"; it does not mean "sacrificed." *Hrm* objects (or people) can be "removed from use" by being given to God (as the metal objects of Jericho are in Josh 6:19), or by being killed or destroyed, but they are not killed *as a means by which to give them to God*, i.e., as a "sacrifice." The phrase translated as "burn as a whole burnt offering" in Deuteronomy 13:15 does not actually use the word for "burnt offering" (*ôlâ*); the word it does use (*kll*)[91] is an adjective that means "entirely," and the word for *burn* is *śrp*, which as discussed above never refers to cultic sacrifice. The metaphor of sacrifice from Isaiah 34:6 is used again in Ezekiel 39:17–19, where the "sacrifice" is not to/for (the Hebrew preposition is the same in either case) Yahweh, or to any deity at all, but rather to/for the "birds and wild animals." For our purposes, the point is that the established practice of *herem* does not constitute evidence for the establishment of institutionalized cultic human sacrifice, since that is not what *herem* is. Further, Yahweh can do it too, so the attestation of the practice in the Moabite stone does not constitute evidence that Chemosh is evil and opposed to the will of Yahweh.

From this brief survey, we can see that the Old Testament never depicts the gods of foreign nations as evil beings morally opposed to Yahweh. The gods occasionally

---

his daughter is an only child (Judg 11:34) and unmarried (Judg 11:37–39) means that her death is also the end of his family line. Thus, Jephthah may be intended to stand as a partial contrast to Abraham, in that Jephthah foolishly offers—and loses—the same thing that Abraham treasures (that is, descendants), was willing to give up anyway, and was allowed to keep.

90. Ahituv, *Echoes*, 409; discussed at length throughout Stern, *Biblical Herem*, 125–35.

91. The NIV uses "whole burnt offering" to translate the collocation *ôlâ kālîl* in 1 Sam 7:9, but in Deut 13:15 the word *ôlâ* ("offering") is not used. Deuteronomy 13:15 should therefore be translated to say "burn it entirely," not "burn it as a whole burnt offering."

oppose Yahweh in a military capacity, but when they do so, the accusation against them is not that they are evil but that they are weak. The idols are depicted as powerless objects made by human hands that should be treated with scorn, not as powerful cosmic antagonists that should be resisted and feared. Worshipping gods other that Yahweh is a violation of Israel's covenant order just as eating certain kinds of animals is, but it is not a violation of Yahweh's universal moral order condemned on principle wherever it is practiced. Nonetheless, despite the lack of moral condemnation of the gods or the practice of worshipping them outside of Israel, or even the moral condemnation of sacrificing humans in the rare cases where it is depicted, and also despite the persistent assertion throughout the text of their weakness and impotence, some interpreters still point to a handful of passages to indicate that the gods are evil and possess demonic power with which to effectively oppose the will of Yahweh. These passages—most notably Daniel 10, Psalm 82, and Genesis 6—we will examine in the next chapter.

Chapter 12

Evil gods and angels

S OME OF THE BIBLE's narrative and poetic literature describes episodes containing beings from the divine realm that are not Yahweh but are also not described as *demons*—that is, depicted using liminal or chaotic imagery, or with words translated as *daimonion* in the LXX. Conflict theologians especially point to the presentation of these beings in the biblical material as empirical evidence that these beings are real. Further, the actions they are depicted as performing are invoked by conflict theologians to argue that the beings are evil and opposed to the will of Yahweh. These accounts are worthy of closer examination.

The sons of God and the Nephilim in Genesis 6

The designation *běnê ĕlôhîm* ("sons of God") occurs relatively few times in the Hebrew Bible. The "sons of God" are assembled in Job 1:6 and 2:1 (NIV "angels"), and they "shout for joy" when the earth's foundation is laid in Job 38:7. The related term *běnê ĕlîm*[1] is used in Psalm 29:1, where the "heavenly beings" are called to praise the LORD, and in Psalm 89:6 none of the *běnê ĕlîm* can be likened to the LORD. A similar term, *běnê ʿelyôn* (NIV "sons of the Most High") might also describe "gods" (*ĕlôhîm*) in Psalm 82:6 (though see below). Additionally, in Deuteronomy 32:8, Yahweh "set up boundaries for the peoples according to the number of the *sons of God.*" NIV translates "sons of Israel" (following the MT), but a common variant reads "angels of God" (e.g., LXX) and scholars have deduced that the variant is probably correct,[2] although a Hebrew rendition of this variant is not attested and so we do not know what the exact Hebrew title should have been. The most likely interpretation of these beings is that they represent Yahweh's divine council.[3] As discussed in chapter 4, the divine council

---

1. The word *ĕlôhîm* is the plural form of *ĕlôhah*; *ĕlîm* is the plural form of *el*. Both words mean *God* and are essentially synonymous.

2. Tigay, *Deuteronomy*, 302–3 and Excursus 31, 513–18; McConville, *Deuteronomy*, 453–55;. Block, *Gods of the Nations*, 25–32; Heiser, "Monotheism, Polytheism, Monolatry, or Henotheism," 17–18.

3. E.g., White, *Yahweh's Council*; Mullen, *Assembly of the Gods*; For discussion of the question, including in early Judaism, see Wright, *Origin of Evil Spirits*, 61–75.

are lesser divine beings whose presence demonstrates the power of the high god and who are delegated to manage the governance of the cosmos. The council is in session in Job 1–2 and Psalm 82, and the "council of the holy ones" is mentioned in Psalm 89:7, which supports this identification. This classification differentiates them from the beings designated "angels" (Heb. *mal'ākîm*), since the *mal'ākîm* have a messenger function while the *bĕnê ĕlôhîm* have a governing function. The taxonomy of the beings is never specified.

The term *nĕpilîm* in Genesis 6:4 occurs only there and in Numbers 13:33, where it refers to the Anakites, one of the peoples of Canaan. As discussed in chapter 9, there are a variety of traditions concerning what the word represents. There is also a degree of uncertainty whether or not the *nĕpilîm*, the *gibborîm* (NIV "heroes"), and the "men of renown" (Gen 6:4) all refer to the same beings, and also whether any or all of these are the same beings as the *bĕnê ĕlôhîm*.[4] However, we are concerned with what can be derived from the text-in-context. Grammatically, the antecedent to the pronoun "they" (as in *"They* were the heroes . . .") could be any of the nouns in the preceding sentence (Nephilim, sons of God, children), but the default should be to associate it with the last noun occurring; therefore it should read, "[the children of the sons of God] were the heroes." However, unlike Enoch and other traditions, the text of Genesis never equates these children with the Nephilim; neither does it say that the Nephilim *appeared* on the earth *because* the sons of God bore children.[5] The text says only that the Nephilim were on the earth at the same time when the sons of God were bearing children with the daughters of men.

If the Nephilim are not the "heroes" and not the sons of God, what are they? Presumably the original audience would have known. The KJV translation "giants" (following the LXX *gigantes*) is derived from the description of the Anakites in Numbers 13:33.[6] However, the designation "Nephilim" applied to these people is rhetorical;[7] we know this because they are also called *rĕpā'îm* (Deut 2:11), which refers to the shades of the dead,[8] but there is no reason to think that the inhabitants of the land were literally spirits. The rhetorical description of the Canaanites as unworldly monsters is the text's way of associating them with the literary trope of the "invincible barbarians"

4. For exhaustive discussion of the various possibilities, see Doedens, *Sons of God*, 68–71; Wright, *Origin of Evil Spirits*, 78–83.·

5. Doedens tries to argue that the word *hāyû* (the *nephilim were* on the earth) ought to instead be rendered "the Nephilim *arose* on the earth (*Sons of God*, 77). However, this argument cannot be sustained grammatically; the proposed parallels in Genesis 6:7, 10 are not really parallel. See also Wright, *Origin of Evil Spirits*, 81–82.

6. And also perhaps from a conceptual similarity to the *gigantes* from Greek mythology, or at least a similarity as understood through the filter of the traditions of the time when the LXX was produced. The *gigantes* were monsters, born of a union between [personified] heaven (Uranus) and earth (Gaia). See Wenham, *Genesis 1–15*, 143.

7. See also Sarna, *Genesis*, 46.

8. H. Rouillard, "Rephaim," 692–700.

(see chapter 9); it is not classifying them anthropologically.[9] In order for that rhetoric to be meaningful, then, the Nephilim must have been understood to be nonhuman beings of some kind,[10] as the sons of God and the *rĕpā'îm* also are. Beyond this the text offers no information. Some interpreters consequently attempt to interpret the term etymologically, based on the Hebrew root *npl*, "to fall." Some interpreters further use this etymology to support an identification of these beings with the "*fallen* angels*.*"[11] However, we should note that the word *npl* never refers to a transition of status, whether moral (from good to evil) or ontological (from angel to demon). It can signify a change in loyalty (i.e., "defect" or "desert"), but does not necessarily carry the negative tones of those English words and refers simply to transition.[12] Further, the pointing of the word *nĕpilîm* would not be translated as "those who are fallen."[13] Finally, etymology is not a reliable guide to determining meaning. The Nephilim are therefore best understood as unidentified unworldly creatures who were on the earth at the same time that members of the divine council were siring mighty heroes among the humans (presumably demi-human rulers or legendary figures such as Gilgamesh; compare to the biblical characters Nimrod [Gen 10:9] and Og [Deut 3:11]).[14] We can now examine what role this information plays in the narrative.

The tradition contained in *1 Enoch*, also reflected in the versification and arrangement of the English Bible,[15] suggests that the activities of the sons of God and the Nephilim were more or less the direct cause of the evil that in turn is the cause of the flood. However, the composition of the text itself indicates that this is not necessarily the case, and the sons of God and Nephilim are not actually associated with the flood at all.[16] As discussed in chapter 10, Genesis is divided into a series of sub-narratives each demarcated by the Hebrew term *tôlēdôt*. The *tôlēdôt* sections are all more or less self-contained; at no point does a narrative arc begin in one *tôlēdôt* and continue in another. Thus, it is vitally important to realize that the *tôlēdôt* section that contains the flood narrative does not begin until Genesis 6:9: "this is the account of Noah and his family."

9. Walton and Walton, *Lost World of the Israelite Conquest*, 148–50.

10. Or perhaps invincible barbarians in their own right; the trope is present in Gen 3–4 in the form of the enemies of Cain (see chapter 10).

11. See for example Sarna, *Genesis*, 46; Wright, *Evil Spirits*, 22.

12. H. Seebass, "נָפַל, *nāpal*," 491. It can also refer to descent; the word in Luke 10:18 translated "fall" (*piptō*) is used frequently in the LXX to translate *npl*. This meaning would be redundant with the observation that they were "on the earth" (i.e., "[the ones who had descended (from heaven to earth)] were on the earth." See chapter 13 discussion of Luke 10:18.

13. The word meaning "those who are fallen" would be *nĕpûlîm* (passive qal) or *nippālîm* (niphal), as opposed to *nĕpilîm*. The "î" vowel in the second syllable would suggest a hiphil (read: "those who cause others to fall"), though the participial form of the hiphil would have a preformative mem with assimilated nun: *mappîlîm*.

14. Stuckenbruck, *Myth of Rebellious Angels*, 3–7.

15. Specifically, the decision to place the beginning of chapter 6 eight verses before the *tôlēdôt* in 6:9. Chapters were inserted into the biblical text as a reference aid in the late Middle Ages.

16. See Sailhamer, "Genesis," 112–13. See also Wright, *Origin of Evil Spirits*, 52.

Genesis 6:1–8 is part of the preceding section that begins in 5:1. Thus, whatever the sons of God and the Nephilim are doing should relate directly to the content of Genesis 5 (the line of Seth), and only incidentally if at all to Genesis 6–9 (the flood).

First Enoch describes the activity of the watchers as a "great sin," but Genesis itself does not indicate that a transgression of any kind has occurred. The traditional assumptions that the sin of the angels is lust, cultic contamination, or mixing of categories (or all of these) are all derived from activities prohibited in Leviticus.[17] Genesis 6 only says that the sons of God "married" and "bore children," neither of which are inherently sinful.[18] Neither does the text give any indication that the sons of God are doing something that they should not be doing. In Genesis 6:3 it is *humans* that the spirit of God will not contend with forever; in Genesis 6:5 God sees the wickedness of the *human* race and the evil of the *human* heart; and in Genesis 6:6 God regrets that he made *human* beings. The text does not imply that the marriage of the sons of God (Gen 6:2) *caused* God to choose to withdraw his spirit (Gen 6:3), or that the presence of the Nephilim on the earth (Gen 6:4) *caused* the wickedness of the human race (Gen 6:5), even though the narrative reports the events in sequence.[19] Together with the *tôlēdôt* structure, we should conclude that the intermarriage of the sons of God, the birth of the heroes, the presence of the Nephilim, the withdrawal of the spirit of God (whatever that refers to), the wickedness and inclination to evil of humans, and God's regret of having made humanity, are all characteristic of the entire antediluvian period from Seth to Noah,[20] precipitated by the multiplication of humans on the earth (Gen 6:1), as opposed to an escalation in the last few centuries before the flood precipitated by the arrival of the sons of God and the Nephilim, as is the case in *1 Enoch*. Therefore, we should ask what role these ongoing conditions play in the context of the narrative.

Because Genesis is embedded in its cognitive environment, we should expect its basic elements to be fairly similar to its ancient Near Eastern counterparts, especially in terms of the issues it chooses to discuss, the details it chooses to record, and the manner in which its information is presented. Two Mesopotamian texts in particular describe the antediluvian period in a manner reminiscent of Genesis 5:1—6:8 (that is, the *tôlēdôt* of Adam's family); the *Atrahasis Epic* and a genealogy called the *Sumerian King List*. *Atrahasis* describes the displeasure of the gods with humanity from their creation up to the time of the flood, as is also seen in Genesis 6:1–8; the *Sumerian King List* describes the succession of kings before the flood and ascribes to them spectacular lifespans (tens of thousands of years), which diminish after the flood (though still lasting hundreds

17. Fröhlich, "Mesopotamian Elements," 15–16.

18. Sailhamer, "Genesis," 115; Wright agrees that reading only Genesis 6, one would not discern any negative behavior. He contends that a negative reading comes from comparing the passage to ancient Near Eastern and Greek myths and the interpretations of the account in Second Temple literature, Wright, *The Origin of Evil Spirits*, 89–90.

19. Wright, *Origin of Evil Spirits*, 95.

20. See Sailhamer, "Genesis," 112. For a discussion of literary recursion in Genesis 6:1, see Longman and Walton, *Lost World of the Flood*, 122–28.

of years), as is also seen throughout Genesis but especially in Genesis 5. By examining these similar documents, we can attempt to discover what meaning the particular features would have had in their ancient Near Eastern context.

In the ancient world, genealogies like the *Sumerian King List* were not historical records as we view them today. Instead they were used to legitimate the status of a person, usually the king, by demonstrating their ancestry.[21] The genealogies in the Bible serve this purpose as well; 1 Chronicles, for example, seeks to identify the returning exiles with the people of Israel who received the covenant of the land and thus affirm their status as the chosen people.[22] Consequently, we should also assume that the genealogy of Genesis 5 has a *legitimation* function. So then, we should ask, *who* is it legitimating, and *how?* When we turn to the ancient Near East, we can see that ancient Near Eastern kings claimed to be descended from bloodlines dating back before the flood. In one inscription, Nebuchadnezzar identifies himself as "distant scion of kingship, seed preserved from before the flood, offspring of Enmeduranki, king of Sippar."[23] Enmeduranki is the Mesopotamian counterpart to the biblical Enoch (Gen 5:23–24),[24] and in the *Sumerian King List* is said to reign for 21,000 years. The long lifespans are a literary convention (as also in Genesis), although there is no scholarly consensus as to what exactly the convention symbolizes or how the specific numbers were calculated. Nonetheless, the Babylonian kings appear to have attached some significance to the possession of an antediluvian pedigree.[25] This feature of the cognitive environment combined with the presence of the genealogies in the Bible indicates that the Israelites may have attached significance to antediluvian ancestry as well. Therefore, we propose that the purpose of Genesis 5 is to establish the bloodline of Abraham—and through him Jacob, and therefore Israel—as stretching back to antediluvian times.[26] While some parts of the Bible downplay the significance of Abraham (i.e., Deut 26:5), Genesis as a whole seems

---

21. Wilson, *Genealogy and History*, 69–72.

22. Johnson, *Purpose of Biblical Genealogies*, 74–76.

23. Annus, "Origin of the Watchers," 294–95, citing W. G. Lambert, "The Seed of Kingship," 427–40.

24. Annus, "Origin of the Watchers," 278.

25. Babylonian priests also claimed physical descent from Enmeduranki: "the ancestry and the legitimacy of the priesthood are traced to the seventh antideluvian king." Orlov, *The Enoch-Metatron Tradition*, 39. "The idea that Enmeduranki's initiation into the assembly of the gods might mark the beginning of the priestly line is significant for a possible association of the king with the priestly office" (ibid. 39). However, Israelite kings are not priests, and Israelite priests are descended from Levi, not from the seventh antediluvian patriarch. The relevant comparison to Nebuchadnezzar, then, is the reference to the "seed preserved from before the flood" more so than the reference to "offspring of Enmeduranki." Israel's antediluvian pedigree is not intended to establish a particular purity to approach the gods, as Enmeduranki's priestly descendants were thought to possess (ibid., 38).

26. See also the *tôlēdôt* of Shem's family line in Gen 11:10–26, which picks up where 5:32 left off and serves the same purpose. Or, more specifically, Genesis 5 legitimates Shem, and Gen 11 legitimates Abraham through Shem.

to portray him as a person of great importance. Genesis 5, therefore, provides the reader with proof of the pedigree of the covenant people.

If Genesis 5 is similar to the *Sumerian King List*, Genesis 6:1–8 is more similar to *Atrahasis*, which describes the state of affairs in the antediluvian period. A group of minor gods, angry at being forced to do labor for the great gods, stage a revolt. The great gods respond by creating humans to do the labor instead. However, the human population increases (compare Gen 6:1) and their noise begins to irritate the gods, which might be comparable to God's "regret" in Genesis 6:6–7. The gods respond by sending a series of three disasters—plague, famine, and drought—each separated by roughly 2 x 600 years; these corrective actions may be comparable to God withdrawing his spirit (whatever that refers to) in Genesis 6:3.[27] (It is worth noting that the full number of years in *Atrahasis* is still far less than the 18,600 year reign of the last antediluvian king in the *Sumerian King List*, just as the 120 years in Genesis is less than the 500 year lifetime of Noah before the flood; we remember that the lifespans are *a literary device* and we should not be concerned with synchronizing the chronology.) Each of these correctives fail to stop the noise. Finally the gods have had enough and determine to wipe out humanity (compare Gen 6:7). The god Enki, however, undermines their plans and warns his favorite human, the eponymous hero Atrahasis. The gods send the flood, but Atrahasis survives by building a boat and preserving the elements of human civilization. When the gods discover this they plan to kill him, but change their minds when they realize that without humans there will be no one to feed them (with sacrifices) or do their work for them. Thus, humans are spared because the gods cannot get by without them.

Both Genesis 6:1–8 and *Atrahasis* describe a state of antipathy between gods and humans. For *Atrahasis*, the antagonism emphasizes the mutual dependence that forms the basis of the Mesopotamian cult system, which we refer to in chapter 7 as the "great symbiosis." Humans and gods do not *like* each other, but they do *need* each other. Genesis takes this same concept of antipathy but spins it in such a way that it picks up the recurring theme of the cosmic history: humans are not very good at establishing order in the world (see discussion in chapter 10). But we must also remember that Genesis 5:1—6:8 are a single literary unit. What does the epilogue in 6:1–8 contribute to the message of the narrative? Without Genesis 6:1–8, interpreters might be inclined to conceive of the antediluvian period as a kind of idyllic golden age where God's faithful servants "called on the name of the LORD" and were blessed with lives spanning centuries, perhaps still overshadowed by the tree of life. This indeed is often done by readers who read Genesis 6:1–8 as a prologue to the flood and who try to connect Genesis 4:17–24 and 5:1–32 as a single unit juxtaposing the evil line of Cain with the godly line of Seth. With Genesis 5:1—6:8 read as a single self-contained unit, however, we see that the antediluvian age is not idyllic.

27. Longman and Walton, *Lost World of the Flood*, 124–25.

Genesis 6:1–8 describes the period as essentially characterized by non-order. This is worthy of further examination.

The Enochian tradition understands the activity of the sons of God to be sinful because of the prohibitions against mixing categories in Leviticus (specifically Lev 19:19).[28] However, the prohibition in Leviticus should not be read to infer that mixing categories is inherently abhorrent and offensive to God. The garments of the priests are made of mixed cloth, and composite creatures (mixed beings, the kĕrûbîm) guard the interior of the sanctuary. Mixed things belong inherently to the liminal or the divine realm and have no place in the order of the human world; this is what the prohibition of Leviticus is intended to emphasize.[29] The divine beings—sons of God—mixing with the human daughters of men is an indication that the order that is supposed to characterize the human world has not been established.

Many commentators observe the parallel between the activity of the sons of God in 6:1 ("[they] saw that the daughters of humans were beautiful [lit. "good"], and they married [lit. "took"] any of them they chose") and that of Eve in Genesis 3:6 ("[she] saw that the fruit of the tree was good . . . [and] she took some and ate it"). This parallel is often invoked to argue that the "sin" of the sons of God is comparable to the "sin" of Eve.[30] Eve's activity should be understood as introducing a disordered state, but chaos does not come because of what she has done, but rather because of what she has taken. Genesis (or any part of the Old Testament, for that matter) does not classify even Eve's activity as "sin"; that itself is a later interpretation (see chapter 10) and cannot be imputed to the sons of God in context. The wisdom that comes from the fruit of the tree of the knowledge of good and evil (Gen 3:6) is what places Adam and Eve ("humanity") in the position to administrate the world order; implicitly, instead of God. The sons of God, however, do not take wisdom; they take wives. What they have taken does not set them up as administrators of order, and they were given no "command" (ṣāwâ, cf. Gen 2:16) not to take wives, explicitly or implicitly. Therefore, the chaos they bring, while still chaos, is of a different nature than that brought by Adam and Eve.

In Genesis 3–4 (which, as discussed in chapter 10, should be read as a part of a single literary unit), the blessing to "be fruitful and multiply" (Gen 1:28) still functions as a blessing. When Eve gives birth to a son "with the help of the LORD" (Gen 4:1) it is a breath of relief: at least this still works. The reason why it works can be traced to Genesis 3:16. "Your desire will be for your husband, and he will rule over you" is not a curse;[31] rather it is a remedy to ease the anxiety (see chapter 10) predicted in the preceding lines. By observing proper social and familial hierarchy—an important component of

28. Fröhlich, "Watchers" 16.

29. Milgrom, Leviticus 17–22, 1659.

30. See for example Page, Powers, 53.

31. Note that the word 'ārar is not used to introduce this proclamation, in contrast to Gen 3:14 and 3:17.

order—they can keep the negative effects of chaos at bay, at least partially. It is important to remember that, while we today sometimes see hierarchy as oppressive and therefore bad, the ancient audience of Genesis would have seen it as good, since hierarchy is a manifestation of order and order is the highest good in the ancient world. The text does not expect us to adopt its values for ourselves—that is not its purpose—and neither does it teach as a universal proposition that family hierarchy is the remedy for social disorder. Those are incidental values of the ancient world that the text is using to convey its message, but we do need to understand what those values *are* if we want to understand what the text is trying to communicate. Eve's [positive] desire for her husband (compare Song 7:10) and Adam's successful rule (demonstrated by giving Eve her name in Gen 3:20) are what allow the blessing of reproduction to function successfully. This is immediately contrasted with the [negative] desire of sin for Cain and his inability to rule over it (Gen 4:7), which promptly brings disorder (Gen 4:8). That disorder is once again mitigated by fruitful reproduction in Genesis 4:25, where God grants Eve another son to replace Abel, thus effectively undoing the damage. However, in Genesis 6:1–8, fruitful multiplication has *itself* become part of the problem; this is why the setting is indicated as "When human beings began to increase in number on the earth and daughters were born to them"[32] and "when the sons of God went to the daughters of humans and had children by them." Successful reproduction is not the final solution to mitigating the chaotic condition.

The failure of the reproductive blessing to perpetuate order on the earth is demonstrated by the mixing of kinds. Not only are "mixed beings"—as the offspring of the sons of God and daughters of men would have been—the natural inhabitants of the liminal realm, and therefore their presence indicates that the world now exists in a liminal state, their presence also indicates that beings are no longer reproducing "according to their kinds" (e.g., Gen 1:25). In the ancient world, it was thought to be possible for animals to give birth to different kinds of animals, such as a cow giving birth to a goat. Mesopotamian omen literature suggests that these occurrences were indicators of divine displeasure; not because hybrid offspring were offensive to deities, but because natural reproduction (e.g., cows giving birth to cows) was a function of the cosmic order that the gods sustained, as opposed to an inevitable function of natural law, as we see it.[33] When the gods allowed the cosmic order to lapse it meant that the gods were angry. Genesis 6 is not an omen text, so we should not infer that the presence of the hybrid offspring itself indicates divine displeasure; rather, we should recognize that the birth of hybrids is an indicator of the lapse in the function of the world order.

32. The verb translated "increase in number" is *rabâ* in Gen 1:28 and *rābab* in Gen 6:1. There is a lot of overlap between a final weak form of the verb, *rb(h)* and a geminate form (last two letters the same), *rbb*. In Gen 6:1, it is a qal infinitive construct ("to be many"), In Gen 1:28, it is a qal imperative of basically the same verb.

33. Specifically see the omen series entitled *šumma izbu;* for publication see Leichty, *Šumma Izbu;* discussion in Koch, *Mesopotamian Divination Texts,* 266–70.

A further indication that the actions of the sons of God are intended to illustrate (as opposed to being blamed for causing) a chaotic state of the world is the statement that they married "whichever they chose" (Gen 6:1). This self-motivation brings to mind the similar condition in the book of Judges, where "everyone did as they saw fit" (e.g., Judg 17:6). Judges illustrates a chaotic condition where there "is no king in Israel"; that is, no underlying structure that dictates what should and should not be. Although the narratives in Judges are written to emphasize Israelites behaving badly, there is no real indication that "what they saw fit" is always necessarily something bad. The phrase emphasizes the lack of control and structure; compare the use of the same phrase in Deuteronomy 12:8 to describe the [sanctioned] worship practices of Israel during their time in the wilderness.[34] It is not the same thing as saying that "the hearts of everyone were inclined to evil all the time" (cf. Gen 6:5).[35] They are not necessarily doing evil—that would have to be determined from context—but whatever they are doing is being done in the absence of any overarching structure, which in an ideal world (at least from the ancient perspective) should be there.

The purpose of the epilogue in Genesis 6:1–8 being added to the account of descent in Genesis 5 is to prevent the antediluvian period from being imagined as an idyllic golden age. The blessing of God continues as the line of Adam persists, but humans are not prospering as a result of setting themselves as the center of order. In fact, we may note the proclamation that accompanies Noah's birth in Genesis 5:29, which anticipates a reversal of the disordered condition and thereby implies that the condition is, in fact, disordered, and known to be such.[36] The antediluvian heritage of Shem, the ancestor of Abram, is recounted with pride—that is the purpose of Genesis 5 by virtue of its genre—but that pride is tempered by the reminder of the chaos of the age in Genesis 6:1–8. True human prosperity within the cosmic order is found within the covenant, not in the glory of ancient kings, either by virtue of an ancient bloodline or the divine heritage of the "heroes of old" and "men of reknown."

The point for our purposes is that nothing in the account indicates that the sons of God and the Nephilim were the *cause* of the disorder (though we might infer that they weren't helping),[37] and therefore we have no basis to infer that they are rebels

34. "At the time of Moses' address, individual Israelites could perform sacrifices wherever they wished." Tigay, *Deuteronomy*, 122.

35. Contra, for example, Block, who wants to interpret "did as they saw fit" as meaning the same thing as "did evil in the eyes of the LORD" (i.e., the common refrain against the kings in e.g., 1 Kgs 11:26; 16:30); Block, *Judges, Ruth*, 483–84. However, we should note that the phrase "did evil in the eyes of the LORD" is itself used frequently in Judges (2:1; 3:7; 3:12; 4:1; 6:1; 10:6; 13:1) and it would be odd to suddenly adopt a different phrase if the same meaning was intended.

36. See discussion in Longman and Walton, *Lost World of the Flood*, 116–18.

37. If the *běnê ʾĕlōhîm* were in fact intended to represent the divine council, we might infer that they were *supposed* to be helping, since government (and therefore establishing and preserving order) is a function of the divine council. However, we do not have enough information to speculate whether their marriage to the daughters of men was an extension of their function, or a deviation or dereliction of it. Many commentators have noted a cosmetic similarity between the reported actions of the sons

or sinners or fallen beings of any kind. Their presence is a feature of the antedilu-vian period; it is not included in the text in order to explain the agencies behind the activities that motivated God's decision to bring the flood. Finally, we must re-assert that Genesis 1–11 is *literature;* it is communicating a message, not providing us with details with which to construct a forensic recreation of the past (see chapter 4). Therefore, it is irrelevant to speculate about whether divine beings can really marry (cf. Matt 22:30—neither passage is interested in the taxonomy of celestial creatures) and whether there were or are really demi-humans running about. It is also irrelevant to speculate about whether angels can sin or not, even though we have asserted that they are not depicted as doing so. The sons of God and the Nephilim are characters in a narrative designed to convey the narrative's message and themes in the cognitive environment of the time; they are not the subjects of a technical study in a bestiary or an entry in a systematic biblical treatment of angels and their nature and behavior, and should not be treated as such.

The princes in Daniel 10

Other than 1 Corinthians 10:20 and Genesis 6:1–8, the other passage that is common-ly thought to provide a behind-the-scenes revelation of the cosmic operations that underlie world events is the vision in Daniel 10, especially Daniel 10:12–13, 20–21. Boyd in particular bases much of his conflict theology on the assumption that Daniel 10 was written in order to convey heretofore unknown information about invisible beings who interfere in God's work in the world.[38] He goes even further to imply that these beings not only prevented Daniel from receiving his message in a timely man-ner (derived from Dan 10:13) but also are ultimately responsible for a wide variety of other ills of which the text makes no mention at all: "how many of us might seriously consider the possibility of a menacing presence of an evil 'prince' over our region as a factor in whether a child is molested, a baby is born healthy or ill, or a group of people accept or reject the gospel?"[39] We should therefore examine the text to find out exactly what the princes are depicted as doing and how familiar the ideas in the vision would have been to the original audience.

---

of God and an ancient Near Eastern concept called *sacred marriage,* wherein a priestess was married to a deity as part of a fertility ritual (e.g., Provan, *Discovering Genesis,* 111–12). Sacred Marriage was not practiced in orthodox Israel, but antediluvian humanity is not Yahwistic and the sons of God are not Yahweh. Consequently, it is theoretically possible that "marrying the daughters of men" would have been seen as one of the legitimate order-bringing functions of divine administrators that, in this case, is nonetheless insufficient to produce order in a world where God is no longer the center. With no clear indication of what exactly the sons of God were supposed to be doing, there is no way we can evaluate whether or not what they actually did is illegitimate, or whether it is legitimate but insufficient to retain order.

38. Boyd, *God at War,* 9–11.

39. Boyd, *God at War,* 10.

One immediate problem comes from the difficulties of determining the date of Daniel. Of course, Scripture is still Scripture regardless of when it was written or by whom, but the date of the document does determine who the original audience was, what ideas from their cognitive environment could have been used to communicate with them, and what the words chosen by the author mean. Daniel 10–12 is an apocalypse that is normally dated to sometime in the second century BCE because that is the time period in which the vision comes to fruition and therefore the audience for which it has the most relevance. For our purposes, the date matters because it makes a difference whether Daniel 10 is invoking an existing Michael tradition (in Dan 10:21 and 12:1), or whether it is the fountainhead of all later Michael traditions. Rather than bog down the discussion with speculations about the date of Daniel, we will examine both options and see what, if anything, changes based on prior knowledge of Michael.

As discussed in chapter 3, apocalyptic literature addresses a community in crisis. The specific crisis that motivates this particular apocalypse is probably the despotism of Antiochus Epiphanes, as is also the case in the visions of Daniel 7–9. Antiochus is represented by the "little horn" (Dan 7:8, 20–22, 24–25), by the "horn" (Dan 8:8–13, 23–25), and by the "ruler" (Dan 9:26–27). Antiochus is the "contemptible person" who takes the throne of the king of the north (Dan 11:21) and also the "king who exalts himself" (Dan 11:36–45). The death of the king in Daniel 11:45 does not match the historical death of Antiochus, which leads scholars to presume that the book was written while he was still alive.[40] Daniel 7, 8, and 9 all describe the death of Antiochus, but the details are vague: in Daniel 7:26 "his power will be taken away and completely destroyed forever"; in Daniel 8:25 "he will be destroyed, but not by human power"; and in Daniel 9:27 "the end that is decreed [will be] poured out on him." Daniel 7:27 further indicates that his death will coincide with the establishment of the reign of the messiah, but provides no details. Daniel 12 picks up on this idea and fills in more of the details, including a timespan of the event, although the numbers in Daniel 8:14 ("2,300 evenings and mornings," or 1,150 days); 12:11 (1,290 days); and 12:12 (1,335 days) are not consistent.[41] The account in Daniel 10–12, therefore, seems to be written to emphasize the final deliverance—from Antiochus, and by extension the exilic state in general—as we would expect from the apocalyptic genre.

Daniel 10:1 states that the vision "concerned a great war." Most interpreters assume that the "war" refers to the battle of the princes in Daniel 10:20—also assumed to be occurring in 10:13—which is reflected on the earth in the battles of the kings of the north and south and finally concluded in Daniel 12.[42] The Hebrew word translated "war" in the NIV (ṣābā') usually means "army," but does sometimes also extend to the actions performed by the army, i.e., "war" (e.g., Num 31:3–6; Deut 24:5). However, some translators think that the "great ṣābā'" refers not to the content of the vision, but

40. See for example Collins, *Daniel*, 390.
41. See Collins, *Daniel*, 317.
42. See, for example, Collins, *Daniel*, 403.

rather to the arduous task of receiving it:[43] so Montgomery, "[it was] a great task,"[44] and Collins, "the service [was] great."[45] The Hebrew text contains no verb and the words "was" (as here) and "concerned" (NIV) have been supplied by the translators. The construct in Hebrew is called a "verbless clause," which consists of a simple indicative statement implying some form of the verb "to be." The translation "concerned" (NIV) is therefore quite interpretive.

Even if Daniel 10:1 is indeed supposed to mean "the vision was [about] a great [army going into battle]," it is unlikely that the battle in question refers to the activity of the princes in Daniel 10:13, 20, since these in no way constitute a "great host."[46] The word used for "fight" in Daniel 10:20 (lāḥam, niphal) can also refer to "war" (2 Sam 8:10; 2 Kgs 8:29; 9:15; 13:12), so if a parallel was intended this would have been the word to use in Daniel 10:1. Indeed, the word ṣābā' is not used again in Daniel 10–12, even to refer to the armies of the kings of the north and south. However, if the text is invoking a pre-existing Michael tradition, then the "great war" is rather obvious; it occurs in Daniel 12:1 when Michael arises and "there will be a time of distress such as has not happened from the beginning of nations until then." This is a reference to the eschatological battle as described in, for example, the Qumran War Scroll (see chapter 9). The reconstructed history in Daniel 11 in this case would be provided in order to situate this final conflict within the flow of history, and Daniel 12:11–12 would provide some indication as to the length of time that will pass until the battle occurs. Within this context, the standoff between the angelic princes, the predations of Antiochus against "the holy covenant" (Dan 11:30–45), and perhaps even the wars of the north and south, are all manifestations of the same ongoing conflict between the minions of light and the minions of darkness, which in turn indicates that the end of the age has not yet come. However, we must recall that, while the text makes use of preexisting knowledge in order to convey meaning, it does not affirm its references. If the author of Daniel is referencing a known Michael tradition from his cognitive environment, he would have already understood that history would be consummated in a battle of dualistic angelic powers, and used that understanding to convey information about God's intention to deliver Israel from their oppressors, but we should not suppose that the Bible—authoritative Scripture though it be—always affirms that what the author believed is true. The authority of the text is vested in the *meaning* it communicates, *not* in the beliefs of the author or audience, and if the author's views

43. Or to the struggle to understand it: see Lucas, *Daniel*, 258; Newsom, *Daniel*, 320. The collocation ṣābā' gādôl occurs only here.

44. Montgomery, *Daniel*, 404.

45. Collins, *Daniel*, 361, with reference to Isaiah 40:2.

46. Collins suggests that the title "prince" implies the presence of their armies as well, but his reasoning is based on the *War Scroll* (where Michael and Beliar are accompanied by their armies) and also on Revelation, not on Daniel itself. Collins, *the Apocalyptic Vision*, 135. Lāḥam ("fight" in Dan 10:20) can refer to single combat (e.g., 1 Sam 17:32), and in every other instance of 'āmad lĕneged (NIV "resisted" in Dan 10:13) the subject is a single individual (Josh 5:13; Dan 8:15; 10:16).

are drawn from his cognitive environment they are especially subject to evaluation regarding what the text is affirming (see chapter 1).

All of that, however, assumes that Daniel is referencing a pre-existing tradition about Michael and the eschatological conflict. Some interpreters alternatively want to suppose that Daniel 10 is actually one of the *sources* of what would eventually give shape to the eschatological conflict tradition, as for example Ezekiel 39 also is. This assumption requires examining the text in a different light. However, as we already saw in the discussion of *1 Enoch* (see chapter 9), we cannot assume that later traditions interpreted their sources in alignment with the source's intentions and context; neither can we assume that New Testament references to those later traditions (in this case, e.g., Rev 12; 20) affirm the accuracy of the interpretations of earlier material (in this case Ezekiel and Daniel) by those traditions (in this case the development of eschatological conflict in Hellenistic literature). Consequently, we will have to examine Daniel itself to see what information we can derive about the princes from the text in context.

The standard interpretation of Daniel 10 holds that the messenger is engaged in battle by the prince of Persia as he travels to deliver his message; the battle delays him from doing so until Michael appears and helps him escape. After escaping, the speaker delivers his message and returns to resume his battle. Conflict theologians rely heavily on this interpretation—that is, God's will (the delivery of the message to Daniel) being thwarted by the hostilities of [angelic] beings—to justify belief in the malicious actions of beings in the cosmic realm that affect humans on earth. In Daniel 10:20, the speaker says that he will "return to fight against the prince of Persia." The word for fight (*lāḥam*) always refers to military combat, and the "support" (*ḥzq* [hithpael] + *'im*) offered by Michael in Daniel 10:21 can refer to military support (1 Chr 11:10; 2 Chr 16:9). The standard interpretation reads "return" (*šuv*) as "go back to doing what I had been previously doing," and on that basis assumes that the "help" (*'zr*) offered by Michael in Daniel 10:13 is conceptually similar to the "support" in Daniel 10:21, and also that the meaning of the words translated "resisted" and detained" in Daniel 10:13 refer to the same general activity as *lāḥam*; that is, to combat of some kind. However, a closer examination of the passage indicates that this standard interpretation cannot possibly be what is occurring.

First, the collocations *'āmad* (qal) + *lĕneged* (NIV "resisted") and *ytr* (niphal) + *šam* + *'ṣl* (NIV "was detained there") in Daniel 10:13 cannot possibly refer to combat, or even adversity, of any kind. The phrase *'āmad lĕneged* means "stood in front of" and also occurs in Daniel 8:15 ("there *before me stood* one who looked like a man"), Daniel 10:16 ("I said to the one *standing before* me"), and Joshua 5:13 ("he looked up and saw a man *standing in front of* him"). The collocation always takes an [angelic] subject—the angelic messenger in Daniel 8:15 and 10:16; the prince of Persia in Daniel 10:13; and the commander of the army of the LORD in Joshua 5:13—and in no instance does the "one standing before" engage the one he stands before in combat; neither do they constrain or harass them in any way.[47] Indeed, in every instance other than Daniel 10:13 the explicit reason for "standing before" someone is in order to *speak to* them. Thus, without any detail of the activity of the prince of Persia, we should assume that his intention is to speak to [the messenger] as well. What exactly he might be saying is unrecorded and is not easily deducible from the information provided.

Similarly, *ytr* + *šam* + *'ṣl* means "remained there beside." It primarily indicates relative location, but can also imply hierarchy or relationship depending on context (e.g., Neh 8:4, where a roster of people stand "beside" Ezra as he reads the law). However, the relationship is never adversarial in nature. The standard interpretation reads that Michael "helps" the speaker so that he is no longer *forced* to "remain beside" the prince (LXX) or king (Hebrew, also NIV) of Persia. However, neither the semantic range of the collocation nor the grammar of the verb[48] allow for an implication of forced detention or restraint. Further, as we have seen, there is no indication that the speaker is "beside" the prince/king of Persia against his will, since *'āmad lĕneged* never implies confrontation and the text does not indicate that he was forcibly detained. What exactly they are doing cannot be determined with certainty, but it is clear that whatever it is they are not fighting or standing in any kind of opposition in any way.

Regardless of the specifics of what the princes are doing, the standard interpretation insists that it stands in opposition to the will of Yahweh. This understanding is derived from a comparison between Daniel 9:23, where the messenger says, "As soon as you began to pray, a word went out, which I have come to tell you," and Daniel 10:12, where the messenger says "Since the first day that you set your mind to gain understanding and to humble yourself before your God, your words were heard, and I have come in response to them." The standard interpretation assumes that the sequence of events in both cases is more or less identical; Daniel's prayer is heard and the messenger is *immediately* dispatched (by Yahweh) to bring a response. The qualification "But the prince of

47. The commander of the army of the LORD stands "with a drawn sword in his hand" in Jos 5:13, but the text does not indicate that he threatens Joshua with it. The collocation "drawn sword" (*šālap* [passive qal] + *ḥereb*) always occurs in conjunction with an angelic subject—the angel of the LORD in Num 22:23, 31 and the plague angel in 1 Chr 21:16—and in Numbers and Chronicles the angel is hostile. However, in neither Numbers nor Chronicles does the hostile angel "stand before" (*'āmad lĕneged*) the one they are threatening; the angel of the LORD "stands in [the road]" (*nāṣab* + *b-*) and the plague angel stands (*'āmad*) with his "hand stretched out." The "stretching out the hand" is the hostile gesture (compare Isa 9), not the "standing." In 2 Sam 24:9 and 2 Kgs 3:26 "those who could draw the sword" (qal) refers to allied swordsmen. Note that Joshua is not sure whether the angel is his ally or his enemy.

48. The key here is that the niphal form is used for the verb "remain." If the text wanted to express "[he] caused me to remain" it would use a hiphil (though this usually occurs with the meaning to spare or preserve, e.g., Ezek 12:16). If the text wanted to convey "I was caused to remain" (now passive/causative) it would use a hophal form, of which there are no occurrences. The niphal form is middle or passive, and with *ytr* is generally middle voice; see 1 Kgs 18:22; 19:10, 14 for the only other occurrences of the first person form. When Hebrew wants to indicate someone being forcibly detained it uses the verb *'ṣr* (see Judg 13:16) or the piel of *'ḥr* (Gen 24:56, and in the passive would be pual, which does not occur).

the Persian kingdom [stood before] me twenty-one days" (Dan 10:13) is read in contrast to "while I was still in prayer, Gabriel . . . came to me in swift flight" (Dan 9:21) and is taken to be a kind of apology for why the messenger did not appear immediately as before. The overall conclusion states that, were it not for the prince of Persia, Daniel would not have had to fast for the whole three weeks (Dan 10:2), which is the same period of time that the prince "stood before" the messenger. Boyd summarizes: "God's messenger literally got caught up in a spiritual battle that seemed to center on the 'prince of Persia' trying to prevent Daniel from getting this message. Were it not for Michael . . . Daniel might have been waiting even longer to hear from God."[49] However, this interpretation is not substantiated by a close reading of the text.

First, Daniel 10 does not say that the messenger *came* as soon as Daniel began to pray; rather it says that they *heard* him from the start. The adversative that begins Daniel 10:13 (*wĕ*, NIV "*but* the prince . . . stood before me") is not necessarily in contrast to the *coming*; it could instead be in contrast to the *hearing* (gloss: "we *heard* you the whole time, *but* we were doing things with the prince of Persia and did not come until now"). Second, the activity that Daniel is doing is different. In Daniel 9:23 the verb is *taḥănûn*, lit "cry for mercy"; in Daniel 10:12 the verbs are "set [your] mind to gain understanding" (*bîn*, hiphil) and "humbled [yourself]" (*ʿānh*, hithpael). The latter occurs only four other times;[50] in Ezra 8:21 it accompanies fasting for a predetermined period of time in the context of a petition to God for a specific favor—there, protection on the road to Jerusalem—which is subsequently granted (Ezra 8:23). This is similar to the situation in Daniel. In Daniel 10:3 Daniel states that "I ate no choice food; no meat or wine touched my lips; and I used no lotions at all until (*ʿad*) the three weeks were over (*mālēʾ*)."[51] The collocation *mālēʾ* + [a period of time] (here "three weeks") always refers to the completion of a more-or-less fixed and pre-established duration; compare especially to the Nazirite vow in Numbers 6:5, "They must be holy until (*ʿad*) the period of their dedication to the LORD (time) is over (*mālēʾ*)."[52] This strongly indicates that Daniel decided beforehand that he was

49. Boyd, *God at War*, 10.

50. Ezra 8:21; Ps 107:17 (NIV "suffered affliction"); twice in 1 Kgs 2:26 (NIV "*shared* our father's *hardship*").

51. The other activity Daniel does—mourning (*ʿābal*, hithpael) in 10:2—is also done by Nehemiah in Neh 1:4, also with a relatively specific objective, in this case to cause the walls and gates of Jerusalem to be rebuilt (Neh 1:3; 2:3). Nehemiah continues to mourn until his petition is granted, but this does not appear to be the case for Daniel; note that Nehemiah sets no duration for his mourning ("until my petition is granted" or "until [X] days have passed" as Daniel does in Dan 10:3 ("until the three weeks were over").

52. Also Num 6:13. Other uses refer to nine months of human gestation (Gen 25:24); Jacob's seven-year labor contract (Gen 29:21); the forty-day embalming of Jacob (Gen 50:3); the seven-day ordination of priests (Lev 8:33); thirty days of purification (Lev 12:4, 6); David's betrothal to Michal (1 Sam 18:26); 400 days of symbolic siege (Ezek 5:2); 180 days of banquets (Esth 1:5); the twelve-month beauty treatments of Xerxes' queens (Esth 2:12); or a time of conscripted service (Isa 40:2). The only time the duration is open-ended is when the period that is over is a lifetime (2 Sam 7:12; 1 Chr 17:11; Jer 25:34; Lam 4:18), but even this is still set in a context of inevitability (royal succession,

going to mourn and fast for three weeks and then proceeded to do so, just as Ezra decided beforehand to fast for three days (Ezra 8:15). Consequently, we would not expect the petition—here, for understanding—to be granted until the prescribed three weeks have passed, regardless of what the messenger was doing in the meantime; this is especially true if Collins is correct that Daniel's mourning and fasting is at least partially undertaken to *induce* the vision.[53] In any case, the collocation [*mālē'* + time] ("[time] is over") never indicates that a spontaneous event has occurred which now allows a person to stop doing what they had been doing, as Boyd suggests that the spontaneous escape of the messenger from the prince of Persia allowed Daniel to stop fasting. The messenger would not have come before the three weeks were over—note that Daniel 9:3 specifies no duration—and Daniel would not have continued fasting once the three weeks were completed. The fact that Daniel 9 and 10 represent differing scenarios is indicated by the different language that is used. We cannot assume that they can be used to interpret one another.

If the princes are indeed evil and opposed to God, then, it must be determined from the language used to describe *them*, as opposed to that used to describe their actions. Once again, an exact identification depends on what the target audience already knows about Michael. Beyond the relation to Michael, the princes are identified only by their title (*śr*) and by the objects of their patronage; "the kingdom of Persia" (*śar malkût pāras*) in Daniel 10:13; Persia (*śar pāras*) and Greece (*śar yāwān*) in Daniel 10:20; and [Israel] in Daniel 10:21. Daniel 10:13 also mentions a "king of Persia" (*melek pāras*), which the LXX amends to also read "*prince of* the king(dom) of Persia" (*archon basieias person*) in parallel to the earlier title with the assumption that both titles refer to the same character (which is possible but not certain—the "king of Persia" that the messenger "remains beside" might be Cyrus). The standard interpretation identifies the princes as the patron deities of the named territories, based on Deuteronomy 32:8: "When the Most High gave the nations their inheritance . . . he set up boundaries for the peoples according to the number of the [sons of God]." The phrase "according to the number of" (*lĕ* + *mispar*) is read to imply that each of the nations or peoples have one of the sons of God *appointed over them* as a ruler or custodian. This interpretation is supported by the observation that ancient Near Eastern nations did indeed have patron gods.[54] In addition to the sons of God in Deuteronomy and the princes in Daniel 10, these same patron gods are also identified by many interpreters with the characters mentioned in such passages as Ezekiel 28:12–19; Isaiah 24:21–22; and Psalm 82. However, *lĕmispar* occurs three other times and never implies distribu-

---

slaughter of livestock, and fulfillment of a prophecy of doom, respectively) and thus is still essentially pre-established. The collocation with the preposition '*ad* ("until") never occurs in the context of a lifetime; that is, it never says "[conditions remained or will remain] until [the uncertain amount of time that constitutes a lifespan] happened to come to an end."

53. Collins, *Daniel*, 372.

54. Page, *Powers*, 63; Collins, *Daniel*, 374; Lucas, *Daniel*, 276; see also Tigay, *Deuteronomy*, 302–3; McConville, *Deuteronomy*, 454.

tion. In Joshua 4:8, the people take stones "*according to the number of* the tribes of the Israelites"; in Ezekiel 4:5, Ezekiel lays on his side for "*the same number of* days as the years of their sin"; in 2 Chronicles 35:7, "Josiah provided for all the lay people who were there *a total of* thirty thousand lambs and goats." The word translated "provided" (Heb. root: *rûm*) does not refer to *distribution to* the lay people; the verb normally refers to making an offering (e.g., Lev 22:15; Num 18:29; Ezek 45:1), so here "provided" should be read to mean "offered on their behalf." In all cases, the element following *lĕmispar* represents a quantity (twelve tribes, 390 days, 30,000 animals) and therefore the collocation indicates "there were this many," not "and all of them got one." A similar phrase in Judges 21:23 indicates that the Benjaminites take one wife for each of them (NIV "each man . . . carried"; lit. "carried off according to the number of them") but the concept of possession is conveyed by the verb *(nāśā')*, NIV "carried off"), not in the collocation *lĕmispar*, which still indicates a number (200; 600 in Judg 20:47 minus 400 in Judg 21:12). The verb in Deuteronomy 32:8 is *nṣb* (NIV "set up"), which means "establish" and does not inherently imply distribution; the collocation "set up boundaries" is used again in Psalm 74:17 as a general order-bringing function (parallel to establishing the seasons) with no mention of the sons of God. Thus, in Deuteronomy 32:8 the "number of the sons of God" should be read as indicating a quantity; this reading is supported by the Masoretic text's decision to change "sons of God" to "sons of Israel," since the seventy nations in Genesis 10 correspond numerically to the seventy sons of Jacob (Israel) in Genesis 46:27 and Exodus 1:5[55] (though, of course, the sons of Israel do not each rule their own nation). Ugaritic texts suggest that there were seventy members of the divine council,[56] and *Targum pseudo-Jonathan* records that "[Yahweh] cast lots on seventy angels (Aram. *mal'ăkîn*) . . . [and] he established the borders of the nations according to the sum of the number of the seventy sons of Israel."[57] The idea that sociopolitical institutions have patron *angels* is attested for the Second Temple period (e.g., Rev 1:20), which Daniel could theoretically be late enough to potentially reference; however, the word used for them is *angelos* ("angels"; also the LXX of Deut 32:8, "angels of God"), not *archon* ("prince"), so even in this case a reference to Deuteronomy is unlikely.[58] The number seventy represents completeness, so the numerical value could be a poetic indication for "the full complement of them." Whatever the number seventy indicates (and who it corresponds to; the divine council, or Jacob's offspring, or both), the text of Deuteronomy 32:8 in context cannot easily be read to say that "Yahweh assigned one of the [seventy] sons of God to each of

55. McConville, *Deuteronomy*, 454; Tigay, *Deuteronomy*, 514–15.

56. CAT/KTU 1.4:VI.46, translation in Parker, *Ugaritic Narrative Poetry*, 140.

57. *Targ. Ps-J.* Deut 3:8.

58. Aram. *śar* refers to Michael in *Gen. Rab.* 78.1, and to the "guardian angel" of Egypt in *Exod. Rab.* 22.2, but this is not the same word the Targum uses for the "angels" in Deut 32:8, so even if a very late pseudo-Daniel is referring to patron angels conceptually (using a Hebrew cognate of a semitechnical Aramaic word) he is still not referencing Deuteronomy.

the [seventy] nations."[59] This assumption should therefore not be used as the basis for identifying the beings described in Daniel 10 (or Ps 82; see below).

Consequently, Deuteronomy itself does not give any information about patron deities beyond what the cognitive environment already assumed about them, especially because the assumption of the known existence of patron deities is one of the warrants for interpreting Deuteronomy 32 in this way. It would be somewhat circular to claim that "we know that the nations have patron deities because Deuteronomy 32 says they do, and we know that that is what Deuteronomy 32 is saying because we know that the nations have patron deities." It is worth noting that the patron gods of the nations (Marduk, Milchom, Chemosh, and so on) are never identified in the Bible as "sons of God" or with the divine council; the preferred term for them is *gods* (*ĕlôhîm* or a near equivalent) or *idols* (various; see chapter 11). Further, neither the sons of God nor the gods/idols of the nations are ever referred to as "prince" (*śar*). Thus, we should not assume that the patron gods of Persia and Greece that are known from the cognitive environment (Ahuramazda and Zeus) are being affirmed as having been appointed over their nations by Yahweh in Deuteronomy 32:8, and in turn are the same beings featured in Daniel 10; there is simply no warrant for such a sweeping conflation.[60]

---

59. The strongest argument in favor of doing so comes from an assumed parallelism between the Lord's "portion" and "allotment" in Deut 32:9 and whatever is represented by the "borders" in Deut 32:8 (see for example Heiser, "Deuteronomy 32:8 and the Sons of God," 70–71). "Border" designates the territories allotted to the tribes of Israel in Josh 13–24, and so Deut 32:8 is read to imply "carving up territory for distribution" in the same way. However, this assumed parallelism is contestable for several reasons. First, the text is problematic as to the particle that introduces the clause of Deut 32:9; some texts read *kî* ("because"; so NIV), others read *wayĕhî* ("and"; so LXX); but neither of these indicates a *contrast* (i.e., they do not say "Yahweh gave the nations to the sons of God, *but in contrast* Israel is his own portion"). Regardless of the meaning of Deut 32:8, Deut 32:9 emphasizes the uniqueness of Israel among the nations; its purpose is not to emphasize the patrons of the nations. Further, Deut 32:8b is best read in parallel with 32:8a; "set up the borders" parallels "gave the nations their inheritance" and "divided mankind," not "the Lord's portion" and "[the Lord's] inheritance." The rhetorical flow of the chapter also connects Deut 32:9 strongly with 32:10 (the antecedent for the pronoun "him" in Deut 32:10 is "Jacob"). Thus, if anything, we should read a hard narrative break between Deut 32:8 and 9, not (as NIV, and also as in this interpretation) between Deut 32:9 and 10.

60. In chapter 7 we argued that the word *šēdîm* of Deut 32:17 and Ps 106:37 also refers to gods (class I spirits) since they receive sacrifices. These gods (*shaddayin*) may have also served on the divine council in Canaanite religion (Burnett, "Prophecy in Transjordan," 158–59; see also Hackett, *The Balaam Text from Deir 'Allā*, 85–89). Whether orthodox Israel considered the divine council to consist of class I spirits that were neglected by sanctioned religious practices, or of domesticated class II spirits (like the Cherubim and Seraphim) pressed into the service of the divine bureaucracy, cannot be determined. The divine council in Canaan may have been understood to have some kind of territorial administrative function (see Burnett, "Prophecy in Transjordan," 160–61; compare perhaps the idea expressed by the Arameans in 1 Kgs 20:23–28), and therefore the council in Israel may have had a similar function, but nonetheless no term designating the divine council is ever clearly used to describe the patron deities of foreign nations in the Hebrew Bible. The Dayr 'Alla text that provides the basis for the etymology does not indicate that the ruling deities of other nations (Marduk, Chemosh, etc.) would have been numbered among the *shaddayin*.

The title "prince" is given to one supernatural being outside of Daniel: the "prince (*śar*, NIV "commander") of the army of the LORD" in Joshua 5:14. This individual is not the same person as the patron deity (Yahweh) of the nation it represents; neither is it the warrior deity of that nation (also Yahweh), neither is it serving on the divine council. Based on the parallel between Joshua 5:15 and Exodus 3:5, the "commander of the army of the LORD" is often identified with the angel of the LORD (compare Exod 3:2). But the angel of the LORD is not a patron deity of a nation and is not one of the sons of God, either. Nonetheless, it is clear from the language that Daniel 10 is intended to invoke Joshua 5. The prince of the army of the LORD "stands before" (*ʿāmad lĕneged*) Joshua in Joshua 5:13, just as the prince of Persia "stands before" the man in linen in Daniel 10:13 and the messenger "stands before" Daniel in Daniel 10:16; Joshua 5:13 is the only occurrence of the collocation outside of Daniel. The conceptual association of Daniel with Joshua should not be surprising; postexilic Israel often conceived of the return and restoration of their land in terms of a new exodus and a new conquest (see chapter 9). By invoking the imagery of Joshua 5, the author of Daniel indicates that his audience are standing on the eve of the new conquest that will restore Israel (which is described in Dan 12). If this is the case then Daniel 10:13 may represent the princes (i.e., military commanders) of the various [divine] forces making their arrangements before the battle commences. We should recall that, in the third year of Cyrus when the vision is set, Israel and Persia are on friendly terms; Cyrus has released the exiles and given permission for the temple to be rebuilt (Ezra 1). Consequently, it should be no surprise that their divine representatives (at any level) are also getting along; remember that they are standing side by side (*ʾeṣel*) in Daniel 10:13. However, Israel's status as a Persian satrapy is not its ideally restored state, as the people are well aware; consequently, at some point the status will change, and Yahweh's armies will turn against Persia and also against Greece (which is what Dan 10:20 and 12:1 refer to) culminating in the final restoration of Israel. But the defeat or destruction of Persia and Greece (and, implicitly, their divine counterparts) for the sake of the restoration of Israel is not the same thing as God's servants having to fight against hostile angels in order to be able to carry out the will of God.

If, on the other hand, the author is referencing an existing Michael tradition, then we can infer some information about the princes based on their relationship to Michael. Michael is not fighting the prince of Persia in Daniel 10:13, but he does fight the princes of Persia and Greece in Daniel 10:20. In the Qumran traditions, Michael is the prince of light, and his opponent is Belial, the prince of darkness; thus, the reader might be expected to associate the princes of Persia and Greece with Belial. Since the Dead Sea Scrolls indicate that Yahweh supports the prince of light,[61] we might therefore infer that the prince of darkness is opposing Yahweh. However, the same documents affirm that Belial is not a rebel; he is established by God to corrupt and deal damage, and also to be eventually destroyed by the victorious sons of

61. 1QS 3.25.

light (see chapter 9). Thus, even in the context of the eschatological battle tradition the princes cannot be seen as angelic rebels against Yahweh obstructing and thwarting his will for his people.

The problem of which of the "princes" (Michael or the prince of Persia) is depicted as representing Yahweh's will (either, both, or neither) remains even if the standard interpretation's identification of the princes as the patron deities of the nations is retained. The standard interpretation of Daniel 10 depicts the prince of Persia as opposing the will of Yahweh. However, if we read Daniel 10 without the influence of Second Temple traditions, we note that Yahweh is absent. In Daniel 10:11 the messenger says that he was sent, but does not say who sent him. Further, the fact that it is *Michael* who represents Israel is significant. In Deuteronomy 32:8–9—the passage that is used to establish the identity of the princes as the sons of God in the standard interpretation—Israel is set aside as "Yahweh's portion" and not delegated to any prince. The fact that Israel has a prince now, in Daniel 10, implies that Yahweh is no longer representing them, which in turn means that the prince of Persia is not opposing *Yahweh*, even within the logic of the standard interpretation; he is only opposing *Michael*. Regardless of when Daniel was written, it is *set* in "the third year of Cyrus King of Persia" (Dan 10:1), and other texts give us information about where Yahweh is and what he is doing in the third year of Cyrus. In Ezekiel 10, the presence of Yahweh departs from the temple, indicating that he has abandoned Jerusalem in preparation for its destruction. The decree for the temple to be rebuilt comes in the first year of Cyrus (Ezra 1:1–2; 6:3), though the temple is not actually rebuilt until twenty years later, and even then no mention is made of Yahweh's return (Ezra 6:13–18; compare Exod 40:34–35; 1 Kgs 8:10–11; Ezek 43:2–7). In Daniel 9, which is also set in the first year of Cyrus,[62] Daniel is informed that more time still is required before the sin of Israel is paid for and the "anointed one" comes (Dan 9:24–25), which will ostensibly coincide with Yahweh's return. Thus, in the third year of Cyrus when Daniel 10 is set, Yahweh has not returned to the side of Israel. Further, Isaiah 45:1 describes *Cyrus*, the Persian king, as Yahweh's "anointed," who he has "raised up" (Isa 45:13). Consequently, if Yahweh is anywhere at the time of Daniel 10, Yahweh should be on the side of *Persia*. Indeed, the messenger affirms that "No one supports me against them except Michael, your prince" (Dan 10:21). Yahweh would be someone, so Yahweh is not supporting them. However, we should not assume that Michael is opposing Yahweh either (perhaps by bringing relief to those subject to God's anger in a kind of Promethean role); it is perhaps best to assume that Yahweh is standing by and taking no role in the interactions among the princes on one side or the other.

Thus, in no case does the text of Daniel 10 in context depict the prince of Persia as having the ability to successfully oppose the will of God or intending to do so. Nothing within the text itself (apart from implications derived from later

62. "Darius son of Xerxes" in Daniel 9:1 probably refers to Cyrus. See Lucas, *Daniel*, 134–37; Lucas, "Daniel," 4:556.

eschatological combat traditions) even indicates that the princes are in any way evil or malicious—and of course we recall that the Bible's references to existing traditions do not affirm those traditions.

The gods in Psalm 82

The princes in Daniel 10 are not depicted as evil or as opposed to God in any way. However, a third passage, Psalm 82, is correlated with both Deuteronomy 32:8 and Daniel 10 to argue that the gods/princes are evil enemies of Yahweh. The psalm begins when "God has taken his place in the divine council; in the midst of the gods he holds judgment" (ESV). This indicates that the heavenly court is in session and God is going to hear a case. The standard interpretation of the psalm, along with the NIV ("he renders judgment among the 'gods'") assume that Yahweh is standing in judgment *over* the gods. However, "the midst of the gods" is paralleled with "the divine council" and simply designates the convening of the court. But who is bringing the case? Most interpreters attribute the statement "How long will you defend the unjust and show partiality to the wicked?" (Ps 82:2) to Yahweh; thus they read the passage as Yahweh sitting in judgment over the gods and accusing them of injustice.[63] The "great assembly" (*ǎdat-ʾēl*) in Psalm 82:1, paralleled to "among the gods," probably refers to the divine council (so ESV)[64] and the standard interpretation of the psalm assumes that these are the same beings—or at least the same kinds of beings—as both the princes in Daniel 10 and the beings in Deuteronomy 32:8. Although we have proposed that such a sweeping conflation is not warranted, we will nonetheless examine what Psalm 82 depicts the "gods" as doing and whether or not the message of the passage is that they are evil beings opposed to the will and purposes of God.

The standard interpretation of Psalm 82 reads verse 2—"How long will you defend the unjust and show partiality to the wicked?"—as an accusation by a judge (Yahweh) addressed to the assembled gods. However, the injunction "how long . . . ?" is familiar from the psalms, where it always indicates that the psalmist, not God, is speaking; usually as a protest, not an indictment.[65] We should note, however, that the normal construction for "how long" as a protest by the psalmist is *ʿad ʾānâ* (e.g., Pss 13:1; 62:3) or *ʿad mâ* (e.g., Pss 79:5; 89:46), while the phrase in Psalm 82:2 is *ʿad mātay*. Outside the psalms, *ʿad mātay* is usually a question about a length of time,[66] but can also be used rhetorically as a protest to God (Jer 4:21; 12:4; Zech 1:12); or rhetorically by God (via a prophet) to complain about Israel (Jer 23:26; 31:2; 47:5; Hos 8:5), or about

---

63. Page, *Powers*, 59; Tate, *Psalms 51–100*, 335; Weiser, *Psalms*, 559; VanGemeren, "Psalms," 624.

64. Tate, *Psalms 51–100*, 329; Page notes that Jesus's statement in John 10:34–36 has often been interpreted to argue that the gods are human (Page, *Powers*, 57). However, New Testament appropriations of Old Testament texts do not tell us what those texts meant in context (see chapter 14).

65. Goldingay, *Psalms 42–89*, 563.

66. 1 Sam 16:1; 1 Kgs 18:21; Isa 6:11; Jer 4:14; 23:26; Dan 8:13; 12:6; Neh 2:6.

Babylon (Hab 2:6); or by others to complain about various things (Exod 10:7; Num 14:27; 1 Sam 1:14; Prov 1:22; 6:9). Nonetheless, in the other seven occurrences in the Psalms, including two others in the Asaph corpus that includes Psalm 82, the phrase is always a rhetorical protest spoken by the psalmist.[67] Thus, Goldingay is correct that we should assume the speaker in Psalm 82:2 is the *psalmist*, not God.[68] Further, in every occurrence of *'ad mātay* in the psalms, the speaker is the psalmist delivering a protest *to God*. Sometimes the referent of the complaint—i.e., person or thing [X] in the construction "How long will [X] [do something]"—is in the third person, as in Psalm 74:10 ("How long will *the enemy* mock you") or Psalm 94:3 ("how long will *the wicked* be jubilant"). These constructions indicate that the psalmist wants God to stop the named persons from doing something. Consequently, if the speaker in Psalm 82 wants God to stop the gods from doing something, the phrase should read, "how long will *they* judge unjustly." In other cases, however, the complaint is addressed directly to God: "How long, LORD, how long" (Ps 6:3); "How long, LORD God Almighty, will your anger smolder" (Ps 80:4); and "How long will it be [until you relent]" (Ps 90:3). In all these cases, the psalmist wants God himself to stop doing something. Complaining that God has acted unjustly is not unprecedented in the Hebrew Bible, especially in laments: Job says the same in Job 7 and (especially) 27, and Habakkuk does as well in Habakkuk 1:2–4, 12–17. This reading would balance nicely with the final appeal for God to "rise up and judge (*špṭ*) the earth" (singular verbs);[69] compare to Psalm 35:17, 23–24 ("how long ['ad 'ānâ] will you look on. . . . [R]ise to my defense, . . . vindicate (*špṭ*) me in your righteousness"). However, we must examine whether a complaint against God—which here extends to the entire divine council as well—makes sense in the context of the psalm as a whole.

Psalms is not an anthology of hymnic and ritual literature compiled randomly; the five books are divided loosely into topics that broadly parallel the history of Israel. Book Three of the Psalter, which includes Psalm 82, leads up to and anticipates the exile.[70] This in turn suggests that Psalm 82 may be conceptually similar to Habakkuk, which also anticipates the exile, also questions the justice of God's decisions (Hab 1:2–4, 12–17; including a "how long" formula in 1:2, though using 'ad 'ānâ), and also expresses hope for the destruction of foreign nations (Hab 3:17). Nonetheless, even if the context fits, we still have to examine the internal logic and language of the psalm itself.

Psalm 82:8 calls on Yahweh (alone, without the council) to judge the earth and take possession (*nḥl*, NIV "inheritance") of the nations. This word is the covenant term for Israel (e.g., Zech 2:12), but here the use is more generic and does not apply the covenant status to the whole earth. In context, the phrase is used as a warrant for

---

67. Pss 6:3; 74:10; 80:4; 90:13; twice in 94:3.

68. Goldingay, *Psalms 42–89*, 563.

69. See Goldingay, *Psalms 42–89*, 568.

70. Wilson, *Editing of the Hebrew Psalter*, 209–14.

why Yahweh should judge the whole earth: *because* you own all the nations.[71] In the standard interpretation the possession of the nations is connected to the death of the gods in Psalm 82:6–7, although whether Yahweh gains possession of the nations by default after the gods are dead[72] or has the right and/or responsibility to kill the gods because he owns the nations already[73] varies by interpreter. The implicit association between the death of the gods and Yahweh assuming rule of the nations is what leads the standard interpretation to assume that the gods in Psalm 82:6 (*ĕlôhîm*) are the same entities that constitute the pantheons of the nations and stand behind the idols, similar to those who are destroyed in Ezekiel 30:13. The psalm as a whole is often extrapolated as an explanation of *why* the idols are destroyed: because they have failed to uphold social justice, which is the presumed indictment in Psalm 82:2–4. This reading assumes two factors: that the gods in Psalm 82 are depicted as evil, and that they do in fact represent the gods of the foreign pantheons. These points are not explicitly stated by the text and are therefore worth closer examination.

The gods who die—implicitly, when Yahweh judges the nations—in Psalm 82:5–7 are usually assumed to be the same figures mentioned in Psalm 82:5 when the speaker claims that "the gods know nothing." Technically the word "gods" supplied by the NIV is absent; the Hebrew says only *"they* know nothing" and does not specify the antecedent. Grammatically it is unlikely that the pronoun refers all the way back to the gods in Psalm 82:1; it might also for example refer to "the wicked [ones]" in Psalm 82:4. For argument's sake, we will follow both the NIV and the standard interpretation and assume that the pronoun refers to whomever is meant by the word "gods" in Psalm 82:6 (see discussion below). The standard interpretation of the psalm takes Yahweh ("God" from Ps 82:1) to be the speaker; accordingly, the statement "I said, 'you are gods'" in Psalm 82:6 is read as a declaration *to* the gods that includes the pronouncement of a verdict: "you will die like mortals" (Ps 82:7). The assumption that Psalm 82:6–7 is a verdict is in turn used to support the idea that Psalm 82:1 depicts Yahweh standing in judgment over the gods. Because the gods are sentenced to death, this interpretation assumes that the gods were evil and identifies their crimes as defending the unjust and failing to uphold social justice; thus Psalm 82:2–4 is read as an indictment from the mouth of Yahweh to the gods. However, several important details should lead us to question this reading.

First, as Goldingay points out, we should not assume that the speaker changes unless this is specifically indicated.[74] The speaker in Psalm 82:8 is the psalmist (since Yahweh is addressed in the second person), and the speaker in Psalm 82:2 is also the

---

71. Goldingay, *Psalms 42–89*, 568; deClaisse-Walford et al., *Psalms*, 642.

72. Hossfeld and Zenger, *Psalms 2*, 335–36; deClaisse-Walford et al., *Psalms*, 643 ("now that the other gods are finished, God is implored to do what they did not").

73. See Goldingay, *Psalms 42–89*, 569; deClaisse-Walford et al., *Psalms*, 643 ("the last line states what was already true: that all the nations, no matter what their god, belong to Israel's great God").

74. Goldingay, *Psalms 42–89*, 559.

psalmist, also addressing Yahweh, as indicated by the "how long . . ." formula. Thus, the speaker who brings the supposed indictment (Ps 82:2–4) and also the supposed verdict (Ps 82:5–7) is still the psalmist. Further, since Psalm 82:2–4 are addressed *towards* Yahweh—again by virtue of the "how long . . ." formula—the statement cannot in fact be read as a criminal indictment; rather, it is a complaint. If Psalm 82:2–4 is a complaint by the psalmist, it is not an indictment by a judge. Consequently, if Psalm 82:2–4 is not a criminal indictment by a judge, then Psalm 82:7 should not be read as a verdict and sentence by a judge. Therefore, we should reexamine these lines to see what else they could mean.

The speaker throughout is the psalmist, who begins in Psalm 82:2 and ends in Psalm 82:8 by addressing Yahweh. This means that Psalm 82:5–7 is probably addressed to Yahweh as well. This makes sense in Psalm 82:5 where the gods—assuming that the pronoun *they* does refer to the gods—are mentioned in the third person ("they [the gods] know nothing"), which would be odd if the gods are supposed to be addressed as in the standard interpretation. However, it means that the statement "I said, 'you are gods'" in Psalm 82:6 is not a declaration *to* the gods, since the statement is still addressed to Yahweh. Rather, we should read the speaker as essentially quoting himself, telling Yahweh what he has said *about* the gods.[75] The statement does not deliver a verdict; it reports an observation. Because the gods will "die like mortals," they are not in a position to reverse the condition described in Psalm 82:2; thus Yahweh himself is called upon to rectify the situation in Psalm 82:8. This observation is well in keeping with the theme of the impotence of the gods that is ubiquitous throughout the Hebrew Bible (see chapter 11).

However, there still remains some uncertainty concerning the identity of the gods in Psalm 82:5–6. Is the psalmist really talking about the gods of the nations? Are these the same gods that form the assembly in Psalm 82:1? In Psalm 82:6 the psalmist identifies the gods as "sons of the Most High" (*běnê 'elyôn*). This title is similar to the designations *běnê 'ělôhîm* ("sons of God"), which describes the divine council in Job 1:6; 2:1, and *běnê 'ēlîm* (NIV "heavenly beings") which describes the divine council in Psalm 89:5–7, and on that basis most interpreters assume that the gods of Psalm 82:5–6 are the same gods that Yahweh is "among" in Psalm 82:1. However, the specific title *běnê 'elyôn* is not used elsewhere. Further, as described above, in *no case* are the gods of foreign pantheons ever described as *sons of God* or as members of Yahweh's council. If *běnê 'elyôn* does refer to the council, Psalm 82:8 would then depict the psalmist "going over their heads" as it were and appealing to Yahweh directly to judge the nations, but these beings are not the same beings as the gods of the foreign nations. If that reading is correct, then Psalm 82:7 is not describing the impotence of foreign gods but rather expressing a lack of confidence in Yahweh's minions. The limitation of

---

75. The very common word "said" (qal of *āmar*) can be used for proclamations or declarations (see Hossfeld and Zenger, *Psalms 2*, 334–35), but it can also introduce quotes.

the divine council is a less prevalent theme in the Hebrew Bible than the impotence of the idols, but the concept is still attested (Job 5:1; 15:15).

A second possible interpretation is that the gods of Psalm 82:5–6 do indeed represent the members of foreign pantheons. However, if this is the case, then the title *běnê 'elyôn* does not identify them with the divine council (the gods from Ps 82:1) since the *běnê 'ĕlôhîm* and *běnê 'ēlîm* are never equated with foreign gods.[76] This reading would explain why neither of these more familiar titles are used, but it also indicates that *běnê 'elyôn* is a reference to something that is not immediately transparent. *'Elyôn* is used occasionally as an epithet for Yahweh (e.g., Ps 50:14), but not in Psalm 82; the title can also be used for the high god of any ancient Near Eastern pantheon.[77] Thus, the designation "sons of *'elyôn*" might simply reference the fact that polytheistic pantheons normally originated through procreation, and would here be paralleled with *'ĕlôhîm* as an affirmation and emphasis of divine status (gloss: "even though you are indeed gods, nonetheless you will die like mortals"). Additionally, it is worth noting that the statement "[the gods] know nothing, they understand nothing" in Psalm 82:5 is repeated in Isaiah 44:18 in reference to idols. This reading would place the observation of their ignorance and impending death within the theme of the impotence of the idols, as discussed above. The point is that gods who will die might be either the members of the divine council (from Ps 82:1 and Deut 32:8), or the idols worshipped as the pantheons of foreign nations, but there is no warrant for claiming that they represent both at once—indeed, the claim that they can be *either* of these is only circumstantial, based on the limited semantic range of the word *'ĕlôhîm* ("gods").

An additional potential identification that still falls within the semantic range of "gods" could be found by reading the references in Psalm 82:5–6 as sarcastic, addressed to individuals who are not in fact divine beings but like to imagine that they are. The statement "you are gods" in Psalm 82:6 is quoted by Jesus in John 10:34 and specifically applied to humans: "those to whom the word of God came." New Testament usage does not tell us what the Old Testament source means in context, but it does indicate that as far back as Jesus's day the interpretation of the "gods" as humans was prevalent enough that it could be meaningfully referenced, even within a cognitive environment that was not materialistic and assumed the real existence of polytheistic deities. Modern scholars who take this position compare the language of Psalm 82:2–4 with injunctions (to humans) to protect the weak in such passages as Exodus 23:6; Leviticus 19:15; Deuteronomy 24:17; Job 19:12–14; Proverbs 14:31; Isaiah 10:1–2; Jeremiah 22:3; and Amos 2:6–7.[78] However, since we have argued that Psalm 82:2–4 is addressed to Yahweh, the

76. The use of a unique title combined with the uncertain referent in Ps 82:6 means that this passage cannot be asserted to definitively *establish* the equation between the divine council (Ps 82:1) and the pantheons (purportedly in Ps 82:6).

77. As is probably the case in Gen 14:19–20; see Elnes and Miller, "*'Elyôn*." 295.

78. Page, *Powers*, 56–57. Another variant of this interpretation points to the unusual use of *'ĕlôhîm* to indicate human judges in Exod 21:6 and 22:8–9, but this case is weak; see ibid. 56 and Tate, *Psalms 51–100*, 340–41. Whether literal or sarcastic, the word *'ĕlôhîm* in Ps 82 refers to divine beings. See also

conclusion that the language identifies the addressees as human is unlikely; the similarity of the language indicates only that upholding order (which is the end to which protecting the weak is a means) is the responsibility of both human rulers and deities.[79] Nonetheless, the practice of sarcastically describing human rulers as divine beings is not unprecedented. In Ezekiel 28:2 the [human] king of Tyre brags "I am a god; I sit on the throne of a god"; to which the prophet replies, "you are a mere mortal" (Ezek 28:2) and then adds, "They will bring you down to the pit, and you will die a violent death" (Ezek 28:8). Similarly, in Isaiah 14:13–14, the (human) king of Babylon boasts, "I will ascend to the heavens; I will raise my throne above the stars of God. . . . I will ascend above the tops of the clouds; I will make myself like the Most High (ʿelyôn)." The prophet immediately contrasts this aspiration with "But you are brought down to the realm of the dead, to the depths of the pit" (Isa 14:15). Both of these passages contrast a (purported) divine status with the (actual) fate of mortal humans, as we also see in Psalm 82:6–7: "You are 'gods' . . . But you will die like mere mortals." Further, both Isaiah 14 and Ezekiel 28 invoke the theme of Yahweh bringing judgment on the nations. In Ezekiel 28, Tyre is punished for "violence" (Ezek 28:16) and for "many sins and dishonest trade" (Ezek 28:18). More closely resembling the particulars of Psalm 82, the [human king of] Babylon in Isaiah 14:5 is called "oppressor" who "struck down peoples with unceasing blows, and in fury subdued nations with relentless aggression" (Isa 14:6); who "made the world a wilderness, who overthrew its cities and would not let his captives go home" (Isa 14:17) and who "destroyed [his own] land and killed [his own] people" (Isa 14:20). In consequence, Yahweh will "rise up against them . . . [and] wipe out Babylon's name and survivors, her offspring and descendants" (Isa 14:22), because "This is the plan determined for the whole world; this is the hand stretched out over all nations" (Isa 14:26). It is worth noting, however, that Babylon's power and disruptive aggression comes through the agency of Yahweh (see for example Hab 1:5–11; Ezek 29:17–20; 30:20–25), just as the condition in Psalm 82:2–4 also comes through the agency of Yahweh. The theme of God (intentionally) empowering people to cause a disordered condition, and then killing them afterwards as judgment for causing that condition, is well established in Israel's prophetic literature, especially in Habakkuk, to which we have argued Psalm 82 is conceptually similar. Thus, the "gods" who die might not be either members of the divine council or the idols of foreign pantheons; they might be humans who hubristically aspire to the station of gods and whose (factual) mortality is being re-asserted. Any of these options is possible within the rhetorical structure of the psalm.

The standard interpretation of the psalm reads the disordered condition of the world in Psalm 82:5 ("all the foundations of the earth are shaken") as a consequence of divine negligence: the gods know nothing and walk in darkness (Ps 82:5) and therefore fail to uphold social justice (Ps 82:2–4), which in turn threatens the collapse

---

Hossfeld and Zenger, *Psalms 2*, 330.

79. Page, *Powers*, 58; Hossfeld and Zenger, *Psalms 2*, 330–31.

of the cosmic order.[80] However, we have proposed that the condition in Psalm 82:2–4 was brought about (or at least indirectly allowed; compare Hab 1:2–4) by Yahweh, not by the gods who know nothing and walk in darkness. Further, the context is unclear whether the ignorance and benightedness of the gods (whoever they are) is the cause of the condition, or another symptom of it. If Psalm 82 conceptually parallels Habakkuk, then the social dysfunction of Psalm 82:2–4 (manifested or anticipated) has been caused by Yahweh, probably in the form of the despoiling of the Mediterranean world by either Assyria or Babylon. In Isaiah 19, Yahweh's wrath on Egypt takes the form of befuddling its leaders: "The officials of Zoan have become fools, the leaders of Memphis are deceived; the cornerstones of her peoples have led Egypt astray. The LORD has poured into them a spirit of dizziness; they make Egypt stagger in all that she does" (Isa 19:13–14). The same combination of "not understanding" (*bîn*) and "not knowing" (*yāda'*) found in Psalm 82:5 is used in Isaiah 6:9 as a manifestation of judgment: "Be ever hearing, but never understanding; be ever seeing, but never knowing" (NIV "perceiving"); and the phrase "walk in darkness" is used to signify calamity in Lamentations 3:2. Thus, the disordered condition that Yahweh has caused and the psalmist petitions him to rectify includes everything in Psalm 82:2–5, from "defending the unjust" to the "walking in darkness." The gods (whoever they are) can be of no help; their impotence and helplessness is itself a symptom—though not a cause—of the problem.

The meaning of Psalm 82, then, is this: Yahweh, presumably in conjunction with his council, has brought about a calamity, which the position of the psalm within Book Three of the Psalter implies should be understood as a reference to the exile (whether impending or manifested, or of the northern kingdom or the southern kingdom, or both). The divine council convenes in Psalm 82:1, and the psalmist comes before them to press his complaint and appeal for relief ("how long will [all of] you . . ."; Ps 82:2). The result of the calamity is that the world order is disrupted; the unjust are defended (Ps 82:2) while the weak and fatherless are not, and the cause of the poor and oppressed is not upheld (Ps 82:3), and nobody rescues the weak and needy from the wicked (Ps 82:4). The catastrophe is so severe that even the gods or kings (it does not matter which) who should preserve order are instead rendered confused and helpless, and the whole cosmos reels on the edge of collapse (Ps 82:5). The psalmist recognizes that the gods or kings (again, it does not matter which) are weak and cannot avail to correct the catastrophe, and so he appeals directly to Yahweh to step in and deliver the world from calamity. This reading is perfectly in line with the themes of Yahweh collapsing the world order and being recognized as the only one who can put it right again, themes that are found throughout the Hebrew Bible, especially in the context of the exile. However, this reading also means that the standard interpretation of the psalm and the theological extrapolations that derive from it are severely misguided.

80. See for example VanGemeren, "Psalms," 625; Page, *Powers*, 58–59.

Most interpreters of Psalm 82 brush over the details of who is speaking to whom and in what context (i.e., the psalmist is speaking to Yahweh in the context of the exile) and instead rush directly into developing a universalized political theology, the main thrust of which is that God always desires the death of anyone anywhere, divine or human,[81] who does not uphold "social justice," the specifics of which can be supplied at the convenience of the interpreter. The assumption that God is speaking in Psalm 82:2 is used to promote "social justice" as an absolute divine ideal, and the extension of the judgment to "the nations" in Psalm 82:8 is used to apply this absolute ideal to all people in all places at all times. So, for example: "Psalm 82 projects, in mythic colors, a highly dramatic 'world picture' that reveals a world full of injustice and violence, and it laments this upheaval as a consequence of the failure of the gods of the nations. The psalm sees no other way out than that these gods must disappear from the stage of the heavens and the world so that Yahweh, the God of Israel, may become the god *of all nations*—as the savior of the exploited and impoverished masses."[82] Conflict theologians further speculate that the purpose of the psalm is not only to reveal God's absolute antipathy to social injustice but also to reveal that the offense is so heinous that it cannot be ascribed to human beings alone: "the angels stand accused of aiding and abetting the wicked in their exploitation of the poor and powerless. . . . [T]he psalmist saw the promotion of inequity and the absence of compassion as grievous sins that are not due to human moral deficiencies alone. So great is the evil of social injustice that it can only be accounted for by the activity of cosmic forces opposed to God."[83] This in turn is invoked both as an example of the Bible's absolute insistence on the reality of such beings[84] and simultaneously used as a basis to comment on the nature of social injustice in principle.[85] Nonetheless, even notwithstanding the contextual reading proposed above or the problems posed by the methodological flaws of sociopolitical eisegesis, this standard interpretation of Psalm 82 still has several difficulties even on its own terms.

First is the problem with the assumption that the gods promote injustice in their domains, that they "aid and abet the wicked in their exploitation of the poor and powerless." Ancient Near Eastern documents testify that the gods of the nations expected and demanded justice from their rulers, in terms very similar to those we find expressed in the Bible. Consequently, a king who promoted social injustice would not be

---

81. The idea that *ĕlōhîm* refers to both gods and humans at the same time is emphasized by, e.g., Page, *powers*, 58; Hossfeld and Zenger, *Psalms 2*, 330–31; Tate, *Psalms 51–100*, 341; see also Goldingay, *Psalms 42–89*, 567.

82. Hossfeld and Zenger, *Psalms 2*, 332. See also Page, *Powers*, 59: "the psalm constitutes both a word of comfort for the disadvantaged and a word of warning for any who would exploit their unfortunate state." Likewise, "the issue of the governance of human affairs is a matter of life and death to God Almighty (Tate, *Psalms 51–100*, 341).

83. Page, *Powers*, 59.

84. See for example Boyd, *God at War*, 131.

85. Wink, *Naming the Powers*, 1:5.

colluding with his gods, but rather *defying* his gods. In the Bible, we see that the people and the kings rarely actually enforced justice, but from that fact alone we would not conclude that they thought they were serving their god (Yahweh) by doing so. Rather, we see clearly that the offense of disorder (when it occurs) is compounded with the offense of impiety; they know more or less what their god wants, but they simply do not care (see for example Jer 36:20–26). The reason why they do not care is because they think their god will be unable to punish them because he needs their sacrifices in his temple; this is the sentiment reflected in Jeremiah 7:3–6. A similar sentiment is represented in the ancient Near Eastern proverb "the man who does not sacrifice to his god can make the god run after him like a dog."[86] Thus, the gods do not encourage injustice because they are evil; rather, they allow injustice because they are codependent. This may well still be reason enough to clear them out of the way, but it provides no basis for speculating that this psalm teaches that social injustice or other evils necessarily derive from the intentional machinations of a demonic source. It is *certainly* not the case that the psalm uses the indictment of the gods as a backhanded condemnation of idolatry in principle,[87] and therefore as a warrant to extend the (purported) behavior of the gods onto all of the various references to idols as if it somehow explained the prohibition of idols to Israel on some sort of moral grounds.[88]

The second problem is that "social justice" in the ancient world was neither an absolute divine ideal nor an end in itself, as it is for example in modern liberation theology. The gods did value and demand justice in society, but justice in society was one manifestation of order (among others), and it was *order*, not justice per se, that the gods valued, since establishing and preserving order is the function of gods. In this regard, Yahweh is depicted similarly to other ancient Near Eastern gods. As discussed in chapter 8, Yahweh's demand for [the ancient Near Eastern conception of] order within Israel is for the sake of his reputation, not because that order reflects his inherent nature or moral character.[89] This is probably just as well, since, while the ancient Near Eastern conception of order, also reflected in the Hebrew Bible, did include care for the poor, it also included many other things that we moderns dislike, such as social hierarchy (including monarchy, aristocracy, and patriarchy), debt slavery, family conventions such as patrilineal inheritance, contractual marriage, and levirate marriage, the entire temple and sacrificial cult system, and legal conventions such as blood vengeance, capital punishment, and talionic law. None of these is considered divine absolutes for all time, and care for the poor should not be, either. It may well be that what we call "social injustice" is in fact bad, and it might even be

---

86. Foster, *From Distant Days*, 387.

87. Contra VanGemeren, "Psalms," 626.

88. For example, "[T]he condemnation of the 'gods' as irresponsible despots implies the condemnation of all human beings who adopt the pagan way of life." VanGemeren, "Psalms," 626.

89. Contra Hossfeld and Zenger, *Psalms 2*, 337: "The true God . . . has tied his divinity to the fate of the poor and dispossessed."

true that we can serve God's purposes in our day by working to eliminate it, but those arguments would have to be presented on their own terms, not by anachronistically misreading and then exploiting proof-texts. Indeed, if we insist on misreading the Bible's text, we will actually lose the basis of knowing what God's messages to us actually consist of, and consequently lose any warrant for the claim that those messages concern social justice—at least, any warrant apart from the assumption that God wants the same things that we want.

The third problem with the logic of the standard interpretation is that Psalm 82:2–5 presents a general picture of a disordered condition; it does not highlight the particular offenses ("social injustice") that especially shake the foundations of the human moral order,[90] as if these particular injustices somehow constituted the root of all evil. Inversions of the world order—i.e., the wicked prospering and the righteous or innocent suffering, as here—occur frequently in the biblical text; the theme is referred to by Bible scholars as the world-upside-down motif. The upheavals can take place in the cosmic realm (e.g., sun going dark, Jer 4:23); in the natural realm (e.g., mountains levelled or valleys raised, Isa 40:4); in the animal realm (e.g., a lion eats grass, Isa 11:6–8); or in the social realm (e.g., rich and poor trade places, Ps 107:40–41).[91] Similar inversions occur in Psalm 82: in the divine realm the gods die (Ps 82:6–7); in the cosmic realm the foundations of the earth shake (Ps 82:5); in the social realm the unjust are defended (Ps 82:2). It is especially significant to note that the use of injury to the gods to represent inversion of the world order is not an image that is unique to Israel; Akkadian prophecies of calamity include references to the destruction of shrines and the deportation of images.[92] Thus, the depiction of the death of the gods is not a judgment on the gods, it is simply an allusion to cosmic upheaval. Gods are not *supposed* to die like mortals, even though in the ancient Near East killing gods is theoretically possible,[93] and so when they do die it signifies that momentous and catastrophic events are occurring.

The world-upside-down motif is morally neutral and signifies a state of upheaval or change, which depending on context can be either a change for the worse (as here in Ps 82) or a change for the better (as in, e.g., Isa 11).[94] We might especially note the use of the motif in Proverbs 30:21–23: "Under three things the earth trembles, under four it cannot bear up: a servant who becomes king, a godless fool who gets plenty to

90. Contra Goldingay, *Psalms 2*, 566: "when faithless people ignore or oppress the poor and no one does anything to rescue them, the very structure of human existence is imperiled." See also Tate, *Psalms 51–100*, 341.

91. Walton et al., *IVP Bible Background Commentary*, 646.

92. Holloway, *Aššur is King*, 195.

93. In both Enuma Elish and Atrahasis a god is killed as part of the process of creating humanity, and in Egypt Osiris is killed by Seth. Thus, it is not the case that death somehow strips them of their divine status (contra, for example, deClaisse-Walford et al., *Psalms*, 643).

94. For a full discussion of the trope, see Van Leeuwen, "Proverbs 30:21–23 and the Biblical World Upside Down."

eat, a contemptible woman who gets married, and a servant who displaces her mistress." The image of the trembling earth is similar to "the foundations of the earth are shaken" in Psalm 82, though the word in Proverbs (*rāgaz*) is different than the one in Psalms (*môṭ*). Nonetheless, the passage in Proverbs is describing a condition of social upheaval, not listing offenses that are particularly abhorrent to Yahweh, and the same is true of Psalm 82. (It is also worth noting that at least two of the conditions mentioned in Proverbs 23—the elevation of the two servants—would be seen as positive events according to modern social ideals, though in context all four are supposed to be negative.) In Israel's prophetic literature the world-upside-down motif is commonly associated with the "day of the LORD," which prior to the exile is negative (indicating the beginning of the exile), but during or after is positive (indicating the restoration). Psalm 82 contains aspects of both, juxtaposing the inverted order of the shaking earth and social chaos (representing the exilic state, or perhaps the state of apostate Israel; compare Hab 1:2–4) with the inverted order of the dying gods (representing the restoration state; compare Hab 3:6, 11). Failing to uphold justice in society *can* be a crime, as we see in, e.g., Exodus 23:6, but the emphasis here on the upheaval of the earth—and, of course, the attribution of the condition to Yahweh, though the standard reading does not acknowledge this—indicate that Psalm 82 is more interested in the condition itself (disorder) than in the act that caused it (potentially, offense). Thus, the imagery of the psalm is a literary device used to convey its message, not a list of offenses that are revealed as particularly and universally offensive to Yahweh.

A final consideration is simply methodological. Several advocates of the standard interpretation note that the particular message they ascribe to the psalm is unique and unprecedented in the Bible.[95] While we should not necessarily expect the Bible to be homogenous, a radical departure from the prevailing trends should serve as a red flag that the interpretation may not be correct and indicate a need for much closer examination, as we have done here and subsequently concluded that the actual message is well in keeping with Old Testament themes. Even if the unique reading does turn out to be correct, a careful systematic theology should treat odd passages as outliers, not use them as the basis of a new theology that radically reinterprets and distorts a large number of clearer texts, as conflict theologians are inclined to do with Psalm 82.

In conclusion, we can affirm that Psalm 82 does indeed depict the *ĕlōhîm* as divine beings distinct from Yahweh, as we would expect to find in the context of the ancient cognitive environment. However, we claim that the biblical text does not affirm its references. The purpose of the psalm is not to affirm for its readers that there really are such beings, or to reveal that certain manifestations of social unrest are in fact caused by these beings. The gods are not depicted as the cause of the chaotic condition of the world and are not depicted as evil or opposed to Yahweh; neither are they sentenced to death for crimes against God and humanity. The point of their death is to demonstrate

---

95. Hossfeld and Zenger, *Psalms 2*, 337: "this psalm, both in terms of the history of religions and in systematic theology, is original and unique." See also Goldingay, *Psalms 42–89*, 569.

a wholesale inversion of the world order, not to reveal, declare, or celebrate that the gods will die. However, the fact that this particular inversion was chosen—as opposed to, say, mountains collapsing or the sun going dark—is not accidental and serves to re-affirm that the gods (or human rulers, whichever the word represents) are impotent and their death is evidence of their weakness. The affirmation of the psalm is not that the gods will be punished for causing chaos, but rather that it is Yahweh alone (and not the gods) who can rectify chaos, and as such it is to Yahweh alone that the psalmist appeals. The psalm is thus fully in keeping with the consistent themes of the psalms and the prophets that deliverance comes through Yahweh alone. It does not give us any information concerning conflict in the divine realm with demonic, rebellious gods of the nations standing against the will of Yahweh, and does not offer a biblical view of cosmic warfare or the role of demons.

Other supposed references to the evil of the gods

Most depictions of the gods of the nations as evil demons opposed to the will of Yahweh are based primarily on Psalm 82, Daniel 10, and Genesis 6, but a smattering of other references are occasionally invoked in support, which we will now briefly examine.

Isaiah 24:21 states that "In that day the LORD will punish the powers in the heavens above and the kings on the earth below." Some interpreters propose that the "powers above" (lit. "host of the heights," *ṣĕbaʾ hammārôm*) refers to divine beings, and compare the event with the death of the gods in Psalm 82:7.[96] This reading is supported by a comparison to Isaiah 34:4, where "All the stars in the sky (lit. "hosts of heaven," *ṣĕbaʾ haššāmayim*) will be dissolved and the heavens rolled up like a scroll; all the starry host (*ṣĕbāʾām*, "their host") will fall." "Host of heaven" and "host of the heights" are seen to be parallel. The same phrase "hosts of heaven" (NIV "starry host") is worshipped by Manasseh in 2 Kings 21:3 and refers to astral deities. The word "punish" (*pqd*) in Isaiah 24:21 means "to put in place";[97] When used with a divine subject, it carries a sense of "decreeing a destiny."[98] The destiny that is decreed can be positive as well as negative: see Exodus 3:16 (NIV "watched over"); Ruth 1:6 (NIV "come to the aid of"); and Psalm 8:4 (NIV "care for"). Further, the destiny is not always decreed on the basis of merit, as all three positive examples show. Here in Isaiah the destiny is negative, paralleled with "shut up in prison" (Isa 24:22). While this fate is different than the death of the gods in Psalm 82, the passage is still often interpreted as confirming that Yahweh will inflict some sort of penalty on the gods for unspecified but nonetheless inferred sins (perhaps from Isa 24:5).[99] However, in context, we should note that both Isaiah 24 and 34 are

96. See for example Page, *Powers*, 60.
97. Creason, "PQD Revisited," 30.
98. Gunnel André, *Determining the Destiny*, 241.
99. See Page, *Powers*, 61.

judgment oracles that invoke the imagery of macrocosmic collapse. In Isaiah 24:18–20 "The floodgates of the heavens are opened, the foundations of the earth shake. The earth is broken up, the earth is split asunder, the earth is violently shaken [*môṭ*, the same word in Ps 82:5]. The earth reels like a drunkard, it sways like a hut in the wind." In Isaiah 24:4 "The earth dries up and withers, the world languishes and withers, the heavens languish with the earth." Likewise, in Isaiah 34:4 "the heavens [will be] rolled up like a scroll" and in Isaiah 34:9–10 "[the] streams will be turned into pitch, [the] dust into burning sulfur; [the] land will become blazing pitch." These are all instances of the "world upside down" that invokes the catastrophic upheaval that accompanies the wrath of Yahweh, which we also saw in Psalm 82, but neither the imagery nor the verb *pqd* indicate that the displaced or disrupted elements have earned their condition. The cosmic collapse is a frequent feature of the "day of the LORD," as for example in Joel 2:10: "the earth shakes, the heavens tremble, the sun and moon are darkened, and the stars no longer shine." However, Joel is not normally read to be passing judgment on the sun and moon. The imagery of the kings and the gods together going down into prison in Isaiah 24:22 is likewise part of the overall state of upheaval, but we should not necessarily assume that they are singled out for offense against Yahweh, any more than we should assume that the shame and dismay of the sun and moon (Isa 24:23) is due to offense against Yahweh. The fall of the kings (macropolitical elements) and of the astral deities (macrocosmic elements) indicates the vast scale of the upheaval of the LORD's judgment, not crimes of the kings and gods per se.

Technically the "hosts of heaven" are the stars, celestial bodies comparable to the sun and moon, but they were also worshipped as gods,[100] just as the sun and moon also were (though these are not "punished" [*pqd*] in Isaiah). The Israelite audience probably would not have distinguished between "the fall of the macrocosmic elements" and the "fall of the things that were revered as gods," and so it is worth examining the implications of this connotation as well. Egypt is turned upside down in Isaiah 19— wise men become fools (Isa 19:11), rivers run dry (Isa 19:6), and brothers will fight each other (Isa 19:2)—and the gods are caught up in it along with their worshippers (Isa 19:1; see also Ezek 30:13). Thus, the fact that the gods are caught up in the chaos emphasizes the impotence of the gods, as we also proposed was the case in Psalm 82. In neither case, however, is the chaos presented as a consequence for anything the gods have done, any more than it is presented as a consequence for anything the sun or the moon have done. The gods (and the kings) are a source of stability for the world and their fall indicates the loss of that stability.

First Samuel 16 contains several references to an "evil spirit from the LORD" that torments Saul (1 Sam 16:14, 16; 19:9). The Hebrew word *ra'* ("evil") is not necessarily a moral designation—its semantic range is similar to English *bad*[101]—and here refers

100. For equation of deities and stars in the ancient Near East see Rochberg, "'The Stars Their Likeness.'"

101. Walton and Walton, *Lost World of the Israelite Conquest*, 153–54.

to the fact that the spirit is inflicting harm. Yahweh threatens Israel with *ra'* in Deuteronomy 30:15 and Joshua 23:15 (NIV "destruction"); Yahweh shoots Israel with "*ra'* and destructive arrows of famine" (NIV "deadly," Ezek 5:16); God brings *ra'* against Egypt (NIV "disaster," Isa 31:2); God brings both prosperity and *ra'* (NIV "disaster," Isa 45:7); Yahweh sends "*ra'* judgments" on Jerusalem (NIV "dreadful," Ezek 14:21); Micah claims that "*ra'* has come from the LORD" (NIV "disaster," Mic 1:12); and Job accepts both good and *ra'* (NIV "trouble," Job 2:10) from God (cf. Eccl 7:14).[102] Thus, we should not see this passage as an affirmation that, while God does indeed have "evil" enemies, they can be co-opted to serve his purposes.[103] There is no indication that the spirit is anything other than an agent of Yahweh.

Similarly, God sends an "evil spirit" (NIV "stirred up animosity") on Abimelech in order to punish him for killing his brothers (Judg 9:23–24). This may be a euphemistic expression for a mood (as NIV) or it could refer to an agent sent to cause disruption. Such an agent is described explicitly in 1 Kings 22:19–22, where the prophet Micaiah observes the divine council in session plotting the downfall of Ahab. One of those present—perhaps a counselor, perhaps not—volunteers to "be a deceiving spirit" and trick Ahab's prophets into predicting victory so Ahab will go to his death. Once again, there is no real indication that this spirit (whatever it is) is *always* a "spirit of falsehood" (*šqr*) that usually opposes God but in this instance is co-opted for his purposes; neither can *šqr* be seen as inherently sinful, because it is credited to Yahweh in 1 Kings 22:23. Page compares this spirit to the *śāṭān* in Job, claiming that "here, as there, it involves an attempt to seduce humans to sin."[104] However, in 1 Kings 22, there is no "sin" involved; the spirit is enticing (*pātah*) Ahab to go to his death in battle, not to sin. Neither should we make too much of the spirit's facilitating false prophecy; Ezekiel 14:9 also shows false prophets being used as an instrument of destruction, although in this case it is explicitly Yahweh who has inspired the false prophecy: "I the LORD have enticed (*pātah*) that prophet."[105] The message of all of these passages is not that Yahweh is sovereign enough to occasionally make use of his enemies to suit his purposes. The message is that the misfortunes experienced by Saul, by Abimelech, by Ahab, and by Ezekiel's contemporaries are manifestations of the judgment of God for specified offenses. The *means* by which that judgment is carried out is not especially significant; the details are not meaningless, but the actions fall within the understanding of what gods could and would do to dispense judgment in the context of the cognitive environment. The audience is supposed to understand God's manifested anger and its cause, not speculate about the operations of cosmic beings.

---

102. Paragraph reused from Walton and Walton, *Lost World of the Israelite Conquest*, 153.

103. Contra Page, *Powers*, 76–77.

104. Page, *Powers*, 78–79.

105. Contra Page, *Powers*, 79: "the primary reason for judging the spirit as evil is, of course, that it performs an evil function—it prompts Ahab's prophets to speak lies."

Finally, we should make note of Psalm 97:7, where the *ĕlôhîm*, also identified as *pesel* and *ĕlîl* (see chapter 11), are called on to worship Yahweh: "All who worship images (*pesel*) are put to shame, [as are] those who boast in idols (*ĕlîlîm*)—worship him, all you gods (*ĕlôhîm*)."[106] The word for "worship" that the gods are called to do (*ḥwh*, lit "bow down") can mean submission or surrender,[107] but in no other place in the Psalter is it used this way. In the Psalms the word signifies a gesture of honor and reverence and is not the kind of action that would be expected of enemies. The servants of the idols are shamed, but the gods themselves are not Yahweh's enemies, because they themselves worship him.

---

106. A textual variant of Deut 32:43 (attested in 4QDeutq but omitted in the MT) adds the line "bow to him, all gods (*ĕlôhîm*)." The LXX amends this to read "*sons of* God" (*huioi theou*), paralleling Ps 29:1 (NIV "mighty [ones]"; Heb. *bĕnê ĕlîm*). See Tigay, *Deuteronomy*, 516.

107. H. D. Preuss, "חוה," 251–52.

Chapter 13

The fall of Satan

T HE TERMINOLOGY OF SATAN'S "fall" (or that of the angels) can be used variously to refer to three different things. It can refer to an ontological transition whereby a creature, usually an angel, becomes a demon. It can also refer to a moral transition by which a good angel becomes a bad angel. Both of these are part of a larger discussion of how demons came to be. The fall can also refer to a transition in location, normally the physical movement from heaven to earth, as we saw in Revelation 12 (see discussion in chapter 10). Sometimes these events are thought to occur at the same time, and sometimes not. As such, the significance of the event for theology can vary by context. We will therefore discuss those passages in the Bible whose message is commonly thought to be conveying information about Satan's fall by providing details of when or why, or simply affirming with authority that such an event occurred.

Satan in the Old Testament

The English proper name *Satan* is a transliteration of the Greek *Satanas*, which in turn is a transliteration of a Hebrew word that means "accuser" or "adversary." In the Old Testament the word is possibly used once as a proper name (1 Chr 21:1) and elsewhere as a title; despite the common English translations in Zechariah 3:1–2 and Job 1–2 as proper names, the Hebrew of these passages includes a definite article (lit. "the śāṭān") and Hebrew does not use definite articles for personal names. Further, the title is not always applied to the *same* individual. The title is given to humans (Hadad the Edomite in 1 Kgs 11:14 and Rezon son of Eliada in 1 Kgs 11:23; NIV "adversary"), to unspecified divine beings (Zech 3:1–2; Job 1–2), and once to the Angel of the LORD (Num 22:22; NIV "to oppose"; lit. "as [a] śāṭān"). Further, *in no instance* is the bearer of the title portrayed as a fallen being in opposition to God. Hadad and Rezon are raised up against Solomon by Yahweh; Yahweh dispatches the śāṭān to strike Job (Job 1:12) and also takes credit for the devastation (Job 2:3). The Angel of the LORD of course is an agent of Yahweh. "Satan" in the Old Testament is an adversary, but not an adversary *of God*; the various individuals who fill this role are appointed *by* Yahweh as adversaries of those that *Yahweh* wishes to oppose.

1 Chronicles 21:1, where Satan is potentially mentioned as a proper name, has a parallel account in 2 Samuel 24:1. In Samuel, Satan is not mentioned; where Chronicles reads "Satan rose up against Israel and incited . . ." Samuel reads "the anger of the LORD burned against Israel, and *he* incited . . . ." The antecedent of the pronoun *he* is unclear, but it in no way refers to Satan. It refers either to "the anger" (a masculine singular noun; Hebrew pronouns match their antecedents in number and gender, even though the proper English idiom would be "it") or to "the LORD." If it means "the anger [of the LORD] incited David," then presumably the wrath of God (for unspecified offense) is being manifested somehow, and, upon observing this, David is inspired to take a census, presumably to collect a tithe to offer as a kind of appeasement. The appeasement mentality angers Yahweh further and leads to the plague. This reading perhaps fits best within the passage's own internal logic. Alternatively, if the passage means "the LORD incited David," then it is difficult to understand David's reaction in 2 Samuel 24:10 ("David was conscience-stricken . . . 'I have sinned greatly in what I have done . . . I have done a very foolish thing'"). God is only the subject of the verb *incite* (*sût*) in one other occurrence (1 Sam 26:19), where God (hypothetically) incites Saul to kill David. When used in a negative sense (i.e., Job 2:3; Isa 36:18; Deut 13:6; Jer 43:3) the action that one is incited *to* is inherently bad or harmful. Thus, this reading would imply something harmful or deleterious about the act of "[counting] the fighting men" that is not transparent to us, and the plague would be punishment for the harm inflicted by the action of the census.

Nonetheless, whichever way we choose to read Samuel, we cannot simply insert *Satan* where Samuel says *he*. In Chronicles, the burning anger of the LORD is not mentioned; therefore we could not possibly read the passage to say, "the anger of the LORD burned against Israel, and Satan used the opportunity to tempt David into taking a census."[1] "Satan," therefore, is portrayed as *an instrument of the* LORD, the agency by which the LORD incited David and/or the instrument by which the wrath that motivated David was manifested. The depiction of the *śāṭān* as an instrument of wrath is consistent with every other Old Testament appearance of the title,[2] which would also explain why "wrath" is not mentioned in Chronicles (since it would be redundant). Alternatively, if Chronicles is written late enough that the Second Temple understanding of "Satan" as a name for the "prince of darkness" character is already established, then the Chronicler could be embellishing the census episode by postulating that character's involvement (implicitly, in David's chosen response to his observation of God's burning wrath; for the significance of associating a person's actions with Satan in Second Temple literature, see chapter 14). However, if this is the case, then Chronicles cannot be *originating* the concept of Satan as a tempter and deceiver since that would be circular, and we recall that the biblical text does not

---

1. Contra Page, *Powers*, 36.

2. Even without the definite article in 1 Chr 21 it can still be a title preceded by an indefinite article, e.g., "an adversary," as is also the case in Num 22:22.

affirm its references (see chapter 1). The point of both 2 Samuel 24 and 1 Chronicles 21 is that David earned a punishment and God relented from carrying it through because of his love for Israel (2 Sam 24:16; 1 Chr 21:15), thus confirming David's affirmation that "[the LORD's] mercy is [very] great" (2 Sam 24:14; 1 Chr 21:13). The exact nature of the offense and the agencies involved are not meaningless but are nonetheless ultimately incidental to this point.

Zechariah 3:1–2 is thematically similar to 1 Chronicles 21 in that its subject is the LORD's relenting from a well-deserved judgment. Joshua the high priest, who is variously thought to represent either himself (unfit to serve), the priesthood in general (contaminated by impurity in a foreign land), or the nation of Israel as a whole (unclean from their covenant infidelity), comes before the LORD, while an accuser (lit. "the śāṭān") stands by to accuse him. The Lord rebukes the accuser (Zech 3:2), removes Joshua's unclean garments, and forgives his sin (Zech 3:4). Of interest to us is whether the śāṭān (which we recall is a title, not a name, contra NIV) is opposing the will and purposes of God as he accuses the high priest, or whether he functions as an instrument of judgment, as for example the angel of the LORD (as a śāṭān) functions against Balaam in Numbers 22:22.

The visions of Zechariah 1–6 as a whole depict the reconstruction of the temple, which also serves as a symbol for the restoration of the land and the renewal of the covenant. Halpern suggests that the imagery employed for the temple reconstruction invokes the *chaoskampf* motif[3] (see chapter 9). Therefore, it is theoretically possible that the śāṭān represents one of the forces of chaos that God is (in this instance, at least) opposing. Page places great emphasis on the "rebuke" of the śāṭān as evidence of his malicious intentions.[4] The same word, *rebuke* (Heb. *gā'ar*), is used to illustrate the *chaoskampf* against the sea in Psalm 106:9 and Nahum 1:4. However, closer examination indicates that the association of the śāṭān with chaos, and therefore with divine opposition, is unlikely. The word *gā'ar* does not necessarily indicate the *chaoskampf* theme or imply malfeasance or chaotic nature on the part of the referent: Ruth can potentially be rebuked for gleaning (Ruth 2:16), and insects in Malachi 3:11 are rebuked (NIV "prevented") from devouring crops. The word is therefore neutral and indicates, "make someone stop doing what they are doing" without commenting on the nature of the person or the action.[5] In fact, no motive is assigned to the śāṭān at all, only an action: "to *accuse* him" (śṭn, the verbal form of the noun śāṭān). In Psalm 71:13, "those who accuse (śṭn) me" is paralleled with 'those who want to harm me,'" and Psalm 109:6 parallels "accuser" (śāṭān) with "an evil person" (ra'). Clearly, then, the presence of the accuser is a very bad situation for Joshua. However, as we saw in chapter 7, ra' does

3. Halpern, "The Ritual Background."

4. Page, *Powers*, 32–33.

5. "Genesis 37:10 [where Jacob rebukes Joseph for his arrogant promulgation of his dreams] is the only passage that implies clear moral disapproval." A Caquot, "גער," 50.

not mean "immoral" or "opposed to God."[6] In Psalm 109, the psalmist is asking *God* to appoint the evil person/the accuser to stand against his enemies: "In return for my friendship they accuse (*śṭn*) me. . . . Appoint someone evil (*ra'*) to oppose my enemy; let an accuser (*śāṭān*) stand at his right hand. When he is tried, let him be found guilty" (Ps 109:4–6). Compare this to Zechariah 3:2: "[the angel] showed me Joshua the high priest standing before the angel of the Lord, and the *śāṭān* standing at his right side to accuse (*śṭn*) him." The parallel image of the accuser "standing at the right" and the trial image in Psalm 109 indicate that Joshua the high priest is on trial. In Psalm 109 the *śāṭān* has been appointed by God to bring misfortune on the psalmist's enemies; there is no reason to assume the *śāṭān* in Zechariah has not been similarly appointed to bring misfortune on Joshua.

The accusations (*śṭn*) against the psalmist in Psalm 109:4, for which the enemies are punished (ironically, by receiving an accuser of their own), are unfounded. However, in Zechariah 3, we see that the accusation against Joshua is not unfounded. Joshua's clothes are indeed filthy (Zech 3:3). The element of chaos that is removed in this passage is the filthy clothes, not the *śāṭān*; there is no indication that the *śāṭān* put the filth there or that he wants it to stay there. Joshua is on trial and the *śāṭān* is the prosecutor. Joshua should by all rights be tried and found guilty, yet he is not. Instead, the prosecutor is forcefully commanded to stand down. The intensity of the command indicates the intensity of God's desire to reinstate Joshua, not the intensity of his desire to be rid of the *śāṭān*, who has nothing to do with Joshua's present condition. Like the plague angel in 1 Chronicles 21:15, the *śāṭān* represents an instrument of wrath and judgment that is withdrawn. There is no indication that the character relishes the chance to accuse Joshua or resents his dismissal, or that his intentions are in any way opposed to the will and desires of God.

The *śāṭān* character in the prologue of Job is more complicated since the episode must be considered in light of the literary shape of the book as a whole. Page argues that the function of the *śāṭān* in Job is similar to his function in Zechariah; that is, he is a prosecutor pressing a case, there against Joshua and here against Job.[7] However, a closer examination of the prologue of Job indicates that it is not actually Job who is on trial.[8] What is actually on trial is an idea called the *retribution principle*, which is ubiquitous in the ancient Near East (and today as well) and states that the righteous will prosper and the wicked will suffer, each in proportion to the degree of their righteousness and wickedness. More specifically, what is on trial is God's policy of running the world in accordance with the retribution principle, as evidenced by his blessing of the righteous Job. The *śāṭān* argues that the practice of blessing the righteous actually inhibits the development of true righteousness, which should "serve God for nothing" (Job 1:9). If the righteous invariably prosper, then righteousness

6. Walton and Walton, *Lost World of the Israelite Conquest*, 153–54.

7. Page, *Powers*, 33.

8. This section adapted from Walton, *Job*.

becomes nothing more than a pragmatic means to achieve prosperity. He proposes that if Job's blessings are removed (Job 1:11) and replaced with afflictions (Job 2:5) that Job will demonstrate that he has no interest in righteousness for its own sake by cursing God to his face. This in turn will demonstrate that the retribution principle is flawed policy and that blessing the righteous inhibits righteousness. Thus, we see that the book overall is concerned with the question of the nature of righteousness, not with the question of Job's guilt or innocence.

It is important to remember that the genre of Job is wisdom literature, not cosmic historiography. All of the characters, including God and the *śāṭān*, are elements in what is essentially a thought experiment.[9] The purpose of the scene in the prologue is not to give a behind-the-scenes glimpse of the heavenly operations that result in suffering. Job is never told of the scene in heaven as an explanation for his ordeal, and we should not appropriate the scene as an explanation for our own experience of evil either. The text is not a theodicy, and its purpose is not to indicate that all human suffering begins with a challenge by Satan in heaven. Instead, the message is twofold. First, the *śāṭān*'s proposal is refuted. Job, despite the urgings of his wife and friends, does not curse God and does not attempt to regain his benefits, thus demonstrating that he did indeed serve God for nothing; blessing the righteous does not necessarily inhibit righteousness. However, in the process, Job offers a policy critique of his own. The *śāṭān* argued that blessing the righteous is counterproductive; Job in his turn argues that afflicting the righteous is unjust. God's response to Job's charge is that his governance of the world is not based on justice, but rather on wisdom. The retribution principle can serve God's purposes, as he demonstrates by restoring Job's blessings, but it is not the iron law by which the universe is governed and fates are decided. Because God's world runs on *wisdom* and not justice, there is not necessarily a reason for his actions (beneficial or otherwise) outside of his wisdom; note that in Job 2:3 God—importantly, *not* the *śāṭān*—has struck Job "without cause." Reasons for human suffering do not necessarily include evil on the part of the human, as Job's friends and the retribution principle imply, but neither do they include accusations and charges on the part of Satan. By construing the prologue as a theodicy wherein suffering is caused by Satan gaining permission to harm us, we in fact miss the point of the entire book.

If the character in Job is described as the accuser or adversary (*śāṭān*), *who* does he accuse and *of whom* is he an adversary? Certainly not Job. Job is introduced to the discussion by God (Job 1:8; 2:3); the *śāṭān* does not bring Job to God's attention. Neither is it implied, as Page suggests, that the "hedge" built around Job in Job 1:10 was specifically intended to prevent the *śāṭān* from harming Job in the past[10] and that he now relishes the opportunity. Similarly, it is difficult to see in what way the *śāṭān*

9. Walton, *Job*, 26–27. This does not necessarily mean that Job was not a real person, but the book of Job is a literary construct and its message and meaning does not change whether its characters are historical or literary (ibid., 27).

10. Page, *Powers*, 27–28.

can be opposing God. It is God who is encouraged to strike Job in Job 1:11 and 2:5; the text reads "stretch out *your* hand and strike," not "give *me* permission to strike." God immediately delegates the task back to the *śāṭān* (Job 1:12; 2:6), but he himself takes credit for the affliction: "you incited *me* against him to ruin him" (Job 2:3; compare Job 1:20 and 2:10 where Job attributes his affliction to God). As suggested previously, what the *śāṭān* is opposing is in fact a *policy*. Given the legal associations of the term in Psalm 109 and Zechariah 3, we should see the title as indicating a legal office. However, the character is not a prosecutor in a criminal case (as in Zechariah) because there is no criminal; neither Job nor God is on trial. Rather, he is more like a plaintiff in a civil suit, similar to the role a constitutional lawyer might play today when they bring a case against a particular law.

Finally, because the *śāṭān* is a character in a thought experiment, there is no use in speculating on his particular characteristics in a systematic treatment of celestial beings. Like any literary character, the attributes he is given serve only to facilitate his function in the narrative. Incidentally, a close examination of God's question "where have you come from?" indicates that the *śāṭān*'s presence is not expected,[11] which in turn indicates that he is not an ordinary member of the divine council (i.e., not one of the "sons of God" from Job 1:6; 2:1; see further discussion in chapter 12) since otherwise he would be expected to be there. This further supports the idea that his presence and subsequent challenge is a unique occurrence, not something that happens routinely whenever someone suffers. Nonetheless, it is useless to speculate on the character's taxonomy because we have also observed that the title *śāṭān* can apply to a wide variety of individuals; nobody today argues, based on Numbers 22:22, that the character in Job is the angel of the LORD. There is no indication in the text of Job that the character is a fallen being who opposes God;[12] further, even if it could be demonstrated that the Old Testament audience *knew of* a fallen being opposed to God, there is no indication that that individual is *this* individual. Two texts in particular are offered to support the idea that the ancient Israelites knew of a fallen being opposed to God; however, neither of them refer to that supposed character as *śāṭān*. Further, the assertion that they describe the fall of a celestial being is highly dubious. This we will now examine.

The kings of Babylon and Tyre: Isaiah 14 and Ezekiel 28

The two Old Testament passages that are commonly interpreted to describe the fall of Satan—Isaiah 14:12–15 and Ezekiel 28:2–19—do not actually mention Satan by name.[13]

11. See the only other occurrences of the collocation in Gen 16:8 (Hagar in the desert) and 2 Sam 1:3 (a foreign messenger [2 Sam 1:8, 13] bringing a report of Saul's death). Observation in class by Edvard Janvier.

12. Helpful discussion in White, *Yahweh's Council*, 109–19.

13. The name *Lucifer* in Isa 14:12 (KJV; NIV "morning star," Hebrew *hêlēl*) refers to the planet Venus and was ascribed to the devil only by association after the translation of the Vulgate. See full discussion of *hêlēl* in chapter 9.

Consequently, the persons they describe can only be inferred to be Satan by association. This in turn tends to make arguments that the passages must refer to Satan rather circular. Historically, the association of the passages with Satan derives from the claim that the qualities ascribed to the persons would not make sense if they were intended to *only* refer to the human kings against which the oracles are specifically directed. So, for example, Origen: "who is there that on hearing, '[You were the seal of perfection, full of wisdom and perfect in beauty. You were in Eden, the garden of God'; Ezek 28:12–13, NIV] or that '[You were anointed as a guardian cherub, for so I ordained you. You were on the holy mount of God'; Ezek 28:14, NIV] can . . . suppose that this language is used of some man?"[14] Thus, we will now examine how the imagery is used in its original context to see if it is true that it makes no sense as a reference to humans.

Isaiah 14 is explicitly a taunt against the king of Babylon (Isa 14:4) that takes the form of a sarcastic funeral lament. Ezekiel 28 is a similar taunt against the king of Tyre (Ezek 28:2, 12). If either of these are supposed to represent Satan, there are two ways in which they might do so. The first is that the prophet might interrupt his proclamation to the human king and begin to address the angelic figure directly. This is more commonly asserted for Ezekiel 28, where the variable titles "ruler (*nāgîd*) of Tyre" in Ezekiel 28:2 and "king (*melek*) of Tyre" in Ezekiel 28:12 are sometimes thought to represent the human and the angel, respectively. The second is that the king might be metaphorically compared to a figure that the original audience would have recognized to be Satan. This is more commonly assumed in Isaiah 14:12–14.

In Isaiah 14:12 the king of Babylon is metaphorically compared to a [presumably] mythographic character named *hêlēl ben šāḥar* (NIV "morning star, son of the dawn"). As discussed in chapter 9, modern scholars have no idea who this character is, though presumably the original audience would have. Consequently, the claim that the reference inherently (though implicitly) invokes a cosmic rebellion against heaven cannot be sustained.[15] None of the character's recorded ambitions—to ascend to the heavens, to sit above the stars and the clouds, to sit on Zaphon, or to be *like* the Most High— involve supplanting the ruling deity and reigning in his place, especially not if *hêlēl* originates from a polytheistic context. Further, the taunt is intended to *contrast* the king's current state with his lofty ambitions, not to *explain* his current status: "You said . . . *but* you are brought down" (Isa 14:13–16), as opposed to "you said . . . *therefore* you are brought down." The contrast between the king's boasts and his current state appears again in Isaiah 14:16–17: "Is this the man who shook the earth and made kingdoms tremble, the man who made the world a wilderness, who overthrew its cities and would not let his captives go home?" After this, an offense is finally ascribed to the king, but

14. Origen, *On First principles* 1.5.4, trans. Coxe, in *ANF* 4.258–59. It is worth mentioning that Origen does not actually identify the [angelic] guardian/ruler of Tyre with Satan or with the character in Isa 14; he only determines that it must be a celestial being and not a human king.

15. Contra, for example, Forsyth, *Enemy*, 134–35, who finds rebellion on the basis of an assumption that *hêlēl* is more or less a direct counterpart to the Canaanite Athtar and Greek Phaethon (see discussion in chapter 9), not on the basis of anything Isaiah says.

it is not the aspiration to rule in heaven, or even any of the sins traditionally ascribed to the devil (pride or envy): "you have destroyed your land and killed your people" (Isa 14:20).[16] If the king is supposed to parallel the mythic character *hêlēl* (whoever that is) in more than hubris and subsequent humiliation, we might suppose that *hêlēl* was an arrogant despot, but the text gives us no reason to assume that he was a rebel and that the desire to rule in heaven was an offense for which he was punished.

Ezekiel 28:2–19 contains two distinct subsections, the first in verses 2–11 and the second in verses 12–19. How they are interpreted varies based on whether they are conceived as a single continuous oracle to a single individual; as two parallel oracles to a single individual; or as two different oracles to two different individuals. If the oracle (linear or parallel) is addressing a single individual, then the situation is much the same as Isaiah 14; the king of Tyre is being metaphorically compared to someone that the audience will recognize by the imagery employed. However, as in Isaiah 14, there is no evidence that the imagery would have been recognized by an ancient Israelite as pointing to the character later called *Satan*. The passage refers to the character as a cherub (Ezek 28:14) in the garden of God (Ezek 28:13), which many interpreters assume is a reference back to the presence of the serpent (= Satan) in the garden in Genesis 3. However, as discussed in chapter 10, the Old Testament never identifies the serpent with Satan, and there is no extant Old Testament tradition that places Satan in the garden.[17] Further, the cherub in Genesis 3:24 is neither Satan nor the serpent, and neither is it fallen; its task is to guard the tree of life. Page suggests that the king is not being compared to an angel, but rather to the first *man*; the metaphor would then indicate that the king of Tyre has rebelled against God just as Adam supposedly did.[18] However, none of the details in Ezekiel (aside from the mention of the garden of God) parallel the account in Genesis in any way. Thus, not only is the imagery not a clear reference to Satan, it is not even a clear reference to *Genesis*.[19] Similarly to Isaiah 14, we can assume that the original audience would have understood who or what the metaphor was referring to, but we cannot identify the referent ourselves with enough certainty to use the association as the basis to speculate about cosmic metaphysics or the nature of characters found elsewhere in the text.

The other suggested option, as we saw above in Origen, is to propose that the second oracle is addressed to some angelic ruler over the city of Tyre, perhaps comparable to the princes of Persia and Greece in Daniel 10. However, this suggestion is problematic for several reasons. First, the title of the princes in Daniel is *śar*, while

16. J. J. M. Roberts suggests that the language specifically refers to Sargon, the contemporary Assyrian king who conquered Babylon and assumed its crown; Sargon died ignominiously and never received a proper burial. Roberts, *First Isaiah*, 207–13.

17. Walton, *Job*, 81.

18. Page, *Powers*, 41–42.

19. "Those who maintain this identification [of the king with Adam] are therefore obliged to posit a variant form of the Eden tradition in Ezekiel." Walton, *Job*, 82.

the title of the ruler of Tyre in Ezekiel 28:12 is *melek*. Second, this reading assumes that the imagery in the passage is not a metaphor, which, given the genre (oracular poetry), there is no good reason to do. Finally, and most importantly, judgment oracles not given against Israel (with the exception of Jonah) *are not actually delivered to the individuals to whom they are addressed.* As discussed in chapter 11, all of the judgment oracles against the nations are delivered to Israelites, in Israel. Prophecy as a genre delivers a declaration of divine intent; it does not predict the future or identify the functionaries behind cosmic operations (see chapter 3). Upon hearing this oracle, the audience would not have been expected to suddenly gain the understanding that Tyre was under the authority of a demonic ruler whose lordship caused its corruption, or to suddenly gain the understanding that the king of Tyre is only a prototype of a much more significant (and heretofore unknown) cosmic malefactor.[20] In general, the oracles against the nations serve as an exemplar for the judgment that is coming to Israel, or (less often, and usually after the exile) promise relief from enemies that Israel will experience. Israel's covenant infidelity stems from a desire to imitate the nations. If the power and splendor of even Babylon and Tyre cannot save them from Yahweh's destructive power, then all of the things that Israel trusts in will not be able to save Israel, either. Thus, even if the passage *is* addressed to Tyre's god, the message is no different than the oracles against the idols found elsewhere: the idols are powerless to prevent their own destruction (see chapter 11). However, the only way the Israelite audience would have identified the referent of the oracle *as* the celestial ruler of Tyre is if they already had an idea that cities were ruled by celestial beings (as we do when we interpret the passage that way). Cities do have patron deities; however, the *kĕrûbîm* are not gods, and so we would not expect to hear a deity identified as a *cherub*. As discussed in chapter 7, the cherubim are the celestial equivalent of domesticated animals; they guard sacred space and pull chariots. They do not rule over things. Further, we would expect the title to be "idol(s) of Tyre," not "king of Tyre" if a god was the intended referent. Consequently, the natural reading would be to assume that the language refers to the human king as a metaphor.

In conclusion, we have no good reason to suppose that any of the references in these passages evidence an ancient Israelite prototypical knowledge of a rebellious angelic character who was punished for opposing God and who would later be clarified to have the name Satan. Of course, even if it did indicate such knowledge, the Bible does not affirm its references; Israelite belief in something does not mean that this thing is the authoritative message communicated by the biblical text. Likewise, there is not enough information in these passages to *provide* the original audience with such knowledge if they did not have it already. The association of the characters in these passages with Satan only occurs after the development of the Satan character in the Second Temple period, which we will now briefly examine.

---

20. Contra Boyd, *God at War*, 160–64.

The fall of Satan in the Second Temple period

As discussed in chapter 9, the character of the devil emerges in the Second Temple period as part of the shifting cognitive environment of the time. In some accounts, the character is created to be as he is; in the Dead Sea Scrolls the prince of darkness is created and empowered to oppose the prince of light (see chapter 9) and in *Jubilees* Mastema (Satan) is given command of a tenth of the demons in order lead humans astray because of their wickedness (*Jub.* 10:8). In other accounts, however, he is depicted as a fallen being who was originally created to be something other than what he became. These accounts influence the way that the various "satan" characters in the Old Testament eventually came to be interpreted.

One of the most detailed accounts of Satan's fall is found in the *Life of Adam and Eve*, which we introduced in chapter 10. The account is found only in the later Latin version of the text, and the antiquity of the passage cannot be determined with certainty. Here Satan is explaining to Adam why he (Satan) has conspired to ruin humankind. When Adam was created, God called all of the angels to worship Adam because Adam was the image of God. Satan responds that he was created before Adam and therefore it is Adam who ought to worship *him*. Michael warns Satan that God will be angry, wherein Satan responds that "if [God] be wrathful with me, I will set my throne above the stars of heaven and will be like the Most High," in reference to Isaiah 14:13–15,[21] at which point he is promptly flung out of heaven. Satan then explains that he wished for Adam to be expelled from paradise in the same way that he was expelled from heaven.[22] This stated motive equates the fate of Satan with the fate of Adam, which, as suggested in chapter 10, was also construed to parallel the fate of Israel. Thus, the pattern of command (here, to worship Adam) → disobedience → expulsion, which Israel experienced at the exile and subsequently read back into Genesis 3, is applied even to Satan.

Most early references to the fall of the devil, however, are either vague or confused. Wisdom of Solomon 2:24 says that "through the devil's envy death entered the world," which refers specifically to envy as the devil's motivation to tempt Adam and Eve, but may also imply that envy motivated him to become the devil, and *2 Enoch* (first century CE[23]) depicts a cadre of angels in torment because they "of their own will plotted and turned away with their prince."[24] These malefactors are distinguished from the followers of Shemihazah (here called *Satanail*) whose offense was described in *1 Enoch* (see chapter 9) and who are seen imprisoned elsewhere (*2 En.* 18.1–9).[25]

21. *Vit. Ad.* 15.3, trans. Andersen, in *OTP* 2:262.

22. *Vit. Ad.* 12.1—16:3.

23. Andersen, "2 (Slavonic Apocalypse of) Enoch," 94–97.

24. *2 En.* 7:3 (long recension), trans. Andersen, in *OTP* 1:114. The short recension reads, "they are evil rebels against the Lord who . . . consulted their own will" (ibid., 115).

25. The long recension adds asides to compare the two groups of angels: "They turned away with their prince and with those who are under restraint in the fifth heaven" in 7:3, and, of the latter group,

Later, however, Satanail is associated with "one from the order of the archangels . . . [who] thought up the impossible idea, that he might place his throne higher than the clouds which are above the earth, and that he might become equal to [God's] power."[26] These two uses of the same name effectively conflate Isaiah 14:14 with *1 Enoch* 6.3–5 (and through Enoch with Gen 6:1 also), a trend that continues throughout the reception history of the material, even though it is unwarranted from either biblical text-in-context. The *Apocalypse of Abraham* (first/second century CE[27]) equates Azazel (from *1 En.* 8.1, identified as a cohort of Shemihazah in *1 En.* 6.7) with the serpent (*Apoc. Abr.* 23.12) and suggests that he deviated from his created state: "the garment which in heaven was formerly [Azazel's] has been set aside for [Abraham], and the corruption which was on [Abraham] has gone over to [Azazel]."[28] Thus, we see that the chronology, conditions, motives, and consequences of Satan's fall are non-systematic and rather muddled. Consequently, we should not imagine that there is a monolithic "fall of Satan" narrative that can be read as a subliminal background to the New Testament. Individual *traditions* may be referenced, but that would have to be determined from context, which we will now examine.

The fall of Satan in the New Testament

Most of the reception of the New Testament's Satan character assumes that he is a fallen being simply by virtue of the fact that he is both evil and extant. Explicit reference to Satan's fall is only made twice, and both are highly dubious as to what exactly they refer to. In Luke 10:18 Jesus states that he "saw Satan fall like lightning from heaven" and Revelation 12:8–9 says that the dragon, identified as Satan, together with his angels "lost their place in heaven" and were "hurled to earth." An additional reference to "angels who sinned" is found in 2 Peter 2:4 and repeated in Jude 6, which is a reference to *1 Enoch* (see chapter 14), but could include Satan as well if Satan and the Enochian watchers are conflated together (which *1 Enoch* does not do but *2 Enoch* does). Finally, 2 Corinthians 11:14 ("Satan himself masquerades as an angel of light") is sometimes interpreted to mean that Satan at one point *was* an angel of light. We will therefore examine these passages to determine what they actually say and whether any of them in context are intended to convey information about Satan or his angels.

Luke 10:18 is set in the context of the dispatch of seventy-two disciples, which is recorded only in Luke (Luke 10:1–23). The disciples are not sent out specifically

---

"similar to them are those . . . who are in the second heaven [i.e., the former group] imprisoned in great darkness" (18:3). The first group are left until the day of judgment, but Enoch encourages the second group to resume their liturgy of praise to the Lord, which they do.

26. *2 En.* 29.3–5, trans. Andersen, in *OTP* 1:148. The account is from the longer recension only.

27. Rubinkiewicz, "Apocalypse of Abraham: A New Introduction and Translation," 683.

28. *Apoc. Abr.* 13.14, trans. Rubinkiewicz, in *OTP* 1:695.

to confront demons; the instructions detailed in Luke 10:3–16 do not include exorcisms.[29] Nonetheless, upon returning, they announce, perhaps with surprise, that "even the demons submit to us in your name" (Luke 10:17). Jesus responds with the reply "I saw Satan fall like lightning from heaven. I have given you authority to trample on snakes and scorpions and to overcome all the power of the enemy; nothing will harm you" (Luke 10:18–19). From the context, the response appears to be intended to explain *why* the demons submit. Thus, we must ask how Jesus's observation of Satan falling from heaven furnishes an explanation.

Many interpreters want to read the passage as a reference to Isaiah 14:12 ("How you have fallen from heaven"), often drawing a parallel between Luke 10:15 ("you, Capernaum, will you be lifted to the heavens? No, you will go down to Hades") and Isaiah 14:13, 15 ("You said . . . I will ascend to the heavens. . . . But you are brought down to the realm of the dead"). In this reading, Jesus's statement is a natural extension of the reference.[30] However, the association is dubious. Luke 10:12–16 are clearly a single unit of discourse, separated from Luke 10:17–20 by a narrative break. It would be very odd, then, for a literary reference to begin in Luke 10:15 and then jump to Luke 10:18. Also, a reference to Isaiah 14 would be more likely to compare Capernaum with Babylon, rather than Sodom, Tyre, and Sidon. Further, the phrase "[be] lifted to the heavens" (*eōs ouranou hupsōtheisē*) is different from "ascend to the heavens" in the LXX of Isaiah 14:13 (*eis ton ouranon anabēsomai*),[31] and Isaiah 14:12 makes no reference to lightning. Further, in Isaiah 14, all of the statements have the same referent (the Babylonian king, perhaps personifying *hêlēl*), and so "fallen from heaven" is essentially a parallel statement to "go down to the realm of the dead." In Luke 10, however, the two statements have different referents; it is unlikely that "Satan" in Luke 10:18 is personifying the city of Capernaum, which has indeed "fallen," as it was prophesied to do in Luke 10:15. Yet that is the most natural reading if Luke 10:15–18 is a reference to Isaiah; Chorazin, Bethsaida, and Capernaum have rejected the disciples (Luke 10:11) and now their fates are sealed (Luke 10:12). Jesus's transitive argument in Luke 10:16 has been confirmed by the power of his name (Luke 10:17), and now the fate of the cities, metaphorically personified as Satan—compare to Matthew 16:23/Mark 8:33 where Peter is metaphorically personified as Satan—will be the same as that of Babylon as

29. Page, *Powers*, 109. Page does, however, note that the commissioning of the seventy-two is similar to the commissioning of the twelve (Matt 10:1–15; Mark 6:7–13; Luke 9:1–6), which does include conferring authority to cast out demons.

30. See for example Green, *Luke*, 418; Edwards, *Luke*, 310.

31. The root in Luke 10:15 is *hupsoō* "to raise high"; cf. John 3:14. The root in Isa 14:13 is *anabainō*, "to move upward." Both are used together in Acts 2:33–34; Christ is exalted (*hupsoō*), but David did not ascend (*anabainō*). However, the concepts are not sufficiently parallel to conclude that the one who is exalted is the one who ascends. *Anabainō* never refers to an increase in status, as *hupsoō* does in both Acts 2:33 and Luke 10:15; the "ascension" of the king of Babylon is hubristic bluster, not a metaphor for social or political advancement. Thus, the "rising up" in Isa 14 and Luke 10:15 are not conceptually similar. Hays, for example, does not even recognize the passage as a reference to Isa 14 at all (Hays, *Echoes of Scripture in the Gospels*).

described in Isaiah. However, no interpreter chooses to read the text in this way, which in turn means the reference to Isaiah is unlikely.

If both the reference and the conventional reading are to be maintained, the reading would presuppose an existing fall narrative such that using the words "Satan" and "fall" (*piptō*) together would automatically invoke Isaiah 14. However, such an existing narrative cannot be clearly attested. Further, while the association of Satan and Isaiah 14 is demonstrably established in Second Temple conception as described above, that association is established by the phrase "I will make myself like the Most High" (Isa 14:14) rather than the phrase "how you have fallen from heaven." The traditions also prefer to describe Satan's fate using transitive or causative verbs (flung out, expelled) rather than intransitive verbs (fell). What exactly the reference would signify in context beyond a generic acknowledgment of an established property of the Satan character cannot be speculated without specific knowledge of the hypothetical narrative that is being referenced.

Alternatively, the statement in Luke 10:18 might not be a reference to Isaiah 14 at all; this is probably more likely. This poses the question of *when* Jesus saw Satan fall from heaven. Most commentators agree that the reference is not likely to be invoking a primordial event. If a primordial event is intended, the statement is comparable to "before Abraham was born, I am" in John 8:58, and would signify Jesus explaining the source of the power of his name (i.e., divine identity). However, Green notes that Luke does not normally emphasize Christ's preexistence,[32] and also that Luke does tend to emphasize demonic activity as persistently *ongoing*, not as an event in the distant past.[33] Combined with the immediate context of the successful exorcisms of the seventy-two, it seems most likely that the fall of Satan occurred as a result of their activities on their mission.[34] Consequently, there is no reason to associate this "fall" with the primordial expulsion from heaven that results from a desire to "be like the Most High" that is found in Second Temple literature.

Nonetheless some question remains as to whether the fall of Satan "like lightning" is a symbol of defeat (as in Isa 14) or a gesture of aggression. Lightning is a weapon of the gods in Israel, in the ancient Near East, and in Greece, although the normal word for Zeus' thunderbolt (*keraunos*) is different than the word used in Luke (*astrapē*), which usually refers to the meteorological phenomenon.[35] In 1 Kings 18:38, fire (Heb. *ēš*, LXX *pur*) "falls from heaven" to consume Elijah's sacrifice.[36] This word is also different from the word in Luke, but does occasionally mean [meteorological]

---

32. Green, *Luke*, 419 n. 68.

33. Green, *Luke*, 419.

34. Bock, *Luke 9:51—24:53*, 1006–7; Stein, *Luke*, 310; Garland, *Luke*, 429.

35. See both used to together (as the attributes of Zeus) in Aristotle, *On the Universe*, 401a15.

36. The word "fall" (Heb. *npl*) is the same in both 1 Kgs 18:38 and Isa 14:12. The word used in the LXX (*exepesa*) is also the same in both and is a variant of *echpiptō*, which in turn shares the same root with the word used in Luke 10:18 (*piptō*).

lightning (e.g., Exod 9:24; Pss 18:12; 105:32; 148:8). In the LXX *astrapē* exclusively translates *bārāq*, which can be a divine weapon (2 Sam 22:15; Pss 18:14; 144:6; perhaps also Deut 32:41; Ezek 21:10; Hab 3:11). If this meaning is intended, then the phrase "I saw Satan [coming down like a bolt of lightning]" would be conceptually similar to Peter's warning that "Your enemy the devil prowls around like a roaring lion looking for someone to devour" (1 Pet 5:8) and in context would be cautioning the disciples not to get too cocky about their ability to command the demons. This warning would then be tempered with the assurance that "I have given you authority . . . to overcome all the power of the enemy; nothing will harm you" (Luke 10:19). However, the inexactness of the words renders the conclusion uncertain. Consequently, most commentators interpret the metaphor of lightning to indicate speed and suddenness[37] rather than destructive violence (i.e., a "flash of lightning" rather than a "bolt of lightning"). The same word is used as a metaphor for brightness or brilliance ("his appearance was like lightning") in Matthew 28:3 (also LXX Dan 10:6), but it is difficult to see how that would make sense in the context of Luke 10:18.[38]

At the same time, we might note that defeat and aggression are not mutually exclusive. In Revelation 12:9, the dragon (Satan) is hurled to earth in defeat, but in Revelation 12:12 he has "gone down . . . filled with fury." Many commentators note the similarity between Luke 10:18 and Revelation 12:9, and indeed speculate that both accounts may be referring to the same event.[39] Revelation does not offer enough details to identify what precisely triggered the "war in heaven," and the suggestion that it was the mission of the disciples in Luke 10 is as likely as any.[40] Once again, then, the war in heaven and the deposition of the dragon in Revelation 12 are unrelated to the traditions of primordial events wherein Satan was expelled from heaven for wishing to be like the Most High. Indeed, if Satan only loses his place in heaven (Rev 12:8) in response to the work of Christ through his disciples, that would mean that Revelation is referring to a different strain of material entirely, one that has nothing to do with the idea of Satan and the angels being expelled from heaven at some point in Genesis.

We have already examined the character of the dragon in chapter 10, where we concluded that the title "serpent" in Revelation 12:9 refers not to the *nāḥāš* of Genesis 3 but to the Leviathan of Isaiah 27, which further removes the content from primordial events and the original tempter of Adam and Eve, and instead associates it definitively with the theme of the eschatological combat. We have already

37. Garland, *Luke*, 429; Stein, *Luke*, 310.

38. If the metaphor was supposed to invoke the shining brilliance of the morning star from Isa 14, it would read "like Heosphoros," not "like lightning."

39. Cf. Stein, *Luke*, 309.

40. Other popular interpretations point to the resurrection (perhaps due to the defeat of death and association of death with the devil in Heb 2:14) or to the ascension (perhaps due to the male child [Christ] being "snatched up to God" in Rev 12:5). However, we remember that the chronology of apocalypses is not necessarily intended literally, even when the referents of the symbols can be clearly identified.

discussed the significance of Revelation 12 in context in chapter 10. However, if Luke 10 and Revelation 12 both refer to the same event, then that would mean that Luke 10 also refers to the eschatological combat. This indeed is how the passage is commonly interpreted; Jesus's name subdues the demons and the devil is hurled from heaven, signaling the appearance of the true messiah and the beginning of the messianic age. However, in the eschatological battle tradition the defeat of the sons of darkness is not especially important in and of itself (see chapter 9); this is why Jesus makes a point to remind his disciples, "do not rejoice that the spirits submit to you, but rejoice that your names are written in heaven" (Luke 10:20). The defeat of the devil is a feature of the messianic age as Luke's audience understood the idea, but it is not the most significant feature and not the one they should emphasize. The real point is that Jesus is shown to be the true messiah and his followers are therefore the true people of God; this is what it means that their "names are written in heaven."[41] Unfortunately, many conflict theologians disregard this emphasis, teaching instead that the point of the passage is to reveal that there *are* such things as Satan and demons and further that an important—or even primary—task of the church is to do battle with them.[42] As discussed already, however, the purpose of the Bible's teaching is not to affirm its references. The eschatological combat has meaning to the original audience of Luke because of the cosmology and eschatology that they have inherited from their cognitive environment, and the text invokes that *meaning* in order to convey its message, which in this case is an affirmation of the identity of Christ and by extension of his people. Its intent is to communicate meaning, not to confirm all of the elements that produced the meaning that was assigned to the image. The text does not reference the material in order to place an authoritative stamp of approval for all time on the things that the audience happened to already believe. Consequently, passages like Luke 10:18 and Revelation 12:9 should be used to affirm the identity of Christ and his people as they were intended to do, not to speculate on the nature and status (or existence) of cosmic entities.

Another reference that the text does not affirm is found in 2 Peter 2:4 and repeated in Jude 6. Both are references to the Enochian tradition of the watcher angels (discussed in chapter 9) and both, in context, are dealing with the issue of various malefactors within the communities they address. Peter is worried about false prophets and false teachers (2 Pet 2:1) while Jude is worried about "ungodly people, who pervert the grace of our God into a license for immorality and deny Jesus Christ our only Sovereign and Lord" (Jude 4). Both include the watcher angels in a list of Old Testament examples of the judgment of God. Peter lists them with antediluvian humanity and Sodom and Gomorrah in contrast to Noah and Lot (2 Pet 2:4–7), while Jude lists them with the wilderness generation in Numbers, Sodom and Gomorrah,

41. See for example Twelftree, *Name of Jesus*, 141.

42. See for example Boyd, *God at War* 190–91; McDermott, *God's Rivals*, 79–80; Arnold, *Powers*, 83–85.

Cain, Balaam, and Korah (Jude 5–7, 11). Peter references the watcher angels in order to emphasize that "the Lord knows how . . . to hold the unrighteous for punishment on the day of judgment. This is especially true of those who follow the corrupt desire of the flesh and despise authority" (2 Pet 2:9–10). Presumably, this last comment is a jab at the "false teachers." As we saw in chapter 9, the Enochian watchers both despised authority and followed the desire of the flesh, and so they serve as prime exemplars of Peter's point. In Jude, the watcher angels serve as a transition between the offenses of the wilderness generation (who implicitly despised their status as the chosen people by "refusing to believe") and Sodom and Gomorrah, who "gave themselves up to sexual immorality and perversion" (Jude 5–7). The Enochian watchers both despised their status—"did not keep their positions of authority but abandoned their proper dwelling" (Jude 6)—and also engaged in sexual immorality (by marrying mortal women). Therefore, the watchers also serve as exemplars of the fate that will befall the malefactors of the community, who are accused of the same offenses of immorality and despising their status by denying Jesus Christ: "They serve as an example of those who suffer the punishment of eternal fire" (Jude 7). Both passages therefore use the fate of the watchers and the details of their offense—which the audience already knew about—as one example among many to make a point about the inexorability of the judgment of God on those who do evil. They are not intended to affirm the actions or qualities of celestial beings and they are not intended to affirm that Enoch's interpretation of Genesis 6 was accurate.

Finally, 2 Corinthians 11:14 does not affirm that Satan used to be an angel of light. It also does not affirm that there is, in fact, a being called Satan who can, in fact, appear as an angel of light, as if this was something the audience did not already know. In *The Life of Adam and Eve* the devil appears as an angel when Eve meets him in the garden,[43] and he again takes the form of an angel in order to trick Eve into abandoning her penance in the Tigris.[44] 2 Corinthians 11:14 is not a discussion on the attributes of celestial beings; rather, it invokes a known quality (deceptive appearance) of a known character (Satan) in order to characterize the false apostles and their ultimate destiny: "Their end will be what their actions deserve," which in turn is a reference to the fate of the sons of darkness in the context of the eschatological combat, since the false apostles are called servants of Satan (2 Cor 11:15; see chapter 14 for the significance of associating people with Satan). The warning is conceptually similar to that of Galatians 1:8, where the teacher of a false gospel should be anathematized even if it is "an angel from heaven," though of course this passage should not be taken to affirm that there *are* angels who preach false gospels, either. The point of 2 Corinthians 11 to warn against deception (implicit "not everyone who looks like an angel is an angel") and also to proclaim the fate of the false teachers using a known concept from the cognitive environment as an illustration, just as was also seen in Peter and Jude.

43. *Ap. Mos.* 17.1–2.
44. *Ap. Mos.* 29.15.

In conclusion, there are no passages in the New Testament that make clear reference to any of the various Second Temple traditions about Satan being cast out of heaven in primordial times for rebellion against God. Further, these traditions do not directly derive from any of the references to Satan in the Old Testament, either. Thus, we must conclude that the fall of Satan is simply not attested anywhere in the biblical text. While Satan (under various names) is a character who appears in the New Testament, and the background of that character as it is understood in the cognitive environment sometimes indicates that he fell, the text does not affirm everything the cognitive environment believes about the character simply by making reference to the character itself or to attributes or qualities it is already known to possess. The character is referenced in order to use the audience's knowledge of him to make a point. This use we will now examine.

Chapter 14

Demons and spirits in the age of the church

V IRTUALLY ALL INTERPRETERS RECOGNIZE that the portrayal of demons in the New Testament is significantly different from that of the Old, at least in terms of the emphasis they receive. Page suggests that the oppression of the Jewish nation under the Seleucids alerted their awareness to finally acknowledge the superhuman dimension of evil, toward which they had previously been more complacent.[1] Russell proposes that the change was motivated by a kind of cultural renaissance that led Israel to divorce itself from the barbarism of its history by partitioning the undesirable traits of its God onto someone else, who in turn became the devil: "The Hebrew sense of good and evil shifted from its previous emphasis upon ritual tabu in the direction of a practical and humane ethic of mutual human responsibility; . . . no longer easy in their minds about ascribing rapine and destruction to the will of their God, the Hebrews sought new theodicies. . . . The malignant destructive aspect of Yahweh was subtracted from him and ascribed to a different spiritual power, the Devil."[2] Some interpreters propose that the change is phenomenological, and that demonic activity on the earth actually increased in anticipation of Christ's incarnation.[3] In chapter 8, we proposed that the change arises from a cultural shift in the understanding of gods. Regardless of the reason, the paradigm shift means that New Testament statements cannot be lifted out of the text as propositions and combined with Old Testament texts lifted in the same way to produce a systematic portrait of demons and spirits. The Bible's texts are not propositions, they are a medium of communication. The Hellenistic world of the New Testament has a different vocabulary of ideas and images with which to convey its message, just as it also has a different language (Greek). But like the Old Testament, its content is chosen in order to convey a message within the context of the cognitive environment shared by the author and audience. That *message* is what we will now examine.

---

1. Page, *Powers*, 87–88.

2. Russell, *Devil*, 181–83.

3. "In the Bible demon possession is part of the upsurge of evil opposing Jesus in the time of his incarnation." Morris, *Matthew*, 208.

The temptation of Christ

The testing or tempting—the Greek word *peirazō* can be used for either—of Christ by Satan in the wilderness is recorded in Matthew 4:1–11; Mark 1:12–13; and Luke 4:1–13. Some interpreters use the narratives in these passages to extrapolate information about the properties and motives of the devil: whether he really has authority over "all the kingdoms of the world" (Luke 4:5–6);[4] whether he really desires to be worshipped (Matt 4:9; Luke 4:7);[5] whether tempting God's servants is a common practice of his such that Jesus's experiences can be vicariously applied to us;[6] whether the initiation of a test by the Spirit proves that Satan is under God's control regardless of his intentions;[7] and so on. However, we propose that the purpose of these passages (along with the rest of the Bible) should be seen as the communication of a message using existing ideas, not as revelation of new information about the devil. Nonetheless, for the sake of argument, we will suppose for a moment that the information about the devil contained in these passages *is* supposed to be new. If we had no prior knowledge of a person named "Satan" or "devil," what would these texts tell us about him?

Our first and most important observation is that, apart from the name, nothing in the character's behavior indicates that he is evil. Jesus is driven into the wilderness by the Spirit (Matt 4:1; Mark 1:12; Luke 4:1) where he meets a character who administers a test (*peirazō*). This is the same word that James 1:13 says that God never does, but it is also the same word that the LXX uses in Genesis 22:1 when "God tested Abraham." The difference between the verbs *tempt* and *test* is that testing hopes the subject will pass, or is interested to see *whether* the subject will pass; tempting hopes the subject will fail. All three Synoptics note that the initiative for the test rests with the Holy Spirit, and the text is ambivalent (again, apart from the name) as to whether the proctor of the test (Satan) has any separate agenda of his own, or whether he is simply carrying out a function he has been assigned as a divine agent, as we commonly see the satan character portrayed in the Old Testament (see chapter 13). However, the character of Satan *is*, in fact, familiar to the Second Temple audience, and his presence in the narrative automatically carries implications about the nature of the encounter. Nonetheless, the Gospel narratives are not *history* as we commonly understand the term; that is, their purpose is to interpret events, not to impartially record the details as a camera would have seen them (see chapter 2). Satan's presence is not a documentation of a phenomenon, reporting the name of the person that Jesus happened to speak to. The Gospels are not a documentary of events that happened in Judea and Galilee; their purpose is to present a particular interpretation of who Jesus is and what he has done. The Satan character, where present, is included in the

4. Page, *Powers*, 98; Boyd, *God at War*, 181; Arnold, *Powers*, 80.
5. Bovon and Koester, *Luke 1—9:50*, 144; Garland, *Luke*, 182.
6. See, for example, Arnold, *Questions*, 98.
7. See, for example, Page, *Powers*, 91, 99.

narrative deliberately by the Gospel writers, not to objectively affirm that he was there and did certain things, but in order to help the text convey the author's chosen message. What that message is in the temptation narrative depends on how the familiar Satan character is being used in this particular instance.

Some interpreters consider the episode to be a confrontation between the prince of light (Jesus) and the prince of darkness (Satan) and therefore see the narrative as invoking the eschatological battle motif.[8] This is theoretically possible, but a number of factors make this interpretation less likely. First, the eschatological conflict is normally depicted as carrying a kind of finality, where the devil will be defeated for the last time to usher in the messianic age. In this passage, however, the devil is not defeated but rather leaves "until an opportune time" (Luke 4:13). Likewise, most eschatological battle references in the New Testament focus on messianic identity; Jesus is depicted in the traditional role of the prince of light in order to convey the message "this is indeed the promised messiah." This does not, however, appear to be the purpose of the temptation narratives, which seem to emphasize Jesus completing a task rather than assuming a role; the ability to resist a personal temptation from the prince of darkness is not normally a feature of the messianic profile. Admittedly, however, the emphasis varies between accounts. In Matthew, the devil is forcefully dismissed, and in both Matthew and Mark the narrative is followed immediately by the proclamation of the dawning of the messianic age ("the kingdom of heaven has come near"; Matt 4:17; Mark 1:15). Page additionally notes that the announcement at Jesus's baptism that immediately precedes the temptation (Matt 3:17; Mark 1:11; Luke 3:21) is an invocation of the [messianic] passages Psalm 2:7 and Isaiah 42:1.[9] Thus, the battle motif is at least implicit and may well explain why the Gospel writers chose to identify the interlocutor with the *devil*, but it is not sufficient to explain why they felt it was necessary to include the temptation narrative in the first place.

Interpreters as far back as Irenaeus have recognized that the narrative of Jesus's life is presented in the [Synoptic] Gospels in such a way that it loosely parallels the history of Israel. Thus, the slaughter of innocents (Matt 2:16) parallels the decree of Pharaoh (Exod 1:22);[10] the flight and return to Egypt (Matt 2:13–14) parallels the exodus;[11] the Sermon on the Mount parallels the giving of the law;[12] the persecution of Jesus by the scribes and Pharisees parallels the persecution of the prophets by the kings;[13] the crucifixion parallels the exile;[14] and so on. The reason for the parallel narrative is to emphasize the resurrection, which reverses the crucifixion and represents

8. See for example Boyd, *God at War*, 187; Longman and Reid, *God is a Warrior*, 95–97.

9. Page, *Powers*, 93.

10. Hays, *Echoes*, 114–15.

11. Hays, *Echoes*, 113–14.

12. Hays, *Echoes*, 144.

13. Turner, *Matthew*, 559; Bock, *Luke 9:51—24:53*; 1122; Green, *Luke*, 475.

14. Hays, *Echoes*, 140.

the restoration, which reverses the exile. However, the resurrection does not merely recapitulate; it brings the two narratives together because the new covenant that the resurrection inaugurates *is* the restoration of Israel. This identification of the new covenant as the promised restoration, and consequently of the people of the new covenant—that is, the Christians—as the remnant of Israel, is arguably one of the dominant themes throughout the entire New Testament. Thus, the vignettes that are found in the Gospels are selected and presented in such a way that they enforce the parallelism of the narratives.

The temptation narrative in particular is important for the parallel narrative structure because, as virtually all commentators recognize, it recapitulates the experience of the Israelites in the wilderness.[15] Consequently, the nature and substance of *the test itself* is derived from the content of Israel's historical narratives, and not, as is commonly supposed, from the motives and desires of the devil. The point of the temptation narrative is that Jesus in the wilderness succeeds where Israel in the wilderness failed. So in Numbers 11:4–34 the Israelites complain to God for food even though they are well-fed on manna; Jesus refuses the temptation for food even though he is genuinely starving (Matt 4:2; Luke 4:2). In Exodus 17:7 the Israelites demand a sign from the LORD even though they had just witnessed the deliverance of the Red Sea and the provision of manna;[16] Jesus refuses the temptation to ask for a sign (Matt 4:6; Luke 4:10–11) even though he has seen nothing so spectacular. Finally, the Israelites worshipped other gods (e.g., Exod 32:1–4; Num 25:1–3), and Ezekiel 16:31–34 implies that they did so even for nothing; Jesus, in contrast, refuses to worship not-God even in exchange for "all the kingdoms of the world" (Matt 4:8–9; Luke 4:6–7). The test proctor offers himself as the object of worship, but any not-God object would have sufficed; we should not infer from Matthew 4:9 and Luke 4:7 that the devil wants to receive worship[17] any more than we should infer from the other tests that the devil wants to see miracles (compare the Pharisees in Matt 12:38). The tests are derived from what *Israel* wanted, *not* from what the devil wants.

Even so, the depiction of the devil in the temptation narrative is not inconsistent with the profile of the devil that exists within the Second Temple cognitive environment, even though—as we saw in chapter 7—that profile is non-systematic and authors tend to pick and choose elements according to the needs of the moment. In the Qumran documents the prince of darkness and his minions seek to lead the sons of light astray,[18] which is the function often given to the devil here by interpreters. The

---

15. Luz, *Matthew 1–7*, 150; Blomberg, *Matthew*, 83; France, *Matthew*, 127–28; Osborne, *Matthew*, 128; Garland, *Luke*, 178; Green, *Luke*, 192–93.

16. The quote "Do not put the Lord your God to the test" in Matt 4:7 and Luke 4:12 is a reference to Deut 6:16, which in turn is a reference to Exod 17:1–7.

17. Contra for example Page, *Powers*, 97.

18. 1QS 3.18–24.

idea that the devil is given authority (compare Luke 4:6) is also found at Qumran,[19] and in *The Life of Adam and Eve* the devil desires to be worshipped by Adam.[20] Thus, the temptation narrative is not a story designed to provide new insight about what the devil is and does; it tells the audience nothing about the devil that they did not already believe. Neither is its purpose to stamp that prior understanding with divine authority for all time. Instead the point is to provide insight about what *Jesus* is and does. Jesus's life, death, and resurrection are tied to the nation and people of Israel and their restoration, and he can accomplish this restoration in part because he was faithful where Israel was not.

Exorcism

Enduring the temptation of the devil is not normally a feature of the messianic profile, but other passages do seem to be written to emphasize Jesus filling the preconceived role of the messiah and his ministry, meeting the expectations of the messianic age. Some of the most prominent passages that serve this function are the exorcism narratives, especially Legion of Gadara (Matt 8:28–34; Mark 5:1–20; Luke 8:26–39) and the Beelzebub Controversy (Matt 12:22–37; Mark 3:23–27; Luke 11:17–22). In general, exorcism narratives are written either to emphasize Jesus's power and authority, invoking the combat imagery of the eschatological battle, or they are written to emphasize the relief brought to the victim, which invokes the themes of healing and restoration that characterize the messianic age. In the combat passages the demons function as agents of opposition and darkness, similar to the way we commonly conceive of them today. In the healing passages, however, the demons are pathogenic and are simply present because in the first-century mindset demons happen to be the efficient causes of particular conditions, as is also their role in the ancient Near East. In this capacity they are more similar to what we call *viruses* than what we call *demons*, and so it is important not to mix the two roles[21] with sweeping conflations; for example, demythologizers often try to classify all demonic activity in the New Testament as disease—usually psychological disorders—in order to preserve their commitment to materialism, while conflict theologians often try to classify all exor-

---

19. 1QS 3.18–22.

20. *Vit. Ad.*, 14.3. It is worth noting that some scholars consider Mark's reference to the animals (Mark 1:13) to be an Adamic image; however, Mark's account does not include the devil's request for worship and the wild animals may be part of the imagery of the wilderness.

21. Admittedly, the ancients themselves in the context of their own cognitive environment would probably not have formed categorical distinctions between the various "aspects" of demons (that is, medical pathogen or supernatural antagonist), as we are suggesting here. At the same time, however, and for the same reasons, they would not have attached the same *significance* to the merging of those categories that we moderns cannot help but do because of the categories we have created in *our* cognitive environment. This categorical distinction is therefore a heuristic for modern readers to help them accurately translate emphasis; it is not an attempt to reconstruct how an ancient person would have described their understanding in their own words.

cism as combat—and thereby extend combat imagery to healing as well—in order to classify all afflictions as essentially demonic and thereby avoid a need to explain why disease and disability can occur in God's world.[22] Examples of "medical" demons are the epileptic spirit (*pneuma alalon*) in Mark 9:17 (see also Matt 17:14–18; Luke 9:39–43) and the demon possessing the daughter of the Canaanite woman in Matthew 15:22 and Mark 7:25,[23] and also probably any occurrence of "demon possession" among a list of physical ailments (e.g., Matt 4:23–24; Acts 5:15–16). These passages are not intended to provide supernatural insight into the causes of diseases beyond what medical science [ancient or modern] could discover, because as far as the ancient world is concerned that *is* the medical science.[24] Likewise, these passages are not intended to emphasize Jesus's ability to master demons any more than passages about healing paralytics are intended to emphasize Jesus's ability to master the human nervous system. They are manifestations of divine power that prove Jesus is sent from God (e.g., Luke 9:43; cf. 5:17–25); they are not manifestation of divine power that prove Jesus is stronger than demons.

Some passages, however, *are* intended to emphasize that Jesus is stronger than the demons and thus invoke the messianic battle theme. One of the most notable examples of what we might call "combat exorcism" is the healing of the Garasene demoniac[25] recorded in Matthew 8:28–34; Mark 5:1–18; and Luke 8:26–39. This particular pericope is also infamous for the inconsistency of its details. Some of these are easy to reconcile, such as the differing names given for the location of the event (Gadara in Matt 8:28; Gerasa in Mark 5:1; Luke 8:26);[26] others are not, such as the varying number of demoniacs (two in Matthew, one in Mark and Luke) or the differences in the dialogue in all three Synoptics. However, we recall that the purpose of the Gospel narratives is to interpret events, not to report phenomena; therefore, the discrepancies in the details of the phenomena are irrelevant. All three Synoptic Gospels interpret the event similarly, although the varying presentation and the details that each author includes are likely in keeping with the general

22. So, for example, Page, *Powers*, 133: "Luke regarded illness as something not part of God's original design for his creation and believed its presence in the world could only be explained by the intrusion of a force whose purposes are inimical to the purposes of God." In contrast, though, see John 9:3.

23. Page notes that both victims are said to be "healed" (Matt 15:28; 17:18; Luke 9:42), which is normally used for disease. *Powers*, 159, 163.

24. For a detailed discussion of the term *selēniazomai* (Matt 15:15, NIV "has seizures") and the condition it indicates, see Stol, *Epilepsy in Babylonia*, 121–30. For a discussion of epilepsy in the Roman world and its supposed causes, see Collins and Attridge, *Mark*, 435–36.

25. For distinction of this account from "healing" narratives, see Bovon and Koester, *Luke 1—9:50*, 326.

26. Some text variants of all three Gospels also read *Gergesa*. All commentators agree that the point of the passage is to identify the region as a "gentile" area, not to document the name of the specific town. For discussion of various interpretive options see Bock, *Luke 1:1—9:50*, 782–84.

themes of each individual gospel.[27] The point is that we should not concern ourselves with which (if any) of the narratives records the "true" event, or with trying to forensically reconstruct the encounter by synchronizing the details from the various passages. Instead, as always, we will examine how the authors are portraying the event and what that portrayal is intended to communicate.

In all three Synoptics the encounter with Legion occurs immediately after the stilling of the storm (Matt 8:23–27; Mark 4:35–41; Luke 8:22–25), which in chapter 9 we argued is a reference to the Old Testament *chaoskampf* motif intended to cast Jesus in the role of the divine warrior. This theme continues in the encounter with the Garasene demoniac. Gadara/Gerasa is outside of Israel;[28] in the Old Testament, the land of Israel (i.e., the land under the covenant) is the center of the world order. If the Gospels are invoking this idea, then Jesus's going across the lake signifies him entering a liminal region beyond the world order (as going to the wilderness in the temptation narrative also does; see also the specific location of the demoniac "coming from the tombs," another liminal image, in Matt 8:28; Mark 5:2), which as discussed in chapter 7 is the traditional abode of demons. All of this indicates that the "demons" here are being presented in their traditional role, inherited from the ancient Near East and the Old Testament, of chaotic and disruptive nuisances, as opposed to the cosmic antagonists who motivate human vices that appear in the Dead Sea Scrolls and the philosophers.[29] This is further supported by the observation that Legion is not causing its victims to *sin*; rather, the demoniacs are violent (Matt 8:28) and self-destructive (Mark 5:3). The point is that when the demons ask not to be tormented (Mark 5:7; Luke 8:28), the "torment" should not be interpreted to mean "punishment for rebellion against God and subsequent facilitation of all the evil in the world."[30] We recall that the profile of demons in ancient texts, including the New Testament, is non-systematic, as authors pick and choose elements that suit their particular purposes (see chapter 7). Some passages do describe demons (or angels) as sinners (e.g., 2 Pet 2:4), but that component of the generic conception of demons is not being emphasized in the Legion story, and if the authors do not emphasize it then the interpreters should not emphasize it either.

The word "torment" (*basanisai*) that the demons think Jesus has come to do is understood by most interpreters to be a reference to eschatological judgment, similar to "the eternal fire prepared for the devil and his angels" in Matthew 25:41. The same word is used in Revelation 20:10, where "[the devil] . . . will be tormented

27. For example, the doubling in Matthew is used throughout his gospel and seems to be a rhetorical device to indicate emphasis. See Nolland, *Matthew*, 375.

28. See for example Osborne, *Matthew*, 320; Luz, *Matthew 8–20*, 24; Morris, *Matthew*, 208.

29. "One of the striking features of the demonological teaching is that it relates almost exclusively to demon possession." Page, *Powers*, 138.

30. For various positions that view the torment as reference to punishment either present or eschatological, see Strauss, *Mark*, 217; Stein, *Mark*, 254; Bovon and Koester, *Luke 1—9:50*, 329; Garland, *Luke*, 358; Green, *Luke*, 340.

day and night." However, in the Gospels, the word commonly refers to suffering from disease (Matt 4:24; 8:6) and is even used to convey the stress on a boat and its rowers (Matt 14:24, NIV "buffeted"; Mark 6:48, NIV "straining").[31] In the Parable of the Unmerciful Servant it refers to the fate of the servant "until he should pay back all he owed" (Matt 18:34), and in the Parable of the Rich Man and Lazarus it refers to the experience of the rich man in Hades (Luke 16:23–28). However, these are not references to eschatological judgment,[32] and Hades (where the rich man is) is not the same place as the lake of burning sulfur in Revelation 20:10 (into which Hades itself is thrown in Rev 20:14). The place where the demons do not want to go in Luke 8:31 is "the abyss," which is where the devil is thrown in Revelation 20:3, but that is not the devil's final judgment and there is no mention of torment. In *1 Enoch* 88.1–3, Azazel and the watchers are thrown into the abyss, but that event occurs concurrently with the flood, not at the eschaton.

Most interpretations additionally try to read the statement "Have you come here to torture us *before the appointed time*" (*pro kairon*) as a reference to the final judgment (so NIV with the adding of the word "appointed"), but Luz notes that the word *kairos* is never used in Matthew as a technical term for the eschaton.[33] He argues instead that the collocation *pro kairon* means "prematurely."[34] The LXX of Sirach 46:19 uses *pro kairon* to indicate the time of Samuel's death, and in Sirach 51:30 it indicates a time of completing work and receiving wages. In 1 Maccabees 6:36 the collocation is used to mean "at [any given] moment" ("the assigned troops would be wherever the [elephant they were assigned to accompany] was *at the moment*");[35] and in Aeschylus it refers to an arrow falling short of its mark (lit. "before the time [of impact]").[36] 1 Corinthians 4:5 says "judge nothing *before the appointed time*" (*pro kairou*) and parallels this to "wait until the Lord comes," but that itself is not enough to prove that *pro kairon* must always mean "before the eschatological enthronement of the messiah and all it entails." Every other occurrence of the term refers to a vague and open-ended concept of time, which would fit in 1 Corinthians 4:5 as well; "judge nothing [until the Lord comes]; wait until the Lord comes" would be redundant, but "judge nothing [prematurely]" or "judge nothing [at this time]; wait until the Lord comes" makes perfect sense. This indicates

31. It can also refer to suffering from affliction of plagues in Rev 9:5; 11:10; to labor pains in Rev 12:2; or distress at the sight of ungodliness in 2 Pet 2:8. It carries connotations of punishment in Rev 14:10–11; 18:7, 10, 15 but for the worshippers of the beast and personified Babylon (= Rome), not the demons.

32. The mention of repayment implies that the servant might theoretically be able to undo his condition (however unlikely due to the vast amount owed), which would not be true of the final judgment. Likewise, in Luke 16 the rich man's brothers are still alive, which would also not be the case at the eschaton.

33. Luz, *Matthew 8–20*, 24.

34. Following LSJ, 3.1b. He concludes that the statement indicates that the demons want to be allowed to live longer (Luz, *Matthew 8–20*, 24).

35. Goldstein, *1 Maccabees*, 313.

36. Aeschylus, *Agamemnon*, 365.

that the demons do not necessarily have a specific pre-ordained time of torment in mind, and we should not read that assumption into their question.

If the "torment" of the demons does not refer to eschatological hellfire—which we propose it does not—then we are free to ask whether Jesus actually intends to torment them at all. Certainly, he is not shown to do so, and there is no reason to assume that the demons accurately perceive Jesus's intentions. The NIV of Luke 8:28 has the demons say, "I beg you, don't torture me!" which is interpreted as an illocution of supplication and paralleled to Luke 8:31, "they begged Jesus repeatedly not to order them to go into the abyss," also rendered as an illocution of supplication. However, the verb in Luke 8:28 is merely the normal word for "say" (*deomai*), and the verb in Luke 8:31 (*parakaleō*) can involve pleading, but ultimately has an illocution of motivation (compare 2 Cor 9:5, NIV "urge"). Several interpreters have noted that the action of the demons is confrontational and aggressive. Where Luke has the demon say "I [say to] you," Mark reads "I adjure you by God" (*horkizō se ton theon*; NIV "In God's name"), which in context functions as a counter to Jesus's command to come out of the demoniac (Mark 5:7–8; Luke 8:28–29). The same word *horkizō* is used by exorcists to command demons[37] and a similar phrase ("I command you in the name of . . .") is used by the hapless sons of Sceva in Acts 19:13. Thus, we should not read the demons' statement "have you come to torture us?" as a kind of pathetic groveling—"please don't hurt us"—rather, it is aggressive, more like a sneer or a taunt. When we combine a defiant illocution with a misconception of what Jesus is there to do—which should be read into the demons' statement in all three Gospels—we can see a direct parallel between the dialogue in Matthew 8:29: "What do you want with us, Son of God (*ti 'emin kai soi . . . huie tou theou*)? Have you come here to torture us?" and the near-identical phrase in the LXX of 1 Kings 17:18: "What do you have against me, man of God (*ti 'emoi kai soi anthrōpe tou theou*)? Did you come to remind me of my sin and kill my son?"[38] The idiomatic "what is there between me and you?" is the same in both,[39] as is the word for "did you come?" (*ēlthes*; aorist of *erchomai*). This suggests that Matthew at least[40] is attempting to invoke a thematic parallel between Jesus's work in Gadara and Elijah's work in Sidon.[41] This in turn might shed some light on the overall purpose of the inclusion of the episode in the Gospels.

In 1 Kings 17, Elijah leaves Israel and goes to stay with a widow in Zarephath in Sidon. While he is there, the son of the widow sickens and dies. In the ancient Near East, having a prophet (a "man of God") around is dangerous, because prophets

37. Collins and Attridge, *Mark*, 268. For demons trying to compel Jesus using a magical formula, see Osborne, *Matthew*, 319; Page, *Powers*, 142–43, 51.

38. Stein, *Luke*, 265.

39. The common phrase is a general expression of consternation or contempt; see 2 Kgs 3:13; Judg 11:12; 2 Sam 16:10; 19:22

40. And also probably Mark and Luke to a lesser extent, although they do not include the title "[X] of God" or the word *ēlthes*.

41. For parallelism between these two stories, see Klutz, *Exorcism Stories*, 61.

attract the attention of the gods and the attention of the gods is not always beneficial to have[42] (compare Job 7:11–21; it is interesting to note that the townsfolk of Gadara do not want to have a prophet around either [Matt 8:34; Mark 5:17; Luke 8:37], though perhaps not for the same reasons). The woman therefore blames Elijah and accuses him of being there to kill her son. Elijah resurrects her son and thereby proves the accusation false. In Matthew 8, Jesus likewise journeys outside Israel and, while there, performs miracles. However, like the widow of Zarephath, the demons (and most commentators) misunderstand why Jesus is there. The misunderstanding is evidenced by their parallel accusations. Elijah did not go to Sidon to perform miracles, or to kill the widow's son; he went there to escape from Ahab (compare 1 Kgs 18:4).[43] Likewise, Jesus did not go to Gadara to perform an exorcism or to torment the demons there: "in Matthew's telling, Jesus's contact with demoniacs, pig herders, and townsfolk here is no more intended than is the encounter with the crowd in [Matt 14:14]."[44] Elijah proves the widow's accusation false by raising her son. Likewise Jesus proves the demons' accusation false when he does not, in fact, torment them; instead he grants their request to go into the pigs (Matt 8:30–32). 1 Kings 17 concludes with the widow's confession: "Now I know that you are a man of God and that the word of the LORD from your mouth is the truth." It is *this affirmation* that is the point of the entire parallel; the *chaoskampf* motif and the reference to 1 Kings in the Gospels are all contrived to say that "Jesus is a man of God (more so: the *son* of God) and the word of the Lord from his mouth is the truth." It is an affirmation of identity, authority, and special divine commission. The miracle itself is not the point; Elijah's miracle is the more spectacular of the two, but the point of the passage in 1 Kings is not "look at what Elijah can do." Likewise, in the Gospels, we miss the point of the passage if we see the message as some variant of "look at what Jesus is able to do to demons." The purpose of Jesus's commission is not to defeat demons any more than the purpose of Elijah's commission was to raise children from the dead.

The miracle itself is not the point of the story (in any of the Gospels), but the details offered to describe it are nonetheless included for a reason. The Gospels are not reminiscences wherein the authors gush about incredible things they saw Jesus do using all of the details they can remember; they are finely *crafted* works of literature and everything they include is intended to help convey its chosen message. Therefore, we should ask, why are there pigs? All three Synoptics include the pigs and the swineherds, which indicates that the detail is important, but there is no counterpart to them in any other exorcism narrative. If nothing else, the pigs serve to emphasize that the episode takes place in gentile territory, beyond Israel. The purpose of this detail is to conceptually invoke Elijah's activity in Sidon (and Elisha's parallel activity in Shunem, 2 Kgs 4),

42. Cogan, *1 Kings*, 428.

43. Cogan, *1 Kings*, 426.

44. Nolland, *Matthew*, 376. Note that in all three accounts the demoniacs come to meet Jesus; he never goes hunting for them.

even in Mark and Luke where the language is not directly parallel.[45] Furthermore, some interpreters have noted that the death of the pigs resembles an elimination ritual, where the demon is transferred from the victim to an object which is then destroyed.[46] Jesus is rarely depicted as using rituals to perform miracles in the Gospels,[47] so the use of a ritual here might be further intended to invoke Elijah at Zarephath and Elisha at Shunem, both of whom use a ritual of some kind to raise the dead (1 Kgs 17:21; 2 Kgs 4:34–36), but do so only rarely and less elaborately to perform signs and miracles elsewhere (e.g., 1 Kgs 17:13–15; 18:36–37; 2 Kgs 1:9–12; 2:8, 14, 21, 24; 4:3–6, 16, 41, 43; 5:10; 6:6, 18). Thus, the pigs serve to establish thematic parallels, and it may be the case that this is *all* they do. However, some additional levels of symbolism are possible. Both Mark and Luke record that the demons' name is Legion (Mark 5:9; Luke 8:30), which is the word for a Roman military unit; additionally, the tenth legion, sometimes stationed in Palestine, had a boar (pig) as its standard.[48] Rome was the contemporary oppressor of Israel, compared to Babylon in Revelation 17. If the pigs are intended to represent the Romans, then there is a level of irony in that the afflictions caused by "Legion" are taken from the current victim and transferred to the pigs = Romans. Further, Luke mentions binding in the abyss, which invokes the fate of the watcher angels in *1 Enoch* 88.3. That passage in Enoch is part of an elaborate allegory of the history of Israel that casts the participants as various kinds of animals; Israel is sheep, and their various oppressors are represented by wild animals. These animals include pigs in *1 Enoch* 89.9, 12, 42–43, 66, where they represent the nations of Genesis 10,[49] Esau and his family,[50] and the Amalekites and Edomites,[51] respectively. Even if Luke is not referencing Enoch directly—the eschatological oppressors in *1 Enoch* are represented by birds of prey, not pigs—the general image of herds of pigs representing foreign peoples would be as easily recognizable as the image of sheep representing Israel (cf. John 10). Spirits in their role as tormentors, which the Gadarene demons are, are instruments of God as often as not; always in the Old

45. "Sometimes Luke will refer in passing to Abraham or Moses or Elijah; . . . more often, however, he will make no explicit reference at all but simply tell the story of Jesus in a way that evocatively echoes the scriptural tales." Hays, *Echoes of Scripture in the Gospels*, 276.

46. Twelftree, *Name of Jesus*, 46; France, *Mark*, 230.

47. Many interpreters make much of this detail and polemically contrast Jesus with the conventional exorcists of his day (e.g., Page, *Powers*, 144–45) However, the details of the Gospels are selected to convey a message, not to record (the extent of) what somebody present would have seen. The Gospels wish to portray Jesus as Israel's messiah, not as a successful professional exorcist. For a discussion of Jesus's recorded actions as compared to the documentation of other exorcists, see Twelftree, *Name*, 42–49.

48. Bovon and Koester, *Luke 1—9:50*, 329. The tenth legion put down revolts after the death of Herod the Great (4 BCE) and participated in the destruction of Jerusalem in 70 CE. Where they were stationed in the meantime is not known with certainty. The name of the tenth Legion, *Fretensis*, means "of the sea straits," so an additional level of irony may be intended in the manner in which the pigs meet their demise.

49. Nickelsburg, *1 Enoch 1*, 377.

50. Nickelsburg, *1 Enoch 1*, 377.

51. Nickelsburg, *1 Enoch 1*, 383, 393.

Testament (e.g., 1 Sam 16:14–16; Num 21:6; Deut 32:24; see chapter 7), and sometimes even in the Second Temple period as well. In *Jubilees* 10:8–9 the demons that are not bound—as the Gadarene demons are not—are allowed by God to remain to punish humans for wickedness. Thus, the act of Jesus sending the agents of affliction into the pigs and the subsequent destruction of the pigs might symbolically prefigure the destruction of Israel's enemies in the messianic age (compare Ezek 38:14—39:29). We should note, though, that the "enemies" that are destroyed are the *pigs*, not the demons, whose fate is unspecified. All we know about what happens to the demons is that they receive what they asked for (Matt 8:31; Mark 5:12; Luke 8:32), which they request in contrast to "torment" or "the abyss" (or "leaving the area" in Mark 5:10), so we cannot assume that their fate is any kind of punishment.[52] This interpretation is of course conjectural, but regardless of any additional layers of symbolism or irony, the main point of the passage—and indeed all exorcism passages—is establishing Jesus's identity as the servant and son of God and Israel's true messiah, and thereby correlating his work (ultimately his death and resurrection, not exorcism) with the promised restoration of Israel. They are not written to report what Jesus did or can do to demons (or to pigs or to gentile economies, for that matter). Focusing on the details of Jesus's actions instead of the affirmation of Jesus's identity misses the point entirely.

A similar though less detailed example of what we have called "combat exorcism," which likewise serves to emphasize Jesus's divine commission and messianic identity, is found in Mark 1:21–27 and Luke 4:31–36, where Jesus performs an exorcism at a synagogue in Capernaum. In both accounts, the demon's taunt is similar to Legion's: "What do you want with us, Jesus of Nazareth? Have you come to destroy us? I know who you are—the Holy One of God!" (Mark 1:24; Luke 4:34).The word for "destroy" (*apollumi*), here used where the Legion narrative uses "torment," likewise *can* refer to eschatological judgment, but does not typically do so, especially not in the Synoptics; the technical-theological "condemn to perdition" (implicitly; contrasted to "save" or "have eternal life") is found mostly in John and in the Epistles.[53] The word *apollumi* can also mean "ruin";[54] "lose";[55] or especially "kill."[56] God can destroy the soul and body

52. Demons do often (eventually) receive punishment in the Second Temple conception, but we recall that the presentation of demons is non-systematic and so we should not use components of the overall profile in our interpretation if the authors do not emphasize them. What will (or might) happen to Legion at the eschaton is irrelevant to what happens to them at Gadara.

53. *NIDNTTE*, "*apollumi*," 1:360. See John 3:16; 6:39; 10:28; Rom 2:12; 14:15; 1 Cor 1:18; 8:11; 15:18; 2 Cor 2:15; 4:3; 2 Thess 2:10; 2 Pet 3:9.

54. Matt 9:17; Mark 2:22; Luke 5:37; further use in John 6:26 ("spoils"); 1 Cor 1:19 (paralleled with "frustrate"); Heb 1:11 (paralleled to "wear out"); Jas 1:11; 4:12; 2 Pet 3:6.

55. Matt 5:29–30 (where *losing* [a body part] is *contrasted* with hellfire [gehenna]); 10:6, 39, 42; 15:24; 16:25; 18:14 ("perish"; compare Luke 15:4–6); Mark 8:35; 9:41; Luke 9:24–25; 15:8–9, 24, 32; 17:33; 19:10; Acts 27:34; further use in John 6:12 ("wasted"); 12:25; 1 Pet 1:7; 2 John 1:8; Rev 18:14.

56. Matt 2:13; 8:25 ("drown"; also Mark 4:38; Luke 8:24); Matt 12:14; 21:41; 22:7; 26:52; 27:20; Mark 3:6; 9:22; 11:18; 12:9; Luke 6:9; 11:51; 13:3–5 ("perish"; paralleled to "died" in 13:4); 13:33; 15:17; 17:27, 29; 19:47; 20:16; Acts 5:37; further use in John 10:10; 11:50 ("perish"; paralleled to "die"); 17:12

in Gehenna (Matt 10:28), but the word is paralleled to generic destruction by fire in Matthew 22:7 ("he . . . *destroyed* those murderers and burned their city"). This, combined with the normally mundane use of *destroy* and the need to specify "in Gehenna," should lead us to think that "final destruction at the eschaton" is not inherently implied in the word *apollumi*. We should also note that in the Synoptics, when the referent is a *person* (as it is here in Mark and Luke), that person is usually Jesus (e.g., Matt 12:14; "the Pharisees . . . plotted how they might *kill* Jesus"). Nowhere else are "demons" or anything equivalent to demons (i.e., any of God's cosmic enemies) the objects or referents of *apollumi*. As was also the case with the "torment" of Legion, therefore, we should not think of the "destruction" as either prefiguring eschatological judgment or as something that Jesus actually intends to do; Jesus does not torment Legion, and neither does he destroy the demon at Capernaum. However, this passage is probably not trying to invoke 1 Kings 17; although the formula "*ti 'emin kai soi . . . elthes*" is the same as both 1 Kings 17 and Matthew 8, too many other grammatical elements are altered or missing.[57] Further, the thematic parallels of leaving Israel and performing a ritual are also absent. Nonetheless, the same point that was made implicitly in Mark 5 and Luke 8 by means of the allusion to Elijah is made explicitly here in Mark 1:27 and Luke 8:36; Jesus, like Elijah in 1 Kings 17:24, is possessed of both power and authority. The ability to command spirits is notable because it demonstrates the power and authority in the context of that particular cognitive environment, but it is the power and authority *itself* that is relevant, not the ability to command demons *per se*.

The "combat exorcism" narratives serve to establish Jesus's divine identity, commission, and authority in a manner that references the themes of the Old Testament and carries meaning in the cognitive environment of Jesus's time, but not all of the exorcism narratives serve this purpose. One "medical exorcism" that appears to be included for a different reason is the epileptic boy in Mark 9:14–29, repeated with less detail in Matthew 17:14–21 (and also Luke 9:37–43, though there with different emphasis).[58] The disciples try to drive out the demon and fail (Matt 17:16; Mark 9:18; Luke 9:40), at which point the victim is brought to Jesus and is healed. When the disciples ask why they failed, Jesus responds that "This kind can come out only by prayer" (Mark 9:29). Boyd suggests that this detail is a warning, revealing that some

---

("lost," compare 18:9; compare also to the fate of Judas, the one who is "lost"); 1 Cor 10:9–10; 2 Cor 4:9; Jude 1:5, 11.

57. The title "[X] of God" that occurs in both Matthew and 1 Kings is omitted here, as it also is in Luke 8 and Mark 5; the pronouncement of the name ("I know who you are . . .") is added after the accusation, and the statement is introduced with an emphatic interjection (*ea*; NIV "go away" in Luke 4:34; untranslated in Mark 1:24), all of which are absent in Matthew and Kings.

58. The version in Luke concludes with the phrase "and they were all amazed at the greatness of God" which indicates that, for Luke, this account serves a similar purpose to the exorcism at Capernaum—that is, to emphasize God's power manifested through Christ. See Bovon and Koester, *Luke 1*, 384; Stein, *Luke*, 289; Fitzmyer, *Luke 1–9*, 810.

demons are stronger than others and require different or greater efforts to deal with.[59] But is this passage really suggesting that some demons are more capable of resisting and opposing God's will (to drive them out) than others?

Because this episode is a "medical" exorcism, it is conceptually similar to Jesus's healing miracles. Importantly, then, the previous chapter of Mark includes another episode of healing that does not work on the first try (Mark 8:22–25). On that occasion both attempts are made by Jesus and involve spitting on the eyes of a blind man; the saliva should be seen as what would have been recognized as a magical reagent.[60] The point of this passage is not to demonstrate that Jesus was correctly able to identify the man's affliction as the kind that can be cured by saliva, in defiance of what modern materialists are inclined to suppose about the causes of blindness.[61] Neither is it to indicate that the first attempt did not succeed because of some deficiency in the persons who attempted it,[62] as many interpreters argue is the case with the disciples' inability to cure the epileptic.[63] The message *certainly* is not to reveal that some cases of blindness are so intractable that they can only be cured by *two* applications of saliva. Most interpreters instead recognize that the man's condition, and the process by which he is healed—specifically, the "failed" first attempt—is symbolic of the reaction of people (especially the disciples) to Jesus's work and teaching; that is, Jesus performs miracles, and [the disciples] begin to "see" a little bit, but still not very well.[64] The emphasis is not on the nature of the condition or on the mechanism used to cure it; rather, the emphasis is on the way people respond to Jesus.

In the story of the epileptic, this same emphasis of reaction to Jesus is made explicitly: "You unbelieving generation . . . how long shall I stay with you? How long shall I put up with you?" (Mark 9:19; also Matt 17:17; Luke 9:41). In Matthew's version, the reason given for why the disciples could not drive out the demon is "Because you have so little faith" (Matt 17:20). Since "the ability to drive out the demon" is symbolic of "properly appreciating who Christ is," the answer that Jesus gives (in both Matthew and Mark) is really an answer about this lack of appreciation, not about the mechanics of exorcism. Prayer (Mark 9:29) is the means by which the disciples will increase their faith, which is lacking in Matthew 17:20. Prayer is not the means by which they will drive out especially intractable demons; many commentators note that prayer is *never* used as an exorcism tool, either here by Jesus (Mark 9:25) or

59. Boyd, *God at War*, 198; see also Page, *Powers*, 164; Strauss, *Mark*, 396, 400; France, *Mark*, 370.

60. Collins and Attridge, *Mark*, 387.

61. Compare Boyd's assessment of the epileptic boy: "Jesus, the Son of God, could [not have] misdiagnosed the condition (while still getting the cure right)." Boyd, *God at War*, 198.

62. Stein, *Mark*, 392.

63. See Lane, *Mark*, 335; Strauss, *Mark*, 400–401; France, *Mark*, 370; Edwards, *Mark*, 276, 281.

64. See Collins and Attridge, *Mark*, 439; France, *Mark*, 323; Strauss, *Mark*, 354; Edwards, *Mark*, 244–45. Most of these indicate that "full sight" comes to the disciples after the resurrection, but Stein argues convincingly that this is not the case (Stein, *Mark*, 393). The "failed" first stage is the symbol; there is no symbolic counterpart to the full healing, at least not that the text chooses to emphasize.

anywhere else in the New Testament. It is *faith* (of the father, Mark 9:24) that allows for the driving out of the demon—which is to say, that allows for a proper perception of Christ. If we think Jesus is talking about exorcism here, we make the same mistake as the disciples in John 4:32–33 (also Matt 16:5–8; Mark 8:15–17) where they think Jesus is talking about food.

Another "medical exorcism" that emphasizes faith (or lack thereof) is the healing of the daughter of a Phoenician woman in Matthew 15:21–28 and Mark 7:24–30. Like the episode at Gadara, this event occurs outside of Israel, and may therefore likewise be invoking the typology of Elijah. However, the themes of this passage are different from those of either Kings or the Legion narrative; where those narratives emphasized the confirmation of divine commission, this story emphasizes the sorry condition of Israel by means of contrast.[65] It is worth noting, however, that Luke does mention Elijah at Zarephath in conjunction with the paucity of faith in Israel in Luke 4:24–26: "no prophet is accepted in his hometown. . . . [T]here were many widows in Israel in Elijah's time . . . yet Elijah was not sent to any of them, but to a widow in Zarephath." The exorcism in Phoenicia might be Matthew and Mark's way of making the same point. The Old Testament itself does not mention that Elijah was sent to Sidon because there was no faith in Israel—it says the opposite, in fact, in 1 Kings 19:18—but the reference in Luke shows that such an understanding was present in the cognitive environment of the Gospels. Nonetheless, in terms of themes in context, the story of the Phoenician woman more closely resembles that of Jonah than that of Elijah. Tyre and Sidon (Matt 17:21; Mark 7:24) are infamous dens of iniquity in Israelite thought;[66] compare Matthew 11:23–24 and Luke 10:13 where Jesus claims "if the miracles that were performed in [Israel] had been performed in Tyre and Sidon, they would have repented long ago, sitting in sackcloth and ashes." This is exactly what the citizens of Nineveh—another infamous city—do in Jonah 3:5–9,[67] which in context serves as a negative foil for Israel's own nonchalant disregard of Yahweh's prophets (compare Matt 12:38–42).[68] The element of Jesus healing from a distance—which is relatively rare; normally Jesus goes to the victim—is also found in Matthew 8:8–9 and Luke 7:68, where Jesus heals the paralytic servant of the centurion;[69] recall that medical exorcisms parallel healings. In that instance, Jesus responds with, "I have not found such great faith even in Israel" (Matt 8:10; Luke 7:9); we should probably read the

65. France, *Mark*, 259.

66. See Strauss, *Mark*, 311.

67. Though the word "repent" (*metenoeō*) here is different than in the LXX of Jonah 3 (*apestrepsan*), the sackcloth and ashes (and general concept of penance and reform by a city of infamous sinners) are similar.

68. See Hays, *Echoes*, 182. For Nineveh as a negative foil for Israel in Jonah, see Sherwood, *Biblical Text and Its Afterlives*, 263.

69. For the parallel to the Centurion, see especially Nolland, *Matthew*, 636; also Morris, *Matthew*, 406; Luz, *Matthew*, 341; Osborne, *Matthew*, 600.

same sentiment into his statement "Woman, you have great faith" in Matthew 15:28.[70] The point of both narratives is that faith correlates to healing, which in this particular context does not bode well for faithless Israel. The nature of the affliction that is healed is mostly incidental,[71] though all of Jesus's healings are intended to invoke the imagery of the messianic age in the context of the cognitive environment (e.g., Matt 11:15), which the healing of the demonized would also do.

A final passage that serves to illustrate both Jesus's divine commission and authority and the refusal of Israel to properly acknowledge it is the so-called "Beelzebub controversy" in Matthew 12:22–37, Mark 3:22–30, and Luke 11:14–22. In Matthew and Luke the controversy is initiated by a medical exorcism (Matt 12:22; Luke 11:14), while in Mark Jesus is accused of being demon-possessed himself (Mark 3:22, 30). Whatever the specific reason, the Pharisees claim that "By Beelzebul, the prince of demons, he is driving out demons" (Matt 12:24; Mark 3:22; Luke 11:15). The name *Beelzebul* is a reference to "Baal-Zebub, the god of Ekron" in 2 Kings 1:2–3, whom Ahaziah of Israel seeks to petition for healing, but the exact meaning of the title *b'l zbb* in Kings is debated.[72] The specific identity of the Philistine deity is less important than the fact that Ahaziah is seeking the aid of a foreign god, as emphasized by Elijah's rhetorical question "Is it because there is no God in Israel that you are going off to consult Baal-Zebub?" (2 Kgs 1:3). Likewise, the primary point of the accusation in the Gospels is to claim that Jesus is invoking a power other than the God of Israel, not to identify that power specifically. In the *Testament of Solomon* (first to third century CE[73]), Beelzebul—there also called "prince of demons"[74]—is bound by Solomon and compelled to summon forth all of the demons, who are themselves then bound, forced to reveal information about themselves, and sent to work building the temple.[75] Additionally, one of the Qumran fragments contains an incantation that may begin by invoking Baal-zebub, though the text is corrupted.[76] The point is that commanding demons by Beelzebul was thought to be something that one could conceivably do.

---

70. Although the language is different; the word for "great" in Matt 15:28 (*megalē*, "large") is not the same word in Matt 8:10 and Luke 7:9 (*tosauten,* "much"), and Mark 7:29 ("for this reply") does not mention either greatness or faith (*pistis*). The comparison is conceptual and derived from parallel circumstance, not linguistic.

71. See Nolland, *Matthew*, 636.

72. The common suggested etymologies for Hebrew *b'l zbb* are a corruption of the Ugaritic titles *zbl b'l* ("Prince Baal") or *ba'al zĕbûl* ("lord of the [exalted] house"); an actual title ("lord of the flies"), which is either honorific or derogatory; or an anachronistic derivative of the Aramaic *be'el debaba* ("enemy"). For extended discussion of the various options, see Lewis, "Beelzebul," 638–39; Herrmann, "Baal Zebub," 154–56.

73. "There is general agreement that much of the testament reflects first-century Judaism in Palestine." Duling, "Testament of Solomon," 942.

74. *T. Sol.* 2.9, trans. Duling, in *OTP* 1:964.

75. *T. Sol.* 3.1–6.

76. Penney and Wise, "By the Power of Beelzebub."

Further, doing so does not necessarily make one evil or a servant of Satan;[77] Solomon could do it, and in Matthew Jesus is compared favorably to Solomon a few verses later (Matt 12:42, "now something greater than Solomon is here"; note also that the messianic title "son of David" used here also happens to be a title of Solomon). Nonetheless, the accusation has an illocution of derision, which can be inferred from the parallel phrases "he is out of his mind" in Mark 3:21 and "he has an impure spirit" in Mark 3:30.[78] However, the purpose of the accusation is not merely to insult Jesus, but rather to neutralize the testimony to his divine commission that his healings represent. As was also the case in 2 Kings, the power of Beelzebul represents a power that is not the God of Israel and is therefore unworthy of attention or respect—here, the attention and respect of the crowd (Matt 12:23; Mark 3:20, Luke 11:14), especially in Matthew, where the accusation is delivered as a direct [negative] response to the question "Could this be the Son of David?" A similar episode occurs in Matthew 9:34, where Jesus is accused of driving out demons by "the prince of demons," who in that passage is not named.[79] Thus, this episode is included in the Gospels to answer the accusation and defend Jesus as truly wielding power from God.

The source of Jesus's authority is questioned again in Matthew 21:23 (also Mark 11:28 and Luke 20:2) where the Pharisees confront Jesus on the Temple Mount, although in this case no alternative source to the implicit "God" is specified. In the passages that follow, the Pharisees and Sadducees try to publicly trap or humiliate Jesus with a series of trick questions (Matt 21:23–27; 22:15–46; Luke 20:2–44). In all these cases, Jesus responds by asking a question that they cannot answer (see especially Matt 21:25–28; 22:45–46; Mark 11:30–33; Luke 20:3–7, 40, 44). This is also his response to the accusation that his power is due to Beelzebul; he presents them with a series of questions and rhetorical statements to which they can give no reply. When Jesus is accused on the Temple Mount, he asks the Pharisees about John's baptism; here he asks them about Satan's house.

The rhetoric of the question "How can Satan drive out Satan?" (Mark 3:23; also Matt 12:26; Luke 11:18) assumes that both Beelzebul and the expelled demon would be recognized by the Pharisees as being somehow associated with Satan. The title "prince of demons" (archōn tōn daimoniōn) is not attested in the NT as a title for Satan; however, Second Temple demonology is non-systematic and there are many names given to prominent or supreme evil beings, including Belial (e.g., the War Scroll), Mastema (Jubilees), Azazel (Apocalypse of Abraham), or Melchirešaʿ (4Q'Amram), all of whom

77. Contra for example Luz, Matthew, 202: "Jesus is in the service of Beelzebul; he makes use of Satanic powers; he performs black magic."

78. Also from the statements in Matt 10:22 and 10:25: "You will be hated by everyone because of me"; "If the head of the house has been called Beelzebul, how much more the members of his household." Using the power of Beelzebul is different from being Beelzebul himself, however.

79. "Here they are obviously countering the awe of the crowds and trying to convince them of the error of their reaction to Jesus." Osborne, Matthew, 360.

are eventually subsumed into the name "Satan."[80] "Beelzebul" may have easily been considered another of these.[81] *Archon* is the title given to Shemihazah and his commanders (including Azazel) in a Greek translation of *1 Enoch* 6.[82] As for the expelled spirit, Luke identifies a woman "crippled by a spirit" (Luke 13:10) as one "whom Satan has kept bound" (Luke 13:16; compare also Acts 10:38), and in *Jubilees* 10:11 a selection of tormenting demons are left on the earth under Satan's command. However, from a biblical-theological standpoint, the point of Jesus's question on the Temple Mount is not to offer any details about the nature of John's baptism, and neither is his point here to offer details about the nature of Satan's house. The point is that any answer the Pharisees give to this question turns out to be bad for them.

Jesus asks, "If Satan drives out Satan, he is divided against himself. How then can his kingdom stand?" (Matt 12:26; Luke 11:18). Mark adds, "if Satan opposes himself and is divided, he cannot stand; his end has come" (Mark 3:26). In the cognitive environment of the Second Temple period, the end of Satan is one of the signs of the arrival of the messianic age (see chapter 9). Further, if the passage is referencing the same tradition later recorded in the *Testament of Solomon*, the last time Satan's house was divided was when the temple was built, which itself was a monumental event in Israel's covenant history, recapitulated in Ezekiel as a sign of the promised restoration. The point is that if the Pharisees admit that Satan is divided and his end has come, they also admit that the time of the restoration is at hand and that they (in theory) should be on the lookout for the messiah. If, in turn, they are looking for the messiah, then there is no good reason for them, like the crowd, not to seriously consider, "Could this be the son of David?" (Matt 12:22). On the other hand, if Satan's house is *not* divided, that also has unpleasant implication for the Pharisees. Jesus's next example is a parable (Mark 3:23) about how to go about robbing a house. The "strong man, fully armed, [who] guards his own house" in Luke 11:21 (also Matt 12:29; Mark 3:27) probably stands for Satan; if his house is not divided, then he is not plundering his own house, so therefore he is inferred to protect it. How does one plunder a house when a strong man defends it? The answer, of course, is that someone stronger than the strong man has overpowered him (Luke 11:22) and tied him up (Matt 12:29; Mark 3:27). Some conflict theologians use this metaphor to argue that the literal "binding of Satan" has been a primary objective of Jesus's ministry;[83] others read it as a warning that evil cannot be overcome without first overcoming supernatural forces (which this

---

80. Russell, *Devil*, 189.

81. Some commentators argue that the epithet "head of the house" (*oikodespotēs*, Matt 10:25) is a wordplay meant to invoke the [presumed] etymology of Beelzebul; *ba'al-zebul*, "lord of the dwelling." If this is true then the title *archon* may also be a wordplay invoking the phonetically similar potential etymology: *ba'al-zabal*, "Baal the prince."

82. Aune, "Archon," 84.

83. "We are not called to bind the strong man ourselves; this has already been done by Christ. We are called to plunder the strong man's possessions by bringing to them the message of redemption and deliverance." Arnold, *Questions*, 106. See also Page, *Powers*, 106–8.

passage presumably teaches underlie that evil) through exorcism or some other form of "spiritual warfare." However, neither of these is really the point. The point is that, if Satan's house is indeed being plundered, then someone stronger than Satan is here; this is what is meant by the statement "But if I drive out demons by the [power] of God, then the kingdom of God has come upon you" (Matt 12:28; Luke 11:20),[84] which immediately precedes the parable about the strong man. The act of "plundering Satan's house" does not refer to the particular exorcism that prompted the controversy, or even to exorcisms in general; the Pharisees' followers can drive out demons too (Matt 12:27; Luke 11:19; see also Matt 7:22; Mark 9:38; Luke 9:49; Acts 19:13), but nobody is calling them "son of David" and claiming that they represent the finger of God. Some commentators offer this as evidence that Jesus's *methods* were radically different from those of other exorcists. However, if Jesus stands as a class apart from all others then his comparison of himself to them—"if I drive out demons by Beelzebul, by whom do your people drive them out?" in Matthew 12:27 and Luke 11:19, another question that the Pharisees cannot answer—would make no sense.[85] Rather, we should see the "plunder" as reflected in the *scale* of Jesus's activities; Jesus is not sneaking in Satan's back window and making off with a few knickknacks. The word *diarpazein* ("plunder") refers in the LXX to the pillage of cities or armies (e.g., Gen 34:27; 1 Sam 14:36; 2 Kgs 7:16) or to wholesale highway robbery (e.g., Judg 9:15; 1 Sam 23:1), not to petty theft (*kleptein*, e.g., Gen 31:19; Exod 22:7). We should not think that the crowd is calling Jesus "son of David" because they saw him do a remarkable trick that other exorcists could not do; rather, it is the *cumulative effect* of everything that Jesus has said and done that leads the crowds to admire him and the Pharisees to fear him.

The Beelzebub controversy is not about the details of Satan or exorcism any more than the confrontation on the Temple Mount is about the details of how John's baptism worked. The point is all about the affirmation of Jesus's commission in the face of those who seek to undermine it. If Satan is plundering his own house, then his kingdom is at an end and the messianic age has come. The last time Satan was turned against himself Solomon did it, but now one greater than Solomon is here (Matt 12:42). However, if Satan is bound and unable to defend his house from another, that means that one greater than *Satan* is here. Either way, the crowds are the ones with the

84. Matthew says "Spirit of God" in reference to the "Spirit of the Lord" that empowered the Old Testament prophets; Luke says "finger of God" in reference to Deut 9:10.

85. Jewish exorcists invoked the power of *Adonai* or *Sabaoth*, and were so effective that the names of power were copied even by non-Jews (see Arnold, *Power and Magic*, 19, 31–32). This is the answer to the rhetorical question "by whom do your followers drive them out?" The comparison of Jesus to the other exorcists forces the Pharisees to extend their assessment of him onto them as well due to the (implicit) assumption that successful exorcism indicates the power of Beelzebul at work. This would either force the Pharisees to claim that the names of Israel's God lack sufficient power, or they must equally insult all Jewish exorcists who claim to be invoking the power of God, neither of which they would be willing to do. However, if Jesus is using radically different methods than other Jewish exorcists, this would be an easy basis to claim that he is drawing on a different power.

proper reaction, and the Pharisees (and any of the reading audience sympathetic to their argument) had best sit up and take note.

In conclusion, the exorcism narratives in the New Testament are not included in order to reveal that some conditions are indeed caused by demons (in defiance of modern medical science), because the New Testament is not a medical textbook and the idea that some conditions are caused by demons was simply part of the cognitive environment of the first century. Whether a modern doctor with a time machine would come to a different diagnosis is not a hypothesis that can be tested and is utterly irrelevant. The purpose is also not to reveal that the mission of Jesus (and by extension his followers) is to hunt down and assault demons wherever they may be found. The disciples are empowered to do so (Matt 10:1–5; Mark 6:7–12; Luke 9:1–2) but they are also empowered to heal the sick, so we should not take this to mean that the essence of Christian ministry is exorcism and therefore all Christians should practice "spiritual warfare" any more than we should take it to mean that the essence of Christian ministry is healing and therefore all Christians should practice medicine. Jesus himself never actively seeks out demons to drive out; demoniacs are brought to him or come on their own. In Acts 16:16 Paul ignores a spirit "for many days" before finally driving it out, not from duty or even compassion but from exasperation (Acts 16:18; see chapter 7). Rather, the point of the exorcisms and other miracles of both Jesus and his followers demonstrate the authenticity of their divine commission. Jesus proves that he is Israel's promised messiah within the context of the messianic expectations of his cognitive environment, and the apostles (e.g., Acts 5:12–16) duplicate his miracles, including exorcism, to demonstrate that they are his true successors and have truly received the Holy Spirit of God. It is the identity and authenticity of Christ and his followers that the text wishes to communicate, not information about demons or about strategies or orders to deal with them.

Warfare and the enemy

Exorcism narratives are not in themselves designed to depict Jesus and his followers conquering the forces of darkness that oppose God and his kingdom, except insofar as the defeat of the demonic symbolizes the arrival of the messianic age in the cognitive environment of the Second Temple period. Nonetheless, some passages do use the imagery of combat and depict demons and (especially) Satan as "enemies." The central thesis of conflict theology revolves around the assertion that the combat is literal; as Arnold writes, "[the Bible] points to the reality of a hostile realm in conflict with the kingdom of God . . . there truly is a war. Satan and his forces fiercely pursue their objective of promulgating all forms of evil in the world. This includes, above all, deceiving people and hindering them from grasping the truth about God's revelation of himself in the Lord Jesus Christ."[86] Note that this argument does not derive from textual examples of demons doing all—or even *any*—of those things; rather, it derives from the idea that demons are the enemies of the kingdom of God and therefore anything that the kingdom does they must be against, whether they are actually shown opposing that activity or not. Therefore, we must examine the language and imagery of warfare, combat, and enemies to see if the message of those passages is really intended to assert the reality of cosmic enemies of God who can be inferred to oppose anything that God endorses on principle.

Our first consideration must be to remember that the concept of the devil and his minions opposing the righteous is part of the cognitive environment of the New Testament. According to the Dead Sea Scrolls, "The authority of the angel of darkness further extends to the corruption of the righteous, . . . moreover, all the afflictions of the righteous . . . occur because of this angel's diabolic rule. All the spirits allied with him share but a single resolve: to cause the sons of light to stumble."[87] The purpose of the Bible's message is not to affirm that the ideas it references are accurate, but rather to use those references to convey meaning. Thus, when Peter writes, "Your enemy the devil prowls around like a roaring lion" (1 Pet 5:8) his purpose is not to inform his audience that they have an enemy, and his name is the devil, and then to inform them of the sorts of things that this enemy does, as if this was something they did not already know. Neither is it to inspire fear of the devil specifically, either for them (for whom it should have come naturally) or for us (who require more persuasion); note that in 1 Peter 5:5 it is *God* who opposes the proud, not the devil who devours them. The specific details of the consequence of "pursuing dishonest gain," "lording it over those entrusted to you," and failing to "submit yourselves to your elders" (1 Pet 5:2–5) is not really the point; the point is that there *are* consequences. We can likewise appreciate that these activities are detrimental, whether or not we also believe that a literal being called the devil will be responsible for delivering them. The same quote from Proverbs 3:34—"God opposes the proud but shows favor to the humble"—is repeated in James 4:6–7, followed immediately by the injunction to "Resist the devil, and he will flee from you." Here the devil is inspiring the pride rather than devouring those who exhibit it, but nonetheless we should not imagine that James is teaching that pride can be specifically countered by resisting a person called the devil, or that "resisting the devil" is the proper and efficacious way of handling pride in contrast to other methods. Neither is it a demonological non-sequitur claiming that demonic activity in general can be mitigated by resistance in general. The proverb about resisting the devil is known from the cognitive environment and here in James is paralleled with "Come near to God and he will come near to you," which is also known.[88] Both of

---

86. Arnold, *Questions*, 20–23.

87. Wise, Abegg, and Cook, *Dead Sea Scrolls*, 130 (1QS 3.21–24).

88. The first statement is repeated almost verbatim in *T. Iss.* 7.7; *T. Dan.* 5.1; *T. Naph.* 8.4. The second statement is a reference to Zech 1:3 and Mal 3:7. See Dibelius and Greeven, *James*, 226.

these statements should be regarded as proverbial sayings, not as mechanistic instructions for how to get God or the devil to do things. Both Peter and James are using the knowledge about the devil that exists in their cognitive environment to make a point about the behavior of their audience, and that point remains valid whether or not they were correct in their understanding of the particulars of the devil.

The term "enemy" (*echthros*, different from *antidikos* in 2 Pet 5:8) is applied to the devil in the Parable of the Weeds (Matt 13:28, 39), and the devil also appears in an adversarial role the Parable of the Sower (Matt 13:19; Mark 4:15; Luke 8:12). In order to understand the significance of the designation "enemy," it is necessary to understand how parables function as a genre. A parable is not a one-for-one allegory such that we expect every attribute of every character to correspond directly to some truth of the world.[89] Specifically, we cannot expect to derive theological details from the particulars displayed by the characters. In Matthew 25:24, the character representing God is called "a hard man, harvesting where you have not sown and gathering where you have not scattered seed," but we normally do not take this as describing what God is actually like.[90] Similarly, in Matthew 13:45–46, the pearl that represents the kingdom of God is bought for a large amount of money, but this does not affirm that the kingdom is something that can be bought (cf. Acts 8:18–21). The affirmations of a parable depend on the message of the parable. The message of the Parable of the Sower is not to explain what the various obstructions to Jesus's words consist of, with the idea that the hearers will do something about it such that more people can hear and understand Jesus. Jesus himself says in Matthew 13:10–17 (also Mark 4:10–13; Luke 8:9–10) that he speaks in parables *specifically so people will not understand him*. In all three Synoptics, he quotes Isaiah 6:9, where incomprehension is produced, not by the devil, but by God. Many interpreters assume that the Parable of the Sower is about evangelism; the sower is the evangelist and the seed is the gospel.[91] Consequently, they assume that the devil here is being identified as a force that hinders the gospel,[92] and therefore also assume that Jesus wants everyone to hear the words and would not obscure his message on purpose. This in turn is used to interpret the parable as informing Jesus's followers about obstacles to their evangelistic efforts; in other words, if they want more of their metaphorical seed to grow they will have to do something about the metaphorical birds (i.e., the devil). However, the Parable of the Sower is not about evangelism; the sower is Jesus, and the "word of God" (Luke 8:11) is not the gospel but rather Jesus's parables.[93] Or, said another way, *if* the "word of God" *is* the gospel, then our understanding of how the gospel works must include the possibility that it can be obfuscated (actively or passively) by God. In 2 Corinthians 4:4 Paul writes that "the god of this

89. Snodgrass, *Stories with Intent*, 26–27.

90. Snodgrass, *Stories with Intent*, 27.

91. See for example Page, *Powers*, 115.

92. See for example Boyd, *God at War*, 222.

93. Snodgrass, *Stories with Intent*, 145–76.

age has blinded the minds of unbelievers." Most commentators assume that *theos tou aiōnos* refers to the devil, but some interpreters, notably John Chrysostom, argued that it must refer to God (in contrast to assertions by Marcionites and Manichaeans), drawing support from Matthew 13:13.[94] The point is that the Parable of the Sower is not intended to instruct the readers as to how they can get more of their metaphorical crop to grow; the intention is to encourage them to be part of the small portion of *Jesus's* crop that *is growing*. The various specific mechanisms that could prevent this are mostly incidental to the point and would all have been familiar within the context of the cognitive environment. Similarly, the Parable of the Weeds is not intended to teach about the mechanism by which the metaphorical crop came to have metaphorical weeds in it. The point of this parable is to explain why the wheat and the weeds are allowed to grow together until the harvest. This serves both as an explanation for why the unproductive and parasitic members of the community are not dealt with by God in real time, and also as a warning that just because someone is not being uprooted, they are not necessarily part of the productive crop. The means by which the weeds were sown is likewise incidental to this point and likewise consistent with what the devil was thought to do within the context of the cognitive environment.

Thus, we can see that, in context, the classification of the devil as an enemy is simply referencing the cognitive environment to convey meaning, not stamping that understanding with approval for all time or providing new information about an adversary that would otherwise remain unknown. Likewise, the imagery of warfare or combat is not intended to provide new information about adversity. Warfare is indeed a metaphor for the Christian life in a variety of passages (e.g., 2 Tim 4:7, Eph 6:10–17), but the critical observation we must bear in mind is that the image is a *metaphor*. Metaphors by definition have some connection with the thing they represent, but at the same time, an over-literal reading of a metaphor has the potential to lead the reader far afield. Warfare is not the only metaphor for the Christian life; another common image is that of a competition or a race (1 Cor 9:24–27; Phil 3:12–14; Heb 12:1–3). However, this image is rarely interpreted to mean that Christians must literally compete against each other for a reward that only the best of them will obtain (e.g., 1 Cor 9:24, "in a race all the runners run, but only one gets the prize"). The presence of literal competitors, and the potential to lose to them, is as integral to the essential concept of competition as the literal presence of enemies, and the potential to lose to them, is to the essential concept of war. However, since we do not take the competition image to mean that we are really competing against anybody [for salvation], we should hesitate to assert that the warfare image must necessarily mean that we are really fighting against anybody, either.

94. John Chrysostom, *Homily on 2 Corinthians* 8.2. He goes on to argue that God does not actively "blind" believers but allows them to persist in their blindness, though whether or not the grammar could support this reading is beyond the scope of this study.

These two observations bring us to the point where we can examine Ephesians 6:12, arguably the most important passage in all of conflict theology: "Our struggle is not against flesh and blood, but against the rulers, against the authorities, against the powers of this dark world and against the spiritual forces of evil in the heavenly realms." Like Daniel 10, 1 Corinthians 10:20, and Psalm 82, this passage is commonly interpreted as providing new revelatory insight into the hidden mechanisms of cosmic operations. In the hands of conflict theologians, it becomes an exhortation designed to awaken materialists to the true nature of the obstacles that oppose them: "We need, more than ever, to gain a revitalized perspective on spiritual warfare. If we are not aware of the subtle and powerful work of our enemy, he will defeat us. Perhaps he already has certain areas of life strongly in his grip, where we have not been aware of his devious work."[95] The idea is that, were it not for Paul, we would probably conceive of our enemies as merely "flesh and blood" and therefore remain largely unable to resist or defeat them. As usual, however, if we want to claim that a passage in context is revelation—new information—we have to examine its teaching in light of what the original audience would have already known or believed.

In his famous series concerning the powers of Ephesians, Walter Wink argues that the various titles offered in Ephesians 6:12—*archon* ("rulers"), *exousiai* ("authorities"), *kosmokratoras* ("powers"), and also *thronoi* ("thrones") and *kuriotētes* ("powers") in Colossians 1:16, and *dunamis* ("power") in Ephesians 1:21—represent "the inner aspect of material or tangible manifestations of power . . . the 'principalities and powers' are the inner or spiritual essence, or gestalt, of an institution or state or system."[96] He goes on to illustrate: "A 'mob spirit' does not hover in the sky waiting to leap down on unruly crowds at a soccer match. It is the actual spirit constellated when the crowd reaches a certain critical flashpoint of excitement and frustration. It comes into existence in that moment, causes people to act in ways of which they would never have dreamed themselves capable, and then ceases to exist the moment the crowd disperses."[97] Wink reads Paul's[98] use of the myth (his term) of the fallen angels in Ephesians as constituting a sociopolitical discourse on the nature of power comparable to Marx's idea of *fetishism*,[99] and reads its message as exhorting his readers to confront the "spirit" (the gestalt or fetish) of the institution rather than merely its structures. He goes on to argue that the early church proceeded to do this:

> When the Roman archons (magistrates) ordered the early Christians to worship the imperial spirit or *genius,* they refused, kneeling instead and offering prayers on the emperor's behalf to God. This seemingly innocuous act was

95. Arnold, *Powers,* 149.

96. Wink, *Naming the Powers,* 104.

97. Wink, *Naming the Powers,* 105.

98. Authorship of Ephesians is disputed by New Testament scholars, but the question of Pauline authorship is irrelevant for our purposes so we will refer to the author as "Paul" for convenience.

99. Wink, *Naming the Powers,* 108–10.

far more exasperating and revolutionary than outright rebellion would have been. Rebellion simply acknowledges the absoluteness and ultimacy of the emperor's power, and attempts to seize it. Prayer denies that ultimacy altogether by acknowledging a higher power. Rebellion would have focuses solely on the physical institution and its current incumbents . . . but prayer challenged the very spirituality of the empire itself.[100]

In chapter 4 we argued that mythography as a literary genre serves as a vehicle to convey observations about the world. However, even if Wink is correct in thinking that the "myth" of the rebellious angels was conceived and propagated to espouse an essentially Marxist conception of power dynamics, the fact remains that Ephesians is not mythography. Paul is not *recounting* the "myth" of the angels and their rebellion, in the way that works like *1 Enoch* and *Paradise Lost* do. The treatment of Ephesians is too cursory to constitute a manifesto; at best, it is a reference to something. But a reference to what? As discussed in the introduction, those who employ a demythologizing hermeneutic—Wink's in particular—find "meaning" in biblical texts by exploring a variety of nonbiblical sources for ideas that *they consider to be meaningful* and then read those ideas back onto the biblical text. Accordingly, Wink's analysis of power is derived from Marx, a theological interpretation of Marx by Franz Hinkelammert, and a smattering of observations from philosophy of religion. Not mentioned and entirely irrelevant to the analysis is St. Paul, because Wink's conception of power can be derived and sustained entirely apart from Ephesians; Paul contributes nothing to the conception, he only (in this theory) references it. But should we really assume that Paul has a proto-Marxist deconstruction of contemporary mythographic imagery in mind when he references the powers in the epistle to the Ephesians?

An alternative potential reference is suggested by Clinton Arnold, who observes that the various terms for power used throughout Ephesians have great significance in the context of Hellenistic magic, which would be particularly relevant for Paul's audience because Ephesus was a major center of magical practice; see also Acts 19:19, where a large amount of magical scrolls are burned in Ephesus. This importance is partly due to the influence of the city's patron deity Artemis (compare Acts 19:24–35).[101] Magic could be used to advance or benefit oneself, or to protect oneself from harmful forces, whether mishaps or accidents, predatory demons, or the curses of other magicians. Especially potent was a series of six names called the *Ephesia Grammata*, which were closely associated with the Ephesian Artemis.[102] By giving up the practice of magic, the Ephesian Christians would lose these benefits; most pressingly, the ability to protect themselves from demons or from hostile magicians, which to them would have been as "real" as anything else. Arnold argues that the purpose of the epistle is to encourage the Ephesians that Christ is more powerful

100. Wink, *Naming the Powers*, 111.

101. Arnold, *Power and Magic*, 15–37.

102. Arnold, *Power and Magic*, 15–27.

than the "powers:" "the convert would no longer need to live in fear that perhaps one or a number of supernatural 'powers' could be equal or superior to Christ."[103] He goes on to conclude that this reference to magic supports the claim that Paul would have conceived of the powers as personalized spirit-beings (specifically in contrast to the institutional gestalt proposed by Wink),[104] and on that basis concludes that the message of the epistle to Ephesians is an affirmation of the reality of such powers for all time and an admonition to the (modern) audience of the pressing need to continue to engage them in battle, but using faith, prayer, and the "armor of God" instead of magic.[105] In the context of Ephesians itself, the pressing need is a means to emphasize an unrealized eschatology,[106] but Arnold's general propositional hermeneutic, consistent with conflict theology in general, means that he sees the author's entire inferred worldview—including both a particular eschatological model and the reality of spirit-beings—as being universally normative for all believers: "If the realm of spirits and angels is a dominant part of the biblical world view, it should thus be a dominant part of the Christian world view in our age."[107] However, while we believe that Arnold has correctly identified Paul's reference, we also believe that the authority of the Bible's message does not necessarily affirm the beliefs of its authors, even as it uses those beliefs as a means to communicate (see chapter 1).

Arnold's understanding of what Paul is referring to when he mentions the powers is probably the more accurate of the two, but nonetheless the conclusions of both Arnold and Wink are misguided because they both assume that the message of Ephesians is fundamentally an instruction to believers (for all time) about how they should deal with manifestations of power. For Wink, the "power" is a social psychology rather than an institution or its structures, and therefore the instruction urges the audience to defy the normalizing self-perception of those institutions instead of legitimating that perception by trying to appropriate the power it avails through revolution. For Arnold, the "power" is personalized spirit-beings rather than human enemies or institutions, or human nature or inclinations, and therefore the instruction consists of a list of specific steps to follow that are to be used instead of magic and (implicitly) also instead of whatever steps would be effective against opposition that is [merely] flesh and blood. However, we propose that the message of the epistle is not about the nature of power or instructions for dealing with power.

Arnold's own thesis emphasizes that the theme of the epistle is the *supremacy of Christ*, written to *encourage* and *comfort* the audience and provide them with assurance in the face of an enemy that they both acknowledged and feared.[108] However, in

103. Arnold, *Power and Magic*, 56; see also ibid., 52–59.

104. Arnold, *Power and Magic*, 50.

105. Arnold, *Power and Magic*, 169–70.

106. Arnold, *Power and Magic*, 155–57.

107. Arnold, *Powers*, 17.

108. Arnold, *Power and Magic*, 56, 58, 64.

point of fact, we moderns are *already* disinclined—for better or worse—to be afraid of the Ephesian Artemis or of any of the other "powers" that Paul references. Thus, we have no need to be assured of their relative powerlessness and thus the epistle would not have been written *to us* using this language because in our cognitive environment the language is meaningless. However, there *are* things that *we* are afraid of that would have been equally meaningless to the cognitive environment of first-century Asia Minor; things for example like climate change, nuclear holocaust, overpopulation, environmental deterioration, or the collapse of the global economy. Paul's teaching *for us*—the reason why the text was written—is also a message of comfort and assurance; whatever we happen to be afraid of, Christ is superior to it. That message in turn is a common theme throughout the biblical text, repeated in such passages as John 16:33 ("In this world you will have trouble. But take heart! I have overcome the world") and Psalm 20:7 ("Some trust in chariots and some in horses, but we trust in the name of the LORD our God"). Trying to use the assurance in Ephesians, or any other passage with the theme of divine supremacy, to deduce technical *details* about the specific nature of the opposition is just as misguided as trying to use cosmogonic passages—which teach that God is in control of the world order—to deduce technical details about the structures of the cosmos, for the same reasons (see chapter 1).

Nonetheless, if the theme of the epistle is supremacy, we must inquire, as Arnold does, as to the reason for the extended discussion of "spiritual warfare" in Ephesians 6:12–17, which in general contributes nothing to this theme and indeed seems to undermine it. Arnold proposes that the passage is the climax to which the entire epistle has been building; the earlier emphasis on divine power is only a precursor to the introduction of the overwhelming cosmic opposition that forms the true subject of his message and that he now authoritatively affirms for all time.[109] We propose, however, that this is not correct. The theme of supremacy is intended to assuage fear, but the caveat of the unrealized eschatology that Ephesians 6:12–17 represents is intended to prevent that assurance from devolving into complacency (as Arnold himself also agrees).[110] Christ *is* supreme and we the church therefore *can* live free of fear, but nonetheless we still have to *do* things. However, just as Ephesians does not provide details concerning the things we ought not be afraid of, it likewise does not provide formulaic instructions for how exactly to deal with them. The "armor of God" does not tell us that prayer and faith will solve all of our problems. However, the juxtaposition of the specific problematic response (magic) with the specific preferred response offered in contrast (the "armor of God") can perhaps provide some insight.

Arnold notes that the primary difference between magic and religion in the Hellenistic world is that magic seeks to compel the deity to action while religion reverently

---

109. Arnold, *Power and Magic*, 121–22.

110. Arnold, *Power and Magic*, 149–50: "Believers do not yet live in a perfect world. . . . [Since they] have not experienced the full installment of their salvation, they need to be admonished and encouraged to live by Christian ethics."

and submissively petitions the deity for aid.[111] He also notes that the "prayer for divine power" in Ephesians 3:14–19 invokes the power of God for believers in terms that are similar to magical incantations.[112] Thus, the Ephesian audience has access to the same *basic tools* as the magicians (divine power), and they are also using those tools to more or less the same ends; that is, to the opposition of spiritual powers in the heavenly realms. However, they are approaching their solution with a different *method* (i.e., not magical manipulation of the deity) and with a different *motive* (not driven by fear). We today do not usually respond to the things we fear by using magic, but we do have our own systems, processes, and tools that we think will be effective in solving our problems, such as political actions or science and technology. Ephesians is not instructing us that we should be using divine power instead of those tools (though there is also no reason why we *couldn't* use divine power, if that happens to work); instead the indication is that the way we approach the problem and the way we use our tools, whatever those respectively are, should be different from the approach taken by those who have no assurance of the supremacy of Christ.

Thus, we would suggest that Arnold fundamentally misunderstands the problem that the epistle is written to address. The problem is not that "the spirit realm may have no more a part of a given Christian's world view than it does of that person's non-Christian neighbor."[113] The "spirit realm" is incidental to the epistle; it comes from the cognitive environment of the first century and any relevance it also has for our culture is a coincidence. The problem, rather, is that any given Christian's *reactions to the things that we are afraid of in our own culture* are essentially identical to those of our non-Christian neighbors. Thus, we respond to our fears by electing corrupt and self-serving politicians; by dumping incomprehensible amounts of money into self-aggrandizing and often destructive science; by instituting abusive and ineffective social policies; by hoarding resources and stockpiling weapons; or by inculcating hate and prejudice against outgroups or "others." That is not to say that there might not be defensible reasons for doing any or all of those things—Ephesians is not a manual for problem solving, note that Paul does not tell the Ephesians that they should not be using divine power as a tool at all—but the point is that whichever way we *do* decide to confront our culture's fears should be done using a fundamentally different *method*—because some methods are more problematic than others, just as magical manipulation of deity is more problematic than reverent petition for divine aid—and with a fundamentally different *motive*, because we are assured of the supremacy of Christ, than what a non-Christian would do, even if we end up using more or less the same tools to achieve more or less the same ends, just as both the Ephesian Christians and magicians used divine power as a tool to combat magical or spiritual opposition. The application of the epistle to the Ephesians in our day is the affirmation that Christ

111. Arnold, *Power and Magic*, 18–19. Citing Aune, "Magic," 1507–57, esp. 1515–16.

112. Arnold, *Power and Magic*, 85–96.

113. Arnold, *Powers*, 16–17.

is supreme, not the affirmation that demons are real. (For a discussion about how conflict theology and its emphasis on spirits actually *discourages* a uniquely Christian approach to adversity, see chapter 16.)

In conclusion, the warfare metaphor in the New Testament indicates a general environment of struggle and adversity, just as the metaphor of competition ("a race") indicates a general striving towards a goal. The warfare image should not be interpreted to be affirming a literal combat with literal enemies, for the same reasons that the competition image should not be interpreted as affirming literal competitors and literal winners and losers. This is especially true in Ephesians, where the supremacy of Christ is asserted in order to comfort and encourage an audience plagued by fear of the adversity caused by practitioners of magic. Whether or not the magic was "real" and they were ever in any actual danger is irrelevant; they *thought* they were, and that is enough. However, we today are not commonly afraid of magic, and so for us the message of comfort should be applied *mutatis mutandis* to whatever is causing adversity and fear in our own time, because we can also be assured that Christ is supreme. Unfortunately, conflict theologians with their persistent emphasis on using Ephesians 6:12 to convince modern readers the overwhelming adversity of the demonic realm are actually using the epistle to *instill fear* rather than alleviate it. Creating fear in the very same realm where the text hoped to assuage it is not "taking the text seriously," it is rather using the text for the opposite effect from the one intended.

Satan as the cause of human evil

Earlier we observed that the demons involved in the possession and exorcism narratives are inflicting injury on their victims, not compelling them to vice. Jesus never drives out a demon that is motivating its host to *sin*. Nonetheless, several references are made to the idea that Satan (especially) is the motivating power behind evil caused *by* humans, and not merely evil that happens *to* humans. We have already mentioned some of these in the discussion of Satan as an enemy in the context of the activity of the prince of darkness leading astray the sons of light and empowering the sons of darkness—beliefs assumed in the cognitive environment of the time—but we will now examine passages that describe specific activities by Satan to see what their inclusion in the text is intended to communicate.

One of the most notable instances of Satan motivating human behavior is when Satan enters Judas as he goes to betray Jesus in Luke 22:3 and John 13:27. Judas is called a "devil" in John 6:70, and Judas' betrayal is prompted by the devil in John 13:2. Most interpreters take these passages to mean that the crucifixion was the devil's idea.[114] Early models of atonement proposed that Jesus's incarnation was a

---

114. See for example Boyd, *God at War*, 255; Page, *Powers*, 127. Many of the commentators recognize the ambiguity of the Greek in this verse, but allow for the possibility that the devil's purposes are being carried out, see for example, Michaels, *John*, 724.

ploy to trick the devil into killing him,[115] thus forfeiting his rightful rulership of the world (inferred from Luke 4:5–6 and John 12:31), but Anselm in the eleventh century rejected this idea in favor of a model wherein the crucifixion is orchestrated by God as a means of paying the debt owed to God by humanity.[116] Regardless of the particulars of atonement theory, the Gospels in general attribute the crucifixion to the designs of God at least as much as to the designs of Satan (i.e., Luke 22:37). In fact, in Matthew 6:23 and Mark 8:33, Peter is called "Satan"—that is, either metaphorically compared to the adversary or indicated to be motivated by Satan—for *opposing* the idea of the crucifixion: "You are a stumbling block to me; you do not have in mind the concerns of God." The "concerns of God" to which Jesus refers are "that [Jesus] must go to Jerusalem and suffer many things at the hands of the elders, the chief priests and the teachers of the law, and that he must be killed" (Matt 16:21; Mark 8:31). So what is the purpose of John portraying Judas as motivated by Satan, if not to teach that Satan wanted Jesus to be crucified?

The key to interpreting these passages is to remember that the audience of the Gospels already knows who Satan is. The purpose of the Gospels as a genre is not to record phenomena (see chapter 2); we should not imagine that John saw an entity named "Satan" enter into Judas, and then sat by with a notepad to see what Satan would make Judas do. "Satan entering Judas" is not really a phenomenon at all; we should not imagine that the disciples saw a kind of black cloud absorb into Judas' body as he took the bread dipped in sauce (John 8:26). We should also not assume that the Holy Spirit dictated to John to write that Satan influenced Judas, even though John would not otherwise have known this; that is not how inspiration works. Instead, the authors are using a reference to a character known from the cognitive environment (Satan) to *interpret Judas' behavior from that moment on*. The aim of the Gospels is not to report phenomena; they *interpret events*, and the ascription of Judas' actions to Satan is a way of interpreting those actions within the logic of their cognitive environment. What the motive of the historical Judas might have been we do not know; real people tend to be complex, and it is likely that there was more to him than the villainous cartoon character that the Gospels (e.g., John 12:6) portray him as.[117] The details recorded in the Gospels are not intended to help us understand *Judas*; they are intended to help us understand the events in which Judas participates. The specific interpretation of Judas' behavior in turn serves two purposes. First, association with Satan in the cognitive environment is always negative. The prince of darkness does not thwart God's plans— he is established by God to do exactly what he does (e.g., 1QS 3.25; 4.16, *Jub.* 10.8–9, see chapter 9)—but nonetheless those who serve him are not to be lauded for serving

115. Boyd, *God at War*, 255–56.

116. Anselm, *Cur Deus Homo*, chapter 7, 11.

117. Note the report of his remorse and suicide, which on the phenomenal level is not the kind of behavior that would indicate a dedicated sociopath, though of course none of the depictions of Judas' actions are included in the text for the purpose of allowing posterity to psychoanalyze him.

that particular role in God's plans. God turns evil to good, but those who do evil, even when that evil serves the purposes of God, always bring destruction on themselves (compare 1QS 4.12–14). This is the meaning of the warning in Matthew 26:24, Mark 14:21, and Luke 22:22: "The son of man will go just as it is written about him. But woe to that man who betrays the son of man! It would be better for him if he had not been born." The subsequent recording of Judas' disgraceful death and ignominious burial also serve to emphasize this point.

The second goal is that the negative portrayal of Judas serves to emphasize the broader interpretation of the passion narrative in general. The Gospels portray Jesus as an innocent victim of a conspiracy, but other interpretations of the same events are possible. As a modern example, Andrew Lloyd Webber's *Jesus Christ Superstar* depicts Jesus as a naïve celebrity with delusions of grandeur, while Judas is depicted as trying to save him (and later his followers) from the consequences of Jesus's self-destruction. Ancient texts indicate that Jesus was often interpreted as a criminal justly executed;[118] in this interpretation Judas would have been a hero, bravely helping to bring a dangerous man to justice. However, the importance of properly interpreting the passion is only incidentally related to Judas, or to Satan for that matter. Jesus's innocence, and therefore his going to his death to fulfill prophecy and to serve the purposes of God and not as a penalty for anything he has done, is ultimately what is important. Judas's influence by Satan, subsequent remorse, suicide, and dishonorable burial all serve to emphasize that Judas is not a hero, but a traitor who helped condemn an innocent man (e.g., Matt 27:3–7, esp. 27:4).

In addition to interpreting the actions of Judas, the involvement of Satan also serves to cast Jesus's death in terms of the eschatological battle motif. John's Gospel in particular, where Satan's role in the passion has the strongest emphasis, draws heavily on the dichotomy of light and darkness that is part of the cognitive environment and also reflected at Qumran. The imagery in John is complex and beyond the scope of this study, but if nothing else it serves to identify Jesus and his followers with the forces of light and therefore as the true people of God and the true Israel who inherit God's promises of restoration. Satan, under various titles throughout the gospel (see below) generally serves to emphasize this theme. However, we recall that the purpose of the Bible's message is not to affirm with authority the accuracy of the imagery that it references. Satan, the forces of darkness, and the forces of light are all concepts that have meaning within the cognitive environment, which John invokes to convey his own message. The purpose of the image is to communicate meaningfully, not to confirm that the world really works that way.

Another passage where people are identified with Satan in order to comment on their motives is found in John 8:44: "You belong to your father, the devil, and you want to carry out your father's desires. He was a murderer from the beginning, not holding to the truth, for there is no truth in him. When he lies, he speaks his native

118. See for example Minucius Felix, *Octavius*, 9, 29.

language, for he is a liar and the father of lies." In the Enochian tradition it is possible for angels to sire children, and sometimes these angels are equated with the devil (e.g., Shemihazah/Satanail in *2 Enoch*; see chapter 13), but the reference here pertains to typology more than biological ancestry. Abraham (John 8:39) is a biological ancestor, but God (John 8:41) is not, and even the relationship with Abraham is described typologically (John 8:39; "If you were Abraham's children . . . then you would do what Abraham did"). However, just as nobody ever takes this passage as a discussion of the devil's progeny and whether he literally has any—although this could easily be done—nobody should take this passage as a discussion of the devil's *attributes*, for the same reasons. The concept of people by virtue of their deeds being numbered among the "sons of Beliar" and thereby having no place in the kingdom of God is well established in the cognitive environment (see chapter 9); Jesus is warning the Pharisees that being biological sons of Abraham (ethnic Israel) does not automatically place them among the sons of light (spiritual Israel). The Pharisees would have already known that such a distinction was possible; for them the delineation is based on those who keep Torah (themselves) versus those who do not (the Hellenizers), which is why they immediately protest that "[t]he only Father we have is God himself" (John 8:41). Of course, this does not imply that they are either claiming the same status of divine sonship that Nicene Christianity eventually attributes to Jesus (compare John 10:36), or claiming to be divine progeny (although gods in the classical world can sire human children), or equating Abraham with God. Since every other element of this discussion is typological rather than literal, it follows that the definition of the devil (as a liar and a murderer) in John 8:44 is also typological rather than literal; that is, it describes the *kinds of things* that the devil character from the cognitive environment would be expected to do. The actions—murder and lies—are chosen specifically for this example on the basis of their correspondence to what the *Pharisees* are doing—i.e., John 8:40, "As it is, you are looking for a way to kill me"; John 8:55, "If I said I did not [know God], I would be a liar like you"—not on the basis of identifying things that a historical person called "the devil" actually did. In fact, it is notoriously difficult to identify who exactly the devil is supposed to have murdered. The satan in the Old Testament never kills anyone except Job's children, which God takes credit for, and the phrase "from the beginning" (*ap arches*) does not imply some kind of primordial activity,[119] although in no tradition is the offense by which Satan becomes the devil considered to be murder. Many commentators argue that the reference is to the role that the devil played in bringing death to humanity in reference to Genesis 3 (compare Wis 2:24, "through the devil's envy death entered the world"; also Heb 2:14). Accordingly, they read this passage as an authoritative identification of the devil's contribution to

---

119. "From the beginning" does not mean either "from the beginning of the world" or "from the beginning of a person's existence"; compare 1 John 3:11, "this is the message you heard from the beginning." The phrase is idiomatic and emphasizes longstanding consistency, similar the English expression "it's always been that way."

the fall of Adam. However, the rare word *anthropoktonos* ("murderer") does not refer to a contribution to the circumstances that cause the death of another, or even to manipulating someone into a circumstance where they take actions to cause their own death, which is the most that the serpent in Genesis can be said to do. In Euripides the word refers to the slaughter and subsequent devouring of men by the cyclops,[120] and also elsewhere refers to human sacrifice rhetorically compared to murder followed by cannibalism: "Now just as I find it incredible that the gods at Tantalus' feast enjoyed the flesh of his son, so I believe that the people here, themselves murderous (*anthropoktonous*), ascribe their own fault to the goddess. None of the gods, I think, is wicked."[121] The actual fate of the victim is less important than the observation that the act represents an atrocity that is unthinkable to ascribe to the gods, and by extension to the godly, which is also the emphasis in John. The only other use of the term in the Bible (1 John 3:15, "Anyone who hates a brother or sister is a murderer") is rhetorical, but it invokes the exposition of the sixth commandment in Matthew 5:21 (*phoneuo*, "kill"); the sixth commandment, in turn, refers specifically to murder (Heb. *rṣḥ*), not to generic contribution to a cause of death.[122] Some interpreters believe that the designation "liar" is a further reference to the serpent in Genesis;[123] however, the term for "liar" in John 8:44 (*pseudos*) is not the same root word that describes what the serpent does in LXX Genesis 3:13 (*apataō*; see also 2 Cor 11:3; 1 Tim 2:14). *Pseudos* indicates neither the activity of the serpent nor an atrocity that is unthinkable to ascribe to the gods. In the LXX it is the word used to describe the "lying spirit" (Heb. *šqr*) sent by the LORD in 1 Kings 22:22–23 (who is not associated with Satan in any way), and it indicates emptiness and insignificance in Psalm 62:9 (LXX Ps 61:9), but it is never used to translate *nsʾ* ("deceived" in Gen 3:13). Additionally, as discussed in chapter 10, full equation of the serpent with the devil is rare in the Second Temple period, and thus we cannot assume that a casual reference to the devil would be meaningfully assumed to also reference the serpent; note that the Wisdom of Solomon cites the devil's *envy* as the medium of death, not the devil's deceit. Consequently, it is highly unlikely that John has a reference to Genesis 3 in mind; or, said another way, if the devil's lies and murder are supposed to implicitly refer to Adam, the tradition through which they do so is not that of Genesis. In 1 John 3:7–15 the typological dichotomy of being

---

120. Euripides, *Cyclops* 127.

121. Euripides, *Iphigenia Among the Taurians* 385–90, trans. Kovacs, in LCL 10:187.

122. "*rṣḥ* [means] culpable killing by use of force . . . it is noteworthy that *rṣḥ* is never used for killing in battle or for killing in self-defense. Neither is it used for suicide." Hossfeld, "רָצַח, *rāṣaḥ*," 632. Targum Onqelos implicitly expands the definition to include suicide (see Grossfeld, *Targum Onqelos*, 57), though Josephus' protest against suicide does not include a reference to the sixth commandment (Josephus, *Jewish War* 3.8.5). However, none of the NT use of *phoneuō*, or references to the sixth commandment either in contemporary Jewish literature or elsewhere in the NT, imply that the sixth commandment has been expanded to include even all forms of direct killing, much less indirect contribution to circumstances that subsequently result in another's death.

123. See for example Page, *Powers*, 125–26.

"children of God" or "children of the devil" (also seen in John 8) is repeated, as is a reference to something the devil has been "from the beginning" ("sinning" in 1 John 3:8; "murder" in John 8:44). In 1 John 3 the exemplar of murder is Cain, not the devil (1 John 3:12), though Cain is specified to have "belonged to the evil one," invoking the same typological relationship that is presented in both passages. Many interpreters throughout history have seen reference to Cain in John 8:44 as well, especially in light of a Jewish tradition that Cain was literally conceived by the devil.[124] A similar typological disparaging of the Pharisees in Matthew 23:25 and Luke 11:51 invokes the death of Abel, in addition to all of the prophets persecuted under the kings (compare Matt 23:31, 27). However, most modern interpreters recognize that, because the imagery here is typological, it is not intended to affirm trivia about the attributes (that is, ancestry or activity) of either Cain or the Jewish leaders. However, because the imagery is typological, it is also not intended to affirm trivia about the attributes of Satan (sinning, lying, murdering), for the same reasons. Being affiliated with the devil, described by the metaphor of sonship, has a very specific meaning within the context of the cognitive environment, but it has that meaning *because* the devil is a character that is already known. The purpose of both John 8:44 and 1 John 3:7–15 is to classify the named persons as being apart from the people of God; it is not to provide or affirm information or beliefs about what the devil is or has done.

Another reference with a different emphasis comes in Luke 22:31, where Satan "has asked to sift all of [the apostles] as wheat." The exact meaning of this comment by Jesus—that is, what Satan wants to happen as a result of the "sifting"—is somewhat obscure. The words "ask" (*exaitein*) and "sift" (*siniasai*) both occur only here in the Greek Bible (New Testament and Septuagint), which may indicate that Luke is quoting something, though if he is we have not discovered the source. Jesus's next statement in Luke 22:32, "I have prayed for you, Simon, that your faith may not fail" indicates that the "sifting" is supposed to cause a failure of the apostles' faith. Most commentators in turn read the general scenario as a reference to Job.[125] In chapter 13, we argued that Job in context does not depict Satan demanding to test Job's faith, but any New Testament reference to Job is not going to refer to the Old Testament in context but rather to the *interpretation* of the text that has filtered through the cognitive environment. The *Testament of Job* (first century BCE–first century CE)[126] describes Job's affliction by Satan, not as a test of Job's faith, but as a punishment for destroying an idol (*T. Job* 2.1—5.3). The "test" of Job consists of whether Job will have the fortitude to endure Satan's onslaught: "Thus says the LORD: if you attempt to purge the place of Satan, he will rise up against you with wrath for battle . . . but if you are patient, I will make your name renowned . . . and you shall be raised up in the resurrection. For you will be like

124. *Targ. Ps.-J.* Gen 4:1; 5:3.

125. See for example Bock, *Luke 9:51—24:53*, 1742; Edwards, *Luke*, 637; Garland, Luke, 869; Green, *Luke*, 772.

126. Spittler, "Testament of Job," 833.

a sparring athlete, both enduring pains and winning the crown."[127] Job's competition with Satan is described in terms reminiscent of Jacob in Genesis 32:24–48: "I [Satan] am weary and I withdraw from you [Job], even though you are flesh and I a spirit. . . . I became like one athlete wrestling another . . . but you conquered my wrestling tactics which I brought on you."[128] This image is similar to that used in Ephesians 6:12, but the theme of endurance in the face of adversity would not be out of place in Luke, either; in Luke 22:46 Jesus tells the disciples to stay awake and pray "so that you will not fall into temptation," not "to prove that you have faith." On the other hand, in *Jubilees* a request from Mastema (Satan) is the occasion for the testing of the faith of *Abraham* (*Jub.* 17:16; cf. Gen 22:1). Regardless of whether Satan is testing the apostle's faith or testing their endurance, most commentators agree that the test is confronted (and failed) when the disciples desert Jesus (Matt 26:56; Mark 14:50) and when Peter denies him (Matt 26:69–75; Mark 14:66–72; Luke 22:54–62; John 18:15–18, 25–26). In both Matthew and Mark the desertion of the disciples has been preordained ("This very night you will all fall away on account of me, for it is written, 'I will strike the shepherd, and the sheep of the flock will be scattered;'" Matt 26:31; Mark 14:27), so the reference to failing a test set by Satan might be yet another reminder that just because an action accords with God's plans does not necessarily mean that the action is good. However, Luke—the gospel that mentions Satan's sifting—makes no mention of the scattering of the disciples. Consequently, the admonition to Peter—"when you have turned back, strengthen your brothers"—is sometimes read as a foreshadowing of Peter assuming leadership of the apostles in Acts,[129] which in turn indicates that the "sifting" of the apostles will be an extended process: "the sifting will not stop after Jesus's passion. It continues as the disciples take up their cross on a daily basis . . . as they are hauled before kings and governors, punished in synagogues and prisons, and led to the gallows."[130] If this is correct, then the "sifting" metaphor here is conceptually similar to the "warfare" metaphor elsewhere; that is, it warns of impending adversity and implies an exhortation to endure.[131] However, like the warfare metaphor, this statement in Luke does not serve to authoritatively identify an enemy, to affirm that there literally *is* an enemy, or to affirm that adversity begins with a request from Satan, since all of these elements are references to ideas that exist in the cognitive environment and are included in the text of Luke in order to convey meaning.

127. *T. Job* 4.3–10, trans. Spittler, in *OTP* 1:841.

128. *T. Job* 27.2–5, trans. Spittler, in *OTP* 1:851.

129. See Garland, *Luke*, 869; Green, *Luke*, 773; Bock, *Luke 9:51—24:53*, 1743.

130. Garland, *Luke*, 875.

131. Many interpreters suggest that the image of "sifting" might be a reference to Amos 9:9: "and I will shake the people of Israel among all the nations as grain is shaken in a sieve, and not a pebble will reach the ground. All the sinners among my people will die by the sword." The "shaking" here is the exile, and the "pebbles" are the sinners who will be separated out and not survive. However, if this reference was intended, we might wonder why Luke does not use the word *likmizō* ("shake," LXX) instead of *siniasai* ("sift").

Additional references to persons being motivated by or affiliated with Satan are Ananias and Sapphira (Acts 5:3); the sorcerer Elymas (Acts 13:10); the gentiles in general (Acts 26:18; "[in] the power of Satan," which might refer to affliction rather than influence since it is contrasted with forgiveness and sanctification, not righteousness, but nonetheless references a concept of Satan's influence in the world at large); "all [those] who do evil" (Matt 13:41, also called "people of the evil one" in Matt 13:38); some of the church's dependent widows (1 Tim 5:15); conceited church leaders (1 Tim 3:6, who "fall under the same judgment as the devil"; compare to the uncharitable in Matt 25:4 and to a long list of offenders in Rev 21:8); or those who follow false teachings (2 Tim 2:25–26). The point of all of these references is to characterize behaviors as negative, at least within the context of the Greco-Roman cognitive environment. Some of these behaviors might incidentally be negative in our modern context as well, but the point of these passages is not to definitively classify for all time what counts as "evil." "Lying to the Holy Spirit" (Acts 5:3) would probably still count as evil in the modern West, but young widows choosing to remaining unmarried (1 Tim 5:14) probably would not. The purpose is also not to identify individuals as tools of the devil in order to examine the behavior of those individuals so as to learn about the kinds of things the devil wants to accomplish. The reference is only meaningful—that is, only places a negative value on the action—because the audience already knows who Satan is, and that what Satan does or wants, or the fate that awaits him, is bad. All of that information, in turn, is already present in the cognitive environment, and we should not assume that the author's intention is to authoritatively affirm the information that he references; that is not the purpose of the text.

A similar conception involves behaviors or activities that either provide opportunity for the devil or represent snares or schemes of the devil: anger (Eph 4:26–27), sexual abstinence within marriage (1 Cor 7:5), improprietous behavior by church dependents (1 Tim 5:14) or leaders (1 Tim 3:7), or failure to forgive (2 Cor 2:10–11). Conflict theologians generally assume that these passages are intended to alert the text's readers to a danger of which they would otherwise be unaware, and also to provide inspired insight into the strategies of Satan. However, we must recall that the target audience of these epistles already has a conception of who the devil is and what the devil does; this is not new information and the Bible's purpose is not to affirm its references. Instead, we must remember that associating persons or behaviors with Satan is a rhetorical indication that those persons or behaviors are outside of or inimical to the community of the people of God. "Do not let the sun go down while you are still angry, and do not give the devil a foothold" (Eph 4:26–27) does not mean that anger will provide someone called "the devil" an opportunity to do something to you that he could not do otherwise; the point is rather that a prolonged nurturing of anger will lead someone to do something, or to become a kind of person, that has no place in the community of the people of God. "Giving a foothold to the devil" (or "belonging to the devil") is thus conceptually similar to "having a part in the table of demons" (1 Cor

10:21), which we discussed in chapter 11. The message of the text is not to describe the devil, but rather to describe the identity of the people of God.

Most conflict theologians read all of these passages as teaching the audience details about who Satan is and what Satan does, as if this was something that they did not already know. As we also saw in the case of the warfare metaphor, this assumption is used to speculate about the nature of particular phenomena[132] (there adversity, here behavior, both of ourselves and others) and also to provide an authoritative guide for managing that phenomenon, in contrast to other potential forms of management that do not take the devil into account.[133] Additionally, great care is taken to emphasize that Satan's involvement does not *exculpate* the victim of wrongdoing: "there is no suggestion that Judas is not responsible for what he does . . . [the image] was not intended to minimalize the guilt of his sin."[134] While it is technically true that the biblical authors never use Satan or evil spirits to exonerate evildoers, the observation also misses the point. The purpose of associating persons or activities with Satan is *to classify something as evil that might otherwise be seen as good or harmless;* it is not to identify the specific cause of something already known to be evil, as opposed to a different potential cause of that evil. Ascribing activity or influence to Satan has meaning because of what the character *Satan* represents in the cognitive environment. The purpose of the references are to convey that meaning, not to provide universal propositions of trivia about what an entity named "Satan" is or does.

Further references to Satan and demons

The Gospels and Epistles contain numerous offhand references to names or titles that are not "Satan" or "devil" but are nonetheless commonly assumed to refer to the same character. The most notable of these are "prince of the world" (*archōn tou kosmou*; John 12:31; 14:30; and 16:11); "Belial" (2 Cor 6:15); and "prince of the power of the air" (*archonta tēs exousias tou aeros*, specified further as "the spirit who is now at work in those who are disobedient"; Eph 2:2). For our purposes, the most important observation about all of these titles is that all of them are self-evidently references. Without an assumed pre-existing profile, there is nothing in the text itself to indicate that all of these titles refer to the same being, let alone that this is the same being elsewhere called "Satan." As it is, though, these references are all well in keeping with the Second Temple understanding of what Satan is and does. In John 12:31 the "prince of the world" is "driven out" in accordance to the "time for judgment on the world," which matches the devil's destiny in accordance with the expectations of the messianic age, and, in context, serves to classify Jesus's passion as the expected messianic event. In

132. So for example, "Such a horrible act of treachery could not be explained without the direct involvement of Satan himself." Page, *Powers,* 127–28.

133. See for example Arnold, *Questions,* 36.

134. Page, *Powers,* 127; see also Arnold, *Questions,* 79.

John 14:30 the "prince of the world" is said to be "coming for" Jesus, which refers to the role Satan plays in Judas's betrayal as discussed above, and in John 16:11 the "prince of the world stands condemned," which likewise invokes the imagery of the messianic age and serves to emphasize Jesus's identity. The "prince of the power of the air" invokes the Middle Platonic idea that demons are the natural inhabitants of the realm of air that extends from the surface of the earth to the orbit of the moon;[135] the title is thus comparable to the epithet "prince of demons" (Matt 9:34; 12:24; Mark 3:22; Luke 11:15). "Belial" is the preferred name for Satan or the prince of darkness in the Dead Sea Scrolls, rhetorically contrasted in 2 Corinthians 6:15 with Christ as an antithesis, which is appropriate since Christ is generally portrayed in the New Testament as filling the role traditionally assigned to the prince of light. The "spirit at work in those who are disobedient" (Eph 2:2, lit. "in the sons of disobedience") also invokes the typological imagery of Qumran. Further references to this same typology are found in 1 John 5:19 ("the whole world is under the control of *the evil one*"; contrasted with "we are children of God"); in 1 John 4:4 ("the one who is in you is greater than *the one who is in the world*"); and in 1 John 2:13–14 ("you have overcome *the evil one*"). Thus, all of these titles probably do refer to Satan, but as always, the purpose of the reference is to convey meaning, not to provide or affirm information or beliefs about Satan.

Another title that is sometimes thought to refer to Satan is the "god of this age" (*theos tou aiōnos*) in 2 Corinthians 4:4, who is said to have "blinded the minds of unbelievers." Most interpreters assume that the title is roughly parallel to "prince of the world" and invokes the devil's established function of leading people astray. This is theoretically possible, but some additional factors should be considered. First, the classification *theos* ("god") is not typically ascribed to the devil. Normally the word *theos* refers to a taxon of beings (the gods), or to beings from another taxon who are nonetheless regarded as gods (for example, LXX Ps 96:5, "the *theoi* of the nations are demons"; "demon" is a taxon. See also e.g., Acts 14:11). Jesus uses the term to refer to humans in John 10:35 (referencing Ps 82), but his purpose in doing so is to trick the Pharisees into contradicting themselves; he is not demonstrating that *theos* can sometimes mean that the being described is not technically divine, because he goes on to compare that claim of divinity with his own: "if [the psalmist] called them 'gods,' to whom the word of God came . . . why then do you accuse me of blasphemy because I said, 'I am God's son'?" In fact, the Nicene *homoousion* relies heavily on the understanding that the designation *theos* (given to Christ in e.g., John 1:1; 20:28) *must* indicate divine taxonomy; it falls to the Arians to argue instead that it can be an idiomatic title for a powerful or exalted cosmic being who is nonetheless not technically divine. On the other hand, if the word *theos* always refers to a deity, it is difficult to read the passage as referring to anything other than triune God of Christianity. The Manichaeans took a taxonomic approach and argued that there were two gods, converting monotheism to dualism; the Marcionites

---

135. See Philo, *de Gigantibus* 2.

took an affirmation-based approach and argued that a being who was not a god had nonetheless been regarded as one, which they took to refer to the god of Judaism and the Old Testament. Theoretically, the "being who is not a god but is considered to be one" could be Satan. However, while the practice of serving *demons* as if they were gods is commonly acknowledged within the cognitive environment through the classification of the "gods" of tradition and popular religion as *daimones* (see chapter 7), the practice of serving the prince of darkness as though he were god is not.[136] As discussed briefly above, John Chrysostom rejected all of these options and concluded that the "god of this age" does indeed refer to the Christian God. The act of blinding those who do not believe is elsewhere ascribed to God in John 12:37–40; Matthew 13:13–15; and Luke 8:10; all of which reference Isaiah 6:9–10. If this reading is correct, the specification "God *of this age*" does not designate a separate entity but is a title given for emphasis; compare to the "God of Peace" (*theos tēs eirēnēs*) in Romans 16:20. However, the point of 2 Corinthians 4:4 is that the disciples should not be discouraged if some people are not listening to them (2 Cor 4:1) because the power of their message comes from God, not from them (2 Cor 4:5), and thus both the message and resistance to the message are beyond their control; their task is simply to present it (2 Cor 4:2, 6). The exact agency responsible for the audience's blindness does not really matter much as far as this point is concerned. Paul's audience would likely have known what the reference specifically meant, but we can understand the message he was conveying even if we do not.

A short parable that refers to demons and exorcism as the basis of its metaphor is found in Matthew 12:43–45 and Luke 11:24–26: "When an impure spirit comes out of a person, it goes through arid places seeking rest and does not find it. Then it says,

---

136. The dragon is *worshipped* (*proskunein*) in Rev 13:4, but as discussed in chapter 10, it is not clear whether the dragon is literally Satan or a human personified as Satan. Worshipping *humans* as gods is attested, e.g., the Beast in Rev 13:4. In the New Testament the verb *proskunein* almost always takes a divine object (often Jesus), but that itself does not mean that the referent of the verb should necessarily be read to mean "something that those performing the action assume to be divine" and consequently as evidence that the object was understood to be a divine being (*theos*) in the cognitive environment. In Matt 4:10 and Luke 4:8 Jesus quotes Deut 6:13 as saying "Worship the Lord your God and serve him only," but the passage in Deuteronomy is not asserting that only Yahweh (or, more broadly, only a *theos*, a class of which Yahweh is the only member) is a legitimate object for the verb *proskunein*. In the LXX *proskunein* commonly translates Hebrew *ḥāwâ* (hishtaphel) and frequently takes human objects who are not Yahweh and who the context does not present as being perceived as gods, including Canaanite people (Gen 23:7), Jacob (Gen 27:29); Esau (Gen 33:3, 6); Joseph (e.g., Gen 37:7); Moses (Exod 11:8); Jethro (Exod 18:7); Boaz (Ruth 2:10); Jonathan (1 Sam 20:41); and Saul (1 Sam 24:8). In Rev 19:10 the speaker tells John not to worship him but instead to "worship God," and in Acts 10:25 Peter tells Cornelius not to worship him because he is also a man. Both characters are claiming to be unworthy of the veneration they are offered, but neither says explicitly that the reason they are unworthy is because they are not beings in the taxon *theos* and only a *theos* should receive worship. Both instead emphasize their equality with the worshipper: "I am only a man myself" in Acts 10:26; "I am a fellow servant with you" in Rev 20:19. The equality in turn refers to status, not ontology. In Matt 18:26 the servant "worships" his master. While the master stands for God in the parable's metaphor, there is no indication within the story that the servant considers his master to be divine.

'I will return to the house I left.' When it arrives, it finds the house swept clean and put in order. Then it goes and takes seven other spirits more wicked than itself, and they go in and live there. And the final condition of that person is worse than the first." Matthew adds "That is how it will be with this wicked generation," which Boyd uses to argue that the purpose of the passage is to authoritatively attribute the cause of the wickedness of the generation to the evil spirits,[137] and in general treats the parable as a propositional exposition on the particulars of demonic behavior which can be freely applied to explain situations beyond those specified in the text itself (he offers Nazi Germany as an example of a "generation" possessed by evil spirits).[138] However, we maintain that biblical passages are not to be read as universal propositions (see chapter 1); further, even within the internal logic of propositional hermeneutics, the method is not applied to the metaphorical structure of parables. We would not use Matthew 13:44 as anthropological data about a Judean practice of burying treasure in fields; we should likewise not use this passage as data about how demons and exorcism work. The Parable of the Restless Spirits is not about demons and exorcism any more than the Parable of the Sower is about agriculture. Someone who interprets the Parable of the Sower as instructing farmers about which circumstances will allow seeds to grow (or not) has missed the point of the lesson; likewise, someone who interprets the Parable of the Restless Spirits as describing what demons will do under various circumstances has also missed the point. The use of the metaphor assumes preexisting knowledge of how demons act, which might be of interest to an anthropologist or historian (just as the reference to the productivity of seeds in various conditions might be useful to someone trying to grow crops or trying to study first-century agriculture), but that information has no value to a theologian except insofar as it is used to convey the message of the text, which in the Parable of the Restless Spirits is that "the final condition of that person is worse than the first." What exactly this means depends on what is symbolized by the metaphor of exorcism. "Hearing Jesus's teaching" is a likely candidate for this; the parable would then be teaching that those who hear Jesus's message and fail to respond to it will be worse off than those who never heard it at all. But for our purposes the important thing is that the passage is in no way a propositional affirmation about anything related to demons or exorcism.

Jude 9 contains a short reference to an incident where "the archangel Michael . . . was disputing with the devil about the body of Moses." Early Christian writers Gelasius (fifth century) and Origen (third century) claimed the passage is an allusion to a work called the *Assumption of Moses*, which some modern scholars believe to be the same work as a document called the *Testament of Moses*,[139] known from a sixth-century Latin manuscript.[140] The text of the *Testament* is incomplete and makes no mention of

137. Boyd, *God at War*, 226.
138. Boyd, *God at War*, 195–96.
139. Priest, "Testament of Moses," 924–25.
140. Priest, "Testament of Moses," 1:919.

a dispute over the body of Moses. A Qumran text called 4Q'Amram describes a vision by Amram, father of Moses, of two angels fighting to take possession of him after his death; one is given the three names "Michael, Prince of Light, and Melchizedek," and the other is given the three names "Belial, Prince of Darkness, and Melchireša."[141] Thus, a tradition of Michael and his evil counterpart fighting over a dead patriarch is attested in the cognitive environment, even if the exact text to which Jude refers has not been preserved. Kobelski suggests that the trope of the devil competing for the soul of the departed might be based on an interpretation of Zechariah 3, which also includes the phrase "the Lord rebuke you" seen in Jude 9.[142] However, Jude's point is not to affirm the authority of his (unknown) source, or to forensically reconstruct an event concerning the body of Moses, or to provide a formula to repel the devil either from claiming one's own body or soul (compare to the spells of the Egyptian *Book of the Dead*) or to counter any of the devil's activates in general (i.e., a formula for exorcism or instructions for "spiritual warfare"). Michael in Jude 9 is contrasted with "ungodly people [who] pollute their own bodies, reject authority and heap abuse on celestial beings," referring to improprieties on the part of certain members of the community. Jude's point is that even Michael, who would have the right to abuse celestial beings if anyone does, did not heap abuse on even the devil, the celestial being who would deserve to be abused more than any of them. If even Michael knew that it was improper to heap abuse on even the devil, then Jude's audience should know that it is far more improper for them, with less status than Michael, to heap abuse on "celestial beings" who deserve it less than the devil. What exactly the malefactors are doing is unclear, but it occurs in a list of things that they should theoretically know not to do, and they are compared in Jude 11 to Cain, Balaam, and Korah. The purpose of the passage is not to authoritatively confirm something that the devil did, or to provide an authoritative formula for confronting the devil in any circumstance.

In 2 Corinthians 12:17 Paul claims to have been "given a thorn in my flesh, a messenger of Satan, to torment me." Who gave it to him is not specified, but the Lord refuses to take it away (2 Cor 12:8), which indicates that it serves God's purpose, specified as keeping Paul from becoming conceited (2 Cor 12:7). Who or what the thorn consists of is not specified. Page suggests illness,[143] but personifying an illness as an "angel of Satan" (*angelos*, NIV "messenger") is unusual, even though demons were indeed considered to cause some illnesses.[144] If the "thorn" is a person (or group of people), however, then affiliating them with Satan is a means of describing their behavior, just as we saw with the association of Satan and Judas. If the thorn is a person, it is also possible that the audience knows who it is. The need to disparage this person and their

141. Kobelski, *Melchizedek*, 28.

142. Kobelski, *Melchizedek*, 76–77.

143. Page, *Powers*, 197.

144. The creatures that cause spirit-induced illness are usually called *pneuma* [something], e.g., *pneuma alalon* in Mark 9:17 or *pneuma ponēron* in LXX 1 Sam 16:14.

obstructive activities might explain why Satan is mentioned at all; the thorn clearly serves God's purpose, so otherwise it is difficult to understand the rhetorical purpose of the reference. There is no indication that the message is intended to teach others that their own afflictions should be attributed to messengers of Satan;[145] Paul's contrast of the condition with his visionary experiences indicate that his situation is not meant to be normative (and, again, the affliction is ultimately attributed to God, regardless of the specifics of the agency). It may even be possible that the "angel of Satan" is a reference comparing Paul to Job. In the *Testament of Job*, Satan's afflictions allow Job to demonstrate patience, which is a virtue that combats pride,[146] which is what Paul's thorn also does; we might also compare the statement "My grace is sufficient for you" (2 Cor 12:9) with the reassurance to Job that "you will know that the Lord is just, true, and strong, giving strength to his elect ones" (*T. Job* 4.11).[147] However, any identification of the thorn is purely speculative, and the message of the text—an admonition not to brag about status or achievement because these are to be attributed to God—is clear regardless of the precise identification of the thorn.

In 1 Thessalonians 2:18, Paul claims that he was prevented from visiting the church by Satan. Boyd argues that these passages prove that Satan is able to oppose God's will for the church and compares the episode to Daniel 10.[148] His assumption is that anything Paul wants, God must also want. However, Paul's missionary desires are thwarted again in Acts 16:7, but there the obstructing agent is the "spirit of Jesus." Clearly, then, the message of 1 Thessalonians 2:18 is not, as Boyd suggests, that any opposition to "ministry" should be attributed to Satan's ability to powerfully resist the will and desires of God.[149] As always, associating something or someone with Satan is a way to comment on the nature of their behavior, not a propositional treatise about cosmic operations or observable phenomena. In Acts 16:7 the obstruction is being interpreted as a positive providential development; in 1 Thessalonians 2:18 it is interpreted as a negative obstacle. Neither passage is intending to identify the agencies behind the obstruction. Or, said another way, if agencies *are* being identified, we must conclude that Jesus can oppose our ministerial efforts as well as Satan can (as we also saw in the discussion of Matt 13:13 and 2 Cor 4:3) and therefore we cannot conclude from a simple observation of obstruction that Satan is responsible. No further speculation about the specifics of Paul's situation is possible without knowing what exactly the opposition consisted of.

145. Contra, for example, Boyd, *God at War*, 277: "Clearly, for Paul, Satan is an ever-present reality ready to inflict physical suffering whenever able to do so."

146. Spittler, "Testament of Job," 845n15e. However, the word for pride in *T. Job*. 15.8 is *hyperephania*, as opposed to the rare *hyperairō* in 2 Cor 12:7.

147. Translated by Spittler, in *OTP* 1:841.

148. Boyd, *God at War*, 53.

149. "The contrast of Paul's earnest desire with Satan's obstruction also says something about Paul's view of just how powerful and successful Satan could be in opposition to the ministry." Boyd, *God at War*, 278.

DEMONS AND SPIRITS IN THE AGE OF THE CHURCH

In 1 John 3:8 the author states that "The reason the Son of God appeared was to destroy the devil's work," and in Hebrews 2:14 the author states that "[Jesus] too shared in their humanity so that by his death he might break the power of him who holds the power of death—that is, the devil." Both of these passages reference the cognitive environment's expectation that the messianic age would coincide with the destruction of the devil in order to further their arguments. In 1 John 3 the emphasis is on the antithetical typological relationship between the sons of light and the sons of darkness; "this is how we know who the children of God are and who the children of the devil are: anyone who does not do what is right is not God's child" (1 John 3:10). In Hebrews the phrase occurs as part of a complex argument defending the integrity of the incarnation. Attridge suggests that the emphasis on the *devil* in connection with death invokes well-established Jewish tradition (e.g., *Jub.* 49.2; Wis 2:24) and is intended to emphasize that the "death" he refers to is the literal departure of physical life, as opposed to the metaphorical uses found occasionally in Paul (e.g., Rom 6), where "death" is a spiritual state of sin, or in Gnosticism, where "death" is a metaphor for spiritual ignorance.[150] This emphasis on literal rather than metaphorical death fits well with the passage's emphasis on literal rather than metaphorical incarnation. Neither passage is intended to reveal or affirm details about the devil's work or the devil's relationship to death, or to provide information about Christ's purpose that the audience would not have already known—both arguments use Christ's destruction of the devil as a premise, not a conclusion. There is certainly no evidence that these passages teach that "the coming of Christ was necessitated by Satan."[151] The eschatological battle tradition that the image references never depicts the messiah as reacting in response to the devil's initiative; both the prince of light and the prince of darkness are established by God to do exactly what they do (see chapter 9).

2 Thessalonians 2:3–12 describes a "man of lawlessness" (2 Thess 2:3) whose appearance "will be in accordance with how Satan works" (2 Thess 2:9). This character is often identified with the beasts from the sea and earth in Revelation 13, who receive their power from the dragon (Satan) in Revelation 13:2, 12. Both passages are allusions to the imagery of Daniel 7–12, where the malefactor is Antiochus Epiphanes (see chapter 9). Here the original audience would have known who the "man of lawlessness" (and also the beast in Revelation; compare to the "man of mockery" in the *Damascus Document* from Qumran)[152] refers to, even if the reference is no longer clear to us. One popular interpretation is that the lawless man is the Roman Emperor Nero, which seems as likely as any. For our purposes, the identification of the man of lawlessness is less important than his association with Satan and the discussion of "how Satan works" in 2 Thessalonians 2:9–12. We should not read the message of this passage to be instruction to the effect of "there is a person called Satan, and he

---

150. Attridge, *Hebrews*, 92.
151. Contra Page, *Powers*, 206.
152. Geniza A 1.14; Wise, Abegg, and Cook, *Dead Sea Scrolls*, 52.

carries out his work through lawless people and through signs and wonders, so now when you see lawless people and signs and wonders you will know that they should be attributed to Satan even though people who have not read this epistle will have other explanations for them." Instead, association of the lawless man (whoever he is) with Satan is another example of the familiar practice of interpreting a person's actions, and the general description of "how Satan works" falls within the Satan character's established function of leading people astray. 2 Thessalonians 2:11–12 specifically states that the "delusion" is sent from God (Gk. *pseudos*, also referring back to the "displays of power through signs and wonders *that serve the lie*" in 2 Thessalonians 2:9; *sēmeiois kai terasin pseudous*); this concept invokes God's deception of prophets in 1 Kings 22:22 and Ezekiel 14:9, and also fits with the general understanding in the cognitive environment that the prince of darkness is empowered by God to do what he does for the purpose of bringing destruction to the wicked (2 Thess 2:12; compare *Jub.* 10:8). The warning contained in 2 Thessalonians 2 is not about the specifics of the devil's methods, but rather a warning against believing lies (2 Thess 2:1–3), the consequences of which are emphasized by associating them with the devil.

Finally, two passages mention members of the community being "handed over to Satan" (1 Cor 5:5; 1 Tim 1:20). Page suggests that "handing over to Satan" refers to excommunication.[153] This is theoretically possible because membership in the community of the people of God and the community of the people of the devil is mutually exclusive, and so appointing someone to one means excluding them from the other, and vice versa (see also 1 Cor 10:20, as discussed in chapter 11). However, it is not clear that "handing over to Satan" means "numbering among the people of Satan." The preferred Greek word for excommunication is *anathema* (NIV "cursed," e.g., 1 Cor 16:22; Rom 9:3; Gal 1:8–9), so this is the word we would expect to see if excommunication were intended. Admittedly, though, as discussed in chapter 11, the reference to Deuteronomy 13:5 in 1 Corinthians 5:13 does invoke the *anathema*. However, this in turn might be a general policy guidance regarding the list of offenders in 1 Corinthians 5:9–11, as opposed to a verdict on the specific individual from 1 Corinthians 5:5; in other words, "expel the wicked person" might not be parallel to "hand this man over to Satan." Further, in 1 Timothy 10:20 the purpose of "handing over" is "to be taught not to blaspheme" and in 1 Corinthians 5:5 the purpose is "that his spirit may be saved," and it is difficult to understand how excommunication would serve either an educative or salvific role; certainly the "expelling" in Deuteronomy 13 does neither. Thus, we should examine the phrase to see if it might indicate something other than excommunication.

The word "handed over" (*paradidōmi*) [to Satan] is the same word used in the LXX of Job 2:6, "he is in your hands," lit. "I [God] hand him over to you [Satan]." We might note that what Satan wants to happen to Job ("strike his flesh and bones") is very similar to what Paul wants to happen to the Corinthian deviant ("hand this man

153. Page, *Powers*, 202–3.

over to Satan for the destruction of the flesh"; the word for "flesh" [*sarx*] is the same in both, though the usage in Paul might be idiomatic). If "hand over to Satan" means "do to them what God did to Job," then we might gain better insight as to what the action signifies. Notably, Job is never considered to have been punished for offense. Paul's statement that he has "passed judgment" (*krinō*) might indicate that the action meted out to the Corinthian deviant is somehow punitive (though a clearer word for "declare guilty and commit to punishment" is the variant *katakrinō*, e.g., 1 Cor 11:32, NIV "condemned"),[154] but nonetheless we should note that neither Corinthians nor Timothy state that the persons are handed over to Satan "to get what they deserve." Thus, while offense might provide the occasion for handing over to Satan, *punishment* is not the intended purpose for Paul's imperative to "hand them over to Satan." In any case, the *circumstances* of the "handing over" are clearly not the same as those that tradition imparts to Job; the referents in the epistles are not being tested for either faith or endurance. However, as discussed above, the *Testament of Job* indicates that Job's affliction will secure him a place in the resurrection (*T. Job* 4.9), which is conceptually similar to Paul's "saved on the day of the Lord" in 1 Corinthians 5:5. Further, the idea that the suffering of those *who remain within the community* can serve to propitiate offense (and be rewarded by resurrection) is well attested in Second Temple period in general (e.g., 2 Macc 7:14, 18). Thus, it seems likely that the individuals in question are somehow subjected to afflictions while still remaining a part of the community. What exactly the "handing over to Satan" consists of is unclear. Certainly, there is no indication that the church leaders were supposed to carry out the destruction of the man's flesh *themselves*, as later inquisitors would be inclined to do.[155] Various references in Ephesians indicate that the power of the Holy Spirit through the church was thought to be able to provide the Christians with protection from Satan (see above), just as God had "put a hedge around" Job in Job 1:10. "Handing over to Satan" might indicate that this protection is removed (as Job's was), leaving the victim (at least in their own perception) vulnerable to the demonic affliction that they acknowledged, anticipated, and feared.[156] Ultimately, however, the point is not to instruct the church for all time in a particular method of discipline, or to offer a technical theological treatise about how salvation works (i.e., through propitiation by affliction at the hands of Satan), or to offer authoritative teaching about whether people outside the church belong to Satan, or to affirm that there really is someone called Satan that people can be "handed over"

---

154. *NIDNTTE*, "*krinō*" 2:748.

155. As always, associating actions with Satan always portrays the people performing the actions negatively, even if those actions ultimately serve God's purposes; nobody in the Second Temple environment would ever want to step in and fill the shoes of Satan.

156. Today in the West we do not usually threaten deviants with demonic affliction because demonic affliction is not real to us and is not generally considered a legitimate danger. However, modern [Catholic and Orthodox] churches have a status called "member in good standing." Those who lose their "good standing" are not excommunicated, but they are cut off from the benefits of the sacraments and other kinds of participation in the community until they restore themselves.

to with the result of producing relatively specific or empirically verifiable phenomena. The concept of giving a person to Satan does not seem to indicate expelling them from the community—compare perhaps to the Old Testament status "outside the camp" (e.g., Lev 13:46) in contrast to "cut off from the people"—but nonetheless the condition of belonging to Satan is negative and undesirable. The reason why they chose this particular idiom (instead of, say, "give them over to God [for judgment]") might be to invoke the negative connotations of belonging to Satan while also distinguishing these individuals from those who suffer afflictions attributed to Satan in the course of "fighting the good fight" and "running the race" (compare Eph 6:13).

After examining all of these passages, we can see that none of them are written for the purpose of providing the audience with information about Satan or demons that they did not already know. If that is not the purpose for which the texts were written, then that is not the purpose for which they should be used. The texts use the audience's existing knowledge of Satan and demons to talk about something else—it is simply a means to an end. If the text is affirming something else, something that has nothing to do with trivia about the Satan and demons, then the text's authority cannot be invoked to affirm trivia about Satan and demons. However, even by its own admission, conflict theology does not typically *derive* its demonology *tabula rasa* from proof-texts; rather it invokes the text as a rationalizing support for a conclusion it has already drawn on philosophical or theological grounds. It is this line of reasoning and not the text-in-context per se that provides conflict theology with its primary warrant, and so these philosophical and theological concerns are worth some brief examination.

Part 4

Conflict Theology on Its Own Terms

Chapter 15

Demons and the problem of evil

CONFLICT THEOLOGY ALWAYS DOUBLES as a theodicy, wherein God's ongoing war with Satan and demons is invoked to explain the phenomenon of evil: "the good and evil, fortunate and unfortunate, aspects of life are to be interpreted largely as the result of good and evil, friendly or hostile, spirits warring against each other and against us."[1] Likewise, "believing in evil spirits may . . . play a significant role in preserving belief in the goodness of God,"[2] and "if we want help from the Bible for dealing with the problem of evil, we must be willing to take seriously what the Bible takes seriously: the intense involvement in life of a figure named Satan and his powers of darkness."[3] The problem of evil as a whole is far too broad a topic for this study, but we will briefly examine the way in which demons are invoked as a means to solve it.

The freewill defense

Invoking demons as an explanation for evil is not new, but the current form of the argument is derived from a corollary of Alvin Plantinga's "freewill defense" described in *God, Freedom, and Evil*, which refutes an argument by J. L. Mackie that Christian theism is inherently self-contradictory.[4] The freewill defense is a specific form of the broader "greater-good defense," which essentially argues that the evil we experience is allowed by God in service of some greater good. Plantinga's argument states that it is theoretically possible that the freedom of free creatures to choose between good or evil is valuable enough—that is, is a great enough good—to justify the evil that they (inevitably) do as a result of using that freedom. He does not claim that this *in fact* is the reason why God allows evil, but as long as it remains possible then there is no logical contradiction within Christianity.[5] The freewill defense, however, covers only the evil that leads from the actions of creatures, it does not extend to what

1. Boyd, *God at War*, 13.
2. Page, *Powers*, 268.
3. Arnold, *Powers*, 11.
4. Plantinga, *God, Freedom, and Evil*.
5. Plantinga, *God, Freedom, and Evil*, 28.

we call "natural evil." Plantinga addresses this issue by pointing out that Christians have traditionally acknowledged powerful spirit-beings who also have free will, who could manipulate natural phenomena.[6] Once again he does not propose free will (of creatures or demons) as the *solution* to the problem of evil; his conclusion is that if Mackie wanted to prove that theisim is inherently contradictory, his argument would require more premises beyond God's omnipotence, omniscience, omnibenevolence, and the existence of evil. In that capacity the argument served its purpose, but subsequent interpreters have extended the argument far beyond its original scope, which has had some limited value for apologetics but has proved catastrophic for theology. The difference has to do with the differences between the respective disciplines, which is worth some brief attention.

Theology (most specifically, *systematic* theology) as a discipline tries to deduce truths about God and God's relationship with the world by deriving them from sources that supposedly reveal the truth of God; almost always the Bible and usually also some combination of tradition, reason, and nature. Apologetics, on the other hand, tries to prove that negative depictions of Christianity are either factually inaccurate or inconsistent with themselves, in terms that those producing the negative depiction are obligated to concede. In order to serve its purpose, the starting premises of an apologist must be the terms, definitions, and assumptions of their anti-Christian interlocutors. A theologian following the proper method of theology will wind up with a conclusion that is consistent with a theologian's premises—that is, the content of the Bible, supplemented perhaps by tradition, reason, and/or nature. On the other hand, a theologian who begins with an argument created by an apologist will necessarily have to adopt the *apologist's* premises—which by definition are the same premises held by those the apologist is trying to refute or persuade—with the result being that the theologian's conclusion will be consistent, not with the Bible, but with the beliefs of anti-Christians. This is unfortunately what has occurred in the case of conflict theology.

The freewill defense works as an apologetic, insofar as it does so, because it incorporates two premises that modern anti-Christians find difficult to reject. The first is the humanistic idea that God's goodness means that God's purposes consist solely or primarily of producing human happiness or human flourishing (see chapter 8), which the freewill defense adopts by conceding the reality of humanist definitions of "evil." The second is the essentially Nietzschian idea that the free exercise of self-will constitutes the highest good. Whether or not the apologist believes that the exercise of the will is valuable is irrelevant; the point is that if the interlocutor is willing to admit that it is valuable, they will lose their basis to complain about evil. Conflict theology runs into trouble when it moves beyond Plantinga and apologetics and actually *affirms* that free will *is* the greater good that God has created to allow evil—in Plantinga's terms, this entails converting a freewill *defense* into a freewill *theodicy*.[7] This conversion

6. Plantinga, *God, Freedom, and Evil*, 58.

7. Plantinga, *God, Freedom, and Evil*, 27–28.

also requires that the free will of the demons be conclusively affirmed as the cause of natural evil; this is what Page means when he says "believing in the existence of the devil and demons is not inherently more difficult than believing in a supreme being who is good and *may, in fact, be implicit in such a belief*. . . . [In the case of natural evil] one can appeal to a free-will defense if one attributes such evil to free moral agents that are not human, namely, to Satan and his angels."[8] This, ultimately, is the warrant for asserting the reality of evil spirits opposed to God; not to follow the evidence of the biblical text-in-context wherever it leads, but to validate a free-will theodicy as a solution to the problem of natural evil.

The problem with this approach is that neither the premise "God's goodness means that God wants to make people happy on their own terms" nor "free beings exercising their self-will is a greater good than if they did not do so" can be affirmed uncritically by theology, if even at all. More importantly for our purposes, the discussion of those questions has nothing whatsoever to do with the information about Satan and demons that conflict theologians produce by way of biblical support; the biblical passages are invoked to try to support the idea that Satan and demons exist, possess will and agency, and exercise a will that is contrary to God's. Because it adopts the framework of an atheistic/humanistic worldview—specifically, the particular definition of human happiness and the value of self-will—as a premise, the conflict cosmology is much more palatable to secular humanists and much more intuitive within a cognitive environment defined by secular humanism than traditional Christianity. However, the price for easy acceptance has been the transformation of this version of Christianity into little more than a nominally theistic derivative of secular humanism (see further discussion in chapter 16).

Cosmology and the greater good

The greater good defense in some form or another has been the church's preferred response to the problem of evil for most of its history, but for the most part it has refrained from trying to define exactly what the greater good consists of. Augustine specifically said that the comprehension of divine goodness was unattainable: "the substantiality of evil is an illusion. . . . Augustine could not, of course, retain this eternal viewpoint. As soon as one loses it . . . evil recovers its substance and power."[9] Traditional Christian theologians understood, as conflict theologians do not, that God's highest good and highest purpose would not necessarily correspond to something that would make sense to us, either in the form of the promulgation of human happiness or the facilitation of self-will. Traditional theology does not believe that God is good on the basis of some empirical measure of goodness, and it likewise does not believe in the "higher good" because it has empirically measured a higher form

8. Page, *Powers*, 268. Emphasis mine.

9. Forsyth, *Enemy*, 417; cf. Augustine, *Confessions*, 7.13–19.

of goodness. The argument that God is good essentially follows the same logic as the argument that God exists; there is too much order and too much *function* to account for, that could not be explained if God were evil.[10]

This observation of cosmic order is actually one of the strongest arguments *against* conflict theology, as expressed by John Chrysostom: "if God had entrusted the whole of this world to [demons'] authority, they would have confused and disturbed everything. . . . And I would ask this of those who say [that the world is under the authority of demons], what kind of disorder they behold in the present, that they set down all our affairs to the arrangement of demons?"[11] Chrysostom's evidence for the wholesale destruction that demonic authority necessarily and instantly produces is derived from the treatment of Job's possessions and the swine of Gadara when they were turned over to demons. While he is not interpreting the texts correctly according to their original context, nonetheless his point remains valid; if demons are what conflict theology claims them to be, and have the power that conflict theology requires them to have, the world should be in a much greater state of disorder than it is. The functional monism of classical theology may have a problem of evil, but functional dualism (i.e., conflict theology) has a problem of *goodness* that is no less pressing. Said another way: if God's relative lack of control over the world and its affairs, which conflict theology requires, still allows for the manifestation of most of the world's order and function, then that order and function exists and operates independently of God in equal degree. This in turn is more or less the same theological system expressed in deism. Once again, the issue of God's successful sustaining of the word order cannot be addressed by pointing at proof-texts that affirm the Bible's authors believed in demons. Nonetheless, a thorough and consistent conflict theology must explain how the world can exist in such a high degree of order and providence that we must conclude that God created it, while simultaneously claiming that the world exists in such a state of chaos and disorder that God could not possibly be in control of its affairs to any significant degree. There may well be reasons to object to the church's classical functional monism, but any argument to that effect needs to address the objections it raised against dualism and also provide an alternative to areas that it legitimately explains, while also maintaining distinction from the deists, agnostics, and atheists in its conception of God, otherwise conflict theology simply becomes a functional derivative of deism, agnosticism, or atheism. None of these are accomplished by using proof-texts to accumulate information about Satan and demons.

Comfort and blame

Evil is not simply a logical problem for abstract philosophy; it presents an acute emotional problem as well. The classical greater-good defense, for better or worse, is

10. See for example Augustine, *De ordine* 1.2.

11. John Chrysostom, *De Diabolo Tentatore*, trans. Brandram, in *NPNF1* 9:184.

largely a construct of abstract deductive theology. Those who affirm it do not necessarily believe that a grieving person will be *comforted* by the assurance that "God is in his heaven and all is right with the world." Conflict theologians sometimes argue that attributing evil to demons is more comforting than attributing it to the inscrutable providence of God. Be that as it may, theologians are not counselors any more than theologians are apologists; a theologian is accountable to truth (through whatever source conveys truth; Scripture, reason, tradition, or otherwise), not emotion, and what is or is not comforting is relative to the psychology of the person in question. Providing comfort is the function of pastors or therapists; they can call on the theologians if theology will help in any given circumstance, but theologians must be attentive to their own functions.[12]

But now we must ask a question that is very hard: are there some things that *should* comfort us, and some things that *should* not? We might imagine the difference between a suffering person who finds comfort in the hope that some benefit may come from it (to themselves or others), and someone who takes a kind of spiteful solace in the knowledge that at least others are suffering as well. If human happiness is an end in itself then there is no difference; humans are humans and all humans should be equally happy. This is the case in secular humanism, where all humans are inherently good and inherently deserving of happiness. But most forms of Christianity, including at least nominally most conflict theology (though see chapter 16), believe that some humans are not good; therefore, since human happiness should correspond to human goodness, there are theoretically some people who *should not* be happy. That of course is not to say that those who are unhappy necessarily deserve it—that is simply another form of the retribution principle (which is useless as a theodicy; see chapter 13) and represents another example of trying to pigeonhole God's higher purpose into something that accords with our sensibilities. "Giving people what they deserve" is not God's higher purpose for allowing evil. The point rather is that the phenomenon of "comfort" is not itself sufficient to prove the truth of a system without some accompanying idea of when and under what conditions human comfort *ought* to occur, which (at minimum) should involve a definition of goodness and an understanding of the "chief end of man." If it turns out that the Bible teaches that humans are inherently good (unless perhaps they do something bad) and that the purpose of humanity is for God to make them happy on their own terms, then so be it, but that cannot be established by pointing to proof-texts about Satan and demons.

The classical Christian stance has been that the Christian should train their mind so that when the (inevitable) suffering comes they will *be able to* take comfort in God's sovereign rule, instead of petulantly "firing" God because he did not see to their happiness. This is often considered to be part of the "training" that Paul mentions in 1 Corinthians 9:25: "Everyone who competes in the games goes into strict training. They do it to get a crown that will not last, but we do it to get a crown that will last

---

12. See for example Plantinga, *God, Freedom, and Evil*, 29.

forever." Paul is specifically talking about the passions of the body, but the concept applies equally to the passions of the mind. In practical terms, this discipline includes cultivating a perception of God who does not serve as merely a means to achieve what we think happiness consists of; whether that means that God is not interested in our happiness at all (e.g., Job 1:21; Eccl 1:13–14) or whether it means the happiness that God intends for us is not appreciable by ordinary human standards (e.g., Heb 12:2; Jas 1:2) is not relevant for this study. The point is that conflict theology, by using demons to defend a concept of God who produces human happiness on human terms, actually serves to undermine this particular discipline. Consequently, the comfort it offers is little different from what a deist or atheist could offer: "bad things happen and God can't do anything about it." Whether God cannot do anything about it because he does not exist (atheism), does not care (deism), or wants to help but cannot because Satan is too strong (conflict theology) is ultimately academic; if atheism offered no comfort, then people would not seek comfort by discarding their faith. Boyd offers an example of a woman who [ostensibly] ascribed to classical monism who lost a child and consequently lost her faith: "[she] admitted that she had never forgiven God for taking away her child."[13] He goes on to imply that his conflict theology would have allowed her to retain it: "what . . . could have led this poor woman instinctively to blame God for her daughter's diabolical death? . . . [W]as it not the entrenched belief that somehow all events, however horrifying, fit into God's plan, and thus . . . must somehow serve a divine purpose?"[14] But there are others who affirm classical Christian providence who also suffer and do not lose their faith; even continent-spanning plagues in the Middle Ages could not empty the churches. The difference is not the theology, the difference is the person.[15] The woman in Boyd's thought experiment did not lose her faith because she believed that God was sovereign; she lost her faith because she had no use for a God who would not or could not act in ways that made her happy. The problem was not that the church taught her that God was all-powerful; the problem was the church taught her (or let her believe) that God is servile, that God's love and goodness means that we should expect him to do everything in his power to make us happy. Boyd's conflict theology advocates the same servile God and would not have helped her. While some people might be able to find some assurance in the fact that "at least God is trying" and thereby forgive his incompetence (as this woman could not), and others may take a more savage solace in the assurance that at least God is suffering too, and still others may hold out hope for a future where God will finally defeat Satan and reshape the world into the form they think it ought to be—none of which deism or

13. Boyd, *God at War*, 40.

14. Boyd, *God at War*, 40.

15. We do not know this person. Boyd chose to use her case for his argument (with or without her knowledge and with what accuracy we do not know; he is quoting a newspaper and speculating, not documenting a personal interview) and we are responding to the caricature in his theological thought experiment, not commenting on the psychology or motives of a real person in a real tragedy.

atheism can offer—it is not clear that any of these approaches are entirely commendable. Ultimately, however, the point is not whether conflict theology is comforting or not, or whether that serves as a point in its favor; the point is that simply assembling a barrage of proof-texts about Satan and demons is not sufficient to support a complete theodicy. The full picture of evil and its solutions has more to do with what we think about the nature and activity of *God* than it has to do with the nature and activity of demons, since demons are defined relative to gods (see chapter 8). This means that, in order to present this theology as representing the authoritative teaching of the Bible, *every aspect* of it needs to be established from the biblical text, including its definition of *goodness* and its definition of *God*. Conflict theologians in general do not attempt to do this; they emphasize the deficiencies of Enlightenment materialism or (in Boyd's case) traditional Christianity and simply assume their entire theological system as the default alternative based on a few proof-texts about the devil. However, we have demonstrated throughout this work that even their understanding of the devil is open to serious question, and the rest of the system remains largely unsupported and undefended (though Boyd at least does try to tie in his demonology with the broader particulars of open theism).

The other problem of evil

The final and most pressing problem with the use of demons to explain evil is that demons are not sufficient to explain all instances of evil. Demons can explain evil that is attributable to demons, but demons cannot explain evil that is attributed to other causes, and cannot explain the demons themselves. Even Boyd admits that "there is still [the question of] why God would create a world in which cosmic war could break out. In this sense the problem of theodicy remains even within a warfare worldview."[16] Thus, the *war itself* is an evil that must be explained, either as something that God could stop but won't, or as something that God wants to stop but can't. If God could stop the war but won't, it means that for some reason he wants the war to occur. If God wants the war to occur, then the war serves some good purpose and the "enemies" are still acting according to God's will even as they engage in battle; this is more or less the position adopted by the Qumran community (see chapter 9). In this conception, the war becomes a cosmetic explanation for certain phenomena but does not explain evil, nor does it avoid attributing that evil to the will and purposes of God. Nonetheless, the activity of demons is important to understand for those who wish to *treat* the problems *caused* by those phenomena; this is Arnold's primary emphasis.[17] As a metaphor, a physician needs to be able to identify which diseases are caused by bacteria (as opposed to viruses or prions) to be able to treat them effectively, but the affirmation that some diseases are caused by bacteria contributes nothing to the question of why we

16. Boyd, *God at War*, 21.

17. See for example Arnold, *Powers*, 201.

live in a world where disease can occur. Bacteria can explain certain manifestations of disease but not disease in general; likewise, demons can explain some manifestations of evil, but not evil in general. Whether or not demons are in fact responsible for *any* phenomena is beyond the scope of this study and cannot be determined by biblical proof-texts (see chapter 6).

On the other hand, if God wants to stop the war but can't, then an explanation apart from the war itself must be postulated as the reason for why the war was able to occur. This is Boyd's position and he attributes the war to limitations, defects, and mistakes on the part of God, in accordance with his open theism. Examining the particulars of open theism is beyond the scope of this study; for our purposes, the important point is that open theism is a *theology proper*, not a demonology, and thus is concerned with establishing the nature and properties of *God*, not the nature and properties of Satan and demons. Once evil is attributed to God's weaknesses, limitations, failures, and mistakes, the secondary agencies that exploit those weaknesses and mistakes (demons) are mostly cosmetic, unless, again, one is trying to engage a specific phenomenon. In either case, once the properties of God are established, the demons become mostly incidental; this is consistent with the observation that demons fill the gaps in a cosmological system left empty by the conception of gods. On the other hand, without establishing the properties of God, the properties of demons are of limited value and cannot be employed as an explanation for evil on their own. More traditional conflict theologians generally argue that the war is evil and that God is trying to end it as fast as he can—this assertion takes the specific form of the insistence of the reality of the war and the genuine opposition of the enemies to God's will—and normally attribute the cause to the supposed greater good of creatures being allowed to exercise their wills. Whether the end of the war will entail removing this supposedly "highest good" so that war will never break out again or by somehow eliminating all creatures whose exercise of will would lead to another war is not explained; neither is it explained why these future conditions were not the conditions established in the first place. Once again, even in a freewill theodicy, demons are only one of many free beings whose exercise of will produces evil; they can be blamed for certain phenomena (i.e., natural evil) but not for evil itself, which is ultimately attributed to a greater good (the free exercise of free will). Thus, Forsyth observes, "Fallen angels are not, in the end, a very useful solution to the problem of evil; they merely push the problem back a stage."[18]

However, there is an aspect of attributing evil to demons that conflict theologians treat as more than merely cosmetic: attributing evil to demons is supposed to provide a motivation for people to fight against it that other presentations of evil cannot. We will examine this and other psychological entailments of conflict theology in the next chapter.

18. Forsyth, *Enemy*, 187.

Chapter 16

The entailments of conflict theology

T HE FINAL WARRANT FOR conflict theology that does not derive from the content of the biblical text is the claim that any other understanding of evil will render the people who ascribe to it unable to effectively work against that evil. Sometimes the claim is mechanistic; evil must be treated according to its cause, just as injury or illness must be treated according to its cause. In this conception, evil caused by spirits must be dealt with differently than evil caused by other sources—namely through "spiritual warfare" of some kind—or else the countermeasures will be ineffective. People who do not acknowledge the reality of the spirits will be unlikely to employ the effective treatment, just as people who do not believe in bacteria would be unlikely to sterilize a wound. We have already discussed this concept in chapter 6 and in chapter 14 in accordance with our examination of Mark 9:14–29 and Ephesians 6:12, upon which the conception is primarily based. Our present concern is a claim that is not mechanistic but psychological: namely, that people will be more *motivated* to oppose evil if they think it is caused by demons than if they think it serves some role in the purposes of God. This claim deserves further attention.

Motivation to fight

> If all evil is believed to serve a higher divine purpose, then clearly one's sense of urgency in fighting it is compromised. . . . [T]his is precisely what has tended to happen within the Christian tradition since at least the time of Augustine. . . . The western tradition has more frequently exhibited a church that is perpetually baffled by evil but singularly ineffective in combating it.[1]

This is Boyd's third warrant for his conflict theology (in addition to its proposed solution to evil, addressed in the previous chapter, and its cosmetic similarity to other cultures, addressed in chapter 5 and further below) and he is not alone. Page adds,

> The person who discerns a satanic dimension in the evils of the world can hardly rest content with the status quo. The belief that the devil ultimately stands behind evil provides a powerful incentive for combating it. If the

---

1. Boyd, *God at War*, 22.

present state of the world is viewed as due in part to forces that are inimical to God, then the various expressions of evil may be attacked without fear that one is opposing God.[2]

In this perception, even if conflict theology cannot be decisively proved, its results are valuable enough that it should be considered to be true anyway, so long as it remains theoretically *possible*. Thus, most conflict theologians concentrate energy on debunking attempts to disprove the reality of spirits, instead of trying to establish each element of their own worldview. But the argument also contains an explicit accusation that the church's classical functional monism—the belief that evil somehow falls in accordance with the will and purposes of God—will necessarily engender a complacency towards evil. For now, the most important aspect of this accusation is that it is not based on *formal doctrine*, but rather on implicit psychological influences.

Very few doctrines of divine sovereignty explicitly state that God's prevailing will means that Christians should not attempt to alter the state of the world. Even the most ardent Calvinists argue that human action—including opposition to evil—is necessary because human action reflects God's will in the world. Whether or not that is somehow internally inconsistent is not relevant for this study; the point is that the conflict theologians' accusation is not based on anything the doctrine claims for itself, but on something that it might conceivably encourage its adherents to do. Undoubtedly, there are some people who use the sovereignty of God as an excuse for complacency or apathy, even in defiance of their own formal theology. Examples could easily be put forth. But if that is a reason to attack the doctrine itself, then it must be said that conflict theology carries some fairly nasty psychological entailments of its own—that is, ideas that are not formally stated in its doctrine but that could easily be derived from its tenets and even asserted to form its natural and logical conclusions. If psychology is to serve as a motive for adopting or avoiding doctrine, then these must undergo careful scrutiny.

The inhibition of Christian enmity

Boyd's assessment about the puzzlement and complacency of the Middle Ages towards evil is patently false on both counts. Even by his own admission, the Roman church was not confused by evil; they filed it under the doctrine of providence and ignored it.[3] As for urgency and enthusiasm in combatting evil, most people would assert that the church of the Middle Ages fought, not too little, but too much. Apathy and complacency are not terms commonly invoked to describe the crusades, inquisitions, and witch hunts that the medieval Christians employed against the devil and his agents. Their method was actually quite similar to the one advocated by some

2. Page, *Powers*, 269.
3. Boyd, *God at War*, 55.

conflict theologians; after determining the demonic character of the enemy through a combination of syncretized pagan theology and selective application of misinterpreted scriptures, they "revolted against all that God revolts against"[4] and went to war. However, conflict theology does not generally advocate the literal *demonizing* of enemies, in the sense of providing a justification to do things to them that one would hesitate to do to "ordinary" humans. That is perhaps possible within conflict theology, but any other theological system can do it just as easily. The real issue is that conflict theology encourages a stance and attitude towards enemies that is not demonstrably different from the enmity exhibited by those who are not Christians.

In the Sermon on the Mount, Jesus teaches, "You have heard that it was said, 'Love your neighbor and hate your enemy.' But I tell you, love your enemies and pray for those who persecute you" (Matt 5:44–45). The imperatives of the sermon are not rules or commands; their content is not unique to Jesus; and their purpose in the discourse is to recapitulate Moses' giving of the law. Nonetheless, the sayings combine to create an impressionistic description of the order of the kingdom of God, just as the sayings of the Torah combined to create an impressionistic description of the covenant order of Israel (see chapter 8). The order the Sermon depicts is an order in which the intuitive logic of the surrounding world is inverted, which is a theme that continues throughout the Gospels and Epistles; the first is the last, the least is the greatest, joy comes through suffering, and so on. The particular *details* are not important; the point is that the logic that governs the order of the new covenant should be radically different from the logic that governs the rest of the world.[5] This includes the logic of how the Christian approaches the concept of *enemies*.

Importantly, the imperative to "love your enemies" is not an imperative *not to have* enemies. Rather, it means to behave charitably towards them *while acknowledging their status as enemies*, as is also demonstrated in, e.g., Proverbs 5:21–22 and Romans 12:20. In the context of modern humanism, however, "love" is defined not in terms of *charity* but rather in terms of *tolerance* and *indulgence*. This is the same thing we usually mean when we say that God "loves" us; he tolerates—that is, "forgives"—our failures and indulges our desires. "Enemies," on the other hand, are defined as those who do things that no moral person could tolerate and no moral person could indulge. Thus, the imperative to "love one's enemies" moves beyond paradoxical to become simply oxymoronic. A solution is reached by combining Jesus's teaching with the homiletic motto "love the sinner, hate the sin" (perhaps derived from Jude 1:23) and the all-important Ephesians 6:12: "our struggle is not against flesh and blood, but . . . against the spiritual forces of evil." In this conception, the ones we *thought* were our enemies, the ones who hate us and persecute us, are not really our enemies at all. They are our neighbors, beloved of God, fellows in the fraternity of good and innocent humanity, driven to evil by some combination of a bad upbringing, oppressive social

4. Boyd, *God at War*, 22.

5. Developed on the scale of a book in Walton and Walton, *Lost World of the Torah*.

institutions, or (most importantly) demonic activity. Because they are our neighbors and not our enemies, loving them is no longer oxymoronic, even if doing so requires a certain degree of courage. But what about our *true* enemies, the "powers of evil in the heavenly realms," whatever they consist of? Nobody ever thinks we should love the devil or pray for the devil,[6] even though he is considered to be our enemy and even though he persecutes us; most everyone agrees, probably correctly, that Jesus's saying was not intended to apply to the demons, although it should be noted that his followers are never instructed to *hate* the demons either.[7] Nonetheless, within conflict theology the hate, fear, and rage that was once reserved for human enemies is now projected onto the devil; as Russell says, "we must fight against this evil with every syllable of our sanity."[8] But is loving those we think of as our neighbors (even if they mistreat us) while hating those we think of as our enemies (even if they deserve it) really the inversion of worldly logic that Jesus and others are talking about?

The imperative to "love your enemies" is not a moral command, though conflict theologians and their propositional hermeneutic would probably treat it as one. Nonetheless, it is good advice, and the reason for this is because the imperatives to love and pray are not for the sake of our enemies, but for the sake of ourselves. The hate, rage, and fear that we direct towards our enemies has harmful effects on our own minds and souls; it hurts us more than it hurts those we direct it against. In classical Christianity, the passions are not inherently *evil*, but they can be harmful and they need to be controlled with the virtue of self-discipline; early ascetics even likened the passions to possessing demons (usually on the basis of such passages as Eph 4:26, 30–31), which is especially relevant in light of conflict theology's own assertion that the beliefs of the early church concerning the nature and form of the demonic should inform our own.[9] The inversion of the world's logic that defines Christian enmity ought to replace hate, rage, and fear with charity and prayer (prayer *for*, not prayer *against*), for our own sake if nothing else. Conflict theology, on the other hand, retains the world's logic of enmity, but redirects it against the devil, thus allowing the hate, rage, and fear to continue to fester in our souls. More than fester, conflict theology actually encourages the *amplification* of the passions; this is the source of the motivation for which conflict theology commends itself. Some people may be saintly enough that they can hate and

6. At least, it is not common. Enoch tried to intercede for the watchers in *1 En.* 13:4–9, and in some systems of universalism the fallen angels will eventually be saved.

7. The word Jesus uses for the hate that is not to be given to enemies (*miseō*) is used only twice as an imperative or commendation (Jude 23 and Rev 2:6, respectively) and takes neither demons nor persons as an object; the objects are a metaphorical description of what is most likely sin, and the "practices of the Nicolaitans," respectively. Romans 12:9 ("hate what is evil") uses a different word (*apostugeō*, a hapax in the Greek Bible) that means *abhor* or *detest* and may expect the audience to react with avoidance (comparable to Heb. *tôʿēbâ*, see chapter 11) rather than hostility; note that the juxtaposed term ("cling to") is also a spacial metaphor, not an attitude.

8. Russell, *Mephistopheles*, 301.

9. See, for example, Boyd, *God at War*, 55; Arnold, *Questions*, 60–61 (although specifically about heresy, the argument still relies on an appeal to early Christian authority).

rage without harm—God himself can do both—but presumably there is a qualitative difference between righteous outrage and the anger that "gives foothold to the devil." If nothing else, the anger and hatred of the Christian should be clearly distinguished from the anger and hatred of the non-Christian. The conflict theologians themselves, however, rely heavily on crass appeals to emotion to incite the passions against things that most non-Christians in the same culture would consider equally hateful—Nazis, tortured children, abused animals, and so on. It is the same hate against the same enemies, and the deleterious effect of negative emotion on the psyche is not lessened by cosmetically hiding its objects behind the label of "demons." Thus, conflict theology subverts the order of the kingdom of God by reinforcing the world's logic that enemies (when properly identified as such) are to be, not loved and prayed for, but hated "with every syllable of our sanity."

The problem of revelation

The problem of undermining the unique logic of Christian enmity is one instance of a larger problem that permeates the whole warrant of conflict theology. The defense that conflict theology provides for itself is twofold. The first is that conflict theology is supposed to be the explicit and authoritative revelation of God through Scripture, and that through Scripture we learn information about the demonic world that we would not have access to elsewhere. Secondly, however, conflict theology is supposed to be highly intuitive; it presents itself as corresponding to the beliefs of most people at most times, and it is supposed to explain evil (and occasionally bizarre behavioral phenomena) more completely and more intuitively than—and therefore on the same terms as—the materialistic explanations of non-Christians. There is something inherently contradictory about claiming that a worldview is so pervasive and intuitive that it could only be denied due to psychological blinders, while simultaneously claiming that it is so unique that it can only be known by special revelation. The conflict theologian's answer to this would likely be something to the effect that, while the reality of demons and their activity is universally known (modern materialists excepted), the victory of Christ and the empowerment of his people to engage in warfare is something that only the Bible reveals. This is a reasonable response, but nonetheless the final systematic understanding of demons within Christianity is still seen to be integrated in a context that includes information or affirmations that other systems would not have access to.

Information derived from a source that others cannot access should result in conclusions that are dramatically different from the conclusions that the others in question can come to, and unless the new information is mostly cosmetic should be fundamentally incomprehensible to them. For example, beginning in the early 1980s, some Christian fundamentalists used an understanding of Revelation 13:17–18 to argue that UPC barcodes represented the "mark of the beast," and therefore the stores and the people who shopped at them were in the service of Satan. For someone who does not know or does not accept that reading of Revelation, the interaction of the fundamentalists with the barcodes is irrational and bizarre, even if one can articulate their internal logic.[10] The interaction remains irrational and bizarre even though the fundamentalists have the same general conception of what a barcode is and does as everybody else (i.e., it is a sequence of numbers used for buying and selling). In the same way, a Christian who has access to information about the victory of Christ should have an attitude towards demons and an interaction with demons that seems bizarre and irrational to those who do not have or do not believe this information—that is, to non-Christians—even if their general conception of what a demon is and does is more or less identical (i.e., a spirit-thing that causes evil). Conflict theology, in contrast, actually presents as one of its warrants the idea that the worldview it espouses is highly intuitive and more or less identical to the worldviews of non-Christian cultures everywhere.[11] A worldview based on revelation should be unintuitive and obtuse to someone who does not have that revelation; as a corollary, if a worldview is not unintuitive and not obtuse to someone who does not have access to revelation, then that worldview is not actually based on that revelation.

Syncretizing the Enlightenment

Conflict theology not only claims to be intuitive in the context of non-Western mythology; it claims to make sense in the context of modern Western culture as well (especially as a satisfying answer to evil; see chapter 15). Nonetheless all conflict theologians take great pains to distance themselves ideologically from the Enlightenment:

> If we modern Westerners cannot "see" what nearly everyone else outside the little oasis of Western rationalism has seen, then perhaps there is something amiss with our way of seeing. It is just possible that the intensely materialistic and rationalistic orientation of the Enlightenment has blinded us to certain obvious realities.[12]

Arnold agrees, "The last 300 years in the west represent the only time in human history that the existence of evil spirits has been treated with widespread skepticism."[13] Specifically, what they are distancing themselves from is "naturalism"

---

10. The *start*, *middle*, and *stop* markers that every UPC code contains are cosmetically similar to the pattern that represents the number 6; thus every UPC code is said to have three 6s in it. The point is that there *is* an internal logic, but merely knowing what that logic is does not make the actions of the fundamentalists seem more reasonable because computer codes have nothing to do with the gematria on which the number in Rev 13:17 is probably based. (The *Testament of Solomon* likewise correlates identities with numbers; specifically Christ bears the number 644 (*T. Sol.* 15.12)).

11. See for example Arnold, *Powers*, 179–81; Boyd, *God at War*, 11–17.

12. Boyd, *God at War*, 18.

13. Arnold, *Powers*, 179. See also Page, *Powers*, 267–68.

or "materialism."[14] However, the Enlightenment worldview covers a much broader scope than cosmology; other notable particulars of Enlightenment thought are (1) the tendency to define "goodness" in terms of the presence of pleasure or the absence of pain ("hedonism"); (2) the tendency to place human happiness as the highest value ("humanism"); and (3) the tendency to place a high value on the free exercise of will ("individualism").[15] All of these are no less foreign to the worldviews of most people at most times than naturalism is—including the worldviews of the various biblical authors. Nonetheless, because conflict theology has failed to give much regard to revelation (by virtue of failing, by its own admission, to distinguish itself substantially from theological systems that do not have this revelation), conflict theology as a worldview remains more or less identical to the prevailing worldview of its cognitive environment in certain respects and therefore, as we will see, continues to affirm the hedonism, humanism, and individualism of the Enlightenment even while trying to reject its naturalism. However, the thinkers of the Enlightenment did not advocate a materialistic cosmology arbitrarily. While the debate over whether materialism derives naturally and necessarily from other Enlightenment values is beyond the scope of this study—materialists say it does, apologists say it does not— in any case there is an undeniable historical correlation, which is worth examining. In other words, if we want to reject materialism, we should at least speculate why anyone wanted to accept it in the first place.

Materialist cosmology derives its warrant from the assumption that "science" is the authority by which we may determine truth. We have discussed the relationship between conflict theology and this assumption in chapter 5, but now we should examine how science *acquired* this authority. The humanistic revolution that gave rise to the Renaissance (and also the Reformation; see chapter 8) placed human happiness as the highest value and also eventually correlated *happiness* with the presence of pleasure and the absence of pain. Consequently, it placed a very high value on anything that could relieve pain and a very low value on anything that tended to cause it. One of the most obvious causes of pain was physical ailments and physical needs. Science brought new understandings and new technologies that allowed for a significant reduction in physical afflictions, at least for the upper classes in the West who defined the cultural narrative; the consequence of industry on the lower classes and the colonies was much grimmer. Science is not good for everything, but what it is good for it tends to do better than any other tool humans have yet developed, including religion. If we want to have rain, we get better results by pouring iodine on the clouds than by pouring wine on the ground or blood on the altar; if we want to cure injury or

14. See Arnold, *Questions*, 28–29.

15. Usually the free exercise of human will is seen as more or less co-identical with the value of human happiness, but one of the more interesting debates of late modernity (taken up most famously by Nietzsche and especially Ayn Rand) is what happens when the two values conflict, and whether "the exercise of the will by those with the strength and courage to do so" (egoism) should replace "the greatest happiness for the greatest number" (humanism) as the highest value.

disease we do better by going to the hospital than by going to sleep in a temple. Thus, even today science is usually affirmed to alleviate more suffering than it causes, even though technology still creates problems for the lower classes (i.e., job loss through automation, or the so-called "digital divide") and even though science occasionally makes things like hydrogen bombs or mustard gas; this is why Arnold can claim that he is "not advocating a complete paradigm shift back to a pre-scientific era."[16] Science itself is not the problem; the value given to science is the problem. But that value does not derive merely from affirming that science is better at meeting certain kinds of needs than religion.

Humans do not experience pain only physically; they experience it psychologically as well. One significant source of psychological pain at the time of the humanistic revolution was the Catholic understanding of sin and guilt before God, identified by Martin Luther as one of the motives for his reform. Medieval theology defined evil in terms of vice rather than pain, and so used guilt and awareness of one's own evil as a means to combat vice, and also as a way of keeping their parishioners, especially those in the upper classes,[17] conscious of their standing before God and therefore submissive to his will, since living in accord with divine will was their highest value. When evil was redefined in terms of pain, however, guilt no longer remediated evil, but contributed to it. Martin Luther found relief in a doctrine of grace that removed his sin, but those who followed him found even more relief in the idea that there had never been any sin in the first place. The inherent goodness and inherent innocence of humanity is one of the defining features of Enlightenment philosophy. Conflict theology usually admits that humans can be responsible for evil,[18] but at the same time broadly accepts that humans are more naturally good than not. This acceptance takes the form of asserting that there are some manifestations of evil that humans could not possibly be capable of and then using these instances as proof of the existence of demons: "the appalling evil that we see around and within us cannot satisfactorily be explained by human perversity alone."[19] Not only does this argument assume that there is such a thing as a limit to "human perversity," it also sets that limit extremely low. By comparison, we should observe that *nature* is generally considered to be morally neutral. Animals are not called *evil* for doing what animals do. While some people do invoke the savagery of nature as evidence against a benevolent creator, nobody argues that animals kill their prey, or their rivals for territory or mates, because they are possessed by demons. Humans of course are held to higher standards of behavior than animals, but the question at hand is what a human might be motivated to do, not what a human should be punished for doing. Apes are intelligent social primates

16. Arnold, *Powers*, 182

17. This is most clearly evidenced by the numerous judgment scenes in medieval art that feature kings, clerics, and other aristocrats subjected to hellfire.

18. See for example Page, *Powers*, 269; Arnold, *Questions*, 34.

19. Page, *Powers*, 268; See also Arnold, *Powers*, 179; Arnold, *Questions*, 30–31.

like humans are, and they also have no "sin nature" and they are not compelled to act by demons. In theory, then, anything an ape is able to bring itself to do a human could also bring itself to do, even without an inherent inclination to sin and even without demonic influence. Yet the kinds of behaviors that are held up as examples of super-human viciousness—brutal cruelty to animals or children (others of their kind, or even their own offspring),[20] violent intimidation,[21] or even systematic destruction of weaker members of the group or members of a rival group[22]—are all things that apes—especially Chimpanzees—are known to do. The claim that humans could not engage in natural primate behavior without the influence of a superhuman force necessarily means that humans are considered inherently morally superior (not only accountable to a higher standard of morality) to ordinary primates.

But the belief that humans are inherently inclined to goodness unless compelled otherwise does not *itself* lead to ascribing higher value to science, except insofar that science does not impose any kind of guilt at all, and indeed frees humans to be able to feel good about engaging in animal behaviors—especially promiscuity, which most societies regulate but "science" does not, and also the abuse and cruelty towards the lower classes that we now call "social Darwinism." Rather, the belief in the inherent goodness of humanity combines with the recognition of human evil to necessitate the identification of a source for that evil that is *external* to the humans who commit it. This source of human evil happens to correlate with a third source of human suffering: social institutions. In the Middle Ages, social structures were seen as morally neutral, established by God along with the rest of the natural order. Whether they facilitated good or evil depended on whether the people running them were good or evil. Thus, the medieval church focused most of its efforts on trying to make the people in charge of those institutions (want to) be good. The "divine right of kings" that was an object of great derision to the humanists originated as a reminder to the king that his office had been established by God and therefore he would be held accountable to God, even though there was (in fact) no human institution that could call him to account.[23] The humanistic revolution correlated the accountability brought by God with an accountability that would be brought by the *people*—"*vox populi, vox dei*"—which in turn correlates to the idea that God's will corresponds to human will and human desire, or at

---

20. Arnold, *Questions*, 30.

21. Arnold, *Questions*, 17–18, 31.

22. Monkeys cannot do this on the same *scale* that humans can (the normal example is the holocaust), but this is because monkeys are less creative and have fewer resources than humans, not because they are lacking in natural viciousness. Hitler did not kill six million people with willpower alone, he needed technology—the trains and the gas chambers—that others before him had no means to produce. Nothing in monkey psychology inhibits them from inflicting as much harm on others of their own kind as their limited resources allow.

23. Kings can be assassinated, but regicide sets a bad precedent; if you killed the last king, the next king can kill you. Even potential usurpers wanted the office they stole to continue to be respected—that is the whole point of stealing it—and therefore they had to respect it themselves.

least to the will and desire of the greatest number of humans. Because the will of the people represented the will of God, the people could do no wrong; thus, evil would be eradicated when the old [inherently evil] authoritarian power structures—notably the church and the aristocracy—were eliminated and replaced with [inherently good] institutions established and approved by the people, most notably democracy, socialism (or communism), and secularism. In this context science was catapulted to prominence because its discoveries were able to undermine the authority of the church, and the church in turn guaranteed the authority of the state. Science was able to do this because the church in the late Middle Ages, following Thomas Aquinas, adopted a theological premise—derived in turn from Aristotle—that the truth of God would be manifested in nature; thus they supported their theology by correlating theological tenets with ideas derived from natural philosophy. Scientists like Galileo and Darwin argued (correctly) that the natural philosophy had been misguided; this observation in turn was used (illegitimately) as a basis to cast doubt on both the theology that corresponded to it and on the church's authority to teach the truth in general.

The reason why the church as an institution had to go—why it was not sanctioned by the will of the people—was not because it taught that the surface of the sun was flawless or that humans appeared as an act of *de novo* creation. Nor was it that the church was particularly oppressive in the sense of inflicting harm on the people; while inquisitions and crusades were trumped up in retrospect, the church as a whole did not do any greater damage than the secular institutions that replaced it. The crime of the church was that it had the audacity to impose its will on the will of the people by telling them what they could and could not believe or think or do, enforced by guilt or (originally) by canon law. In a cognitive environment where the free exercise of the will is a great good, inhibiting the free exercise of the will is a great evil. The Reformers tried to hold human will accountable to Scripture alone and the deistic Enlightenment philosophers tried to hold human will accountable to reason; both were equally deemed oppressive and replaced in their turn. As long as *God* exists, even in the abstract deistic sense, he represents a law that can be imposed on human will. Therefore, in order to preserve the supremacy of human will, God must either be removed from the cosmology entirely or else reclassified in a role where he legitimizes, or at least approves, the free exercise of human will. Materialism, justified by the now-established authority of science, was the means to the former; conflict theology, by virtue of adopting a freewill theodicy, is an example of the latter. Conflict theology thus retains the *values* of materialism and of the system that produced it, even while cosmetically rejecting its specific tenets.

Conflict theology likewise locates the motive to human evil as something external to the human: namely, demonic influence. Sometimes this influence comes through the same institutions as those vilified by the secularists; Martin Luther[24] said the Ro-

24. Arnold argues that "[the] understanding of [war against] the devil was central to the reformation" (Arnold, *Questions*, 23). Boyd, on the other hand, says that Luther still placed too much emphasis

man church was a tool of the devil, and all conflict theologians claim that Hitler and the Nazis were demonically inspired. Sometimes different institutions are similarly identified, typically those associated with non-Christian religions (i.e., yoga schools, mosques or temples, or new-age cult centers), or those associated with conservative Christian vices (i.e., bars or brothels). Sometimes the "forces of Satan" are simply allowed to stand as an institution of their own. Also like their secular counterparts, conflict theologians argue that the solution to this evil is to replace those old institutions with new ones, usually church-based institutions of some kind. But by choosing to focus on the materialism alone, the hedonism, humanism, and individualism that form the pillars of the Enlightenment worldview are allowed to stand unchallenged. Is Arnold correct that the problem we should be concerned about is that "the spirit realm may have no more a part of a given Christian's world view than it does of that person's non-Christian neighbor?"[25] Or is a greater concern that the Christian may not have a conception of God, of God's relationship to humanity, of the nature of goodness, and of the purpose of humanity in God's plan, that is any different from that of their non-Christian neighbors?

In the end, the atheists are most likely right, at least on this count: a God whose purpose is primarily to make humans happy on their own terms probably does not exist, and so if we are interested in achieving happiness on our own terms we are better off trying to see to it ourselves. Boyd is also correct when he notes that this conception of God has virtually nothing in common with the idea of God as presented in classical Christian theology.[26] Christians are not supposed to be interested in achieving our own desires and gaining happiness on our own terms: "not my will but thy will be done, on earth as it is in heaven." The "problem of evil" that conflict theology explicitly seeks to address can only exist as a problem in an environment where human happiness and human will are given high value and prominence; the problem is absent from the Bible and absent from classical Christian theology. The reason is not because they were *unaware* of the paradox between God's goodness and power and the reality of evil—Augustine addresses it specifically in a dialogue about the nature of the world order[27]—but they did not regard it as problematic or as a reason to doubt God's power, benevolence, or existence. Consequently, the modern "problem of evil" is commonly attributed to David Hume, not to Augustine's sixth-century interlocutors, and exists specifically within the cognitive environment of the Enlightenment. By adopting the

---

on the sovereign will of God (Boyd, *God at War*, 47). Whether or not Luther and the Reformers would actually qualify as "conflict theologians" (i.e., those who understand conflict with the devil as a central and essential feature of Christian doctrine) is beyond the scope of this study.

25. Arnold, *Powers*, 17.

26. "The warfare worldview . . . does not square with either our modern Western materialistic view of the world or many traditional Christian assumptions about God." Boyd, *God at War*, 17.

27. "[T]hose who ponder these matters are seemingly forced to believe either that divine Providence does not reach to these outer limits of things or that surely all evils are committed by the will of God. Both horns of this dilemma are impious, but particularly the latter." Russell, *Divine Providence*, 7.

problem as a problem and by addressing it in a manner that is consistent with Enlightenment values and categories of thought, conflict theology essentially appropriates and affirms all of the values and categories of the Enlightenment; this is what we mean that it has *syncretized* with the Enlightenment, and in doing so actually substantiates and legitimizes the very same worldview it claims to undermine and reject.

As a final note, it is interesting to realize that the definition of evil as *pain* actually *reduces* the role of the devil from what it was considered to be in earlier eras of Christianity. Conflict theology views the activity of the devil mostly in terms of harm, so that when we suffer harm we blame the devil and therefore are spared from having to blame God. In earlier modes of Christian thought, however, the devil could tempt as well as harm; he could offer pleasure as well as pain. Thus, today when we (for example) receive a promotion, win an award, or fall in love, it never even occurs to us to blame the devil; instead we thank God for his provision because we assume that all goodness—by which we mean pleasure—must come from God. While there does remain a general sense that temporary pleasures can have painful consequences, there is very little conception that the things we like might have a capacity to harm us in ways that we never experience as pain, if we are even consciously aware of them at all. By defining evil in terms of pain and goodness in terms of the absence of pain—and therefore of pleasure—we attribute all pleasure to God and all pain to the devil. Conflict theology—which professes a desire to *increase* awareness of the devil and the devil's work—not only encourages a tendency to attribute God's activity (potentially, pain) to the devil, but also a tendency to attribute the devil's actions (potentially, pleasure) to God.

Conclusions concerning conflict theology

It is important to recognize that none of the elements discussed in this chapter are formally expressed as doctrine. Conflict theologians do not explicitly affirm the values of humanism, hedonism, and individualism—and would probably reject them if asked—just as conventional classical theologians do not explicitly advocate complacency towards evil and would likewise reject the idea if asked. Neither does the observation that conflict theology is syncretized with the Enlightenment and might potentially encourage a conception of God that places him subservient to human will necessarily mean that conflict theology is *wrong*, for the same reasons that the observation that classical theology is syncretized with Greek philosophy and might potentially encourage a conception of God that makes him indifferent to evil—both of which are true—does not mean that classical theology is wrong. *If* conflict theology is wrong, the reason why it is wrong is not to be found in its psychological entailments; the reason is because it is derived from an unsound hermeneutic and (conversely) because a methodologically defensible hermeneutic, when applied consistently, cannot establish any scriptural warrant for it. At the same time, though, it does not seem unreasonable to expect that a worldview that claims to be based on unique revelation should be able to distinguish itself meaningfully from worldviews that do not have that revelation. Neither does it seem unreasonable to expect that a worldview that claims to distance itself from its own culture would not simultaneously syncretize with it. Likewise, we might not expect a worldview that claims to increase awareness of demons and demonic activity based on early Christian definitions to pay relatively little heed to demonic functions other than causing pain, such as exciting the passions, misrepresenting revelation, or syncretizing the gospel. But none of these issues have anything to do with information that the Bible does or does not offer about Satan, demons, or spirits.

Conclusions

This study began with the observation that much of the theological discussion of demons and spirits in biblical theology occurs in a debate between interpreters who favor a "demythologizing" approach to the text and those who favor a systematic theology wherein conflict between God and God's people on the one side and literal spirit-beings (Satan and demons) on the other is given particular prominence; we defined this trend heuristically as "conflict theology." We argued that neither of these approaches can adequately locate the warrant for its conclusions within the Bible's text. Against the demythologizers, we argued that the text contains a message that can still be meaningfully read and therefore any appeals to the text's content must reflect the content of that message. Against the conflict theologians we argued that the purpose of the message was not to convey a series of logical propositions designed to be organized into proofs by systematic theologians. Thus, this study is as much about the process of biblical theology as it is about the specific study of demons and spirits.

The text contains a message that we can read, but that message is not written in English and is not presented according to the logic of the modern West; the language and logic are both derived from the documents' original cultural setting, which we called its "cognitive environment." This means that in order to be able to receive the message we must first translate the text, both in terms of words and internal logic. If we want to receive the communication that God has given us, we cannot "read the Bible" by looking at the English text and guessing at its meaning based on our own intuition. Sometimes the English does not render the Hebrew (or Greek) accurately, as we saw in Daniel 10; other times the words and grammar are correct but our modern perspective does not accurately represent the logic, as we saw in Psalm 82 and 1 Corinthians 10:20. Accordingly we described what the relevant internal logic behind the passages might have been by describing what various terms thought to refer to "demons" meant—both in the ancient usage and in our own conception—and how the logic of the text's cognitive environment would have understood the idea of enmity and conflict involving the gods. Finally we examined every passage in the

Bible thought to contain information about Satan or demons and tried to discern its message based on all of the information about genre and the meanings of words, combined with discourse analysis, comparative studies, and (in the case of Old Testament passages reflected in the New Testament) history of reception. We concluded that the text contains no new information about demons or spirits that its original audience would not have already believed, and that it does not affirm as truth the beliefs of the original audience, for the same reasons that it does not affirm their beliefs about cosmic geography. Demons, like the physical structures of the cosmos, are mentioned in the text as a means to an end to affirm something else.

Finally, we took some time to address conflict theology on its own terms. We observed that conflict theology does not present itself only as a result of following the evidence of exegesis wherever it happens to lead; it also claims to be able to address the problem of evil and to represent a more universal and culturally-aware worldview than other expressions of theology. We examined these claims and also drew attention to some difficulties that conflict theology may entail that other expressions of theology may not, and concluded that, if conflict theology is to stand as a representative of biblical authority, it must present greater evidence in greater detail than can be obtained by simply examining proof-texts to construct a theology of Satan and demons.

In the end, we cannot offer any "biblical" conception of demons and spirits because our study has indicated that the Bible does not contain one—it contains only references to beliefs widespread in the cognitive environments in which it was written. Anything we can "know" about spirit-beings, we must discern in the same manner that we discern information about other subjects on which the Bible does not speak. Nonetheless, based on our research and the relationship of demons to other elements of systematic theology, we can propose a heuristic that Christians might be able to use to locate demons and spirits within a larger modern worldview. In general, we propose that demons and spirits should be best regarded similarly to the way we regard such things as *wild animals* or *viruses*. This is similar to how they were conceived in the world of both the Old and New Testaments, and as such the portrayal fits well with other aspects of biblical theology. We can thus briefly address some things to keep in mind when thinking about this conception of demons.

First, demons are *natural*. By this we mean that they are created as part of God's world and have their place in his purposes. It does not necessarily mean that "science" will be able to verify them empirically, though if the conflict theologians are correct that current models of psychology and disease cannot explain spirit-induced phenomena then science may discover them eventually. This would be useful for those who wish to *treat* demonic affliction, but would do nothing to counter metaphysical materialism or cast doubt on the benevolence of God, any more than any other phenomenon of nature would do.

Second, demons are *not evil*. Bears, sharks, and ebola are not evil. Nonetheless, they are extremely dangerous and can be extremely inimical to healthy human life. They can also be quite terrifying to encounter. Demons are likewise dangerous and terrifying, as many accounts of supposedly spirit-based phenomena can verify. None of this means that they cannot have a place in God's world, but it does mean that they must be treated with caution, just like dangerous animals or contagious diseases must be.

Third, demons are *not active everywhere*. We should not feel a need to extrapolate demonic causes for things that can be otherwise explained. Tigers are real, and if I go to certain places I might encounter a tiger. If I encounter a tiger there is a good chance it would hurt me. But that does not mean that any time I get hurt a tiger was somehow involved. Likewise, if I go to certain places I might encounter demons and they might hurt me. But that does not mean that demons are involved every time I get hurt. Identifying causes is important for managing effects. Attributing demonic afflictions to non-demonic sources limits the ability to deal with those afflictions, as conflict theologians point out. But for the same reasons, attributing non-demonic phenomena to demons limits the ability to deal with those, either. For example, attributing the Holocaust to demonic possession of Hitler and the Germans means that one is less likely to seriously consider the various sociological, philosophical, economic, or otherwise human factors that allowed the Holocaust to occur, which in turn means that those same elements will be allowed to stand unchallenged elsewhere. Discernment is important, not assumptions based on a hypothetical profile cobbled together either from cosmological assumptions or from biblical proof-texts.

Readers may note that these conceptions deal primarily with the activity of inflicting pain. For better or worse, that is what "evil" means in our culture and so those are the terms that are most meaningful to us. Nonetheless, it is worth giving brief consideration to the conception of demons as motivating vice and inhibiting the gospel, both of which are affirmed in conflict theology. As far as the motivation to vice, it should be noted that humans do not generally need any help with this. Neither is it sufficient to simply will ourselves to be righteous, because our will itself is part of the problem (e.g., the argument of Rom 7:15–20). Righteousness can only come by the grace of God, whether that entails deliverance from demons or deliverance from ourselves. Attributing the inclination to vice to demons can be helpful if it prompts us to depend on God's assistance as opposed to our own efforts, but it can likewise be harmful if it motivates us to overestimate our own righteousness and innocence. The same is true in the case of demons being thought to inhibit the gospel. The church has innumerable ways to make itself odious to potential converts, and blaming demonic interference for its failures might discourage self-awareness and self-discipline. At the same time, it may be encouraging to remember that receptiveness to the gospel is ultimately beyond our control (e.g., 2 Cor 4:1–6). In both cases, discernment once again becomes important, although it is not clear that replacing a self-motivated process (personal or institutional discipline) with a different self-motivated process ("spiritual warfare") would ultimately be helpful in either case. If we are trusting in God's power to remove demonic obstacles, God can do it regardless of the methods we choose to use because divine power is not manipulated by mechanism (see chapter 6). But if we are trying to wield divine power through our own efforts (even when we call those efforts "prayer") then we are neither placing our trust in God nor giving attention to those areas that are genuinely our own responsibility. Once again the key is discernment, both in terms of identifying the causes of problems and also identifying when it is our responsibility to act and when it is our responsibility to trust in God.

Finally, no matter what exactly they are doing, *demons have no power that God does not allow them to have*. Like the lions in Daniel 6:22 or the snake in Acts 28:5, God can protect us from the activity of demons if he chooses to do so. At the same time, that does not mean I can feel free to go to the zoo and stand in the lion cage. Because they are dangerous, demons, like contagious pathogens or wild animals, should be left alone. If they are present, we should treat them with as much fear and caution as prudence dictates, exactly as we would treat a predator. But we do not need to be paranoid. God has the strength to protect his people. Battling demons might be the vocation of some people, just like curing diseases or hunting animals might be. But those who do not have this calling should pay less attention to the activity of demons and concentrate on whatever their own function happens to be in service of the body of Christ.

Bibliography

Abusch, T. "Witchcraft and the Anger of the Personal God." In *Mesopotamian Witchcraft*, 27–63. AMD 5. Leiden: Styx and Brill, 2002.

Adalı, Sellim Ferruh. *The Scourge of God: The Umman-Manda and its Significance in the First Millennium BC*. SAAS 20. Helsinki: The Neo-Assyrian Text Corpus Project, 2011.

Aelian. *On Animals, Volume III: Books 12–17*. Translated by A. F. Scholfield. LCL. Cambridge: Harvard University Press, 1959.

Ahituv, Shmuel. *Echoes from the Past*. Jerusalem: Carta, 2008.

Alexander, Philip. "3 (Hebrew Apocalypse of) Enoch." In *OTP* 1.223–315.

Allen, Leslie C. *Psalms 101–150*. WBC. Waco, TX: Word, 1983.

Andersen, F. I. "2 (Slavonic Apocalypse of) Enoch: A New Translation and Introduction." In *OTP* 1:91–213.

Andersen, Francis I., and David Noel Freedman. *Hosea*. AB. New York: Doubleday, 1980.

Anderson, Bernhard W. *Creation Versus Chaos*. New York: Association, 1967.

Anderson, Gary A. "The Penitence Narrative in the Life of Adam and Eve." In *Literature on Adam and Eve: Collected Essays*, edited by Gary Anderson et al., 3–42. Leiden: Brill, 2000.

———. *Sin: A History*. New Haven: Yale University Press, 2009.

André, Gunnel. *Determining the Destiny: Pqd in the Old Testament*. Coniectanea Biblica Old Testament Series 24. Lund: Gleerup, 1980.

Annus, Amar. "On the Origin of Watchers: A Comparative Study of the Antediluvian Wisdom in Mesopotamian and Jewish Traditions." *JSP* 19 (2010) 277–320.

———. *The God Ninurta in the Mythology and Royal Ideology of Ancient Mesopotamia*. SAAS 14. Helsinki: Neo-Assyrian Text Corpus Project, 2002.

Arnold, B. T. "Divination and Magic." In *Dictionary of Scripture and Ethics*, edited by J. B. Green, 238–42. Grand Rapids: Baker, 2011.

Arnold, Clinton E. *Power and Magic: The Concept of Power in Ephesians*. Reprint, Eugene, OR: Wipf and Stock, 1989.

———. *Powers of Darkness*. Downers Grove, IL: IVP, 1992.

———. *Three Crucial Questions about Spiritual Warfare*. Grand Rapids: Baker, 1997.

Attridge, Harold W. *Hebrews*. Minneapolis, MN: Fortress, 1989.

Aune, David E. *Apocalypticism, Prophecy, and Magic in Early Christianity: Collected Essays*. Grand Rapids: Baker, 2008.

———. "Archon." In *DDD*, 82–85.

———. "Magic in Early Christianity." In *Aufstieg und Niedergang der römischen Welt* 2.23:2, edited by Wolfgang Haase, 1507–57. Berlin: de Gruyter, 1980.

————. *Revelation 6–16*. WBC. Waco, TX: Word, 1998.

————. *Revelation 17–22*. WBC. Waco, TX: Word, 1998.

Averbeck, R. A. "Ancient Near Eastern Mythography as It Relates to Historiography in the Hebrew Bible: Genesis 3 and the Cosmic Battle." In *The Future of Biblical Archaeology: Reassessing Methodologies and Assumptions*, edited by J. K. Hoffmeier and Alan Millard, 328–56. Grand Rapids: Eerdmans, 2004.

Ballentine, Debra S. *The Conflict Myth and the Biblical Tradition*. Oxford: Oxford University Press, 2015.

Barr, James. "The Question of Religious Influence: The Case of Zoroastrianism, Judaism, and Christianity." *JAAR* 53 (1985) 201–35.

Barré, M. L. "Rabişu." In *DDD*, 682–83.

Batto, Bernard F. *Slaying the Dragon: Mythmaking in the Biblical Tradition*. Louisville, KY: Westminster John Knox, 1992.

Beal, Lissa Wray. *1 & 2 Kings*. AOTC. Downers Grove, IL: IVP, 2014.

Beale, G. K. *The Book of Revelation*. NIGTC. Grand Rapids: Eerdmans, 1999.

Beale, G. K., and Sean M. McDonough. "Revelation." In *Commentary on the New Testament Use of the Old Testament*, edited by G. K. Beale and D. A. Carson, 1081–1161. Grand Rapids: Baker, 2007.

Beaulieu. P-A. *The Pantheon of Uruk during the Neo-Babylonian Period*. Leiden: Brill, 2003.

Beckman, Gary *Hittite Diplomatic Texts*. Atlanta: Society of Biblical Literature, 1996.

Blair, J. M. *De-Demonising the Old Testament*. Tübingen: Mohr Siebeck, 2009.

Bloch-Smith, Elizabeth. *Judahite Burial Practices and Beliefs about the Dead*. JSOTS 123. Sheffield, UK: JSOT Press, 1992.

Block, Daniel I. *Judges, Ruth*. NAC. Nashville, TN: Broadman and Holman, 1999.

————. *The Gods of the Nations*. Grand Rapids: Baker, 2000.

Blomberg, C. *Matthew*. NAC. Nashville: Broadman & Holman, 1992.

Bock, Darrell. *Luke 1:1—9:50*. BECNT. Grand Rapids: Baker, 1994.

————. *Luke 9:51—24:53*. BECNT. Grand Rapids: Baker, 1996.

Bodi, Daniel. "Ezekiel." In *ZIBBCOT* 4:400–517.

Bokser, B. M. "Messianism, the Exodus Pattern, and Early Rabbinic Judaism." In *The Messiah*, edited by James H. Charlesworth, 239–60. Minneapolis, MN: Fortress, 1992.

Bottéro, J. "The 'Code' of Hammurabi." In *Mesopotamia: Writing, Reasoning, and the Gods*, 156–84. Chicago: University of Chicago Press, 1992.

————. "The Substitute King and His Fate," in *Mesopotamia: Writing, Reasoning, and the Gods*, 138–55. Chicago: University of Chicago Press, 1992.

Bovon, F., and H. Koester. *Luke 1—9:50*. Hermeneia. Minneapolis, MN: Fortress, 2002.

Boyd, Gregory A. *God at War: the Bible and Spiritual Conflict*. Downers Grove, IL: IVP, 1997.

————. *Satan and the Problem of Evil: Constructing a Trinitarian Warfare Theodicy*. Downers Grove, IL: IVP, 2001.

Brown, Jeannine K. *Scripture as Communication*. Grand Rapids: Baker, 2007.

Bultmann, Rudolf. "New Testament and Mythology." In *Kerygma and Myth: A Theological Debate*, vol. 1. London: SPCK, 1961.

Burnett, Joel S. "Prophecy in Transjordan: Balaam Son of Beor." In *Enemies and Friends of the State*, edited by Christopher A. Rollston, 135–206. University Park, PA: Eisenbrauns, 2018.

Caquot, A. "גער." In *TDOT* 3:49–53.

Carroll R. (Rodas), M. Daniel. "Hosea." In *The Expositor's Bible Commentary*, edited by Tremper Longman III and David E. Garland, 8:213–305. Rev. ed. Grand Rapids: Zondervan, 2008.

Charlesworth, James H. *The Good and Evil Serpent*. New Haven, CT: Yale University Press, 2010.

Chavalas, Mark W., and Murray R. Adamthwaite. "Archaeological Light on the Old Testament." In *The Face of the Old Testament*, edited by David W. Baker and Bill T. Arnold, 59–96. Grand Rapids: Baker, 1999.

Choi, J. H. "Resheph and Yhwh Ṣeba'ot." *VT* 54 (2004) 17–28.

Christensen, Duane L. *Nahum*. AB. New Haven, CT: Yale University Press, 2009.

Ciampa, Roy E., and Brian S. Rosner. *The First Letter to the Corinthians*. Grand Rapids: Eerdmans, 2010.

Cogan, Mordechai. *1 Kings*. AB. New Haven, CT: Yale University Press, 2001.

Collins, Adela Yarbro, and Harold Attridge. *Mark*. Minneapolis, MN: Fortress, 2007.

Collins, B. J. "The Puppy in Hittite Ritual." *Journal of Cuneiform Studies* 42 (1990) 211–26.

Collins, John J. *The Apocalyptic Vision of the Book of Daniel*. HSM. Cambridge: Harvard University Press, 1977.

———. *Daniel*. Hermeneia. Minneapolis, MN: Fortress, 1993.

Conzelmann, Hans. *1 Corinthians*. Hermeneia. Minneapolis, MN: Fortress, 1975.

Copan, Paul. *Is God a Moral Monster? Making Sense of the Old Testament God*. Grand Rapids: Baker, 2011.

Craigie, Peter C. "Helel, Athtar and Phaethon (Jes 14:12–15)." *ZAW* 85 (1973) 223–25.

———. *War in the Old Testament*. Grand Rapids: Eerdmans, 1978.

Cranfield, C. E. B. *Romans 9–16*. London: T. & T. Clark, 1979.

Creason, Stuart. "PQD Revisited." In *Studies in Semitic and Afroasiatic Linguistics Presented to Gene B. Cragg*, edited by Cynthia Miller, 27–42. SAOC 60. Chicago: University of Chicago Press, 2007.

Cunningham, G. *Deliver Me from Evil: Mesopotamian Incantations 2500–1500 BC*. Rome: Pontifical Biblical Institute, 1997.

Day, John. *God's Conflict with the Dragon and the Sea*. Cambridge: Cambridge University Press, 1985.

———. *Yahweh and the Gods and Goddesses of Canaan*. JSOTS 265. Sheffield, UK: JSOT, 2002.

Day, Peggy L. *An Adversary in Heaven: śāṭān in the Hebrew Bible*. Atlanta: Scholars, 1988.

de Jong, Albert. "Iranian Connections in the Dead Sea Scrolls." In *The Oxford Handbook of the Dead Sea Scrolls*, edited by Timothy Lim and John J. Collins, 479–500. Oxford: Oxford University Press, 2010.

de Jonge, Marinus. "The Literary Development of the *Life of Adam and Eve*." In *Literature on Adam and Eve: Collected Essays*, edited by Gary Anderson et al., 239–49. Leiden: Brill, 2000.

De La Torre, Miguel A., and Alberto Hernandez. *The Quest for the Historical Satan*. Minneapolis: Fortress, 2011.

deClasse-Walford, Nancy, Rolf A. Jacobson, and Beth LaNeel Tanner. *The Book of Psalms*. NICOT. Grand Rapids: Eerdmans, 2014.

Del Monte, Giuseppe F. "The Hittite Herem." In *Memoriae Igor M. Diakonoff*, edited by Leonid Kogan et al., 21–45. Babel und Bibel 2. Winona Lake, IN: Eisenbrauns, 2005.

del Olmo Lete, G. "Deber." In *DDD*, 231–32.

Dewrell, Heath D. *Child Sacrifice in Ancient Israel*. Winona Lake, IN: Eisenbrauns, 2017.

Dibelius, Martin, and Heinrich Greeven. *James*. Minneapolis: Fortress, 1998.

Doedens, Jaap. *The Sons of God in Genesis 6:1–4*. Kampen: Theologische Universiteit van de Gereformeerde Kerken, 2013.

Duling, D. C. "Testament of Solomon: A New Translation and Introduction." In *OTP* 1:935–87.

Dunn, James D. G. *Romans 16–20*. WBC. Dallas, TX: Word, 1988.

Edwards, James R. *The Gospel according to Luke*. PNTC. Grand Rapids: Eerdmans 2005.

———. *Mark*. PNTC. Grand Rapids: Eerdmans, 2001.

Elnes, E. E., and P. D. Miller. "*'Elyôn*." In *DDD*, 293–99.

Euripides. *Trojan Women. Iphigenia among the Taurians. Ion*. Edited and translated by David Kovacs. LCL 10. Cambridge: Harvard University Press, 1999.

Evans, Craig A. "The Messiah in the Dead Sea Scrolls." In *Israel's Messiah in the Bible and the Dead Sea Scrolls*, edited by Richard S. Hess and M. Daniel Carroll R., 85–102. Grand Rapids: Baker, 2003.

Fee, Gordon. *1 Corinthians*. NICNT. Grand Rapids: Eerdmans, 1987.

Ferguson, Everett B. *Backgrounds of Early Christianity*. 3rd ed. Grand Rapids: Eerdmans, 2003.

Fitzmyer, Joseph. *Luke 1–9*. AB. New York: Doubleday, 1982.

Forsyth, Neil *The Old Enemy: Satan and the Combat Myth*. Princeton, NJ: Princeton University Press, 1987.

Foster, Benjamin. *From Distant Days*. Bethseda, MD: CDL, 1995.

Fox, Michael V. *Proverbs 10–31*. AB. New Haven: Yale, 2009.

France, R. T. *Matthew*. NICNT. Grand Rapids: Eerdmans, 2007.

Fritz, Volkmar. *1 & 2 Kings*. Minneapolis, MN: Fortress, 2003.

Fröhlich, Ida. "Mesopotamian Elements and the Watchers Tradition." In *The Watchers in Jewish and Christian Tradition*, edited by Angela Kim Harkins et al., 11–24. Minneapolis: Fortress, 2002.

Garland, David. *1 Corinthians*. BECNT. Grand Rapids: Baker, 2003.

———. *Luke*. ZECNT. Grand Rapids: Zondervan, 2011.

Garroway, Kristine. *Children in the Ancient Near Eastern Household*. Winona Lake, IN: Eisenbrauns, 2014.

Geller, M. *Evil Demons: Canonical* Utukku Lemnutu *Incantations*. SAACT 5. Helsinki: Neo-Assyrian Text Corpus Project, 2007.

German, Igal. *The Fall Reconsidered*. Eugene, OR: Pickwick, 2016.

Gersh, Stephen. *Middle Platonism and Neoplatonism, the Latin Tradition*. 2 vols. Notre Dame, IN: University of Notre Dame, 1986.

Ginzberg, Louis. *The Legends of the Jews*. 7 vols. Philadelphia: Jewish Publication Society of America, 1968.

Goldingay, John. *Psalms 42–89*. Grand Rapids: Baker, 2007.

———. *Psalms 90–150*. Grand Rapids: Baker, 2008.

Goldstein, Jonathan A. *1 Maccabees*. AB. New York: Doubleday, 1976.

Gray, John. *1 & 2 Kings*. OTL. Philadelphia: Westminster, 1976.

Grayson, A. Kirk. *Assyrian Rulers of the Early First Millennium BC I. 1114–859 BC*. RIMA. Toronto: University of Toronto, 2002.

Green, A. R. W. *The Role of Human Sacrifice in the Ancient Near East*. Missoula, MT: Scholars Press, 1975.

Green, Joel B. *Luke*. NICNT. Grand Rapids: Eerdmans, 1997.

Grossfeld, Bernard. *The Targum Onqelos to Exodus*. ArBib 7. Wilmington, DL; Glazier, 1988.

Hackett, Jo Ann. *The Balaam Text from Deir ʿAllā*. HSM 31. Chico, CA: Scholars, 1980.

Halpern, Baruch. "The Ritual Background of Zechariah's Temple Song." *CBQ* 40 (1978) 167–90.

Hamilton, Victor P. *The Book of Genesis: Chapters 18–50*. NICOT. Grand Rapids: Eerdmans, 1995.

Harkins, Angela Kim, et al., eds. *The Watchers in Jewish and Christian Tradition*. Minneapolis: Fortress, 2002.

Hayes, Christine. *What's Divine About Divine Law? Early Perspectives*. Princeton, NJ: Princeton University Press, 2015.

Hays, Christopher B. *A Covenant with Death*. Grand Rapids: Eerdmans, 2015.

Hays, Richard B. *Echoes of Scripture in the Gospels*. Waco, TX: Baylor, 2016.

Heider, George C. "Molech." In *DDD*, 581–85.

———. *The Cult of Molek: A Reassessment*. JSOTS 43. Sheffield, UK: JSOT, 1985.

Heiser, Michael S. "Deuteronomy 32:8 and the Sons of God." *BibSac* 158 (2001) 52–74.

———. "Monotheism, Polytheism, Monolatry, or Henotheism? Toward an Assessment of Divine Plurality in the Hebrew Bible." *BBR* 18 (2008) 1–30.

———. *The Unseen Realm*. Bellingham, WA: Lexham, 2014.

Heltzer, M. "New Light from Emar on Genesis 31: The Theft of the *Teraphim*." In *Und Mose schrieb dieses Lied auf*, edited by M. Dietrich and O. Loretz, 357–67. Münster: Ugarit-Verlag, 1998.

Hendel, R. "Vampire." In *DDD*, 887.

Herrmann, W. "Baal Zebub." *DDD*, 154–56.

Hesiod. *Theogony. Works and Days. Testimonia*. Translated by H. G. Evelyn-White. LCL 57. Cambridge: Harvard University Press, 1914.

Hoehner, Harold W. *Ephesians*. Grand Rapids: Baker, 2002.

Hogan, Karina Martin. "The Watchers Traditions in the Book of the Watchers and the Animal Apocalypse." In *The Watchers in Jewish and Christian Tradition*, edited by Angela Kim Harkins et al., 107–19. Minneapolis: Fortress, 2002.

Holladay, William L. *Jeremiah 1*. Minneapolis, MN: Fortress, 1986.

———. *Jeremiah 2*. Minneapolis, MN: Fortress, 1989.

Holloway, Steven W. *Aššur is King! Aššur is King!* Leiden: Brill, 2002.

Hossfeld, F. "רָצַח, *rāṣaḥ*." *TDOT* 13:630–40.

Hossfeld, Frank-Lothar, and Erich Zenger. *Psalms 3*. Minneapolis: Fortress, 2011.

Hundley, Michael B. "Here a God, There a God: An Examination of the Divine in Ancient Mesopotamia." *AoF* 40 (2013) 68–107.

Hutter, M. "Abaddon." In *DDD*, 1.

Jackson, Bernard S. *Wisdom-Laws*. Oxford: Oxford University Press, 2006.

Janowski, B. "Azazel." In *DDD*, 128–31.

———. "Satyrs." In *DDD*, 732–33.

Jewett, Robert. *Romans*. Hermeneia. Minneapolis, MN: Fortress, 2007.

Johnson, Marshall D. "Life of Adam and Eve: A New Translation and Introduction." In *OTP* 2:249–95.

———. *The Purpose of Biblical Genealogies*. Eugene, OR: Wipf & Stock, 2002.

Joines, K. R. *Serpent Symbolism in the Old Testament*. Haddonfield, NJ: Haddonfield House, 1974.

Kang, Sa-Moon. *Divine War in the Old Testament and the Ancient Near East*. Berlin: de Gruyter, 1989.

Katz, Dina. *The Image of the Netherworld in the Sumerian Sources*. Bethesda, MD: CDL, 2003.

Keener, Craig. *Acts: An Exegetical Commentary*. Grand Rapids: Baker, 2015.

———. *Miracles*. Grand Rapids: Baker, 2011.

Keil, C. F., and F. Delitzsch. *Isaiah*. Grand Rapids: Eerdmans, 1954.

Kelly, Henry A. *Satan: A Biography*. Cambridge: Cambridge University Press, 2006.

———. *Satan in the Bible, God's Minister of Justice*. Eugene, OR: Cascade, 2017.

Kilmer, Anne Draffkorn. "The Mesopotamian Counterparts of the Biblical Nephilim." In *Perspectives on Language and Text*, edited by Edgar W. Conrad and Edward G. Newing, 39–43. Winona Lake, IN: Eisenbrauns, 1987.

Kitchen, Kenneth A., and Paul N. Lawrence. *Treaty, Law and Covenant in the Ancient Near East*. 3 vols. Wiesbaden: Harrassowitz, 2012.

Klijn, A. F. J. "2 (Syriac Apocalypse of) Baruch: A New Translation and Introduction." In *OTP* 1:615–52.

Kloos, Carola. *Yhwh's Combat with the Sea*. Leiden: Brill, 1986.

Klutz, Todd. *Exorcism Stories in Luke-Acts*. Cambridge: Cambridge University Press, 2004.

Kobelski, Paul. *Melchizedek and Melchireša'*. CBQMS 10. Washington DC: Catholic Biblical Association of America, 1981.

Koch, Ulla Susanne. *Mesopotamian Divination Texts*. Münster: Ugarit-Verlag, 2015.

Koester, Craig R. *Revelation*. AB. New Haven: Yale University Press, 2014.

Kwasman, Theodore, and Simo Parpola. *Legal Transactions of the Royal Court of Nineveh, part 1: Tiglath-Pilesar III-Esarhaddon*. SAA 6. Helsinki: Helsinki University Press, 1991.

Laato, Antti, and Lotta Valve. "Understanding the Story of Adam and Eve in the Second Temple Period." In *Adam and Eve Story in the Hebrew Bible and in Ancient Jewish Writings including the New Testament*, edited by Antti Laato and Lotta Valve, 1–30. SRHB 7. Winona Lake: IN: Eisenbrauns, 2016.

Lambert, W.G. "The Seed of Kingship." In *Le Palais et royauté (archéologie et civilisation). 19e Rencontre Assyriologique Internationale*, edited by P. Garelli, 427–40. Paris: P. Guethner, 1974.

Lane, William L. *The Gospel of Mark*. NICNT. Grand Rapids: Eerdmans, 1974.

LeFebvre, Michael. *Collections, Codes and Torah: The Re-characterization of Israel's Written Law*. London: T. & T. Clark, 2006.

Leichty, Erle. *The Omen Series Šumma Izbu*. TCS 4. Locust Valley, NY: Augustin, 1970.

Lemaire, André. *The Birth of Monotheism: The Rise and Disappearance of Yahwism*. Washington, DC: Biblical Archeological Society, 2007.

Lewis, C. S. *The Screwtape Letters*. New York: MacMillan, 1982.

Lewis, Scott M. "'Because of the Angels': Paul and the Enochic Traditions." In *The Watchers in Jewish and Christian Tradition*, edited by Angela Kim Harkins et al., 81–90. Minneapolis: Fortress, 2002.

Lewis, Theodore J. "Beelzebul." *ABD* 1:638–40.

Liverani, Mario. *Assyria: The Imperial Mission*. Translated by Andrea Trameri and Jonathan Valk. Winona Lake, IN: Eisenbrauns, 2017.

Livingstone, A. *Court Poetry and Literary Miscellanea*. SAA 3. Helsinki: University of Helsinki Press, 1989.

Longman, Tremper, III, and Daniel G. Reid. *God is a Warrior*. Grand Rapids: Zondervan, 1995.

Lucas, Ernest C. "Daniel." In *ZIBBCOT* 4:518–75.

———. *Daniel*. AOTC. Downers Grove, IL: IVP, 2002.

Lundbom, Jack R. *Jeremiah 1–20*. AB. New York: Doubleday, 1999.

Luz, U. *Matthew 1–7*. Hermeneia. Minneapolis, MN: Fortress, 2007.

Malul, Meir. *Knowledge, Control, and Sex: Studies in Biblical Thought, Culture, and Worldview*. Tel Aviv: Archeological Center Publication, 2002.

Marincola, John. *Authority and Tradition in Ancient Historiography*. Cambridge: Cambridge University Press, 1997.

McConville, J. Gordon. *Deuteronomy*. Downers Grove, IL: IVP, 2002.

McDermott, Gerald R. *God's Rivals*. Downers Grove, IL: IVP, 2007.

Meeks, D. "Demons." In *Oxford Encyclopedia of Ancient Egypt*, edited by D. Redford, vol. 1, 375–78. New York: Oxford University Press, 2001.

Michaels, J. Ramsey. *The Book of John*. NICNT. Grand Rapids: Eerdmans, 2010.

Milgrom, Jacob. *Leviticus 17–22*. AB. New York: Doubleday, 2001.

Montgomery, James A. *A Critical and Exegetical Commentary on the Book of Daniel*. ICC. Edinburgh: T. & T. Clark, 1927.

Moo, Douglas J. *The Epistle to the Romans*, NICNT. Grand Rapids: Eerdmans, 1996.

Morris, Leon. *The Gospel according to Matthew*. PNTC. Grand Rapids: Eerdmans, 1992.

Mullen, E. Theodore. *The Assembly of the Gods*. Missoula, MT: Scholars, 1980.

Newsom, Carol A. *Daniel*. OTL. Louisville, KY: Westminster John Knox, 2014.

Nickelsburg, George W. E. *1 Enoch 1*. Hermeneia. Minneapolis, MN: Fortress, 2001.

Niditch, Susan. *Chaos to Cosmos*. Atlanta: Scholars, 1985.

Niehr, H. "תנין." In *TDOT* 15:726–731.

Noll, Mark. *The Scandal of the Evangelical Mind*. Grand Rapids: Eerdmans, 1995.

Nolland, John. *The Gospel of Matthew*. NIGTC. Grand Rapids: Eerdmans, 2005.

Orlov, Andrei A. *The Enoch-Metatron Tradition*. Texte und Studien Zum Antiken Judentum 107. Edited by Martin Hengel and Peter Schäfer. Mohr Siebeck: Tübingen, 2005.

Ornan, T. "In the Likeness of Man: Reflections on the Anthropocentric Perception of the Divine in Mesopotamian Art." In *What Is a God? Anthropomorphic and Non-Anthromorphic Aspects of Deity in Ancient Mesopotamia*, edited by B. N. Porter, 93–151. TCBAI 2. Winona Lake, IN: Eisenbrauns.

Osborne, Grant R. *The Book of Revelation*. BECNT. Grand Rapids: Baker, 2002.

———. *The Hermeneutical Spiral*. 3rd ed. Downers Grove, IL: IVP, 2006.

———. *Matthew*. ZECNT. Grand Rapids: Zondervan, 2010.

Oswalt, John N. *The Book of Isaiah: Chapters 1–49*. NICOT. Grand Rapids: Eerdmans, 1986.

Otzen, B. "בְּלִיַּעַל *bĕliyaʿal*," In *TDOT* 2:131–36.

Page, Sydney H. T. *Powers of Evil*. Grand Rapids: Baker, 1995.

Pardee, D. *Ritual and Cult at Ugarit*. SBLWAW 10. Atlanta: Society of Biblical Literature, 2002.

Parker, Simon. *Ugaritic Narrative Poetry*. Atlanta: Society of Biblical Literature, 1997.

Parpola, Simo. *Letters from Assyrian and Babylonian Scholars*. SAA 10. Helsinki: Helsinki University Press, 1993.

Parpola, Simo, and Kazuko Watanabe. *Neo-Assyrian Treaties and Loyalty Oaths*. SAA 2. Helsinki: Neo-Assyrian Text Corpus Project, 1988.

Patterson, Richard D., and Hermann J. Austel. "1, 2 Kings." In *The Expositor's Bible Commentary*, edited by Tremper Longman III and David E. Garland, 3:615–954. Rev. ed. Grand Rapids: Zondervan, 2008.

Pelikan, Jaroslav, and Valerie R. Hotchkiss, eds. *Creeds and Confessions of Faith in the Christian Tradition: Volume I: Early, Eastern, and Medieval*. New Haven, CT: Yale, 2003.

Penney, Douglas L., and Michael O. Wise. "By the Power of Beelzebub: An Aramaic Incantation Formula from Qumran (4Q560)." *JBL* 113 (1994) 627–50.

Puech, Émile. "*11QPsApa*: Un rituel d'exorcismes. Essai de Reconstruction." *RevQ* 14 (1989–1990) 377–408.

———. "Dead Sea Scrolls: Forty Years of Research." *STDJ* 10 (1992) 64–89.

Philo. *On the Cherubim. The Sacrifices of Abel and Cain. The Worse Attacks the Better. On the Posterity and Exile of Cain. On the Giants*. Translated by F. H. Colson, G. H. Whitaker. LCL 227. Cambridge: Harvard University Press, 1929.

———. *On the Creation. Allegorical Interpretation of Genesis 2 and 3*. Translated by F. H. Colson, G. H. Whitaker. LCL 226. Cambridge: Harvard University Press, 1929.

———. *Questions on Genesis*. Translated by Ralph Marcus. LCL 380. Cambridge: Harvard University Press, 1953.

Pitard, Wayne. "The Combat Myth as a Succession Story at Ugarit." In *Creation and Chaos*, edited by Joann Scurlock and Richard Beal, 199–205. Winona Lake, IN: Eisenbrauns, 2013.

Plantinga, Alvin. *God, Freedom, and Evil*. Grand Rapids: Eerdmans, 1974.

Plato. *Lysis. Symposium. Gorgias*. Translated by W. R. M. Lamb. LCL 166. Cambridge: Harvard University Press, 1925.

Plutarch. *Moralia, Volume V: Isis and Osiris. The Oracles at Delphi. The Oracles at Delphi No Longer Given in Verse. The Obsolescence of Oracles*. Translated by Frank Cole Babbitt. LCL 306. Cambridge: Harvard University Press, 1936.

Pongratz-Leisten, Beate. "The Other and the Enemy in the Mesopotamian Conception of the World." In *Mythology and Mythologies. Methodological Approaches to Intercultural Influences*, edited by R. Whiting, 195–231. Melammu 2. Helsinki: The Neo-Assyrian Text Corpus Project, 2001.

———. "Sacrifice in the Ancient Near East: Offering and Ritual Killing." In *Sacred Killing*, edited by Anne Porter and Glenn M. Schwartz, 291–304. Winona Lake, IN: Eisenbrauns, 2012.

Porter, Paul A. *Metaphors and Monsters: A Literary-Critical Study of Daniel 7–8*. Lund: Gleerup, 1983.

Preuss, H. D. "גלולים." In *TDOT* 3:1–5.

———. "חוה." In *TDOT* 4:248–56.

Priest, J. "Testament of Moses: A New Translation and Introduction." In *OTP* 1:919–34.

Provan, Iain. *Discovering Genesis: Content, Interpretation, Reception*. London: SPCK, 2015.

Ratzinger, Joseph. *'In the beginning . . .': A Catholic Understanding of the Story of Creation and the Fall*. Grand Rapids: Eerdmans, 1986.

Reynolds, Bennie H. "Molek: Dead or Alive?" In *Human Sacrifice in Jewish and Christian Tradition*, edited by K. Finsterbusch et al., 132–50. Leiden: Brill, 2007.

Riley, Andrew J. "Zeru, 'To Hate' as a Metaphor for Covenant Instability." In *Windows to the Ancient World of the Hebrew Bible*, edited by Bill T. Arnold et al., 175–85. Winona Lake, IN: Eisenbrauns, 2014.

Riley, G. "Demon." In *DDD*, 235–40.

———. "Midday Demon." In *DDD*, 572–73.

Roberts, J. J. M. *First Isaiah*. Minneapolis, MN: Fortress, 2015.

Rochberg, Francesca "'The Stars Their Likeness': Perspectives on the Relation between Celestial Bodies and Gods in Ancient Mesopotamia." In *What is a God*, edited by Barbara Nevling Porter, 41–92. Winona Lake, IN: Eisenbrauns, 2009.

Rouillard, H. "Rephaim." In *DDD*, 692–700.

Rubinkiewicz, R. "Apocalypse of Abraham: A New Introduction and Translation." In *OTP* 1:681–705.

Runia, D. T. "Logos." In *DDD*, 525–31.

Russell, Jeffrey Burton. *The Devil: Perceptions of Evil from Antiquity to Primitive Christianity*. Ithaca, NY: Cornell University Press, 1977.

———. *Lucifer: The Devil in the Middle Ages*. Ithaca, NY: Cornell University Press, 1984.

———. *Mephistopheles: The Devil in the Modern World*. Ithaca, NY: Cornell University Press, 1986.

———. *Satan: The Early Christian Tradition*. Ithaca, NY: Cornell University Press, 1981.

Russell, Robert P. *Divine Providence and the Problem of Evil: A Translation of St. Augustine's de ordine*. New York: Helenson, 1942.

Rüterswörden, U. "Horon." In *DDD*, 425–26.

———. "King of Terrors." In *DDD*, 486–88.

Saggs, H. W. F. *The Encounter with the Divine in Mesopotamia and Israel*. London: Athlone, 1978.

Sailhamer, John. "Genesis." In *Expositor's Bible Commentary*, edited by Tremper Longman III and David E. Garland, 1:21–331. Rev. ed. Grand Rapids: Zondervan, 2008.

Sanders, E. P. "Testament of Abraham: A New Translation and Introduction." In *OTP* 1:871–902.

Sarna, Nahum M. *Genesis*. JPS Torah Commentary. Philadelphia: Jewish Publication Society, 1989.

Sasson, Jack M. *Jonah*. AB. New York: Doubleday, 1990.

Schreiner, Thomas R. *Romans*. BECNT. Grand Rapids: Baker, 1998.

Schwienhorst, L. "מָרַד." In *TDOT* 9:1–5.

———. "מָרָה." *TDOT* 9:5–10.

Scurlock Joann. *Magico-Medical Means of Treating Ghost-Induced Illnesses in Ancient Mesopotamia*. Leiden: Brill and Styx, 2006.

Seebass, H. "נָפַל, *nāpal*." In *TDOT* 9:488–97.

Sherwood, Yvonne. *A Biblical Text and Its Afterlives: The Survival of Jonah in Western Culture*. Cambridge: Cambridge University Press, 2000.

Smith, Mark S. *The Origins of Biblical Monotheism*. New York: Oxford University Press, 2001.

Snodgrass, Klyne R. *Stories with Intent*. Grand Rapids: Eerdmans, 2008.

Spittler, R. P. "Testament of Job: A New Translation and Introduction." In *OTP* 1:829–68.

Spronk, K. "The Incantations." In *Handbook of Ugaritic Studies*, edited by W. G. E. Watson and N. Wyatt, 276–82. Leiden: Brill, 1999.

Stavrakopoulou, Francesca. *King Manasseh and Child Sacrifice*. Berlin: de Gruyter, 2004.

Stein, Robert H. *Luke*. NAC. Nashville, TN: Broadman and Holman, 1993.

———. *Mark*. BECNT. Grand Rapids: Baker, 2008.

Sterling, Gregory E. *Historiography and Self-Definition: Josephos, Luke-Acts and Apologetic Historiography*. Atlanta: Society of Biblical Literature, 1992.

Stern, Philip D. *The Biblical Herem: A Window on Israel's Religious Experience*. Atlanta: Scholars, 1991.

Stol, M. *Epilepsy in Babylonia*. Groningen: Styx, 1993.

Stone, M. E. "Greek Apocalypse of Ezra: A New Translation and Introduction." In *OTP* 1:561–79.

Strauss, Mark L. *Mark*. ZECNT. Grand Rapids: Zondervan, 2014.

Stuart, Douglas. *Hosea-Jonah*. WBC. Waco, TX: Word, 1987.

Stuckenbruck, Loren T. *The Myth of Rebellious Angels*. Grand Rapids: Eerdmans, 2014.

Tate, Marvin E. *Psalms 51–100*, WBC. Waco, TX: Word, 1990.

Thiselton, Anthony. *1 Corinthians*. NIGTC. Grand Rapids: Eerdmans, 2000.

Tigay, Jeffrey. *Deuteronomy*. JPS Torah Commentary. Philadelphia: JPS, 1996.

Tsumura, David. *Creation and Destruction*. Winona Lake, IN: Eisenbrauns, 2005.

———. *The First Book of Samuel*. Grand Rapids: Eerdmans, 2007.

Turner, David. *Matthew*. Grand Rapids: Baker, 2008.

Twelftree, Graham H. *Christ Triumphant: Exorcism Then and Now*. London: Hodder & Stoughton, 1985.

———. *In the Name of Jesus*. Grand Rapids: Baker, 2007.

Van de Mieroop, Marc. *The Ancient Mesopotamian City*. Oxford: Oxford University Press, 1997.

———. *Philosophy before the Greeks: The Pursuit of Truth in Ancient Babylonia*. Princeton, NJ: Princeton University Press, 2016.

van den Broek, R. "Apollo." In *DDD*, 74–77.

van der Leeuw, G. *Religion in Essence and Manifestation*. Translated by J. E. Turner. London: Allen & Unwin, 1938.

van der Toorn, Karel. "The Nature of the Biblical *tĕrāpîm* in the Light of the Cuneiform Evidence." *CBQ* 52 (1990) 203–22.

———. "The Theology of Demons in Mesopotamia and Israel: Popular Belief and Scholarly Speculation." In *Demons: The Demonology of Israelite-Jewish and Early Christian Literature in Context of Their Environment*, edited by K. F. Diethard Römheld and Hermann Lichtenberger, 61–83. Tübingen: Mohr Siebeck, 2003.

VanGemeren, Willem A. "Psalms." In *Expositor's Bible Commentary*, edited by Tremper Longman III and David E. Garland, 5:21–1011. Rev. ed. Grand Rapids: Zondervan, 2008.

van Henten, J. W. "Python." *DDD*, 669–71.

Vanhoozer. Kevin J. *Is There a Meaning in this Text?* Grand Rapids: Zondervan, 1998.

———. "Lost in Interpretation: Truth, Scripture, and Hermeneutics." *JETS* 48 (2005) 89–114.

Van Leeuwen, Raymond C. "Proverbs 30:21–23 and the Biblical World Upside Down." *JBL* 105 (1986) 599–610.

Venema, Dennis R., and Scot McKnight. *Adam and the Genome*. Grand Rapids: Brazos, 2017.

Wakeman, Mary K. *God's Battle with the Monster*. Leiden: Brill, 1973.

Walton, John. "The Anzu Myth and Daniel 7?" In *The Book of Daniel: Composition and Reception volume one*, edited by John J. Collins and Peter W. Flint, 69–89. Leiden: Brill, 2001.

———. "Creation in Gen 1:1—2:3 and the Ancient Near East: Order out of Disorder after Chaoskampf." *Calvin Theological Journal* 43 (2008) 48–63.

———. "Demons in Mesopotamia and Israel: Exploring the Category of Non-Divine but Supernatural Entities." In *Windows to the Ancient World of the Hebrew Bible: Essays in Honor of Samuel Greengus*, edited by Bill T. Arnold, Nancy Erickson, and John H. Walton, 229–46. Winona Lake, IN: Eisenbrauns, 2014.

———. *Genesis*. NIVAC. Grand Rapids: Zondervan, 2001.

———. *Genesis One as Ancient Cosmology*. Winona Lake, IN: Eisenbrauns, 2011.

———. *Job*. NIVAC. Grand Rapids: Zondervan, 2012.

———. "Jonah." In *ZIBBCOT* 5:100–119.

———. *Lost World of Adam and Eve*. Downers Grove, IL: IVP, 2015.

———. *Lost World of Genesis One*. Downers Grove, IL: IVP, 2009.

———. *Old Testament Theology for Christians*. Downers Grove, IL: IVP, 2017.

Walton, John H., and D. Brent Sandy. *The Lost World of Scripture*. Downers Grove, IL: IVP, 2013.

Walton, John H., and J. Harvey Walton. *Lost World of the Israelite Conquest*. Downers Grove, IL: IVP, 2017.

———. *Lost World of the Torah*. Downers Grove, IL: IVP, 2019.

Walton, John, et al. *IVP Bible Background Commentary: Old Testament*. Downers Grove, IL: IVP, 1999.

Watson, Rebecca S. *Chaos Uncreated: The Reassessment of the Theme of "Chaos" in the Hebrew Bible*. Berlin: de Gruyter, 2005.

Watson, W.E.G. "*Hêlēl*." In *DDD*, 392–94.

Weinfeld, Moshe. "Divine Intervention and War in the Ancient Near East." In *History, Historiography, and Interpretation: Studies in Biblical and Cuneiform Literatures*, edited by H. Tadmor and M. Weinfeld, 121–47. Leiden: Brill, 1984.

Weinfeld, Moshe, and S. David Sperling. "Moloch, Cult of." In *EJ* 14:427–29.

Weiser, Artur. *The Psalms*. OTL. Philadelphia: Westminster, 1962.

Wenham, Gordon J. *Genesis 1–15*. Waco, TX: Word, 1987.

Westbrook, R. *History of Ancient Near Eastern Law*. Leiden: Brill, 2003.

Westenholz, Joan Goodnick. *Dragons, Monsters and Fabulous Beasts*. Jerusalem: Bible Lands Museum, 2004.

———. *Legends of the Kings of Akkade*. Winona Lake, IN: Eisenbrauns, 1997.

White, Ellen. *Yahweh's Council*. Tübingen: Mohr Siebeck, 2014.

Whitney, K. William. *Two Strange Beasts: Leviathan and Behemoth in Second Temple and Early Rabbinic Judaism*. Winona Lake, IL: Eisenbrauns, 2006.

Wiggermann, F. A. M. *Mesopotamian Protective Spirits: The Ritual Texts*. Groningen: Styx, 1992.

Wildberger, Hans. *Isaiah 13–27*. CC. Minneapolis, MN: Fortress, 1997.

———. *Isaiah 28–39*. CC. Minneapolis, MN: Fortress, 2002.

Wilson, Gerald H. *The Editing of the Hebrew Psalter*. Chico, CA: Scholars, 1985.

Wilson, Robert R. *Genealogy and History in the Biblical World*. New Haven, CT: Yale, 1977.

Wink, Walter. *Naming the Powers*. Philadelphia: Fortress, 1984.

———. "Towards a New Paradigm for Bible Study." In *Walter Wink: Collected Readings*, edited by Henry French, 11–30. Minneapolis: Fortress, 2013.

Wise, M., M. Abegg, and M. Cook, *The Dead Sea Scrolls*. New York: HarperSanFrancisco, 1996.

Wolterstorff, Nicholas. *Divine Discourse: Philosophical Reflections on the Claim that God Speaks*. Cambridge: Cambridge University Press, 1995.

Wright, Archie T. *The Origin of Evil Spirits*. Tübingen: Mohr Siebeck, 2005.

Wright, Christopher J. H. *The Mission of God*. Downers Grove, IL: IVP, 2006.

Wright, R. B. "Psalms of Solomon." In *OTP* 2.639–70.

Wyatt, N. "Qeteb." In *DDD*, 673–74.

————. "The Religion of Ugarit: An Overview." In *Handbook of Ugaritic Studies*, edited by W. G. E. Watson and N. Wyatt. Leiden: Brill, 1999.

————. *Religious Texts from Ugarit*. Sheffield, UK: Sheffield University Press, 1998.

Yamauchi, Edwin M. "Did Persian Zoroastrianism Influence Judaism?" In *Israel: Ancient Kingdom or Late Invention?* edited by D. I. Block, 282–97. Nashville: B & H, 2008.

Author Index

Subject Index

Scripture Index

2 Samuel

1 Kings

2 Kings

Jeremiah

Lamentations

Ezekiel

Mark (continued)

Luke

2 Peter

2:1	226
2:4–7	226
2:4	34, 113, 115, 222, 226, 235
2:8	236n31
2:9–10	227
3:6	240n54
3:9	240n53
5:8	250

1 John

2:13–14	266
3	262, 271
3:7–15	261–62
3:8	38, 262, 271
3:10	271
3:11	260n119
3:12	262
3:15	261
4:4	266
5:19	266

2 John

1:8	240n55

Jude

4	226
5–7	227
5	241n57
6	113, 115, 222, 226–27
7	227
9	33, 35n2, 268–69
11	227, 241n57, 269
23	287, 288n7

Revelation

1:20	193
2:6	288n7
5	32
9	31
9:2	71

9:5	236n31
9:11	71
11:10	236n31
11:15	112, 112n54
12	31, 144, 189, 212, 225–26
12:1	144
12:2	236n31
12:3	104, 144
12:4	144
12:5	225n40
12:7–12	144–45
12:8–9	222
12:8	225
12:9	128, 143, 146, 225–26
12:12	225
12:13	144
12:14–15	143–44
12:16	144
12:17	144–45, 145n52
12:19	225
13	271
13:2	271
13:4	267n136
13:12	271
13:17–18	289
13:17	290n10
14:10–11	236n31
17–19	146
17	31, 239
18:2	67
18:7	236n31
18:10	236n31
18:14	240n55
18:15	236n31
18:23	146
19:10	267n136
19:20	146
20	107, 115, 144, 189
20:1–3	115
20:1	71
20:2	128, 143–44, 143n47
20:3	236
20:7–8	115
20:10	146, 235–36
20:14	236
20:19	267n136
21	31, 104
21:1	104
21:8	264
21:25	104
22:20	141

Primary Sources Index